SOCIAL CONSTRUCTIONISM AND THEOLOGY

EMPIRICAL STUDIES IN THEOLOGY

EDITOR

JOHANNES A. VAN DER VEN

VOLUME 7

SOCIAL CONSTRUCTIONISM
AND THEOLOGY

EDITED BY

C.A.M. HERMANS
G. IMMINK
A. DE JONG
J. VAN DER LANS

BRILL
LEIDEN · BOSTON · KÖLN
2002

This book is printed on acid-free paper.

Library of Congress Cataloging in Publication Data

Social constructionism and theology / edited by C.A.M. Hermans ...
[et al.].
      p. cm. — (Empirical studies in theology, ISSN 1389-1189 ; v. 7)
   Includes bibliographical references and index.
   ISBN 9004123180 (cloth : alk. paper)
   1. Theology, Practical. 2. Deconstruction. I. Hermans, C. A. M.
   (Chris A. M.) II. Series.

   BV4. S63 2001
   261.5—dc21
                                                        2001043341
                                                        CIP

Die Deutsche Bibliothek – CIP-Einheitsaufnahme

Social Constructionism and Theology / ed. by C.A.M. Hermans..........
– Leiden ; Boston ; Köln : Brill, 2001
   (Empirical studies in theology ; Vol. 7)
   ISBN 90–04–1231–80

          ISSN   1389-1189
          ISBN   90 04 12318 0

PRINTED IN THE NETHERLANDS

CONTENTS

SOCIAL CONSTRUCTIONISM AND PRACTICAL THEOLOGY: AN INTRODUCTION

Chris A.M. Hermans

Within the discipline of practical theology there is a growing self-understanding which is moving away from defining this discipline as applied theology. The concept of action or practice plays a central role in this new self-understanding. Practical theology starts its theological reflections from practices, aims at empirically analyzing practices, and should be directed towards the transformation of these practices. Practical theology aims at developing a hermeneutical action-theory (Heitink, 1993) or a hermeneutical-empirical approach to human actions (Van der Ven, 1999, p. 331). From this practice-orientation there is a strong connection between practical theology and the social sciences. This can be compared with the strong relationship which exists between the exegetical study of the holy scriptures and rhetorical theory in literary sciences. Social constructionism is a growing theory within the social sciences. There is a rapidly growing body of publications with the term "social constructionism" included in their titles. What is more, many scholars within the field of the psychology of religion and the sociology of religion adhere to some form of social constructionism. For practical theology, it is important to reflect on this emerging concept of social constructionism within the social sciences. This is the aim of this volume.

In the introduction we will first introduce the emerging self-understanding of practical theology inclining towards the study of religious practices (section 1). Afterwards we will turn to the theory of social constructionism. Social constructionism is not a paradigm in the Kuhnian sense. Social constructionist scholars share some presumptions about the nature of social reality and the way to analyze social reality in order to reveal its cultural and social dynamics. We will give special attention to one of the main aspects where social constructionists differ, namely whether there exists a reality that is independent of our discourse about reality. This topic is one of the most contentious battle grounds between social constructionism and the mainstream within the social sciences. We cannot introduce social constructionism without addressing this problem.[1] In the last section (3) of this introduction we will give an overview of the chapters in this volume.

1. *The Practice-orientation within Practical Theology*

All scholars working within the field of practical theology agree on the fact that their discipline cannot be defined as applied theology. This idea is clearly expressed in a recent volume by leading scholars within the International Academy of Practical Theology (Schweitzer & Van der Ven, 1999). According to Osmer three elements of practical theology set it apart from dogmatic theology and Christian ethics, namely:

> (1) a performative orientation, based on this literature's interest in how best to perform a particular practice or activity in concrete circumstances;
> (2) a theory of formation and transformation guiding the praxis of the Christian life over time; and
> (3) a practical theological hermeneutic of the field in which an action or practice takes place, locating the actors involved in moral time and space' (Osmer, 1999, p. 126).

These three elements together constitute the distinctive rationality of practical theology, which 'attempts to provide reasons for how and why to perform an action or practice in a manner that corresponds to and participates in the praxis of God' (Osmer, 1999, p. 126).[2]

According to Browning (1996), practical theology is characterized by a practice-theory-practice model which breaks the application model that has only two elements, namely theory-practice. Theology

---

[1] In particular, we will position Gergen in this debate. Gergen, who is one of the leading social constructionists, was invited to a conference of the research group of practical theology and social sciences in the Netherlands in December 1999. Ken Gergen was one of the speakers at this conference organized by prof. Gerrit Immink (University of Utrecht). The idea of a volume on social constructionism and theology was born at this conference. We were glad to get the interest of Gergen in this project.

[2] We will not differentiate between practices and praxis. We take a more abstract perspective in this section and subsume these concepts under the heading of human actions. Human actions can be defined by the fact that they are intentional, i.e. goal-directed (Searle, 1983). We also skip the discussion about when practices or praxis are to be defined as religious practices or religious praxis and how this is related to Christian practices or praxis. The meaning of intentional actions studied by practical theology implies the binary code of transcendence versus immanence.

can be practical if we bring practical concerns to it from the beginning. 'When a religious community hits a crisis in its practices, it then begins reflecting (asking questions) about its meaningful or theory-laden practices' (Browning, 1996, p. 6). And practice also returns after the theoretical reflections. The crises in the practice of the community from which we started can be transformed according to the insights that we have achieved (such as change in preaching or worship). This is where theology gets practical in a full or concrete sense. Browning (1996; 1999) speaks about a 'strategic practical theology'.

Heitink defines practical theology as an action science: 'the empirical-oriented theological theory of the mediation of the Christian faith within the praxis of the modern society' (Heitink, 1993, p. 18). In relation to his definition he speaks about two types of praxis, namely the mediation of the Christian faith as praxis 1 and the context of the modern society as praxis 2. Praxis 1 points to the fact that the typical object of practical theology is the transformation of the intentional actions of persons or groups. Praxis 1 can never be understood without praxis 2. Sometimes praxis 2 is supportive of praxis 1, but sometimes it puts constraints on praxis 1. It is precisely this interaction between praxis 1 and praxis 2 which breaks the model of practical theology as applied theology. It makes it impossible to reduce the object of practical theology to predefined theological categories. Or to put it positively, it puts the living faith ('sensus fidei') of people within the context of society at the core of practical theology.

Van der Ven posits the interaction between theory and praxis starting from a cyclical or, rather, spiral model, namely the so-called empirical cycle (Van der Ven, 1993, pp. 157–224; 1999, pp. 330–335). The first phase is the development of the theological problem and goal. In this phase the researcher participates in the field of research of the subjects whose lives she or he investigates (for example, liturgical practices of initiation in a religious community). One cannot develop a theological problem and goal only from an outside perspective ('allo-perspective'). In the second phase, the so-called theological induction, this rather global conception of the actions and practices is specified by a systematic reading of theological literature in close interaction with the actions and practices under investigation. This phase ends with a theological research question which is always practice-oriented: it starts from an understanding of the practices in which people are involved and aims at transforming these practices. In the third phase, the so-called theological deduction, the experiences and reflections of the second phase become the object of conceptualization. This phase focuses on the formulation of a conceptual model which forms the core of the empirical-theological research. Although this phase has a theoretical scope, it is also practice-oriented in the sense that it implies the operationalization of concepts in observable, measurable and verifiable actions. The fourth phase is called empirical testing. In this phase empirical data from the actions and practices of people are gathered, either by qualitative or quantitative methods, and analyzed from the perspective of the theological research questions. The last phase is the so-called theological evaluation. This evaluation is directed towards both the practices in which people are involved, and the theological theory which forms the conceptual framework of the research. In the light of the results of the research the practical theologian reflects on the way in which these practices can be transformed. But these results will also give rise to an evaluation of the theological framework that was formulated in earlier phases of the research.

This practice-orientation brings practical theology in close contact with the social sciences which study the same actions. Logical though this may seem, in the development of practical theology as a discipline this cooperation has been a contested notion. In Germany, for example, there was a close relationship between the social sciences and practical theology at the beginning of the 20th century. The period between the 1920s and the 1960s was characterized by non-cooperation due to the influence of dialectical theology and of Neo-Lutheranism on protestant theology (Schweitzer, 1999, p. 310). From the 1960s until today, new forms of relationship between the social sciences and practical theology have been emerging. From an international perspective, this is the case in most countries of the world.[3]

Cooperation is not the only type of relation between practical theology and the social sciences. From a logical point of view, three types of relationship can be differentiated (see Schweitzer, 1999).[4]

---

[3] For example, the first chair of practical theology at the Catholic University of Nijmegen was created in the 1960s in close connection with the chairs of the psychology of religion and the sociology of religion.

[4] Schweitzer (1999) distinguishes four types. In my opinion the second type is only a sub-model of the first type because it uses social-scientific insights only as 'input' within theological theory and not as an independent science. I will use the typology of Van der Ven (1993; 1999) to differentiate within the cooperation type. I believe that his 'multi-disciplinary model' has the same meaning as Schweitzer's first type (namely the *ancilla model*).

The first type is the *ancilla model* according to which the social sciences are considered as "ancillary models" of practical theology. Within practical theology one draws on insights from the social sciences, but it is practical theology that defines the meanings of these insights. There is an asymmetry between practical theology and the social sciences in the sense that the social sciences are subordinated to practical theology. Within this model one can differentiate a sub-model which makes use of the social-scientific critique of assumptions, methods and procedures which may be found in practical theology, church and religion. 'The difference between the perspective of the social scientist and [that of] the practical theologian leads to the possibility of greater awareness as to what may be hidden to an exclusively theological analysis, for example, the ideological abuse of religion in politics and society' (Schweitzer, 1999, p. 312). Although the social sciences are used as a critical source, this "use-of" or instrumental character does not breach the subordination of the social sciences to theology.

The second type is the model of *cooperation between practical theology and the social sciences*. The defining characteristic of this type is the fact that practical theology and the social sciences are on an equal footing from a theoretical point of view. Practical theology and the social sciences share a research perspective which is common to both. Although the disciplinary framework is different, both disciplines share a common research question and research aim (see the first phase of the empirical cycle: above). There must also be a conceptual relationship between theological and social-scientific theory within the conceptual framework of the research (see the third phase of the empirical cycle: above). These two criteria have to be met in order to be able to speak of "cooperation" between practical theology and the social sciences. Cooperation implies a co-construction of the research question and aim, and the theoretical framework. Two sub-models can be distinguished within this type. The first is called the *interdisciplinary model* (Heitink, 1993; Van der Ven, 1993). Within this model, the research is a joint enterprise between the practical theologian and the social scientist. It is not important whether these scholars are located within different departments or within the same department. Both settings are possible. What is important is that both criteria are met. The second sub-model is called the *intradisciplinary model*. The difference between this sub-model and the interdisciplinary model is the fact that there is just one scholar incorporating

both theoretical perspectives within his or her research. This model
implies that the practical theologian conducts practical-theological
research with the help of empirical methodology. But it also implies
that the practical theologian has enough knowledge of social-scientific
concepts to do justice to this theoretical frame of reference.

The third type subsumes practical theology under the social sciences. Schweitzer calls this the *practical theology as social science* model
(Schweitzer, 1999, p. 313). As the empirical study of actions of religious people, practical theology is not different from disciplines such
as the psychology of religion or the sociology of religion. The research
question and aim are formulated from a social-scientific perspective.
Theological questions and interests are subordinate to social-scientific
questions and interests. In addition, practical theological concepts are
subsumed under social-scientific concepts. As the research question
and concepts are dominated by the social sciences, so too are the
evaluations of the research. There can be an evaluation of the research
in the light of the transformation of practices within the Church
or religion, but again it is social-scientific theory that guides the
evaluation.

Within the discipline of practical theology most scholars will argue
for the second type of cooperation between practical theology and
the social sciences (Schweitzer & Van der Ven, 1999). I believe that
the main difference among scholars is whether one should opt for
an interdisciplinary approach or for an intradisciplinary approach.

2. *Social Constructionism as an Emerging Social-scientific Theory*

One of the first publications that spoke about the social construction of reality was the book by Berger and Luckmann (1966). The
thesis of Berger and Luckmann is that we experience everyday reality as something fixed that is taken for granted within society. This
"taken for granted" character of reality hides the fact that our knowledge of reality is constructed socially through human activities. 'Any
body of "knowledge" comes to be socially established as "reality"'
(Berger & Luckmann, 1966, p. 3). Since the 1960s the number of
publications with the term "social constructionism" included in their
titles has increased exponentially. This growing number of publications hides the fact that the concept of social constructionism has
not been clearly defined. Social constructionism is still an emerging

social-scientific theory, as we formulated in the title of this section. It is not up to us to define social constructionism, if social scientists have not yet completed this theoretical debate among themselves. The aim of this section is more modest. Firstly, we will formulate what the core thesis of social constructionism is. We will do so from a critical perspective provided by the study of social constructionism by the Canadian philosopher Ian Hacking (1999). Secondly, we will ask what is being constructed. We will differentiate between facts and concepts or ideas.[5] Thirdly, we will go into the question of relativism which is the main point of critique of social constructionism. We will show that there are different positions within social constructionism with regard to the acknowledgement of an extra-linguistic reality. Some social constructionists (such as Gergen, 1999) repudiate the existence of facts apart from human discourse; others opt for a coexistence thesis of natural facts and social construction (such as Harré, 1999).

What do scholars say when they claim that a phenomenon (X) is constructed? The starting point of social constructionism seems to be thesis (1), that the existence or character of X is not determined by the nature of things.

> (1) 'X need not have existed, or need not be at all as it is. X, or X as it is at present, is not determined by the nature of things; it is not inevitable' (Hacking, 1999, p. 6).

An illustration. Feminist authors have shown that sex-specific behaviour is not attributable to "natural" differences between the sexes. The fact that men never, or to a much lesser degree, undertake domestic tasks is socially and culturally determined. This need not be so at all. The same applies to poor children or children of poor parents. The existence of children who have to live in poverty is not a natural fact. Hacking, however, poses the question whether thesis (1) really is the central thesis of social constructionism. If everyone knows that X (sex-specific behaviour, poor children) is an accidental outcome of the way in which society is constructed, it then becomes pointless to talk about the social construction of X. After all, if everything is contingent there is no point in arguing that it is a social

---

[5] Berger and Luckmann (1966) speak about "knowledge", as one can see in the subtitle of their book: 'A treatise in the sociology of knowledge'.

construction. It has become a redundant argument. Underlying thesis (1), however, is another premise (0) which is debated by social constructionists:

> (0) In the present state of affairs, X is taken for granted; X appears to be inevitable (Hacking, 1999, p. 12).

In the absence of thesis (0) there is no reason to talk about the social construction of X. In the current relationships among men and women in our society, sex-specific behaviour seems to be a self-evident fact. Social constructionists, however, dispute its self-evident nature. The concept of womanhood, manhood or poor child is a social-cultural construction whose meaning, independently of context, is rooted in the nature of the thing itself.

X is not so self-evident as it seems if one examines the construction of X. This is where the term social constructionism is derived from. X has cultural origins and is socially constructed. In this context X can refer to the product, but also to its construction as a process. Sex-specific behaviour as a product comes into existence within social structures. It is the outcome of a history in which social and cultural factors play a role. The process of constructing sex-specific behaviour is also socially structured in the sense that social and cultural factors interact in the creation of sex-specific behaviour. Particular conduct by a girl will be corrected by adults because it is seen as non-feminine and cultural motives will be provided (for example, 'the emotional bond with the mother is so important for children'). Linked to this Hacking formulates the aim of social constructionism as:

> displaying or analyzing actual, historically situated, social interactions or causal routes that led to, or were involved in, the coming into being or establishing of some present entity or fact (Hacking, 1999, p. 49).

Things which appear self-evident to us—like particular behaviour, emotions, the poor child, the teaching profession—have been generated by historical and social-cultural processes. Their self-evident nature is less obvious than it seems. It could also have been otherwise. Is all reality therefore relative? At this point we may raise the fundamental criticism of social constructionism, that is, whether social constructionism does not run the risk of sliding into total relativism? To illustrate this we refer to four working hypotheses which Ken Gergen (1999) states as central within social constructionism.

The first working hypothesis says that the way in which we understand our world and ourselves is not demanded by that which exists (Gergen, 1999, p. 47). There is no world independent of language. Everything that is can be described differently. 'There is nothing about "what there is" that demands these particular accounts; we could use our language to construct alternative worlds in which there is no gravity or cancer, or in which persons and birds are equivalent, and punishment adored' (idem). From a constructionist perspective our understanding of the world is a linguistic convention. And this convention is not self-evident.

The second working hypothesis is that the way in which we describe and explain things is rooted in the relationships among people. The meaning of the world is not something peculiar to separate individuals but forms part of the coordination of actions among individuals. Language and all other forms of representing the world are rooted in relationships.

The third working hypothesis is that by our description, explanation or representation we simultaneously determine the future of reality. 'As our practices of language are bound within relationships, so are relationships bound within broader patterns of practice—rituals, traditions, "forms of life"' (Gergen, 1999, p. 48). Without the shared language in which institutions are described and explained, these institutions would not exist in their present form. By describing reality differently we transform our world.

The fourth working hypothesis points at the importance of reflecting on the ways in which we understand and explain reality. There are no universal answers to the question of which is "the right one". Good reasons, good explanations or good values always depend on some tradition which accepts certain constructions as being right or real. 'For constructionists such considerations lead to a celebration of reflexivity, that is, the attempt to place one's premises into question, to suspend the "obvious", to listen to alternative framings of reality, and to grapple with the comparative outcomes of multiple standpoints' (Gergen, 1999, p. 49).

The question is whether Gergen with these working hypotheses does not slide into a universal constructionism? Gergen's premise is that no reality exists independently of our linguistic representations of reality. Only that which is talked about exists. This notion appears to be flawless. What would the street in which someone lives be without that person's description of it? Or what would poverty represent apart from the meaning which we ascribe to it? Of course, language is an important medium through which we understand and represent reality. But this does not mean that we can reduce reality to words (embedded in relationships and practices) which we use to discuss it. Hacking (1999, p. 24) refers to this as linguistic idealism. We can avoid this danger if we distinguish between that which we refer to when speaking and the statements we construct about that which we refer to. Our statement about the tree in front of our house presupposes the existence of a tree in front of our house. The existence of the tree is a precondition for our statement. In this connection John Searle (1995) distinguishes between "ontological objective" and "epistemological subjective". Searle calls the existence of the tree a fact which can be verified by any competent speaker independently of the way in which reality is represented by ourselves. There is a reality corresponding to our statements. It is pointless to ignore the existence of the tree and attempt to walk right through it. At the same time, however, we presume a cognisant subject who refers to this tree in his or her description. And one can argue about this description. Is it a tree or perhaps a shrub? Why is it important to mention this tree? Why does one resident mention this tree in front of the house, while another speaks about other houses in the street and the people who live there? Such differences in the construction of the location where someone lives can be amply accommodated while at the same time acknowledging the existence of objective facts in reality independently of our statements. If one denies the latter one ends up in radical relativism.It is true that social reality contains a distinction from "natural" objects like trees, stone walls or volcanoes. A piece of paper represents a 10 Euro note on the basis of the status or function of money value which has been given to it. Likewise, a certain form of cohabitation represents marriage on the basis of the meaning ('status') ascribed to this particular form of cohabitation. The constituent rule ('X is Y in C') is indissolubly linked to this social practice. Moreover, it is only through this rule that this practice is created. This is a major difference between social facts and natural facts. No social reality exists unless it is given a linguistic meaning. However, this does not mean that all social reality may be reduced to language. 'A socially constructed reality presupposes a non-socially constructed reality' (Searle, 1995, p. 191). People of flesh and blood must exist in order to be able to speak about a marriage. There is no point in going to the town hall to marry an "imaginary" partner who only exists in my dreams. And if I do not repay my debt, a bailiff will arrive sooner or later to recover the out-standing loan. You can, by means of language, construct a different reality in which neither money nor debt to other people exists, but this will prove to be fairly futile.

As is clear from Gergen's four working hypotheses, social con-structionism aims to prove the non-necessity of X. This refers to X as an idea rather than a fact (Hacking, 1999, p. 28). Social con-structionism refers to the construction of concepts, or "knowledge" as Berger and Luckmann (1966) would say. It is the classification of certain behaviour as sex-specific that is debatable. The concept of poverty can be challenged. According to Anne-Marie Ambert (1998, pp. 115–116), 'In Western societies, but particularly in North America, children are socially constructed as the sole responsibility of their parents, especially their mothers'. The result of this concept is that children's poverty is tied to their family's income, which comes down to the mother in absence of support by a father. Social reality is constructed, and can also be constructed differently if we use different concepts or change the description of our concepts. And the latter is possible because these concepts are culturally determined and cre-ated in the course of history. By unmasking their self-evident nature, people regain the possibility to be in control of their own future. This emancipatory or transforming intention is clearly visible also in Gergen's third and fourth working hypotheses. The realisation that a certain idea of reality is a construct may help people to deal with this construction in a critical and reflective manner and make other choices (see also Hacking, 1999, p. 58).

3. *An Overview of this Volume*

The chapters in this volume are divided into three parts. The first part contains reflections by social scientists about the meaning of social constructionism for their field of research. The second part contains reflections by practical theologians about the meaning of social constructionism for their discipline. The third part contains two evaluative chapters. The selection of the chapters in part I is based on the following reasons. In the first place there is a strong debate about social constructionism within the psychology of religion (see for example Alma, 1998; Jablonski, Hermans & Van der Lans,

1998; Vergouwen, 2001). We therefore asked three scholars in the field of the psychology of religion each to write a chapter in this volume (Van der Lans, Popp-Baier, Day). In the second place we were glad to find Kenneth Gergen, as one of the leading scholars within social constructionism, prepared to write an introductory chapter on social constructionism. The selection of the chapters in part II is based on the fact that we wanted to include reflections from all sub-disciplines within practical theology in this volume. There is an ongoing debate within practical theology about the division of the discipline into sub-disciplines. We will not go into this debate. Whatever typology is used, you will find an article on that topic. In part III there are two evaluative chapters: one from a social-scientific point of view and one from a theological point of view.

Part I opens with a chapter by *Kenneth Gergen* in which he gives his view on central ideas within social constructionism. Gergen starts with some epistemological assumptions which seem to be central in many current constructionist analyses. He then asks what it means to have knowledge of religious practices from a constructionist view. He stresses the fact that individual subjectivity in Western society is seen as the cornerstone of communal existence. Relationships are seen as inter/actions between finite individuals. In many cases the relationship of the individual self to God may be a reflection of this individualist conception of the self. Social constructionism interprets the self as a relational self, and communication as coordinated action between relational selves.

Van der Lans starts his contribution with two points of criticism of mainstream psychology as voiced by Gergen. The first point of criticism is directed against the focus on the individual mind to account for individual behaviour, and the second against the claim of objective truth associated with it. According to Van der Lans, both points of critique also relate to the psychology of religion. He then gives an overview of research within the psychology of religion based on the social-constructionist viewpoint. An introduction of the social-constructionist approach into the psychological study of religion involves a radical change in procedure. Van der Lans has five changes in mind: a central focus on religious communication; the dyad or group as unit of analysis; the researcher as participant in the research; knowledge of the lived narratives of the religious tradition in which the research participants are involved, and a multiplicity of research methods. He ends with a critical observation in respect of social constructionism as it has been developed so far, namely the lack of a systematic methodology. Not all social constructionists will agree with him on this point (see Gergen in this volume) but according to Van der Lans this is necessary for social constructionism in order to evolve into a strong research alternative to mainstream psychology.

Social constructionism can best be examined by studying a religious phenomenon in its historical genesis within relationships. Religious conversion is a perfect research topic to be investigated from the framework of social constructionism. *Popp-Baier* (chapter three) gives an overview of classical and contemporary conversion research. Narrative conversion research is compatible with the social constructionist point of view. She formulates three methodological steps for analyzing conversion narratives and illustrates this methodology with reference to data from her own research project on religious orientations and experiences of women in the Charismatic-Evangelical women's group Aglow. Conversion narratives must be seen as the result of a process in which people learn to use religious language within relationships. Popp-Baier ends her chapter by stating the importance of narrative and discourse analysis to capture this communicative basis of religious communication.

The chapter by *Day* is directed to religious development. Religious development as researched by Oser and Fowler is also of central interest to practical theologians. Both theories of religious development stand within the framework of constructivism of which Piaget can be seen as the founding father. Day formulates three core problems of constructivism: the seemingly universal character of the development is an artifact of research methodology; differences between religious voices of the participants are ignored; and the hierarchy between the stages might be more a matter of personal style and factors of the social and historical context. At the heart of the constructivist conception is the idea of an individual epistemic subject. What is needed, according to Day, is a shift to the discursive framework of interpersonal relationships. This implies a shift from "what" is being said in religious discourse to "whom" it is said to. Day ends with some notions that are important for the concept of development in a constructionist frame.

Part II contains seven theological contributions. The first two chapters (five and six) focus on a general theme for practical theology, and for theology in general, namely religious communication. Chapter five by *Wallace* focuses on the topic of religious speech in a post-modern society. Wallace starts with the Heideggerian-inspired move in contemporary theology away from metaphysical founda-tions. Freed from the need to secure God in metaphysical founda-tions there can be renewed attention for the biblical witness as a model for human becoming. Wallace opts for a post-modern theol-ogy with an emancipatory intent which can escape the dilemma of a universal versus sectarian theology. According to Wallace the aware-ness of the self as social construct is a formidable challenge to the dominant model of selfhood in the West, namely the self as a free, independent, rational "monad". Social constructionism substitutes for this "monad" a self in communication with others within the con-text of coordination of actions. Referring to Ricoeur, the self is also "other" to itself. One element in this "otherness" is the phenome-non of being called by the voice of conscience. Within social con-structionism there is, according to Wallace, a certain tone deafness to the importance of otherness in the formation of selfhood.

Hermans (chapter six) begins with the epistemology underlying the intersubjective conception of communication within social construc-tionism. Can there be ultimate meaning within a social constructionist conception of communication, as developed by Gergen? Hermans refers to two characteristics of the understanding of communication within social constructionism, which could be very helpful in cur-rent debates on religious communication, namely meaning in rela-tionships and transformative dialogue. In religious communication we construct a life-narrative in which God is the author and we are the "hero". This model of "God as author" and "man as hero" stems from Mikhail Bakhtin. Bakhtin distinguishes between two mod-els, namely a monologic Author-God and a polyphonic Author-God. The last model is in accordance with the social-constructionist view-point on human discourse. At the end of his chapter Hermans eval-uates the two models of religious communication. He then points to major repercussions of social constructionism on how we conduct research into religious communication. Finally, he analyzes what ulti-mate meaning could be from a theological point of view.

Immink (chapter seven) also focuses on the issue of religious com-munication, but more specifically in relation to the act of preach-ing. Immink first analyses the idea of social constructionism (more specifically that of Gergen) that human discourse should be under-stood in terms of performative action. This, however, ignores the fact that human discourse is also a matter of illocutionary action.

From this perspective Immink argues that the social and institutional dimension of language has a normative import and is not merely a matter of choice and convention. According to Immink, illocutionary action requires some form of metaphysical realism. The second part of this chapter is directed to human discourse in the act of preaching. Immink first describes three specific features of preaching as communicative acts. He refers to two models in homiletical discourse and argues that in successful communication the noetic act precedes the performative act.

Schweitzer (chapter eight) opens up the dialogue between social constructionism and religious education. Schweitzer enters this dialogue with a specific aim in mind, namely the search for theoretical tools that can help religious educationists in meeting the challenges of religious education in a multicultural and multireligious society. First, Schweitzer refers to some basic theoretical notions that are shared between social constructionism and religious education such as narrative, metaphor, a relational self, community and dialogue. Even more important is the fact that the conception of the self of social constructionism is open for religion, an openness that other conceptions of the self (such as that of Habermas) lack. Schweitzer subsequently formulates two points of criticism. Firstly, he does not agree with some social constructionists (such as Gergen) that we need to go beyond constructivism. According to Schweitzer, what is needed is a combination of both approaches. Secondly, it is important for theology to preserve the activity of the Word of God together with the activity of the creation of meaning in relationships.

Church organization and organizational change is the topic of chapter nine by *De Jong*. This chapter starts with an outline of the evolution within theological literature on church development over recent decades. De Jong relates the different emphases within church development to a social constructionist approach. He sees three shortcomings in Gergen's social constructionist approach with regard to the institutional facts, namely reductions within language, insufficient cognizance of facts and a reduction of intentionality to intersubjectivity. According to De Jong these problems can be overcome by Searle's theory about the construction of social reality. He gives three illustrations of the contribution made by Searle to the field of research into church development. In the last section of this chapter De Jong reflects on the dimensions of power and polyphony within global corporations. He applies the social constructionist approach to global corporations to the Catholic Church (as a religious 'multinational').

Schilderman (chapter ten) addresses the question of personal religion and pastoral care. Schilderman starts his contribution with a reflection on one aspect of modernity that entails a great problem for personal religion, namely religious individualism. This phenomenon results from a tendency to rely less on religious intermediaries and to stress a moral appreciation of religious authenticity. What is religious identity against the background of this emerging emphasis on personal, authentic religion? With the help of Rom Harré's model of personal identity , Schilderman develops a model of religious identity. Identity as ('identifying') activity may be understood as a persuasive attempt to integrate personal and social assent. Personal religion is the interpreted and narrated result of these persuasive processes. This notion is illustrated by three cases of personal religion based on a pastoral care method known as spiritual inquiry. This method is an application of the self-confrontation method, based on the valuation theory of Hubertus Hermans. This chapter ends with three challenges to the view presented of personal religion, namely religious individualism, religious instrumentalism and religious relativism.

The last chapter in part II is on social constructionism and moral identity. *Hermans* and *Dupont* start with an analysis of the social constructionist conception of the self as a narrative construct influenced by the socio-cultural context in which a person lives. This theoretical perspective forms the background to a narrative approach to moral development. The debate between this narrative approach to moral development and the Kohlbergian approach to moral development has not been very fruitful as yet. The authors trace both theoretical perspectives back to different types of ethics. It connects the social construction of moral identity with the so-called 'concrete ethics' (Bakhtin, Levinas). The moral criterion of concrete ethics is the subjective irreducibility of the other as the groundless ground of ethics. The relevance of this concept is illustrated in a conversation between four physical therapists. At the end of their chapter the authors argue that on the basis of concrete ethics the four points of criticism of the Kohlbergians' narrative approach can be countered.

Part III contains two reflections on the preceding chapters. The first reflection is by *Gergen* (chapter twelve). Gergen first addresses the problem of moral action. Secondly, he takes up the question of the real (or objectivity), which seems to be discredited by social constructionism. Finally there is an elaborate discussion with regard to the sacred. According to Gergen a sophisticated constructionism will lead to abolition of the distinction between the sacred and the profane, and in so doing opens new possibilities for the sacralization of everyday life.

Van der Ven (chapter thirteen) starts his reflection with a proposition about the material and formal object of practical theology. Fundamental questions regarding the material and formal object of practical theology should be dealt with primarily in terms of the categories and concepts of practical philosophy, rather than those of speculative philosophy. From the perspective of practical philosophy Van der Ven points to four aspects which need to be discussed within theology as a practical science. From an ontological perspective a fundamental question for practical theology is whether the core concept is action or interaction, act or communication. From an epistemological perspective Van der Ven points to language as speech acts, narratives as related to actions, and the open plot of a life-narrative. There are also ethical aspects which are important for the definition of the object of practical theology. Van der Ven identifies three agencies (I/we, you [singular and plural] and he/she/they) and refers to the ethical attitudes towards them. In so doing he wants to avoid ethical relativism which could be luring in social constructionism. The last section of this chapter is on God-talk. Can we know God outside the speech acts in which we establish a relationship to God? Can we do justice to the dialectic of the presence and absence of God in the images of God that we use? Can we leave room for the extralinguistic 'reality' of God?

References

Alma, H.A. (1998). *Identiteit door verbondenheid. Een godsdienstpsychologisch onderzoek naar identificatie en christelijk geloof* [Identity through belonging. Research in the psychology of religion on identification and Christian faith]. Kampen: KOK.

Ambert, A.-M. (1998). *The web of poverty. Psychosocial perspectives.* New York: The Haworth Press.

Berger, P. & Luckmann, Th. (1966). *The social construction of reality. A treatise in the sociology of knowledge.* New York: Anchor Books.

Browning, D. (1996). *A fundamental practical theology: descriptive and strategic proposals.* Minneapolis: Augsburg Fortress.

—— (1999). Toward a fundamental and strategic practical theology. In: Schweitzer, F. & Ven, J.A. van der (Eds.). *Practical theology—International perspectives* (pp. 53–74). Frankfurt a.m.: Peter Lang.

Gergen, K. (1999). *An invitation to social construction.* London: Sage Publications.

Hacking, I. (1999). *The social construction of what?* Cambridge Mass.: Harvard U.P.

Harré, R. (1998). *The singular self. An introduction to the psychology of personhood.* London: Sage Publications.

Heitink, G. (1993). *Praktische theologie. Geschiedenis, theorie, handelingsvelden* [Practical theology history, theory, action domains]. Kampen: KOK.

—— (1999). Practical theology: An empirical-oriented approach. In: Schweitzer, F. & Ven, J.A. van der (Eds.). *Practical theology—International perspectives* (pp. 265–272). Frankfurt a.M.: Peter Lang.

Jablonski, P., Hermans, C. & Van der Lans, J. (1998). Understanding religious language as mediated action: Vygotskian perspective. In: Ploeger, A. & Sterkens, C. (Eds.). *Search for meaning. Education into realms of meaning in a plural society* (pp. 191–218). Kampen: KOK.

Osmer, R.R. (1999). Practical theology as argument, rhetoric, and conversation. In: Schweitzer, F. & Ven, J.A. van der (Eds.). *Practical theology—International perspectives* (pp. 113–140). Frankfurt a.M.: Peter Lang.

Searle, J.R. (1983). *Intentionality. An essay in the philosophy of mind.* Cambridge: Cambridge U.P.

—— (1995). *The construction of social reality.* New York: The Free Press.

Schweitzer, F. (1999). Practical theology, contemporary culture, and the social sciences—Interdisciplinary relationships and the unity of practical theology as a discipline. In: Schweitzer, F. & Ven, J.A. van der (Eds.). *Practical theology—International perspectives* (pp. 307–322). Frankfurt a.M.: Peter Lang

Van der Ven, J.A. (1993). *Practical theology. An empirical approach.* Kampen: KOK.

—— (1999). An empirical approach in practical theology. In: Schweitzer, F. & Ven, J.A. van der (Eds.). *Practical theology—International perspectives* (pp. 323–339). Frankfurt a.M.: Peter Lang.

PART ONE

SOCIAL-SCIENTIFIC CONTRIBUTIONS

SOCIAL CONSTRUCTION AND PRACTICAL THEOLOGY:
THE DANCE BEGINS

Kenneth J. Gergen

Introduction

It is quite possible that the closing of the 20th century represents
the twilight of the modernist project of knowledge. This project—
with deep roots in Enlightenment philosophy and subsequent instil-
lation in our institutions of democracy, public education, law, and
public morality—casts individual knowledge as the critical bench-
mark of cultural achievement. In the modernist world, knowledge is
defined as a condition of the individual mind. And, while the object
of such knowledge could be mental or spiritual life, the modernist
project has become increasingly identified with the individual's knowledge of the "external" or material world—objective as opposed to
subjective. In this sense, scientific knowledge stands as the crowning
achievement of Western culture, with individual scientists singled out
for their unique accomplishments. It is this desideratum of individual knowledge to which we can also trace the flourishing of the social
sciences within this century, and the increasingly central place occupied by the natural sciences in society. And it is the conflation of
individual knowledge with science that has functioned antagonisti-
cally to longstanding beliefs in knowledge of the sacred (subjective,
mystical), and served within the 20th century to recast religious studies as a social science.

   Yet, for increasing numbers of scholars and scientists the longstanding romance with individual knowledge has grown stale. Indeed,
for many such a valorization of the individual mind seems detri-
mental to human well-being, and its global diffusion little short of corrosive. The sources of discontent are many. Surely the role of science
in the systematic extermination of Jews, the eradication of Hiroshima
and Nagasaki, the napalm incineration of Vietnamese, and the global
destruction of natural resources has left a broad wake of skepticism.
Either the process of knowledge production is without moral posture, or its implicit morals are monstrous. The failure of the modernist promise of unfettered progress and prosperity—the "grand

narratives" of the West—has also deposited a residue of disillusion-
ment (Lyotard, 1984). With every "advance" that rationalizes the
presumption of individual knowledge, humankind seems to confront
a wave of rapacious repercussions—increasingly powerful weapons
of destruction, environmental desecration, and human degradation
among them.

In the intellectual world, wave upon wave of cutting critique has
been directed toward the modernist vision of human knowledge.
Although boasting knowledge free of value, modernist accounts of
the world are found replete with androgynous, racist, elitist, materi-
alist, colonialist, and individualist biases. Favored by this conception
of knowledge are forms of relationship that are hierarchical, instrumental, competitive, and manipulative. Literary and rhetorical theorists have effectively challenged the modernist presumption that
knowledge claims can serve as accurate pictures or maps of the world—
demonstrating the lodgement of such claims in traditions of text and
rhetoric (cf. McClosky, 1984, Simons, 1984). Truth claims, for theorists such as Michel Foucault (1979, 1980), serve as vehicles for
enhancing the power of the scientific establishment and reducing to
puppetry all those who would find them credible. Adding weight to
these critical incursions, innumerable inquiries in history and sociology now bear out the disturbing implications of Thomas Kuhn's,
The Structure of Scientific Revolutions, to whit, that which we call knowledge
issues from shared paradigms of understanding and practice within
communities of interlocutors. Scientific theories and facts are not so
much reflections of the real as they are communal accomplishments.

We find ourselves moving, then, through the agonies of broad and
trenchant critique of longstanding assumptions about self and world.
Indulging in such critique, we cross the threshold into the vertiginous
space variously termed post-Enlightenment, post-positivism, post-empi-
ricism, post-foundationalism, post-structuralism, and post-modernism.
Yet, while quick to name the space of deliberation, we have little
been able to articulate its own presumptions and potentials for the
future. Thus far the primary form of deliberation has been critical
in character; its contours are determined primarily by that to which
it is opposed. And, while successfully opposing the array of inter-
locking assumptions making up the modernist worldview, critics have
been little capable of offering a successor project. For many, such
efforts are virtually precluded, for to make claims to a superior rationality or truth would be to recapitulate the very orientation in ques-

tion. Thus, many find the entry into the intellectual world beyond modernism deeply compelling—but despairingly directionless.

It is precisely at this juncture that many of us find enormous potential in the emerging dialogues on social construction. Is it possible, we ask, to locate within the array of critical argumentation a unique composite of suppositions that will enable us to break the containment of modernism, and offer promising new visions and potentials without recapitulating the litany of modernism itself? The challenge is not an easy one, nor do I believe, should we view it as one that can (or should) ever be completed. However, in the present offering I wish to develop in brief some of the most promising and pivotal ideas to emerge from dialogues that now move across the globe. The participants in such dialogues issue from many and varied sectors of scholarly and professional life, and while disagreements are rife, a core set of working suppositions can be termed social constructionist. In what follows I shall first develop a rudimentary outline of these suppositions. This will set the stage for opening discussion on several issues of special relevance to practical theology. My hope is that together these discussions can serve as an adequate invitation to the dance of dialogue constituting the ensuing chapters of this volume.

Premises for a Social Constructionist View of Knowledge

One may conveniently trace elements of contemporary constructionism to early work in the sociology of knowledge, with Karl Mannheim (1951), Ludwig Fleck (1979), and Berger and Luckmann (1966) serving as leading exemplars. All were concerned with the extent to which knowledge claims were lodged within communities of understanding. However, the watershed period of development—that in which constructionist thought acquired its robust revolutionary significance—resulted from the emerging confluence of three different forms of post-1960s critique: an ideological critique in which the moral and political significance of seemingly neutral claims to knowledge became manifestly apparent, a literary/rhetorical critique that underscored the demands of literary and rhetorical traditions on descriptions and explanations of the world, and a social-historical critique which made apparent the social processes required to legitimate claims to knowledge. Thrown into critical question were not

only all authoritative claims to truth, but indeed all transcendent
claims to facts, rationality, truth and objectivity. As these various
lines of critique amalgamated in various ways, so also were marginal
traditions of inquiry given new life (e.g. hermeneutics, rhetoric, discourse analysis, media studies, film studies), and new domains of
inquiry set in motion—including for example, women's studies, cultural
studies, narrative studies, queer studies and interpretive studies.

Yet, in trying to assay these various movements, it is also clear
that there are no assumptions shared by all participants. Indeed,
there are significant areas of tense disagreement. In my view it is
most useful to characterize our current condition as one of active,
ongoing dialogue, and to treasure the prevailing impulse to avoid
terminating debate with new canons or codes. At the same time, for
purposes of our present discussion, there are advantages to freezing
the frame momentarily, and selecting out a reasonably coherent array
of suppositions around which there tends to be reasonably broad
agreement. In this way we appreciate more fully what is at stake for
developments in practical theology. In my view the following suppositions appear to be central to many current constructionist analyses (Gergen, 1994, 1999).

— *The terms by which we account for the world and ourselves are not dictated
by the stipulated objects of such accounts.* There is nothing about what is
the case that demands any particular form of sound, marking, or
movement of the kind used by persons in acts of representation or
communication. This orienting assumption grows in part from the
incapacity of scholars to make good either on a logic of induction
by which general propositions can be derived from observation, or
a correspondence theory of language in which single words can be
tied unambiguously to observational atoms. It owes a special debt
to Saussure's (1983) argument for the arbitrary relationship between
signifier and signified—word and object. It benefits directly from the
various forms of semiotic analysis and textual critique demonstrating how accounts of worlds and persons can function independently
of their putative referents. It is also informed by analyses focussed
on social conditions and processes in science that privilege certain
interpretations of fact over others— irrespective of observations themselves. In its most radical form, it proposes that there are no principled constraints over our characterization of existing states of affairs.
In terms of description and explanation, we confront a condition of

"anything goes." What is possible in principle, however, is beyond practical possibility. A second assumption furnishes the reason.

– *The terms and forms by which we achieve understanding of the world and ourselves are socially derived products of historically and culturally situated interchanges among people.* For most constructionists, descriptions and explanations of the world are not driven by "what there is," but rather, have their origins in human relationships. Prominent are those relations in which linguistic meaning is achieved. To achieve intelligibility is to participate in a pattern of social coordination, or if sufficiently extended, a cultural tradition. It is only by virtue of sustaining a coordinated pattern of relationship that we can make sense at all. And in this way, accounts of the world and self are everywhere and at all times constrained. If there is sufficient univocality in language use, various descriptions may acquire the veneer of objectivity, the sense of being literal as opposed to metaphoric. Or, in Alfred Schutz' (1962) terms, understandings become "culturally sedimented," constituents of the taken-for-granted order.

Yet, this emphasis on "truth through tradition" is incomplete without taking into account the forms of interaction in which language is embedded. It is not simply the shared repetition of a vocabulary that leads to its reification, but the entire pattern of actions-within-context of which such discourse is a part. It is thus possible to maintain a deep concern with "justice" and "morality"—terms with a high degree of referential pliability—because they are embedded within more general patterns of relationship. We carry out elaborate social procedures—such as "blame and forgiveness" on the informal level, and court proceedings at the institutional level—in which terms such as "justice" and "morality" play a key role. To remove the terms from these traditional or institutionalized patterns of relationship, would be to destroy traditions. To remain within the accustomed traditions is to know that justice and morality can be achieved.

It is in the same way that scientific communities can draw conclusions that carry the sense of transparent objectivity. By selecting certain configurations to count as "objects," "processes," or "events," and by generating consensus about the occasions upon which the descriptive language is to apply, a social world is formed of which the sense of "objective validity" is a byproduct. Thus, as scientists we may come to agree that on certain occasions we shall call various configurations "aggression," "prejudice," "unemployment" and so on—not because there simply is aggression, prejudice and unemployment "in the world"—but because these terms allow us to index various configurations in ways that we find socially useful. It is thus that communities of scientists can reach consensus, for example, about "the nature of aggression," and feel justified in calling such conclusions "objective." However, cut away from the communities responsible for establishing and negotiating reference, the conclusions turn strange, suspect, or possibly oppressive.

– *The degree to which a given account of world or self is sustained across time is not principally dependent on the objective validity of the account, but relies on the vicissitudes of social process.* This is to say that accounts of the world and self may be sustained without respect to perturbations in the world they are designed to describe or explain. Similarly, they may be abandoned without regard to what we take to be the perduring features of the world. In effect, the languages of description and explanation may change without reference to what we term "phenomena," and the latter are free in principle to change without necessary consequences for theoretical accounts. This view owes a debt first to the Quine-Duhem thesis that through progressive elaboration of its ancillary and implied clauses a theory may be sustained across a sea of observations that might otherwise function as refutations. It further reflects much history of science study of the social processes responsible for paradigm change or stasis (Kuhn, 1962). Further, it benefits from the sociology of knowledge emphasis on the negotiation of meaning in scientific laboratories (cf. Latour, 1987). It is featured in the present summary primarily to underscore the implications of social constructionism for scientific approaches to "religious behavior." For as this position makes clear, methodological procedures, regardless of rigor, do not act as principled or transcendent correctives to the languages of scientific description and explanation. In effect, empirical methodology is not a knock-down device for adjudicating the adequacy of competing scientific accounts. Politically speaking, this is to open the door to alternative voices within the culture, voices long scorned for their lack of acceptable ontology, epistemology, and accompanying methodology. Such voices are no longer silenced because they lack the necessary empirical data.

At the same time these arguments do not lead to such dangerous conclusions as: observations are irrelevant to scientific description, could be abandoned without affecting the corpus of scientific writing, and have no bearing on the credibility of the scientist or the societal value of the scientific effort. What is being advanced here is that controlled observations do not in themselves furnish a warrant for holding certain descriptions and explanations transcendentally more accurate—"more objective," "truer"- than others. However, within scientific communities empirical methods can be (and typically are) used in ways that bear on truth claims, the confidence of conclusions, the veracity of the investigator, and the implications of the scientific effort for society. Methodological practices can be used to ascertain the "existence of the phenomena," their co-occurrence with other established phenomena, and the probability of their existence within larger populations. Further, community members may build up mutual trust in the report of such events, and legitimately chastise or expulse those who play the game incorrectly or guilefully. The texts of science will amply express the results of such activities, and if one enters into the appropriate rituals predictions can indeed result. But in the end, these are practices of historically and culturally situated communities and their warrant is derived from within these communities. It is the claim to transcendent truth—beyond the local culture—to which the constructionist objects.

– *Language derives its major significance from the way in which it is embedded within patterns of relationship.* In their critique of the correspondence view of language, critics lay to rest any simple view of an observational basis of language meaning. As outlined above, propositions, are not so much "reality driven" as they are culturally determined. At this point most constructionists ally themselves with Wittgenstein's (1953) view of language as owing its meaning to its use within relationships. For Wittgenstein words acquire their meaning within language games, that is, through the ways they are used in patterned exchanges of words. The term "score" in football acquires its meaning from the particular way in which it is used within the tradition of the game, or in Wittgenstein's terms, the "form of life." Observations may thus play a part in the generation of meaning, but only within the "rules" or conditions of a particular "game" or form of life. This view of meaning as derived from micro-social exchanges, embedded within broad patterns of cultural life, lends to social constructionism a strong pragmatic dimension. That is, it draws critical attention to the way in which languages—including scientific theories—are used within a community and extended outward into the culture. The

constructionist analyst is not likely to ask about the truth, validity,
or objectivity of a given account, what predictions follow from a theory, how well a statement reflects the true intentions or emotions of
a speaker, or how an utterance is made possible by cognitive processing. Rather, for the constructionist samples of language are inte-
gers within patterns of relationship. They are not maps or mirrors
of other domains—referential worlds or interior impulses—but out-
growths of specific modes of life, rituals of exchange, relations of
control and domination, and so on. A preeminent question to be
asked of knowledge claims is thus, how do they function within a
community, in what rituals do they play an essential role, what activities are facilitated and what impeded, who is harmed and who gains
by such claims?

— *None of the propositions making up the social constructionist web are candi-
dates for truth.* The wave of critiques giving rise to constructionism
undermines both the traditional conceptions of truth—namely as
inhering in a privileged relationship between mind and world ("seeing
the world as it is"), or between words and world ("describing the
world as it is"). Rather, we are lead to view the term "truth" as a
discursive integer, acquiring its meaning from particular traditions
of usage. On the positive side, the declaration "it is true" functions
as a guaranty to one's interlocutors that one's words are conforming
to a shared tradition. To declare in a court of law that "It is true
that I was in Utrecht on the night of December 12" is to assent to
common traditions of coordinating language within a particular sub-
culture. From a critical standpoint, however, "truth talk" has too frequently functioned as a means of circumscribing dialogue, of privileging
certain traditions while silencing all contenders. In effect, the phrase,
"It is true,"often functions to eliminate or disparage resistant voices.

   In this context constructionist descriptions and explanations of language, meaning, culture and the like must also be viewed in terms
of cultural function. There is no attempt, then, to safeguard constructionist arguments against all criticism, or to replace other orientations to knowledge, language, social process and the like. Rather,
one is invited to explore the implications of constructionist deliberations
in terms of how we go on in intellectual, scientific, cultural and
global life. What forms of reflection are invited, what new modes of
understanding are encouraged, what kinds of practices emerge, what

happens to our relationships together? In confronting these questions, a search for "the answer" is replaced by open-ended dialogue.

It is this last line of argument that also saves constructionist deliberations from the charge of self-refutation. As it is said, how can constructionism claim that truth is socially constructed without simultaneously undermining its own claims to truth? Such critiques are misdirected, however, as constructionism makes no such claims for itself. As I see it, constructionist arguments function not so much like truth claims as invitations to enter a domain of intelligibility—wear it like a new coat, dance with its melodies, explore its pathways. If the domain expands the potentials for life, then perhaps this is sufficient. In any case, there is no attempt here to erect yet another "first philosophy," or to wage war with existing traditions. Rather, constructionist thought invites us into an appreciative stance with respect to all traditions—even while it asks us to look carefully into their suppressive potentials.

Social Construction and Practical Theology

Constructionist dialogues have given rise to an enormous expansion in the range and forms of scholarly inquiry, and a virtual explosion of new practices—in organizations, therapy, education, counselling, social work, community building and more. And, while there is a substantial corpus of scholarship relating religious and spiritual issues to postmodernism (cf. Taylor, 1984; Berry, P. and Wernick, 1995; Milbank, 1990), the dialogue between constructionism and practical theology is only in its infancy. The present volume is only one indication of the possibilities inherent in this dialogue. It would be impossible to lay out in advance all the paths that might be taken as the conversation develops. However, as an incitement to these discussions, I shall make some preliminary inroads into three significant domains—knowledge of religious practice, the self, and communication. In each case constructionism will pose challenges to much traditional thinking on such matters, and open avenues to alternatives of significant potential. Throughout these discussions I must beg both for the reader's patience and assistance. I shall speak into issues of practical theology, but I will do so without the privilege of a conversational history. My proposals will undoubtedly prove insensitive to much that has been spoken and written within this domain; they may fall short in some instances and prove unintelligibly radical in others. These are challenges that will demand further dialogue, and it is precisely the possibilities of generative dialogue that I hope may be invited by these remarks.

Knowledge of Religious Practice: A Constructionist Vision

How are we now to understand what it is to possess knowledge about religious practices? How does a constructionist view transform the study of such practices? At the outset, it is important to realize that while critical of the assumptions of traditional empirical study, constructionism is not set against the battery of empirical practices— for example, systematic observation, interviews, statistical records, standardized measures—that comprise the tradition. Nor does it attempt to undermine the conclusions based on such studies. Indeed, such information may be of enormous practical importance to the religious community, if not the society more generally. Further, much constructionist inquiry is itself indebted to an empiricist heritage. Cosntructionists have been particularly engaged in the study of discourse, the ways in which meanings are generated, sustained, or disrupted in relationships (cf. Edwards and Potter, 1992; Antaki, 1988). The rhetorical power of such work is derived primarily from its colorings of objectivity.

Constructionist writings, do, however, invite us into a reflective posture about traditional empirical inquiry—including its own. At the outset, we are asked to remove the mantle of "truth beyond perspective" from the conclusions of such work. We are asked to consider the grounding assumptions that ultimately shape the concepts, observations, and arena of conclusions. From what standpoint is the inquiry taking place; what values are at stake; whose voices are silenced by approaching the work from this particular standpoint? All become pertinent questions. We are also invited to consider the implications of treating empirical conclusions as working truths. If, for example, fundamentalist religious sects are characterized as "close minded," what does such a characterization imply with respect to our subsequent actions toward these groups? If such a conclusion is indeed alienating, then we might ask whether it is to an alienated world we hope our findings will contribute. Finally, we might wish to ask whose voices are being suppressed by such work, and whether we might not augment our practices of inquiry so as to be more inclusive. Have we, for example, simply translated the voices of those we study into a framework of our own choosing, or have these voices been granted authenticity in their own right? The outcome of such reflection cannot be determined in advance; however, with each question new departures may be invited.

It is in this latter sense that the constructionist dialogues do far more than provoke critical reflection. They also invite new forms of methodology, theory, and practice. In the domain of research methodology, constructionists point to the ways in which differing methodologies construct their objects in various ways. Experimentation will necessarily demonstrate that persons are caught within a deterministic world of cause and effect, while trait measures will yield linear hierarchies of good and bad (e.g. high self-esteem vs. low, high neuroticism vs. low)—not because causal relations and hierarchies are simply there in the world, but because the choice of method is inevitably a choice of ontology. Further, all methodologies harbor political, moral and ideological ramifications. Most existing methods, for example, create the reality of a subject-object divide—the knowing scientist as opposed to the subject of study. In this way they foster an atomized picture of society in which each of us exists separately and independently of others. We shall return to this issue shortly.

For now the important point is that because of the constraints of existing methodologies, many constructionists have been moved to seek alternatives. Such methods create different constructions of human activity and harbor different values. For example, many researchers have established means of working cooperatively with those they might otherwise study as "the other." Participatory action researchers attempt to work with various marginalized groups to establish the kinds of knowledge necessary to enhance their life conditions. Others use various narrative methodologies to give voice to otherwise silenced sectors of society. Polyvocal methodologists attempt to give expression to the multiple voices or selves possessed by both the researcher and the researched. And still other scholars search for more aesthetic means of representing their subject matter; performance, poetry, multi-media, music, and art are all added to the compendium of methodologies. The range and number of the newly emerging "qualitative methodologies" cannot be underestimated (cf. Denzin and Lincoln, 2000).

At the theoretical level, constructionism again invites the scholar into a creative mode. If it is not the world as it is that determines our descriptions and explanations, but rather the network of pre-suppositions that constrains what it is we can ultimately say about the world, then all existing presumptions become optional. There are no necessary grounds, taken for granted principles, or ontological certainties from which we must begin the task of articulating the world. And, should the world that is constructed by the existing presumptions seem problematic for humankind, we are invited then to develop alternatives. We may wish, then, to replace the concept of theoretical accuracy with generativity. A *generative theory* is that which can unsettle the taken for granted assumptions and offer new alternatives for both "seeing" and for action (Gergen, 1994). Theorists such as Freud and Weber served a generative function within the worlds they occupied. What alternatives do we now wish to pursue? We should be less guided in such theorizing by "what there is" than "what may become."

The constructionist also points to the limited gains to be achieved through highly abstract and abstruse theorizing. Theory for the constructionist is not a map of the world, but a communicative act within a range of relationships. To create theory which can function only within the narrow range of the academy is perhaps a squandering of dialogic resources. We might rather prize those forms of expression that bring greater numbers of communities into common dialogue. The implications of these remarks on theory will be clarified in the following discussion.

From the Bounded to the Relational Self

Most western religions—at least in their contemporary configurations—are highly congenial to the individualist presumptions of knowledge. That is, there is a strong tendency to view individual subjectivity as the cornerstone of communal existence. Whether in terms of consciousness, agency, rationality, conscience, beliefs, desires, or motives (and their various cognates) "the mind" is a pivotal determinant of individual action. Or, more broadly, we see individuals as fundamentally bounded, with the mind (or possibly the soul) somewhere toward the center of individual being. From this perspective, it is the inter/action among bounded individuals that creates relationships—

in families, friendships, romances, communities, and societies. When we speak of the relationship of the individual agent to God we again instantiate this tradition. While constructionism places us in a position to appreciate the fruits of the individualist tradition, we simultaneously find ourselves inquiring into the limitations. For, if we view our constructions of the real and the good as relational achievements, placed in jeopardy are all ontological posits concerning the nature of individual minds. That is, all that we can intelligibly say about mental events (including the conscience or the soul) does not derive from the "nature of the individual interior" in itself, but from the social negotiation of reality. In effect, presumptions about individual minds are derivative of relationship, and thus optional.

Within this clearing, we are first free to consider both the gains and shortcomings of the individualist tradition for the culture more generally. To be sure, most would agree that in its contribution to our traditions of democracy and public education, for example, the individualist tradition has been invaluable. Further, many would view cultural life as deeply nourished by the prevailing beliefs in individual reason, free choice, the emotion of love, and private conscience. Yet, we also find that these same cultural legacies are purchased at a price. Increasingly scholars have come to see the individualist view of the self as contributing to deeply problematic forms of life. To define the self in terms of a bounded region of the interior is to define cultural life in terms of atomized units. As Winston King (1988) has put it, "Mind, soul, or consciousness alone within the citadel of individual selfhood looks out at everything else, whether human or nonhuman, as 'other.'" (p. xi) The very definition of self is that which sets one apart from others—which is to say, fundamentally isolated and unknown by others. In this sense, the traditional conception contributes to a sense of alienation and loneliness, and in more extreme conditions a sense of "all against all." One is invited into caring for the self first, ensuring that "number one" is satisfied above all. This form of narcissism defines relationships as secondary—to be sought primarily when one needs them for personal gain or gratification. We may not wish to abandon the individualist tradition, but its limitations certainly invite deliberation on expanding the range of alternatives.

For the constructionist, then, what follows from these critiques? As one commentator (Johnson, 1999) has averred, "Social construction makes for lively polemics, but does not add much to our knowledge. It is not enough merely to be subversive." (p. 45) It is the case that much of the constructionist literature has been critical in posture. Focal has been the challenge of unmasking the face of authority and liberating human action from the taken for granted. In my view, however, such forms of deconstruction are only pre-liminary to the more exciting and expansive challenge of *reconstruction*. If we locate problems and limitations in existing conceptions of the real and the good, how might we forge alternative intelligibilities of promise? And how can these alternatives inspire new forms of personal or societal action? There are no principled answers to such questions, no convenient formulas or heuristics for developing new languages and related practices. We move here from playing what James Carse (1986) would call a *finite game*—in which the rules are already established—to an *infinite game*, in which we play together with the rules to create anew.

In my view, the process of generative reconstruction is indeed in progress, and has already lead to a range of exciting and practically promising innovations (see my 1999 review). For the present, I shall focus on only one of these developments, represented in what might be called the *narrative turn* in our understanding of the self. In this case we begin with the premise that the self is indeed a social con-struction. This possibility is not so much a dismantling as an invi-tation to explore the potentials of such a view. One of the primary vehicles in constructionist analyses is the narrative—a rhetorical device by which we can simultaneously create the sense of relationship among events, impart a directionality to them, imbue them with moral significance, and come to understand them as temporally located. Many constructionists find it useful to view individual iden-tity in terms of narrative construction. One comes to understand and communicate about oneself in terms of stories. To possess a sense of self derives in part from the capacity to tell a story about a sin-gle individual, emerging from a set of events in the past, lodged within a present, and moving toward one or more goals in the future.

Most important in terms of its challenge to the individualist tra-dition, narrative theorists and practitioners see narratives as em-bedded within the socius. This is so most obviously the case in terms of the cultural and historical variations in narrative forms. Different story forms emerge across varying cultures and periods of history; narrative forms may be lacking in some cultures and richly elabo-rated in others. Further, children must learn to acquire these linguistic conventions in order to participate within the culture. Thus, to narrate the self at all is to participate in a cultural (communal) action. Equally important, however, is an understanding of narratives as communicatively embedded. That is, making sense in narrative is essentially a linguistic act. To sustain a narrative account one must be linguistically intelligible to one's interlocutors (real or imagined). The intelligibility of the self is thus born of relationship. And too, because one's interlocutors are typically embedded within one's stories ("the supporting cast"), narrative negotiations are deeply formative of "how the story of self" can be told. Self-narratives are thus inter-stitched with others.

It is largely the socially embedded quality of narration that has lead moral scholars and researchers to trace moral action to narratives of the self. For example, as Alasdair MacIntyre (1981) proposes, the "story of my life is always embedded in the story of those communities from which I derive my identity." (p. 205) If one's life story is embedded in one's communal relationships, one essentially understands oneself in terms of the moral traditions of the community. To live out one's narrative identity within the community will constitute moral action according to its standards. It is also this socially embedded quality of narratives that has inspired therapists around the world to focus their practices on narrative change. "Restorying" is a key to forging new patterns of relationship (cf. White and Epston, 1990). And it is this same concern with the formative and sustaining power of narration that has lead many organizational specialists to focus on the circulation of stories in organizations. It is largely through the sharing of stories that organizational culture is built and shared visions are made possible (Czarniawska-Jeorges, 1996).

Narrative theory and practice represent an important step toward redefining the self as fundamentally relational. However, there are additional moves in this direction that may be better understood as we confront the challenge of communication.

Toward Communication as Coordinated Action

As a final incitement to conversation, let us consider the issue of communication—a pivotal process for the practical theologist. For example, how are we to address diverse interpretations of religious texts, how can those with divergent or conflicting beliefs reach common understanding, and how is it that communication functions to change or sustain belief within a community? These are only a few questions of abiding concern. Yet, attempts to answer such questions have traditionally issued from the individualist tradition just discussed. To communicate, it is typically advanced, involves the sharing of private meanings. To understand another is to comprehend his/her subjectivity—thoughts, attitudes, feelings, values and the like. And the site of comprehension is one's individual psyche. Good communication, from the traditional standpoint, requires *intersubjective* resonance. As might be supposed from the critiques outlined above, approaching questions of communication from this standpoint leads to enormous conceptual problems. How can one ascertain the character of one's own thoughts or feelings, such that they can be properly communicated? How is it possible to access another's private meanings? For hermeneutic theorists, questions such as this have rendered the problem of accuracy in communication insoluble. What alternative to the individualist orientation to communication can constructionism provide? Again, a constructionist view of knowledge does not require any particular conception of communication—the door is open to multiple perspectives. At the same time, by extending assumptions within the metatheory we do find it inviting to consider communication as a relational achievement. Helpful here is Wittgenstein's (1953) advisory, "Try not to think of understanding as a 'mental process' at all. For that is the expression which confuses you. But ask yourself: in what sort of case, in what kind of circumstances, do we say, 'Now I know how to go on.'" (p. 97) Drawing from Wittgenstein's view of word meaning as derived from language games, we can explore the possibility that understanding is not a mental act but successful participation in a form of life. There is much to be desired in this idea, as it usefully expands the intelligibility of relational selves. Let us explore:

In my work on this subject I have found it useful to view the minimal unit of meaning as constituted by both a communicative *action* and a *supplement*. That is, meaning docs not inhere in the isolated utterance (and/or action) of the individual, but comes into meaning as another supplements it with yet another utterance (and/or action). For example, the utterance, "How old are you?" contains no meaning in itself. It begins to acquire meaning as "a question" when another responds with what we take to be "an answer," such as "I am now 52." In contrast, if one responds to the utterance with silence, it could be viewed as an "undesirable intrusion." Or, to reply with, "What is this, implicit ageism?" may define the initial utterance a form of prejudice. Yet, we cannot fasten on these accounts of what is meant, for each supplement is *itself* a form of communicative action. It too remains unfinished in terms of its potential meaning. For the interrogator to reply to the respondent's answer, "I am now 52" with "I don't believe you," would rob the utterance of meaning as an answer, and to suggest that it is dissimulation. But of course, the conversation does not terminate here . . . meaning continues to unfold. In this sense, there is no ultimate comprehension; meaning is always open to the next supplemental move.

As this line of argument is carried forward, several features become increasingly significant. First we see that there can be no private meaning, that is a space of significance that is not already embedded within a sea of cultural signification. We come into meaning only within the process of relationship. Or, to embellish the relational view above, the articulation of an "I" (after all, an integer in language) requires a preceding process of relationship. Second, we find that the movement into meaning requires difference. A supplement that duplicates the communicative action that precedes it, stands as empty as the action itself. It is in precisely this way that a child who echoes everything a parent says to him or her, robs the adult of the capacity to mean. And, as we expand the range of differences that are possible, so do we expand the potentials of any communicative act to mean something. Finally, we come to appreciate the ways in which persons, acting in a face to face relationship, largely owe their capacities to create meaning to traditions, to histories of relating in which various action/supplement sequences have become recognized as meaningful. There is no act of friendship, courage, passion or love that is one's very own. Centuries of relationship have been required to offer up these possibilities.

The present reasoning also carries important implications for relations among those with contrasting faiths or beliefs. As suggested above, differences are required in order to sustain a domain of meaning. It is from the matrix of difference that meaning comes into being. Thus, as we confront a sea of differences we shift from registers of alienation to appreciation. Without contrasting traditions, the significance of one's own becomes pallid—becoming the ocean which the fish cannot appreciate as such. Moreover, we may especially prize the emergence of new amalgams, forms of religious practice that draw from otherwise conflicting traditions. As we entwine the differences, so do we "dance new meanings into being." Further, it may be said that it is a strength of Christianity that it is a polyglot tradition, braiding together strands of Hebrew, Greek, and Roman traditions to form a set of practices that sustain these various traditions (even if the origins are often suppressed.) And, in spite of the broad critiques of New Age spiritualism, the movement must be appreciated for its unbridled amalgamation of otherwise alienated religious forms (Wexler, 1996).

In Conclusion

The social constructionist dialogues have largely been spawned within a context of critique of modernist assumptions of individual knowledge. Yet, as the conversation has broadened and gathered momentum, so is it possible to discern movements that far exceed critical reflection. As I have tried to outline here, the constructionist dialogues furnish us with the rudimentary beginnings of a far richer array of possibilities—both conceptual and practical. Further, as the implications are extended, we find fertile ground for new conversations—such as those represented in the present volume. The intersections between constructionist thought and issues in practical theology are many and vital. In the present chapter I have tried to open the door to mutual concerns with knowledge of religious practice, the relational reconstruction of the self, and the nature of human communication. I have not yet touched on issues of moral action and the nature of the sacred, both of which are very important to me. However, perhaps the ensuing chapters will open a space for such discussion. And, most likely, we shall find ourselves moving into new spaces of conversation, scarcely imagined in the preceding. Therein lies the beauty of continuing the dialogue.

References

Antaki, C. (Ed.) (1988). *Analyzing everyday explanation: a casebook of methods*. London: Sage.
Berger, P. & Luckmann, T. (1966). *The social construction of reality*. New York: Doubleday.
Berry, P. & Wernick, A. (Eds.) (1995). *Shadow of spirit, postmodernism and religion*. New York: Routledge.
Carse, J. (1986). *Finite and infinite games, A vision of life as play and possibility*. New York: Free Press.

Czarniawska-Jeorges, B. (1996). *Narrating the organization*. Chicago: University of Chicago Press.
Denzin, N. & Lincoln, Y. (2000). *Handbook of qualitative methods*. 2nd ed. Thousand Oaks, CA: Sage.
Edwards, D. & Potter, J. (1992). *Discursive psychology*. London: Sage.
Fleck, L. (1979). *Genesis and development of a scientific fact*. Chicago: University of Chicago Press.
Foucault, M. (1979). *Discipline and punish: The birth of the prison*. New York: Random House.
—— (1980). *Power/knowledge*. New York: Pantheon.
Gergen, K.J. (1994). *Realities and relationships*. Cambridge: Harvard University Press.
—— (1999). An invitation to social construction. London: Sage.
Johnson, D. (1999). "Are you for real?" A review of I. Hacking's *The social construction of what? New York Times Review of Books*, Dec. 12, 1999. (p. 45)
King, W. (1988). Foreword, to Nishitani, K. (1988) *Religion and nothingness*. Berkeley: University of California Press.
Kuhn, T. (1962). *The structure of scientific revolutions*. Chicago: University of Chicago Press.
Latour, B. (1987). *Science in action*. Cambridge: Harvard University Press.
Lyotard, J.F. (1984). *The post-modern condition: A report on knowledge*. Minneapolis: University of Minnesota Press.
MacIntyre, A. (1981). *After virtue*. South Bend, Ind. Univ. of Notre Dame Press.
Mannheim, K. (1951). *Ideology and Utopia*. New York: Harcourt Brace.
McCloskey, D.N. (1985). *The rhetoric of economics*. Madison: University of Wisconsin Press.
Milbank, J. (1990). *Theology and social theory: beyond secular reason*. Oxford: Blackwell.
Saussure, F. de (1983). *Course in general linguistics*. London: Duckworth.
Schutz, A. (1962). *Collected papers: The problem of social reality*. The Hague: Martinus Nijhoff.
Simons, H. (Ed.) (1994). *Case studies in the rhetoric of the human sciences*. Chicago: University of Chicago Press.
Taylor, M.C. (1984). *Erring, A postmodern A/theology*. Chicago: University of Chicago Press.
Wexler, P. (1996). *Holy sparks, Social theory, education and religion*. New York: St Martins.
White, M. & Epston, D. (1990). *Narrative means to therapeutic ends*. New York: Norton.
Wittgenstein, L. (1953). *Philosophical investigations*. Oxford: Blackwell.

IMPLICATIONS OF SOCIAL CONSTRUCTIONISM FOR THE PSYCHOLOGICAL STUDY OF RELIGION

Jan M. van der Lans

Introduction

The founding fathers already saw clearly that psychology should not confine itself to the study of the isolated individual. There is not a single psychological phenomenon that can be understood without connecting it to its social impulses. George Herbert Mead is often cited as an early advocate of this view, but many others could be mentioned. In one of his studies on the social origin of the self, Mead (1925) remarked that "any self is a social self, [. . . .] restricted to the group whose roles it assumes, and it will never abandon this self until it finds itself entering into the larger society and maintaining itself there" (p. 276).

Before Mead, the German psychologist Georg Simmel, whose work was recently rediscovered (Levine, 1971; Fuhrer & Josephs, 1998), had introduced the concept of cultivation. Cultivation refers to the continuous process of unfolding of the inherent potential of the developing individual by interaction with sociocultural resources. "The cultivated mind is constructed through transaction of the person with his cultural environment, i.e. permanently changing cultural forms, such as personal possessions, places, settings, institutions. These cultural forms are mostly overlooked in contemporary developmental theorizing and research" (Fuhrer & Josephs, 1998, p. 277). In the 1920s, both Piaget and Vygotsky emphasized the role of social interaction in learning processes. They drew attention to the fact that learning is not just a matter of imitation and passive reproduction of what is transmitted to children, but a process of construction in which both child and educator are actively involved. However, Piaget's conceptual approach differed markedly from that of Vygotsky. Piaget investigated how, through the dual action of assimilation and accommodation, the developing child builds mental representations of its world of experience. Vygotsky approached learning as co-construction taking place when cultural tools for thinking and acting are mediated in the interaction between child and educators. Nevertheless,

Vygotsky was also primarily interested in intra-mental functioning
(Fuhrer & Josephs, 1998).[1]

In this respect, social constructionism brought a radical change.
In search of a psychological explanation of behavior, scholars belonging to the social-constructionist movement[2] focus on processes of
social interaction and cultural mediation. Social constructionists are
primarily interested in dynamic interpersonal processes of construction, especially discursive interaction. In their view, human subjects
achieve a sense of self mainly through discourse (Gergen, forthcoming). "If we create our worlds largely through discourse, then we
should be ever attentive to our ways of speaking and writing" (Gergen,
1999, p. 115). For social constructionists, the intra-mental world of
cognitive representations and its development is no longer the object
of study. They concentrate on discursive processes in which a shared
world of experience is constructed. Individual psychological characteristics are only studied as dynamic elements of socio-cultural action.
Social constructionists criticize mainstream psychology generally for
its aspiration to uncover the universal essentials of mental functioning.
Social constructionism contends that only the investigation of the
dynamics of social practices can open the door to understanding the
individual self. Evidently, this outlook entails methodological implications as well.

This chapter will discuss the significance of social-constructionist
theory for the psychology of religion.[3] As in the other chapters of
this book, social constructionism is conceived here as it has been
voiced by Kenneth Gergen. I will first go into the question of whether
Gergen's criticism of mainstream psychology is also applicable to the

---

[1] For an extensive comparison of the theoretical approaches of Simmel, Piaget
and Vygotsky I refer to Fuhrer & Josephs (1998).

[2] Leading authors are Kenneth Gergen, Ron Harré, John Shotter, Michael Billig,
Jonathan Potter, Margaret Wetherell. Gergen's focus is the interdependence of self-
knowledge and relationships, Shotter focuses on dynamic interpersonal processes of
construction ("joint action"), Harré on language as social action. As 'discourse psychologists', Potter, Wetherell and Billig investigate the performative function of language in social action.

[3] What exactly is psychology of religion? Psychology of religion wants to explain
the phenomena of religion, both individual (belief, experience, practice, religion in
the biography) and social (relationship between type of religious orientation on the
one hand, and group life, intergroup relations, societal issues on the other), using
psychological concepts and theories. Note, that there is not one psychology of religion but a diversity of approaches. Most current theoretical approaches in the psychology of religion are inspired by either social psychology or psychoanalysis.

psychology of religion. Next, I will give an outline of research in the psychology of religion based on a social-constructionist viewpoint. Finally, some implications of the social-constructionist approach will be discussed.

1. *Is Gergen's Criticism on Mainstream Psychology also Applicable to Research in the Psychology of Religion?*

Ken Gergen has voiced many objections against mainstream psychology, particularly experimental social psychology. His main points of criticism are directed against (1) the focusing on the individual mind to account for human behavior, and (2) the claim of objective truth associated with experimental research.

To state that 'the isolated individual' (Gergen, 1995) is the object of study in psychology would be an exaggeration. The social context of individual behavior is nearly always given some measure of attention. However, the social context is mostly conceived in a limited fashion, in terms of some general static background variables. It is generally true that, by focusing on internal mental states and structures, psychology overlooks the impact of social interdependency. In the social-constructionist approach relational processes replace the individual person as the central concern of psychological research and reflection. Not intra-mind processes but social interaction is the object of research, particularly the intersubjective exchange of meaning and the co-construction of narratives. Social constructionism is not so much a new psychological theory for, as was said earlier, social interaction has been recognized as a significant theme from the beginning. But after the dominance of Cognitivism since the 1950s,[4] social constructionism is certainly a new perspective on what should be the object of psychological research.

Another reason for Gergen (1998b; 1997; 1999) to criticize mainstream psychology regards the philosophy of knowledge underlying

---

[4] The new interest in studying cognitive processes, which in the late fifties replaced "the cold winter" of behaviorism and objectivism, was initially "welcomed as a revolution intended to bring 'mind' back into the human sciences" (See Jerome Bruner's almost autobiographical report in the first chapter of his Acts of Meaning, 1990). Very soon, however, computation became the leading model in research. Cognitive processes were equated with the information processing in computer programs. The new cognitive scientists soon appeared to be no less reductionistic than the former S-R learning theorists.

the empirist methodology. Epistemology is a main theme in social constructionism. Gergen challenges the claim that the testing of hypotheses, if conducted in accordance with methodological and statistical rules, reveals objective truth. Gergen argues that from a social-constructionist viewpoint there is no reason to attribute special authority to this kind of methodology, because all its strategies (e.g. random sampling, tests of significance) cannot change the fact that scientific interpretations rest on local sociocultural conventions. Both the so-called objective methods and the conclusions drawn from the data are historically and culturally situated. Our conceptions of the psychological reality are products of social construction, instead of representing real internal facts or structures.

These two criticisms also hold for the psychology of religion. First, the psychological study of religion is focused on the individual as "a self-determining and self-contained being" (Gergen, 1996, p. 498). Although textbooks in the psychology of religion generally agree with Clifford Geertz' well-known definition of religion as a meaning system or discourse that people share and a system of social practices (Geertz, 1973, p. 90), this conception of religion as an interactional phenomenon is surely not a leading principle for research in this field. Religiosity is usually investigated as one of the characteristics of an individual person. Religious behavior is not approached as relational practice, i.e. a practice of sharing something with others who are of concern to the individual. Neither are religious beliefs studied as negotiated understandings of meaning. The research is carried out based on the assumption that a systematic investigation of the relationships between religiosity and other personality characteristics in various samples will be conducive to finding universal psychological determiners that can account for variation in individual religiosity.[5]

It is not difficult to find examples of this kind of 'essentialistic thinking' in the Anglo-American oriented social psychology of reli-

---

[5] In qualifying specific beliefs and behavior as religious, psychology of religion conforms to common parlance. In spite of the increasing cultural heterogeneity of society, the fact that the criteria for identifying religious belief, attitude, experience, motivation are highly circumscribed by culture and social context is not yet a topic of discussion in the psychology of religion. This is even valid for the concept of religion itself. We use concepts to sort out life into separate domains. But the yearly procession with the statue of the goddess Sarasvati in villages in India will surely not be categorized as religion by the local people. The concept does not even exist in their vocabulary.

gion. It occurs in the many studies into types of religious orientation that remains a main topic of research since Gordon Allport's introduction of the classical distinction between intrinsic and extrinsic religiosity. Religious types are conceived in these studies as internal mental structures and described in terms of their correlation with personality characteristics. Essentialistic thinking also occurs in psychological studies of fundamentalism and orthodoxy that explain these religious phenomena by correlating them with scores on personality scales (e.g. Leak & Randall, 1995; Gritzmacher, Bolten & Dana, 1988; Furnham, 1982). Although correlational analysis does not permit conclusions about causality, such studies refer to internal mental structures to account for these types of religious belief. In my own research into people's construction of the meaning of biblical narratives, I started out with the simple idea that a cognitive skill like metaphor competence would give me the key to understanding why people choose either a literal or a metaphorical interpretation of a religious utterance. However, analyzing the research data we found that not cognitive skills but social interaction accounted for the variance. People who were active members of a religious community preferred a literal interpretation and people who preferred the metaphorical meanings practiced religion privately without being involved in a religious community (Lans, J. van der, & Jablonski, P., 1994).

A bias towards internal mental structures can also be recognized in research into religious development. Under the influence of the Piagetian paradigm, structural differences of religious thinking are often reduced to distinct stages of individual cognitive development instead of being related to social and cultural conditions (e.g. Goldman, 1964; Fowler, 1981).

A focus on intra-individual mental processes is not less characteristic for psychoanalytic studies on religion. Based on the work of Freud, these studies account for people's concepts of God by relating them to hidden underlying psychic structures. Nevertheless, a social-constructionist researcher will probably find more affinity here than with the social-psychological or cognitive approach to religious behavior, because in psychoanalytic studies people's narratives are of central concern. An individual's religious beliefs are studied as narratives, the personal meaning of which is determined by social interactions in one's biography, especially in early childhood. Also in psychoanalysis, the religious reality, in which an individual believes, is studied as "a world created through discourse", be it that a psychoanalyst is primarily interested in the implicit and hidden affective discourse between parents and child, and will approach religious narratives as vehicles of relational experiences that are of concern for the person (e.g. Rizzuto, 1979).

Gergen's epistemological criticism seems to be valid for the psychology of religion as well. Every psychologist of religion knows the classic methodological principle of the 'exclusion of the transcendent', that was formulated by Theodore Flournoy (1903). Following this principle, the psychology of religion abstains from making truth claims concerning a metaphysical reality.[6] Truth claims concerning a psychological reality, however, are found in every academic journal of the psychology of religion, just as is the case in mainstream psychology. Here, too, there is consensus about the belief that successful hypothesis-testing reveals the truth of our theories with respect to the psychological determinants of religious behavior. With that goal, lots of scales and pre-structured questionaires have been constructed, considered to be objective measures of various aspects of religious thinking, experience, feeling and action. Data have been collected with these instruments, hardly ever in a religious context, most of the times from first-year students before or after a lecture. As if religious believers are "self-contained" individuals. Hood (1997), one of the most experienced empiricists in the psychology of religion, distances himself from methodological claims to truth, however. Referring to Gergen's criticism of mainstream psychology, he affirms that "what constitutes an empirically derived theory, is in no sense resolved" (p. 224).

2. Examples of Research in the Psychology of Religion Based on the Social-Constructionist Viewpoint

After having indicated the type of research that demonstrates that the criticisms launched by social constructionism against mainstream psychology also bear on the psychology of religion, I will mention some investigations into religious behavior that have been conducted in accordance with the basic ideas propounded by social construc-

---

[6] Yet, in spite of this principle, several experimental studies were set up to proof that prayers are answered. To my view, such studies should be considered experimental theology instead of psychological.

tionism. These studies are rather heterogeneous in regard to their topics of research, but they are alike in the fact that the religious individual is studied as a social actor involved in a community of interlocutors.

Religious Experience

It is appropriate to call to mind here first the scholarly work of Hjalmar Sundén who some decades ago introduced a new approach in the study of religious experience, by studying these phenomena as imaginative discursive interaction. He demonstrated in several case studies that religious experience in which a person has the sense or feeling of the presence of "a beyond", becomes psychologically understandable when it is analyzed as an internal dialogue. He analyzed religious experience as a process of role-playing and role-taking guided by a biblical (or other) religious narrative with which the person is very familiar and which under specific situational conditions becomes the reference frame for the construction of reality (Sundén, 1960; 1987). Because of this approach of religious experience as relational action, Sundén may be considered a social constructionist *avant la lettre*. His conception replaced the previous romanticist view that religious experience arises from an innate human sensitivity for the sacred (Vergote, 1984, p. 125) and is therefore beyond social construction.

A study by Szuchewycz (1994) can be mentioned as a recent example of a similar constructionist approach. Performing a micro-analysis of speech acts in a charismatic prayer meeting, he revealed various discursive strategies which help the believer to create an experience of divine human communication.

Religious Belief as Discursive Social Action

Two examples can be mentioned here. In setting up a study into religious belief, James Day (1993) adopted one of the main principles of social constructionism, namely that language is social action. On the basis of narrative interviews he concluded that religious belief "depends on an audience by whom the believer can be understood", and that "there is no belief independent of the narrative forms that fund its construction, reformation, and communication" (p. 225). His study clearly demonstrates that the religious beliefs of an individual person are not the outward expressions of an inner state but elements in an ongoing process of negotiation about meaning. To investigate religious belief in the context of interaction with an audience is quite a new approach in the psychology of religion. In a comment to Day's article, Gergen (1993) emphasized the important implications of Day's analysis for the psychology of religion as well as for religious institutions: "Rather than viewing beliefs as private possessions of unfathomable minds. . . . the present emphasis is on beliefs as they function within relationships. This relational view gives honor to community, interdependence, and the inherent connection of all people." (pp. 234–235). Community and interdependence is what makes or breaks religious beliefs. We also refer here to Ulrike Popp-Baier's research (1998) into religious orientations of women in a charismatic movement in Germany. Her theoretical frame was not social constructionism in the strict sense but the 'hermeneutic social psychology' of Fritz Schütze (originating in phenomenological sociology and symbolic interactionism) and his methodology of the narrative interview. Popp-Baier's study should be mentioned here because she steered clear of an essentialistic approach to the religious orientation of her participants, by conceiving it not as a mental structure but as a construction accomplished during the narrative interview. Moreover, the study is worthwhile because of its thorough methodology.

Religion as a Context Factor in Self-construction

In research in pastoral psychology and clinical psychology of religion, a narrative approach is sometimes used to investigate the role of religion in the discursive construction of identity (e.g. Barbarin & Chessler, 1986; Bilu & Witztum, 1994; Ganzevoort, 1998; Van Uden & Pieper, 1996). Susan O'Neill (1999) interviewed an obsessive-compulsive patient and found in her account of living with this disorder that religion was a key discourse in her self-presentation.

Social Perceptions of or About Religious Groups

The resource mobilization theory has frequently been used in the past to account for the growth and decline of cults (Bromley & Shupe, 1979) or of social movements in general. Recently, Kebede & Knottnerus (1998) discovered that a social-constructionist perspective offers a more fruitful approach because it focuses on social-psychological processes. They observed how, during small group discussions called 'reasoning', adherents of the Rastafari movement construct a collective identity and collective action frames, in which Biblical symbolism plays a significant role. In another study, Bartkowsky (1998) related negative perceptions about Voodoo-ism in the cultural discourse to typifications of Voodoo in the media.

Popp-Baier, in her contribution to this book, explains that a social-constructionist approach is suitable to examine changes in religious identity in research on religious conversion, since it perceives the convert as a social actor involved in a community of interlocutors and conversion narratives as products of social interchange.

3. *Some Implications of the Social-constructionist Approach*

To introduce a social-constructionist approach into the psychological study of religion involves a radical change of procedure, in several respects. Some implications will be mentioned here. The main implication regards the question of what should be the object of research. After the preceding argumentation it will be evident that the key to understanding an individual's religiosity can only be found in research into communication processes in which individuals are involved. I will argue that internal dialogues should also be part of this research, and discuss Wertsch' concept of mediated action as another refinement.

Does social constructionism also provide us with a new methodology for the study of religious communication? Addressing this issue, I will mention some points that require further discussion.

Religious Communication Deserves Particular Attention

The introduction of the social-constructionist paradigm into the psychology of religion will strongly encourage studies into religious communication processes. From a constructionist point of view, religious faith is primarily social, not psychological. This view is in keeping with the importance that religious agencies attribute to tradition. Tradition is always a central concern of a community of faith since it contains its roots as well as the condition for its existence. The word tradition refers to a product as well as a process. The product-aspect is often emphasized, for instance when church authorities argue that the heritage should be preserved unaltered. This policy may cause a fossilization of the religious tradition. In living religions, tradition is not a static system of inmutable ideas and conventions, but a continuous process of acts of communication. When a living religion is the object of study, then research into tradition-as-process is of primary importance. This is true for studies of religion as a socio-historical institution as well as for psychological studies of the nature and function of an individual's religiosity. From the perspective of social constructionism, the royal way to understanding an individual's religion is to investigate the discursive transactions and negotiations of religious meaning in the social networks in which the individual is involved. This is the only adequate way to study topics like religious identity or religious experience. It is important to note that it would be a mistake to focus solely on manifest transactions within a physical social network. The psychological study of an individual's religiosity should also cover the internal dialogue between the self and another who is virtually present in memory or imagination. What matters is that religiosity must always be studied as dialogical activity in which meanings are negotiated.

Unit of Analysis

In a social-constructionist perspective, the unit of analysis should not be the individual but discursive interaction in a dyad or a group. The power of this approach is that it throws light on psychological phenomena that may remain invisible in case of an exclusively individual focus, for example the way in which different social contexts evoke different selves. But is it a matter of either/or or of and/and?

If we shift the focus exclusively to social action and interaction, we may run the risk of marginalizing the individual side of the social construction process. Human beings are conscious, reflective animals who, while participating in a concrete social context, can at the same time be involved in other virtual discourses, by way of memory and imagination. If we were to only take dyadic or group discussions as the units of analysis, we could miss these inner dialogues between the self and another, or between different self-positions, which may be highly effective in the construction of meaning, identity, self-concept, etc. For some purposes, therefore, it will be better to take the individual as the unit of analysis. Not as an isolated object but as a self who, by way of memory and imagination, may be involved in a dialogue with more social contexts than the present external one. As already mentioned, some psychoanalytical studies of religion show that we should not draw a sharp distinction between mental structures and relational action. There should be a balance in research designs between an individual-oriented and a social context-oriented approach.

James Wertsch (1999) suggested for this same reason that 'mediated action' should serve as our basic unit of analysis. Mediated action is defined as "human action, carried out by an individual or group, that employs a 'cultural tool' or 'mediational means'. . . . If one accepts the claim that cultural tools play an inherent role in mediated action, one is led to recognize that there is an important sense in which such action can never be attributed solely to individuals. Instead, cultural tools must be viewed as doing some of our acting for us, or, more accurately, we *and* cultural tools act in tandem" (p. 152). Examples of cultural tools in the field of religion are narratives derived from the holy books or hagiography, religious aphorisms, rituals, symbols, devotional objects, etc. Another advantage of taking mediated action as research focus is that it will draw the investigator's attention to a significant characteristic of human action. "It involves an irreducible tension, or dialectic, between mediational means, on the one hand, and their unique use by an individual or individuals, on the other hand. Leaving either of these elements out of the picture almost inevitably leads to reductionism. . . . Mediated action is best thought of in terms of a tension between cultural tools, with all their potential to shape action in accordance with convention, on the one hand, and the unique use of these cultural tools, with all its unpredictability and creativity, on the other" (id., pp. 152–153).

Attention for this dialectic tension is very important in research in the domain of religion. It is through this tension that religious communication is a living tradition. It is also the key to understanding alterations in a person's religious identity as well as religious changes in the culture at large.

The Researcher: Distant Investigator or Involved Participant?

Social constructionism puts great weight on the idea that the investigator is not a distant observer. She/he should realize that a research situation is also relational in the sense that the investigator her-/himself is a participant. This regards data collection (interview or observation) as well as data analysis. In an interview, the respondent

constructs a self-narrative, guided by questions and reactions of the
interviewer. Methodological handbooks present rules in order to prevent interviewer bias. However, social constructionism seems to
demand more than prevention. It points to the fact that an interview is not only a method of collecting data. It is a dyadic relationship, itself performing a social function. The interviewer is part
in the game. This makes a discursive analysis of an interview pro-
tocol extremely complicated. I am afraid that this issue is not nearly
given as much attention as it deserves. For example, if the interview
method is used in order to compare how young and grown-up believers construct their images of God, the interviewer must be conscious
of the fact that the interview protocols are not an objective reproduction of the God-narratives of his/her respondents, precisely because
of the fact that the interviewer has played an active part in the construction process. Also, the way in which the researcher, sitting behind
her/his desk, will read and understand the interview protocols, will
in turn be influenced by her/his personal attitudes and virtual social
networks, and will lead to an all but 'objective' summary of the God-
narratives of the respondents. Not to mention the problem of the
relationship between their experiences of God and their narratives
about this experience.[7]

It becomes clear, that once social constructionism has sensitized
us to the contextuality of our research data, some of the common
technical terms of our methodological discourse, such as 'validity',
'reliability', extrapolarization' and 'representativeness' need revision.

Should the Investigator be Familiar with Religious Discourse?

One consequence of the "relational embeddedness of all significant
human activities" (Gergen, 1997) is that neither religious beliefs, nor
religious experiences nor praying can be investigated without paying
attention to the religious tradition in which the individual is embedded
(conceived as the complex of religious narratives). An individual's
religion is based on shared language. Religion is a discursive artifact.

A significant implication for research is that being familiar with
the lived narratives of the religious tradition in which the research
participants are involved is a necessary prerequisite for the investi-

---

[7] This problem of the relationship between 'experience' and 'narrative' is treated
extensively by Popp-Baier.

gator. Without this familiarity a dialogical relationship between investigator and participant is hardly possible. Because of this, it seems extremely difficult for a psychologist of religion born and grown up in the Western world, to study the religious mental representations of people from a non-Western religious culture. This applies not only to beliefs but also to ritual behavior. From a social-constructionist viewpoint, Milton Yinger's famous one-liner needs correction. Yinger (1970) once warned students of religion to "look for rituals first, then for the beliefs connected with them" (p. 17). However, ritual and narrative are inextricably entwined. Being a lived narrative, a religious ritual does not have any sense in it self, prior to discourse, but owes its meaning to the narratives shared by the community. As soon as the sharing of the narratives stagnates (e.g. because of a loss of plausibility), the significance of the ritual is no longer generally accepted and the community will disintegrate. Religious rituals cannot be understood without knowledge of the narratives.

Ambiguity with Respect to Methods

The key question is of course what to do with traditional research methods? The keystone of social constructionism is the idea that our conceptions of psychological and social reality are time- and culture-bound. In Gergen's philosophy of knowledge, objective truth does not exist. Gergen rejects the possibility of mapping reality in a decontextualized manner (Gergen, 1985). What does this mean for methods of the social sciences such as laboratory experiment, survey questionnaire, standardized psychometric tests and personality scales?

Gergen's philosophy of science has been labeled anti-empirical (Kukla, 1986). But this label regards his rejection of the concept of empirical truth. "Scientific formulations would not be the result of an impersonal application of decontextualized, methodological rules, but the responsibility of persons in active, communal interchange." (Gergen, 1985, p. 272). However, Gergen is not against the application of empirical methods. "We need not abandon our attempts to predict and control" (Gergen, 1998[a], p. 102). And in his recent book he lists specific ways in which empirical research can be useful (Gergen, 1999).

Yet, this leaves us in an ambivalent state of mind. Social constructionism makes it difficult to go on believing in the standard methods. On the other hand, it does not provide an elaborate alternative overall methodology, apart from specific methodologies that have been worked out for discourse analysis and for narrative approaches. Methods and theory are interdependent. If conservative research procedures are still considered to be useful, then, after the attacks on the positivist ground beneath traditional psychology, they need a new methodological justification.

Psychological research into religion can benefit from a multiplicity of methodologies. A traditional survey with structured questions may provide an overview of the diversity of religious practices, thus allowing a preliminary classification (a fine example is Hutsebaut, 1998). Following this global approach, the inquiry may switch to another method that allows a more profound analysis of these practices as mediated action within social communities. The study of social practices in combination with the accompanying narratives (negative or regressive as well as positive or progressive) remains of primary importance for the study of religion.

Final Remark

During the century that has just come to an end, academic psychology has more than once seen theories arriving on the scene which opposed its one-sided focus on the individual mind and stood up for the study of the individual in context (e.g. Vygotsky's sociocultural theory and Symbolic Interactionism). Until now, these approaches have had little or no influence at all on mainstream psychology. According to Gergen, the time is now ripe for a turnover. "As we approach the 21st century, psychological essentialism is undergoing a subtle but increasingly discernible erosion" (Gergen, 1996, p. 128). In his view, the need for a social-constructionist psychology is bound up with changes in the broader society. The profusion of communication technologies causes the self to be thrust into an ever-widening array of relationships (Gergen, 1991; 1996).

I have read several of Gergen's articles and books. I like his challenging writing style and his fresh ideas, and also his attempt to bridge realist and constructionist positions (Gergen, 1998; 1999). Over the years I found that his ideas are also appealing to students. In the department where I worked, Berger & Luckmann's *The social construction of reality* (1966) had already been required reading for the students since the early 70s and the seed of social constructionism fell into fertile ground.

But I also found that the majority of my colleagues in other psychology departments are not responsive and even antagonistic to this approach. Despite the fact that positivistic psychology has been the target of criticism from both inside and outside for over a quarter of a century, and even though an authoritative key-expert in this country such as H.C.J. Duijker already condemned psychology's disregard for the historical, social, and cultural context of its object as early as 1979, mainstream psychology continues to pursue its dream, in The Netherlands as elsewhere, of being a natural science and will not give up its belief in the truth warrants of the experimental method. That makes me less optimistic than Ken Gergen about the possibility of a paradigm change within social psychology.

What are the obstacles? Is it because social constructionism does not offer alternative criteria for truth? (Gergen, 1985, p. 272). This is certainly an important reason. However, truth warrants are currently under great pressure in all sciences. But there are more reasons for the rejection of social constructionism. One might be the lack of a systematic methodology. Research reports based on this approach often leave behind the impression of being too intuitive. But the social context may well be the most unfavorable factor. The high social status of the natural sciences, which is also reflected in strong financial support by the government, strengthens the position of psychological research according to the man-machine model. Access to financial resources and to academic journals is far easier for this type of psychological research. It is not difficult to understand why real innovations are so rare in academic disciplines.

References

Berger, P. & Luckmann, Th. (1966). *The social construction of reality*. Garden City, NY: Doubleday.
Bilu, Y. & Witztum, E. (1994). Culturally sensitive therapy with ultra-orthodox patients. The strategic employment of religious idioms of distress. *Israel Journal of Psychiatry, 31*, 170–182.
Bromley, D. & Shupe, A. (1979). *'Moonies' in America. Cult, Church and Crusade*. London: Sage Publications.
Bruner, J. (1990). *Acts of Meaning*. Cambridge, MA: Harvard University Press.
Day, J.M. (1993). Speaking of belief: language, performance, and narrative in the psychology of religion. *International Journal for the Psychology of Religion, 3* (4), 213–230.
Duijker, H.C.J. (1979). *De problematische psychologie en andere psychologische opstellen* [Problematic psychology and other psychological essays]. Meppel/Amsterdam: Boom.
Flournoy, Th. (1903). Les principes de la psychologie religieuse. *Archives de Psychologie, 2*, 33–57.
Fowler, J. (1981). *Stages of Faith. The Psychology of Human Development and the Quest for Meaning*. San Francisco: Harper & Row.

Fuhrer, U. & Josephs, I.E. (1998). The Cultivated Mind: From Mental Mediation to Cultivation. *Developmental Review, 18,* 279–312.

Furnham, A. (1982). Locus of control and theological beliefs. *Journal of Psychology and Theology, 10* (2), 130–136.

Ganzevoort, R. (1998). Religious coping reconsidered, Part Two: A narrative reformulation. *Journal of Psychology and Theology, 26* (3) 276–286.

Geertz, C. (1973). *The Interpretation of Cultures.* New York: Basic Books.

Gergen, K.J. (1985). The Social Constructionist Movement in Modern Psychology. *American Psychologist, 40* (3), 266–275.

—— (1991). *The Saturated Self.* New York: Basic Books.

—— (1993). Belief as relational resource. *The International Journal for the Psychology of Religion, 3* (4), 231–236.

—— (1995). Singular, socialized, and relational selves. In Lubek, Ian, Van Hezewijk, R. a.o., (Eds.). *Trends and issues in theoretical psychology* (pp. 25–32). New York, NY, USA: Springer Publishing Co.

—— (1996). Technology and the self: From the essential to the sublime. In Grodin, Debra, Lindlof, Thomas R., a.o. (Eds.). *Constructing the self in a mediated world. Inquiries in social construction* (pp. 127–140). Thousand Oaks, CA, USA: Sage Publications, Inc.

—— (1996). Psychological Science in Cultural Context. *The American Psychologist, 51* (5), 496–503.

—— (1997). Social theory in context: Relational humanism. In Greenwood, John D. *et al.* (Eds.). *The mark of the social: Discovery or invention?* (pp. 213–230). Lanham, MD, USA: Rowman & Littlefield Publishers, Inc.

—— (1998ª). From control to co-construction. New narratives for the social sciences. *Psychological Inquiry, 9* (2), 101–103.

—— (1998ᵇ). Constructionism and Realism: How are we to go on? In Ian Parker (Ed.), *Social Constructionism, Discourse and Realism* (pp. 147–156). London: Sage Publications.

—— (1999). *An Invitation to Social Construction.* London: Sage Publications.

—— (forthcoming). Narrative, Moral Identity and Historical Consciousness: a Social Constructionist Account.

Goldman, R. (1964). *Religious Thinking from Childhood to Adolescence.* London: Routledge & Kegan Paul.

Gritzmacher, S.A., Bolton, B. & Dana, R.H. (1988). Psychological characteristics of Pentecostals: A literature review and psychodynamic synthesis. *Journal of Psychology and Theology 16* (3), 233–245.

Heritage, J.C. (1989). Current developments in conversation analysis. In D. Rogers & P. Bull (Eds.), *Conversation: An interdisciplinary approach.* Clevedon: Multilingual Matters.

Hood, R.W. (1997). The Empirical Study of Mysticism. In B. Spilka & D.N. McIntosh (Eds.), *The Psychology of Religion. Theoretical Approaches* (pp. 222–232). Boulder, Co.: Westview Press.

Hutsebaut, D. (1998). Omgaan met geloof en godsdienst: ontwikkeling of bepaald door opvoedingsmodel? [Dealing with faith and religion: development or determined by type of education?]. In J. Janssen, a.o. (Eds.). *Schering en Inslag. Opstellen over religie in de hedendaagse cultuur* (pp. 18–31). Nijmegen: KSGV.

Jablonski, P.T., Hermans, C.A.M., & Lans, J.M. v. d. (1998). Understanding religious language as mediated action: Vygotskian perspective. In A. Ploeger, & C. Sterkens (Eds.), *Search for meaning. Education into the realms of meaning in a plural society* (pp. 191–218). Kampen: Kok.

Kebede, A.S. & Knottnerus, J.D. (1998). Beyond the pales of Babylon: The ideational components and social psychological foundations of Rastafari. *Sociological Perspectives, 41* (3), 499–517.

Kukla, A. (1986). On Social Constructionism. *American Psychologist, 41* (4), 480–481.

Lans, J. van der, & Jablonski, P. (1994). Religious language interpretation. In K. Krenn, H. Petri, & G. Roth (Hrsg.), *Archiv für Religionspsychologie*, Band 21 (pp. 208–219). Göttingen: Vandenhoeck & Ruprecht.

Leak, G.K. & Randall, B.A. (1995). Clarification of the link between right-wing authoritarianism and religiousness. The role of religious maturity. *Journal for the Scientific Study of Religion, 34* (2), 245–252.

Levine, D.N. (Ed.) (1971). *Georg Simmel on sociability and social forms.* Chicago: Chicago University Press.

Mead, G.H. (1925). The Genesis of the Self and Social Control. *International Journal of Ethics, 35,* 251–277.

O'Neill, S. (1999). Living with obsessive-compulsive disorder: A case study of a woman's construction of self. *Counselling-Psychology-Quarterly, 12* (1), 73–86.

Pattillo-McCoy, M. (1998). Church culture as a strategy of action in the Black community. *American Sociological Review, 63* (6), 767–784.

Popp-Baier, U. (1998). *Das Heilige im Profanen. Religiöse Orientierungen im Alltag. Eine qualitative Studie zu religiösen Orientierungen von Frauen aus der charismatisch-evangelikalen Bewegung* [The Sacred in the secular. Religious orientations in everyday life. A qualitative investigation of women of the Charismatical-Evangelical movement]. Amsterdam/Atlanta, GA: Rodopi.

Rizzuto, A. (1979). *The Birth of the Living God.* Chicago: University of Chicago Press.

Sundén, Hj. (1966). *Die Religion und die Rollen* [Religion and roles]. Berlin: Töpelmann.

—— (1987). Saint Augustine and the Psalter in the Light of Role-Psychology. *Journal for the Scientific Study of Religion, 26* (3), 375–382.

Szuchewycz, B. (1994). Evidentiality in ritual discourse: The social construction of religious meaning. *Language-in-Society, 23* (3), 389–410.

Van Uden, M. & Pieper, J. (1996). Mental Health and Religion: a complex relationship. In Grzymala-Moszczynska, H. & Beit-Hallahmi, B. (Eds.). *Religion, Psychology, and Coping* (pp. 35–56). Amsterdam-Atlanta: Rodopi.

Vergote, A. (1984). *Religie, geloof en ongeloof. Psychologische studie* [Belief and unbelief. Psychological perspectives]. Antwerpen: De Nederlandsche Boekhandel.

Wertsch, J.V. (1999). Sociocultural research in the copyright age. In Lloyd, Peter, & Fennyhough, Charles (Eds.). *Lev Vygotsky. Critical Assessments.* Vol. IV. (pp. 144–163). London: Routledge.

Yinger, J.M. (1970). *The scientific study of religion.* London: The Macmillan Company.

CONVERSION AS A SOCIAL CONSTRUCTION: A NARRATIVE APPROACH TO CONVERSION RESEARCH

Ulrike Popp-Baier

1. *Introduction*

"Constructionism" and "constructivism" are deeply rooted in western philosophical tradition.[1] In his well-known statement (B 1) Protagoras, the oldest of the sophists, asserted: "Of all things the measure is man, of things that are that they are, and of things that are not that they are not" (cf. Sprague, 1972, p. 18). Throughout the history of philosophy, different versions of this statement have been formulated to challenge the belief in any kind of reality independent of human efforts and in the notion of true knowledge as the accurate representation of an objective order. The statement reflects the basic assumption of all theories that the world as we know it is *our* world.

The paradigmatic programme for a "constructive" theory of knowledge is apparent in Kant's transcendental philosophy: "Something dawned on all investigators of nature when *Galileo* let balls, of a weight chosen by himself, roll down his inclined plane; or when *Torricelli* made the air carry a weight that he had judged beforehand to be equal to the weight of a water column known to him; or when, in more recent times, *Stahl* converted metals into calx and that in turn into metal by withdrawing something from the metals and then restoring it to them. What all these investigators of nature comprehended was that reason has insight only into what it itself produces according to its own plan; . . ." (Kant, *Critique of Pure Reason*, B XIII). According to this description, knowledge cannot be a reflection of a given reality but is the construction of a world. This notion that knowledge includes in a certain sense also the construction of the

---

[1] Many authors draw no distinction between "constructionism" and "constructivism" (cf. e.g. Hacking, 1999) and evaluate this tradition in general as relativism, scepticism and subjectivism (cf. e.g. Nagel, 1997). A detailed discussion of the different deliberations on reality construction, however, requires distinguishing between the main positions in contemporary dialogues concerning these issues. For a brief description of different forms of constructionism and constructivism with their different emphases and outlooks, cf. for example Gergen (1999).

object of this knowledge is elaborated in Kant's transcendental theory of knowledge.

Contemporary pragmatist or post-modern philosophy stresses the dependence of knowledge on language, social practices and social relationships. In the philosophy of science "constructionists" argue that even in fundamental physics, scientific findings result from processes of social interaction and the mobilization of disparate rhetorical or representational resources.[2] Explicitly constructionist projects aim to display or analyze actual, historically situated social interactions underlying the establishment of entities or facts presented in the physical and social world, in sciences and humanities.[3]

In psychology Kenneth Gergen is one of the most prominent protagonists of the social constructionist movement. From "Social Psychology as History" (1973) to "An Invitation to Social Construction" (1999), Gergen has challenged empiricism and realism in psychological inquiry and devised a social constructionist perspective, which sheds a new light on standard research topics such as emotions, memory, the self or mental disorder. His social constructionism provides an ambitious paradigm of psychological thought. According to Gergen, the present dialogues (in social constructionism) "not only unsettle the grounds for all that we know to be real and good; they also offer unparalleled opportunities for creative deliberation and action. They invite us into new spaces of understanding from which a more promising world can emerge" (Gergen, 1999, p. vi).

In this paper I will not explore the fundamental debates about social constructionism, relativism or subjectivism in psychology and search for the "last word" (cf. Nagel, 1997). The aim of this paper is modest. I will start by considering Kenneth Gergen's perspective and examining whether it is a reliable tool for conducting conversion research in psychology of religion.

---

[2] Sokal's reactions to different forms of this "epistemic relativism" epitomized the so-called science wars which focused on social construction (cf. Sokal & Bricmont, 1997).
[3] For example, Jeffery's (1998) "The Social Construction of Indian Forests", Kitzinger's (1987) "The Social Construction of Lesbianism", Pickering's (1984) "Constructing Quarks: A Sociological History of Particle Physics" or Tonkin's (1992) "Narrating Our Pasts: The Social Construction of Oral History".

2. *"Social Construction of What?"*[4]

Social constructionism offers fruitful prospects for research in the social sciences when the overarching attitude is related to local claims about the social construction of a specific X. According to Hacking (1999), social construction critiques an assumed status quo, and the logic of social constructionist arguments implies two theses. The first thesis is the precondition for every kind of social constructionist claim about a certain X. It is the fundamental basis (i.e. the 0 level) for an argument that X is socially constructed:

"(0) In the present state of affairs, X is taken for granted; X appears to be inevitable" (Hacking, 1999, p. 12).

The next thesis is the starting point for social constructionist arguments:

"(1) X need not have existed, or need not be at all as it is. X, or X as it is at present, is not determined by the nature of things; it is not inevitable." (Hacking, 1999, p. 6).

An example of an influencing social constructionist perspective on a certain subject is the core argument of early gender theorists that biological differences between the sexes do not determine gender, gender attributes, or gender relations. Before early feminists started their work, thesis (0) concerning a variety of gender attributes and gender relations as biologically determined was almost common sense and thesis (1) became the starting point not only for social constructionist arguments but also for emancipatory politics and life politics (cf. Giddens, 1991).[5] On the other hand, as Hacking (1999, p. 12) argues, nobody claims that banks, the tax system, cheques, money, dollar bills, the Federal Reserve, or the British monarchy are based on a social construction. These are all contractual or institutional objects, and everybody today understands that contracts and institutions are the result of historical events and social processes. Therefore,

---

[4] I borrow this title from Ian Hacking's (1999) book "The Social Construction of What?"

[5] Contemporary debates concerning these issues are more complicated. For example Judith Butler challenges the distinction between "sex" and "gender" and maintains that the construct called "sex" is as culturally constructed as "gender." In addition to this argument she suggests a new understanding of "construction" (cf. Butler, 1990, 1993).

nobody will defend thesis 0, the precondition for a social constructionist argument concerning these objects. Claiming thesis 1 would
be pointless, because everybody would agree with thesis 1. Generally,
a social constructionist argument concerning a certain X (object,
characteristic of an object or subject, classification. . . .) makes sense,
if someone defends a thesis claiming that X is taken for granted, is
determined by the nature of things, and is inevitable. This is the
precondition for a social constructionist thesis about X. Otherwise,
the social constructionist argument would be trivial.

Moreover, the "construction" metaphor retains one element of its
literal meaning, namely that of building or assembling from parts.
According to Hacking (1999, p. 50) "anything worth calling a construction has a history. But not just any history. It has to be a history of building." Calling X a social construct therefore implies a
historical perspective on X in social scientific research. If we claim,
that X has been socially constructed, we need to examine how X
has been constructed historically in the context of social relationships.

What are the consequences of this point for a social constructionist viewpoint in psychological research? If we want to relate the
overarching attitude of social constructionism to local claims about
the social construction of a specific X, we have to specify thesis 0
as the precondition for social constructionist arguments concerning
psychological research.

With respect to the state of the art in psychological research, claims
about X as socially constructed are useful if at least one of the following three theses receives general support within the academic
community, if at least one of the following three theses represents a
kind of status quo concerning the classification of a certain X in
psychology:

(1) X is the effect of the cause Y.
(2) X is a physiological or a mental state.
(3) X is an individual act or the product of one.

Invoking emotions, thought, memory, knowledge, and the like as
social constructs is equivalent to arguing, for example, that emotions
are not the effect of a cause and are not mental states or the product of individual acts as is maintained in current research on emotions (cf. e.g. Frijda, 1986). In a social constructionist perspective
emotions could be conceptualized as situated contributions to a discourse which depend on the use of shared language and a certain

common background of social knowledge and experience and which have a history. Empirical research in the framework of this "social constructionist" perspective on emotions explores the functions of emotional displays in the episodes of everyday life, the different kinds of emotional displays in various sub-cultures and their respective construction over time. In addition, the social constructionists might engage in interesting debates with defenders of the idea that emotions are states of individuals or physiological reactions to environmental stimuli. Emphasizing that social conflicts are socially constructed would be pointless, as most psychologists would not defend (1), (2) or (3) concerning the "nature" of social conflicts. A social conflict is rarely believed to be the effect of a cause, a physiological or mental state, or the product of an individual act. And of course, social conflicts have a history, as any "empiricist" or "realist" will agree. Social constructionist arguments are not necessary for a historical perspective on social conflicts.

After this prelude I will examine whether the social constructionist perspective can be related to conversion research in psychology of religion in a useful way.

3. *Classical and Contemporary Conversion Research*

Considering conversion research in psychology of religion reveals that the conceptualization of conversion as a transformation of the self is prominent (cf. e.g. the overview in Hood *et al.*, 1996 or the review of Paloutzian, Richardson and Rambo, 1999). According to Richardson (1985), a classical research paradigm can be distinguished from a contemporary research paradigm. In the classical paradigm, empirical research conceptualizes conversion as a sudden event in which a passive subject is influenced by forces which may be variously identified. The conversion process is seen as more emotional than rational. The contemporary paradigm conceptualizes conversion as a gradual process in which the convert figures as an active, seeking agent. It is rational rather than emotional. One question that remains to be answered concerning the classical and the contemporary paradigm is: to what does the "self" refer? Zinnbauer and Pargament (1998, p. 164) borrow their definition from the ego-psychology and describe the self as a person's inner world that includes the person's beliefs about the world and about himself or herself. The change in the self brought about by conversion is therefore a change in the core elements of this belief. This mental interpretation ties in with many conceptions of the self in conversion research (cf. Hood *et al.* 1996, as an exception cf. Ullman 1989). Other authors maintain that for a psychological conceptualization of conversion a description of a certain change "in the person" is essential (cf. Paloutzian, Richardson and Rambo, 1999, p. 1053).

In the 1970s the so-called new religious movements elicited great interest among social psychologists and sociologists. In this context the contemporary conversion research paradigm was elaborated, although the classical paradigm persisted and contributed to the debate about these movements as well. Two models—one of the classical research paradigm and one of the contemporary research paradigm—reflect opposite ends of the spectrum concerning the conversion to new religious movements: the model of conversion as "brainwashing" and the model of experimental conversion.

According to Hood *et al.* (1996, p. 324), the term "brainwashing" has entered the vernacular as a summary term for some loosely defined techniques of coercive persuasion that presumably can make persons adopt beliefs and conform to behaviours they would normally reject. The term was originally used to describe the ideological changes of US military personnel who were taken prisoner and indoctrinated by Chinese communists during the Korean War (1950–53). In a body of academic literature published during the Cold War era, techniques of thought reform were analysed as mechanisms of social control characteristic of totalitarian societies and in a second step as characteristic of (fundamentalist) religious groups (e.g. Sargant, 1957, Lifton, 1961). From the late 1960s onward, when the activities of world-rejecting religious movements came under close scrutiny in the West, their socialization practices were compared with these techniques of persuasion (cf. e.g. Halperin, 1983). In this context, some authors produced new variations of the brainwashing thesis, as Conway and Siegelman (1978) have in their book *Snapping*. They describe the manipulative recruitment techniques of the new religious movements as a kind of information bombardment that leads to an "information disease." The authors submit that this information disease explains the drastic personality change of the people who eventually join the group. Ultimately, the conceptualization of this kind of conversion— as brainwashing, as thought reform, as mind control or as coercive persuasion—matters little, as it is combined with a theory about mental changes that are caused by certain techniques. This kind of conversion theory thus implies thesis (1) X (= Conversion) is the effect of Y, and thesis (2) X is a physiological or mental state.

The other extreme of the contemporary research paradigm is the paradigm of the experimental conversion (cf. Dawson, 1999).[6] According to this model, conversion to a new religious movement can be conceptualized at best as the rational act of an individual who wants to change his or her lifestyle. In this case conversion is seen above all as a kind of rational calculation and conscious lifestyle experimentation. Converts are regarded as being aware of their situation, assessing circumstances and weighing the advantages and disadvantages of affiliation. Dawson (1990) uses the rational action theory to analyse conversion processes. According to this concept, the individual chooses to convert and may likewise choose to deconvert, if and when the time is right for him of her. "What we need is a better understanding of the criteria that inform their choices" (Dawson, 1999, p. 309). This conception clearly supports thesis (3): X is an individual act.[7]

Conversion as brainwashing and conversion as an experimental activity are two extreme examples for the conceptualization of conversion in the classical and the contemporary research paradigm. Despite the ongoing popularity of the brainwashing thesis, most scholars in the academic conversion research today reject nearly all versions of the brainwashing model of conversion (cf. Melton, 1999). The model does not fit the general attitude of tolerance and respect for the religious beliefs of "others" that most researchers in religion would like to sustain. Above all, empirical research has clearly demonstrated that the data do not support the model, because most studies show that people joining these movements are extremely likely to drop out of them after a short time (cf. e.g. Barker, 1984). On the other hand, the model of the experimental conversion does not accommodate adequate descriptions of the influence of the religious

---

[6] For an attempt to distinguish between types of conversion (intellectual, mystical, experimental, affectional, revivalist and coercive), cf. Lofland and Skonovod (1981).

[7] In a research report on conversion to the new religious movements of Ananda Marga and the Divine Light Mission in the Netherlands in the 1970s, Van der Lans (1981) stresses the influence of individual dispositions of the converts *and* the influence of social-affective relationships between the potential converts and members of the movements on the process of conversion. Therefore, this report may already be viewed as linking the contemporary research paradigm with a more social-constructionist perspective on conversion.

groups, their recruitment techniques or their communicative and
rhetorical devices. Nevertheless, the two extremes reveal the general
tendencies of the classical and the contemporary research paradigm
in conceptualizing conversion.[8] By defining conversion as a kind of
personal change, mental descriptions are central, and the act of conversion is seen as the act of an individual. If we question the usefulness of this conceptualization and accept Gergen's invitation to
perform social construction in conversion research, we have to look
for another mode of conversion research. Fortunately, we need not
invent a new research paradigm, as we already have the paradigm
of narrative conversion research.

4. *Narrative Conversion Research*

Empirical research efforts to describe and explain conversion have
until now relied primarily on converts' verbal accounts as records of
past events and experiences. Conversion stories were not studied as
such but were thought to convey the conversion procedure and were
thus regarded—at least implicitly—as fairly accurate accounts of a
conversion event.

Research based on the "linguistic turn" in social sciences valued
conversion stories differently. Especially in conversion research within
sociology of religion, conversion stories were no longer interpreted
only in terms of their possible referential function but were understood primarily as acts of speech and communication and were
analysed as such (cf. e.g. Beckford, 1978, Knoblauch, Krech &
Wohlrab-Sahr, 1998, Luckmann, 1987, Snow & Machalek, 1984,
Staples & Mauss, 1987, Stromberg, 1993, Ulmer, 1988, 1990). Considering conversion from the perspective of conversion stories involves
two types of empirical research.

One involves emphasizing the aspects that can be "observed" and
described in the process of telling conversion stories. Such aspects
are the communicative reconstructions in conversion stories, of which
the structure is conducive to empirical analysis. In his attempt to

---

[8] Rambo (1993) tried to develop a more comprehensive framework for analysing
conversions by formulating a stage model which includes historical, theological, social
and psychological aspects of a possible conversion process. This model, however,
has yet to be "tested" empirically (cf. Paloutzian, Richardson, Rambo, 1999).

identify communicative genres (cf. Luckmann, 1986), which he applies to the conversion stories, Luckmann (1987) stresses that conversion stories conform to special preconceived models. Converts telling their stories adopt, according to Luckmann, communicative models of their conversion experiences; more accurately, they adopt models of *telling* conversion experiences. Conversion stories become models of a reconstructive genre that presumes to relate "actual" experiences. In an empirical study of conversion stories, Ulmer (1988, 1990) aims to elaborate both the genre's general traits and the basic components of such stories and their function in the overall composition of such a reconstructive genre.

The other type of empirical research, which focuses on the conversion stories, is associated with a new narrative conceptualization of conversion. This kind of narrative conversion includes e.g. the sociological study by Staples & Mauss (1987) and the psychological anthropological study by Stromberg (1993). Staples and Mauss are inspired by the work of Snow & Machalek (1983, 1984), who interpret conversion according to George Herbert Mead's concept as a change of the universe of discourse. This universe of discourse concept designates the socially constructed frame of reference of self-evident assumptions about mankind and the world in which individuals structure their actions and experience them as purposeful. Staples & Mauss (1987) focus on a certain aspect of such a fundamental change, namely on the change in the way a person thinks and feels about himself or herself. They recommend interpreting this change primarily as self-transformation and the corresponding acts of speech as methods for converts to achieve such self-transformation. Compared to Zinnbauer and Pargament (1998, see above), Staples and Mauss (1987) take a functionalist approach to language and maintain that it is primarily through language that individuals transform themselves. The authors do not look for an "inner world" that changes but for particular kinds of language and rhetoric used by converts to achieve self-transformation. Their empirical study on conversions of Christian Evangelicals reveals that *biographical reconstruction* is the specific rhetorical indicator for a conversion story. According to the approach of Staples and Mauss (1987), converts exhibit this pattern of language because it is only this act of speech that will enable the so-called self-transformation and the adoption of a new universe of discourse in a manner that allows the converts to describe themselves as having undergone fundamental change.

This narrative conceptualization also implies that conversion stories are told as life stories, and that they are a special form of a "self-narrative."[9] Creating a self-narrative involves devising a story about oneself as a temporal being that has a past and relates the present to this past in order to form a perspective for the future. The deliberations of Paul Ricoeur (1991) concerning the narrative function of the so-called plot help us explore other meanings. Referring to Aristotle's Poetics, Ricoeur (1991) defines the act of plotting as an integrative process, which provides the dynamic identity of a narrated story. According to Ricoeur, the plot is a synthesis of the heterogeneous in three respects:

1) It is a synthesis of multiple events or incidents with the complete and individual story.

2) It unifies "components as widely divergent as circumstances encountered while unsought, agents of actions and those who passively undergo them, accidental confrontations or expected ones, interactions which place the actors in relations ranging from conflict to cooperation, means that are well-attuned to ends or less so, and, finally, results that were not willed. . . ." (Ricoeur, 1991, p. 426).

3) It synthesizes a succession of incidents (a pure chronology) into a meaningful temporal unit characterized by a beginning, integration, culmination and ending and derives a configuration from a succession.

These characteristics of stories in general are also typical of self-narratives. Accordingly, we can view conversion stories as self-narratives structured by the plot of the communicative model of conversion. That implies a decisive change in the life of the story's implicit author as a main issue in this kind of story.

The psychological anthropologist Stromberg (1993) follows this conception of conversion. In his analysis of conversion stories from Evangelical circles in the United States, he assumes that religious

---

[9] Gergen's term self-narrative "refers to an individual's account of the relationship among self-relevant events across time. In developing a self-narrative we establish coherent connections among life events" (Gergen, 1994, 187). In contrast to other narrative approaches placing their major emphasis on the individual, Gergen wishes to consider self-narratives as forms of social accounting or public discourse. In this sense, narratives are conversational resources and are open to continuous alteration as interaction progresses. Self-narratives function much like oral histories or morality tales within a society. They serve social purposes such as self-identification, self-justification, self-criticism and social solidification. Narratives are by-products of people's attempts to relate through discourse (cf. Gergen, 1994, 188, 189).

discourse is decisive in enabling believers to reconcile conflicting desires or to express verbally embodied aims and consequently to transform themselves. Borrowing from speech act theory, Stromberg (1993) identifies two forms of communicative behaviour: the form of the *referential* and that of the *constitutive*. When we use linguistic symbols in a *referential* manner, we assume implicitly a general consensus in a certain social reference group concerning the meaning of these symbols. Communicative behaviours that are visible as activities in which one communicates by doing something are designated as *constitutive* communicative behaviours. Their meanings depend upon the contexts in which they occur. According to Stromberg (1993, 10) these behaviours always entail a breakdown between communication and situation. For example, when I say "I have a headache" that may be a referential communicative behaviour if I want to tell someone that I feel pain in my head, and I assume that everyone who knows English will understand this utterance. In a different context, however, the same statement may form a *constitutive* communicative behaviour, i.e. a polite hint that someone should leave. In this case the meaning of the communicative behaviour depends on the social context. Another example of constitutive communicative behaviour is communication that occurs through symbolic systems other than verbal language. For example, I choose to convey the message that I am wealthy by purchasing an expensive car (Stromberg, 1993, 10).

Stromberg (1993) submits that converts who relate their conversion story use a type of speech that always comprises both the referential and the constitutive forms of communication: canonic discourse, which refers to a certain religious context of meaning, becomes constitutive (i.e. meaningful) in a broader sense by linking canonic language directly with individual experience. Stromberg (1993) argues that this connection enables verbal expression of previously inaccessible or unacceptable desires while deepening the commitment to faith. In this sense the conversion narrative constitutes the narrator's self-transformation. Usually this kind of self-transformation takes place and will dialogically be sustained by a variety of social interactions within the respective religious groups. According to this perspective, conversion does not seem like a singular occurrence in the life of an individual. Rather, it concerns a gradual procedure in which subjects attribute meaning to their experiences in a social context. This attribution of meaning is not contained within a single story that is

constantly repeated with each narration. Rather, Stromberg stresses—
in part by regarding the conversion story as a ritual—that the story's
actual performance is an essential constituent of the procedure that
may be perceived as conversion in the sense of self-transformation.

This approach is perfectly compatible with the constructionist metatheory. Kenneth Gergen (1994, 185) proposes a relational view of
self or identity "one that views self-conception not as an individual's
personal and private cognitive structure but as *discourse* about the
self—the performance of languages available in the public sphere."
Conversion to a certain religious belief is related to a kind of discursive practice, to the elaboration of a progressive self-narrative that
relates a more or less radical change of oneself according to the
specific features of the communicative genre of conversion story,
depending on the religious group or groups concerned. Conversion
therefore means religious communication through the ongoing construction and performance of self-narratives as products of social
interchanges—informed, sustained, and restricted by the respective
religious group's canonical language. From the convert's perspective,
his or her psychological task is to assimilate the new religious language to the familiar language she or he has used until now for
public accounts about herself or himself and to accommodate the
familiar language with the new one.

To explore the process of linguistic construction in more detail,
Gergen (1999, p. 64) suggests employing three different lenses: "First,
we shall treat *discourse as structured*, that is, as a set of conventions,
habits or ways of life that are stable and recurring. . . . We then consider a variation on the image of discourse as structure, namely, *discourse as rhetoric*. Here the emphasis is on the way in which conventions
or structures of language are used to frame the world and thus
achieve certain social effects. . . . Finally, we abandon concern with
structure altogether, and put on the lens of *discourse as process*. In particular, we shall be concerned with the ongoing flow of social interchange, the conversations, negotiations, arguments and other processes
by which we are constituted." Using this framework allows us to
relate the approaches of Luckmann (1987), Staples & Mauss (1987)
and Stromberg (1993) to each other to achieve an adequate narrative analysis of conversion conceptualized as a social construction.
The methodical steps for analysing conversion narratives are therefore as follows:

1) We look at conversion narratives as dependent on a structured discourse. That means that we examine the respective canonical religious language providing a certain structure and topics for conversion narratives.

2) We analyse conversion narratives as rhetoric by considering the use of religious language in these narratives as a means of achieving certain social effects or the way that religious language generates effects. As Stromberg has stated, we consider how canonical language becomes constitutive.

3) Last but not least, we have to realize that conversion narratives are always constructed in the context of particular social interactions. As the result of specific flows of social interchange, conversations, and arguments, their meaning always depends on these processes.

5. *"God Made my Marriage New"—An Example of a Narrative Analysis of a Micro-story in a Conversion Macro-story*[10]

In the context of my research project on religious orientations and experiences of women in the Charismatic-Evangelical women's group Aglow,[11] I conducted biographic-narrative interviews (cf. Schütze, 1983, 1992, Rosenthal, 1993) with women who had joined Aglow. In analysing the interviews, I explored the biographical reconstructions structured by the conversion plot (cf. Popp-Baier, 1998). One of my interview partners (I will call her Mrs. King) told me a typical progressive self-narrative about the changes in her life after her conversion. She stressed that her marriage had improved and told me the following micro-story, which is part of her conversion story.

> Her marriage has been bad from the very beginning. Her husband has always been a tyrant and has terrorized her and her two sons. When he came home from work and felt tired and stressed, he recovered by blaming his family and shouting at his wife and sons. Her

---

[10] Gergen (1994, 203) distinguishes macro-narratives from micro-narratives with regard to the narrated time: "*Macronarratives* refer to accounts in which events span broad periods of time, while *micronarratives* relate events of brief duration." I base my distinction between macro-stories and micro-stories on the narrating time.

[11] I use the term Charismatic-Evangelical to refer to the religious orientations of all groups and movements influenced by the Evangelical and the Pentecostal movements.

husband's behaviour literally made her sick. Usually she would burst into tears and became so exhausted that she had to go to bed when her husband's attack ended. She seriously considered divorce but could not manage it, in part because of financial reasons. These problems continued in their family for years and became more and more unbearable for Mrs. King. She submitted to her husband. Because he was such a strong personality, neither she nor her sons could resist him. She and the children had been an anxious group and were forced to obey. She did everything in the world for the sake of peace and quiet but never got either. This situation changed when Mrs King delivered her life to Jesus Christ and became born-again. She worked through her past with her pastoral counsellor and received advice on communicating with her husband according to the rules of her new belief. She learned that she had to love him, obey him and to forgive him for everything he had done to her or might do to her in the future. In the beginning she doubted whether she could do this but tried anyway. What happened seemed like a miracle. Her marriage changed completely. First, she adopted a totally new attitude toward her husband. For example, one day after an attack from her husband she told him: "Do you know that I love you very much?" She had not planned to say something like that and became frightened when she heard her own words. Then she continued: "Yes, and Jesus Christ also loves you and wants me to tell you this." Her husband became very frightened by her words but seemed to accept it. And Mrs. King no longer felt hurt and no longer withdrew. She was able to forgive him. Her husband's rages and shouting fits decreased. Once when he was shouting a lot again, he became sick and had to go to bed. Previously, Mrs. King had been the one to get sick and take to her bed. Now her husband was in bed and had to recover from his own shouting. And sometimes, when he had just finished his shouting, she asked him: "Would you like a cup of coffee?"

According to the first of the three analytical steps above, this micro-story reflects certain conventions that belong to the canon of the Charismatic-Evangelical belief.

First of all Mrs. King's story about her marriage makes sense in the framework of her conversion account, which conforms to the preconceived model of this genre. The biographical reconstruction of the marriage is also structured by the conversion plot as a meaningful temporal unit that relates a "good time" after conversion to a "bad time" before the turning point of conversion. The "good time" after conversion is constructed as the consequence of this act. This construction's content depends in part on conventions in canonical language, on a specialized vocabulary of motives that identify important features of Charismatic-Evangelical life, especially forms of relationships or activities (cf. Csordas, 1987, 1994, 1997).[12] Mrs. King's marriage story is informed by two motives: the recommended patriarchal relationship between husband and wife in a marriage and the communicative scheme of forgiveness.[13] In Mrs. King's self-narrative these elements of the canonical language of the Charismatic-Evangelical movement are linked to the changes in the marriage after conversion. The main character in the micro-story changes from a passive victim to an active agent able to cope with the situation by following the new rules of behaviour she has learned.

In the second step we interpret the changes by analysing the social effects of the language conventions used in the framework of the story. That means that we can try to analyse how the canonical language becomes constitutive communicative behaviour. Perhaps we can also interpret the marriage story to infer that the main character (the storyteller herself) changes her tyrannical husband's behaviour by using a certain communicative strategy. Before her conversion, her husband's rages and shouting fits made her sick, and she reacted by bursting into tears. After conversion she responded to her husband's shouting fits by telling him "I love you," "Jesus Christ loves you," or "Would you like a cup of coffee?" These reactions can be conceived as a strategy of paradoxical communication that frightens the aggressor because his aggressive behaviour ceases to generate the intended effect that it produced for so long. The teller of the marriage story has achieved her goal (changing her husband's behaviour) through the symbolic transformation of her communicative behaviour into the canonical language of the Charismatic-Evangelical Christianity, which produces effects and becomes constitutive as a strategy of paradoxical communication. Of course, this psychological interpretation is not the "true" interpretation of this story but only one possible interpretation. And—as Stromberg (1993) admits— the interpretation of a certain communicative behaviour as constitutive is always disputable.

In the third step we interpret this marriage story in the context of the relationship between the interviewer and interview partner.

---

[12] According to Csordas (1994) these motives are words or combinations of words with a specific religious connotation that circulate constantly in the genres of ritual language.

[13] These motives can change over time. I conducted my empirical research in a German city in the early 1990s. Since then, some Aglow groups have reconsidered the relationship between wife and husband in a "Christian" marriage.

Among the several aspects of the social interchange that contributed to the construction of this story, I will mention only one here: Born-again Christians have to witness the way that God has changed their lives. Relating one's personal conversion experience is conceived mostly as a testimony and serves to convince the listener to devote his or her life to Jesus Christ. Mrs. King also viewed the interview as an opportunity to provide such testimony and tried to convince me (the interviewer) to convert. This overarching attitude colours both the conversion macro-story and the micro-stories contained within this story, which need a positive end to convince the listener that life with God is better than life without God.

According to Stromberg (1993) this interview is part of my inter-view partner's conversion (as self-transformation). It is one of the opportunities for my interview partner to re-interpret (or rather to re-construct) her past and plan her future in the framework of the Charismatic-Evangelical language and consequently to construct a life story as a typical conversion story in which the different micro-stories reflecting various temporal perspectives become coherent within the macro-story of her life. Her ultimate task is to construct a nar-rative religious identity step-by-step as a born-again Christian woman.

From a constructionist point of view, narrative multiplicity is im-portant primarily because of its social implications. "Multiplicity is favored by the variegated range of relationships in which people are enmeshed and the differing demands of various relational contexts" (Gergen, 1994, p. 204). When people are pressured by the demands of the various relational contexts, however, they become entangled. Alternatively, if some relational contexts are very frightening, peo-ple may long for a strong and clear relationship with a certain social group. The respective narrative constructions—at the micro and macro levels—are also essential linguistic tools to interpret, defend and accommodate the "master social relationship" according to one's own life and to negotiate with the other existing social relationships. We might also say with respect to social relationships that the con-struction of conversion narratives reconciles the variety of social rela-tionships in one framework of meaning.

6. *Conversion as Religious Communication—Concluding Remarks*

In this chapter I have tried to outline an understanding of religious conversion as a kind of religious communication, in which a self-narrative is constructed. The special characteristic of this self-narrative is a decisive change in the life of the story's implicit author. According to the narrative approach of Peter Stromberg (1993) this self-transformation in conversion narratives is due to a type of speech which comprises referential and constitutive forms of communication: Canonic discourse (e.g. the language of Evangelical Christianity), which refers to a certain religious context of meaning, becomes meaningful (i.e. constitutive) in a broader sense by linking canonic language directly with individual experiences. Stromberg (1993) argues that this connection enables a.o. verbal expression of embodied aims or unacknowledged purposes or inaccessible or unacceptable desires while deepening the commitment to faith.

Arguing that the "constitutive" meaning is the "real" meaning of a certain religious communication would miss the point of Stromberg's argument. The "referential" and the "constitutive" are two sides of the same coin. In the story of our interview partner Mrs. King "forgiveness" and "paradoxical communication" are justifiable meanings of Mrs. King's communicative behaviour within the framework of the story. When Mrs. King explains to me that God changed not only her marriage but her whole life as well, I can agree with her in a certain sense. At a linguistic level I can interpret the self-transformation in her conversion narrative as a symbolic transformation of constitutive meanings into the referential meanings of the canonical language of the Evangelical-Charismatic movement, which become constitutive again themselves. The "embodied aim" of my interview partner to change the behaviour of her husband is transformed into the acceptance of a patriarchal relationship between her and her husband and into the communicative form of forgiveness. Accommodating these symbolic forms in a certain situation, however, constitutes the meaning of paradoxical communication, a communicative strategy that is in this case successful for "knocking down" an aggressive opponent.

The background to this kind of understanding of self-transformation in religious conversion reflects a conception of language and how it functions that contradicts certain widespread common-sense understandings of these topics. Such a common-sense understanding comprises a kind of essentialism concerning meanings which are classified as mental states, as belonging to the "mind." Utterances are interpreted as references to unseen entities such as ideas, feelings, and so on. According to this understanding, language merely gives public form to a distinct private thought that takes shape before it will be expressed in words. We think of utterances as carrying meaning like a surrounding essence, regardless of context, and perceive the mind as the source and location of such essences. According to Ryle (1949), this understanding belongs to a kind of official doctrine which he calls "the dogma of the Ghost in the Machine." In this official doctrine the mind occupies the body in precisely the way that meaning occupies an utterance. Both are non-corporeal essences which are responsible for the concrete manifestations we actually encounter in the world as actions and utterances.

Another view of language is unfolded in Gergen's social constructionism which depends to a great extent on Wittgenstein's language philosophy. According to Gergen (1999), people do not use language to share the contents of their minds. Instead, language and all other forms of representation derive their meaning from the ways they are used within relationships. "What we take to be true about the world or self, is not thus a product of the individual mind. The individual mind (thought, experience) does not thus originate meaning, create language, or discover the nature of the world. Meanings are born of coordinations among persons—agreements, negotiations, affirmations. From this standpoint, relationships stand prior to all that is intelligible" (Gergen, 1999, p. 48).

That means for our converts that they learn to use a certain religious language in the context of certain social relationships—especially in the context of the religious reference group they have joined.[14] By reconstructing or reframing their life story within this language, the coordinated and negotiated meanings of the macro-story and the different micro-stories arise both from the social context of the religious reference groups they have joined and from the other social contexts that have influenced the ongoing production of this story. Nonetheless, the life story's (re)construction as a conversion story coincides with the social and cultural valuation of the referential meanings of the canonical language. Therefore these meanings will be classified as produced by the mind, by the "I" or by another

---

[14] For a constructionist interpretation of religious language in general, see Day (1993)

transcendental source, by God. The obvious changes can be interpreted as personal transformations. The corresponding constitutive meanings emerging from other social processes or from other aspects of the same social processes are mostly unavailable to the narrator on a reflexive level.

Research on this kind of religious communication is to be conceptualized as narrative and discourse analysis, in which the details of social processes of communication, commitment, and creativity can be analysed. Studies of actors formulating and making sense of new and current religious language must consider the interplay of the constitutive with the referential and should seek to clarify the constitutive meanings that arise in various aspects of the narratives and discourses. These meanings can be "identified" via interpretation by an "outsider", although their construction is also the result of social relationships and social processes and has no specific epistemological status.[15] Under certain circumstances, if the interpreter serves as a counsellor to the "convert," this kind of interpretation may broaden the convert's reflexive conceptual horizon and consequently expand his or her options to act. Nonetheless, such interpretations abound with limitations and snares. I will therefore conclude with a quotation from Kenneth Gergen (1999, p. 86), which captures this point: "So the bottom line for me is to underscore the limitations and partialities of all analyses. I think we gain most if we appreciate these analyses not as reports on objective truth, but as 'frames' or 'lenses' on our world—to shake us up, reconstruct, give further dimension, and open new vistas of action. There is always more to say—for which we should be thankful."

References

Barker, E. (1984). *The Making of a Moonie*. Oxford: Basil Blackwell.
Beckford, J.A. (1978). Accounting for Conversion. *British Journal of Sociology, 29*, 249–262.
Butler, J. (1990). *Gender Trouble: Feminism and the Subversion of Identity*. New York: Routledge.
—— (1993). *Bodies that Matter*. New York: Routledge.

[15] Of course there is an important difference between meaning construction in a social scientific context and in everyday life. In social scientific contexts the interpretative analyses are usually *methodically* constructed and evaluated according to various criteria for research quality whenever possible. There is a growing body of literature about qualitative methods in psychological research concerning these issues. In my study I have elaborated my interpretative analyses in the context of a grounded theory approach (cf. Popp-Baier, 1998).

Conway, F. & Siegelman, J. (1978). *Snapping: America's Epidemic of Sudden Personality Change*. Philadelphia: J.B. Lippincott.

Csordas, Th.J. (1987). Genre, Motive, and Metaphor: Conditions for Creativity in Ritual and Language. *Cultural Anthropology, 2*, 445–469.

—— (1994). *The Sacred Self: A Cultural Phenomenology of Charismatic Healing*. Berkeley: University of California Press.

—— (1997). *Language, Charisma, and Creativity. The Ritual Life of a Religious Movement*. Berkeley: Cambridge University Press.

Dawson, L.L. (1990). Self-Affirmation, Freedom, and Rationality: Theoretically Elaborating "Active" Conversions. *Journal for the Scientific Study of Religion, 29*, 141–163.

—— (1999). Cult conversions: controversy and clarification'. In: Lamb, Christopher & Bryant, M. Darrol (Eds.). *Religious Conversion. Contemporary Practices and Controversies*. London: Cassell.

Day, J.M. (1993). Speaking of Belief: Language, Performance, and Narrative in the Psychology of Religion. *The International Journal for the Psychology of Religion, 3*, 213–229.

Frijda, N.H. (1986). *The emotions*. Cambridge: Cambridge University Press.

Gergen, K.J. (1973). Social psychology as history. *Journal of Personality and Social Psychology, 26*, 309–320.

Gergen, K.J. (1994). *Realities and Relationships. Soundings in Social Construction*. Cambridge, Mass.: Harvard University Press.

—— (1999). *An Invitation to Social Construction*. London: Sage Publications.

Giddens, A. (1991). *Modernity and Self-Identity. Self and Society in the Late Modern Age*. Oxford: Polity Press.

Hacking, I. (1999). *The Social Construction of What?* Cambridge, Mass.: Harvard University Press.

Halperin, J. (Ed.) (1983). *Psychodynamic Perspectives on Religion, Sect and Cult*. Boston: PSG.

Hood, R.W., Spilka, B., Hunsberger, B. & Gorsuch, R. (1996). *The Psychology of Religion. An Empirical Approach* (2nd ed). New York, London: The Guilford Press.

Jeffery, R. (1998). *The Social Construction of Indian Forests*. Edinburgh: Centre for East AsianStudies.

Kant, I. (1996). *Critique of Pure Reason* (transl. by Werner S. Pluhar. Introduction by Patricia Kitcher). Indianapolis: Hackett Publishing Company, Inc.

Kitzinger, C. (1987). *The Social Construction of Lesbianism*. London: Sage Publications.

Knoblauch, H., Krech, V. & Wohlrab-Sahr, M. (Eds.) (1998). *Religiöse Konversion. Systematische und fallorientierte Studien in soziologischer Perspektive* [Religious conversion. A sociological perspective on systematic and case studies]. Konstanz: Universitätsverlag Konstanz.

Lans, J. van der (1981). Volgelingen van de goeroe. Hedendaagse religieuze bewegingen in Nederland [Disciples of the guru. Religious movements in the Netherlands today]. Baarn: Ambo.

Lifton, R.J. (1961). *Thought Reform and The Psychology of Totalism*. New York: Norton.

Lofland, J. & Skonovd, N. (1981). Conversion Motifs. *Journal for the Scientific Study of Religion, 20*, 373–385.

Luckmann, Th. (1986). Grundformen der gesellschaftlichen Vermittlung des Wissens: Kommunikative Gattungen [Basic Forms of Social Mediation of Knowledge: Communicative Genres]. *Kultur und Gesellschaft. Sonderheft 27 der Kölner Zeitschrift für Soziologie und Sozialpsychologie*, 191–211.

Luckmann, Th. (1987). Kanon und Konversion [Canon and Conversion]. In: Assmann, Jan (Ed.). *Kanon und Zensur. Beiträge zur Archäologie der literarischen Kommunikation II* [pp. 38–46]. München: Fink.

Melton, J.G. (1999). Anti-cultists in the United States: an historical perspective. In: Wilson, B. & Cresswell, J. (Eds.). *New Religious Movements. Challenge and Response*. London: Routledge.

Nagel, Th. (1997). *The Last Word*. New York, Oxford: Oxford Universiy Press.

Paloutzian, R.F., Richardson, J.T. & Rambo, L.R. (1999). Religious Conversion and Personality Change. *Journal of Personality*, 67, 1048–1079.

Pickering, A. (1984). *Constructing Quarks: A Sociological History of Particle Physics*. Edinburgh: Edinburgh University Press.

Popp-Baier, U. (1998). *Das Heilige im Profanen. Religiöse Orientierungen im Alltag. Eine qualitative Studie zu religiösen Orientierungen von Frauen aus der charismatisch-evangelikalen Bewegung* [The Holy in the Profane. Religious Orientations in Everyday Life. A Qualitative Study of Religious Orientations among Women from the Charismatic-Evangelical Movement]. Amsterdam: Rodopi.

Rambo, L.R. (1993). *Understanding religious conversion*. New Haven, Conn.: Yale University Press.

Richardson, J.T. (1985). The Active vs. Passive Convert: Paradigm Conflict in Conversion/Recruitment Research. *Journal for the Scientific Study of Religion*, 24, 119–236.

Ricoeur, P. (1991). Life: A Story in Search of a Narrator. In: Valdés, M.J. (Ed.). *A Ricoeur Reader: Reflection and Imagination* [pp. 425–437]. New York: Harvester/Wheatsheaf.

Ryle, G. (1949). *The Concept of Mind*. Harmondsworth: Penguin Books.

Rosenthal, G. (1993). Reconstruction of Life Stories: Principles of Selection in Generating Stories for Narrative Biographical Interviews. In: Josselson, R. & Lieblich, A. (Eds.) *The Narrative Study of Lives. Volume 1* [pp. 59–91]. Newbury Park: Sage Publications.

Sargant, W. (1957). *Battle for the Mind*. London: William Heinemann.

Schütze, F. (1983). Biographieforschung und narratives Interview [Biographical Research and Narrative Interview]. *Neue Praxis*, 3, 283–294.

—— (1992). Pressure and guilt: War experiences of a young German soldier and their biographical implications. *International Sociology*, 3, 187–208.

Snow, D.A. & Machalek, R. (1984). The Sociology of Conversion. *Annual Review of Sociology*, 10, 167–190.

Sokal, A. & Bricmont, J. (1999). *Intellectual Impostures. Postmodern philosophers' abuse of science*. Bury St Edmunds: St Edmundsbury Press.

Sprague, R.K. (Ed.) (1972). *The Older Sophists*. Columbia, SA: University of South Carolina Press.

Staples, Cl.L. & Mauss, A.L. (1987). Conversion or Commitment? A Reassessment of the Snow and Machalek Approach to the Study of Conversion. *Journal for the Scientific Study of Religion*, 26, 133–147.

Stromberg, P.G. (1993). Language and self-transformation. A study of the Christian conversion narrative. New York: Cambridge University Press.

Tonkin, E. (1992). *Narrating Our Pasts: The Social Construction of Oral History*. Cambridge: Cambridge University Press.

Ullmann, Ch. (1989). *The Transformed Self. The Psychology of Religious Conversion*. New York, London: Plenum Press.

Ulmer, B. (1988). Konversionserzählungen als rekonstruktive Gattung. Erzählerische Mittel und Strategien bei der Rekonstruktion eines Bekehrungserlebnisses [Conversion Stories as a Reconstructive Genre. Narrative Devices and Strategies in Reconstructing a Conversion Experience]. *Zeitschrift für Soziologie*, 17, 19–33.

—— (1990). Die autobiographische Plausibilität von Konversionserzählungen'. [The Autobiographical Plausibility of Conversion Stories] in Walter Sparn (ed.) *Wer schreibt meine Lebensgeschichte? Biographie, Autobiographie, Hagiographie und ihre Entstehungszusammenhänge*. Gütersloh: Gütersloher Verlagshaus, pp. 287–295.

Zinnbauer, B.J. & Pargament, K.I. (1998). Spiritual Conversion: A Study of Religious Change Among College Students. *Journal for the Scientific Study of Religion*, 37, 161–180.

RELIGIOUS DEVELOPMENT
AS DISCURSIVE CONSTRUCTION

James M. Day

Introduction

In his recent collection of essays, Gergen (1999) suggests that constructivist models of psychological functioning may be distinguished from constructionist ones on the grounds of their contrasting emphases on the place of the self in the field of human action, and the ways in which interaction between self and world are represented in language. In contrast to the constructivist emphasis on internal constructions of reality, of which language is considered an accurate rendering, constructionist emphases incline us to view the self as constructed through the discursive possibilities which social interactions furnish. As some readers may be aware, the shift Gergen proposes traces a parallel interest in my own work at the interface of constructivist and constructionist models in the psychology or moral and religious development. It is in this context of psychological research and practice in moral and religious development and education, as well as an abiding interest in the implications of such work for pastoral practice that I write here.

In order to establish a framework for moving beyond constructivist assumptions to constructionist ones, this chapter will begin with a brief outline of the constructivist model and a critique of some of what I take to be its deficits both of internal consistency and empirical verifiability. We shall then embark upon a quest for more promising alternatives. If we find the constructivist canon and case unsatisfying, what alternatives might we discover, on what grounds, and toward what ends? If we are to take a constructionist turn, what of the idea of religious development? Does it remain tenable, and how so? Finally, I shall hope to show that this constructionist turn may indeed hold promising avenues for practice in pastoral theology.

As I have suggested elsewhere, such a turn invites readers to move from a vision rooted in internalist conceptions of individual human beings as epistemic subjects, toward a constructionist perspective where speech, language, and narrative serve as foci for understanding

religious development in terms of interpersonal relationships. Readers
are thus invited to move "from the cognitive-developmental emphasis on cognitive deep structures and their supposed reorganization
within individuals to an emphasis on religious discourse as *relational
and* performative, and are enjoined to re-imagine religious language
not so much as a factotum of *individual* operations, but, rather, as a
dynamic that *does something communicatively.* I propose a move from a
focus on such supposedly representative religious language and what
it would tell us about what is *internally* held, to alertness to the ways
in which religious language may alternatively both make possible
and inhibit the richness of human relationship. This in turn implies
a move from a conception of human beings as *univocal* epistemic subjects moving from heteronomous error to autonomous apprehension
of universally recognizable truth(s) to a *discursive or dialogical* self forever woven into being through conversation, forever embedded in
and constrained by the conventions and possibilities of communication in relationship" (Day, in press).

Constructivist Fundamentals in the Psychology of Religious Development

A working familiarity with the basic and dominant models in the
psychology of religious development, namely those of James Fowler
and of Fritz Oser and Oser's colleague Helmut Reich, is assumed
here, though a brief outline of the same is furnished below. Readers
may find ample descriptions by the leading authors in the constructivist canon elsewhere (Fowler, 1981, 1996; Kohlberg, 1969,
1981, 1984; Oser & Reich, 1990; Oser & Gmünder, 1991; Piaget, 1965,
Reich, 1997. See also Day, in press; Day & Youngman, in press; Day
& Naedts, 1995, 1999).

   Fowler is concerned to describe *faith development,* by which he means
"an orientation of the total person, giving purpose and goal to one's
hopes and strivings, thoughts and actions". This development involves
"a dynamic pattern of personal trust in and loyalty to a center or
centers of value" whose orientation can be understood in relationship to the person's trust in and loyalty to core "images and realities of power" and "to a shared master story or core story" (Fowler,
1981). Fowler's model is clearly affected by notions derived from liberal protestant theology (Niebuhr and Tillich are both clearly represented in Fowler's notions of faith, and of faithing as a human

activity) and from the field of religious studies, with the particularly phenomenological accent given the field by Wilfred Cantwell Smith and his associates in the Faculties of Arts and Sciences and of Divinity at Harvard, though it has earned popularity as a practical as well as theoretical model well beyond the confines of Cambridge, Massachusetts, of Emory University where Fowler is professor, and of liberal protestant circles. (Day & Youngman, in press).

Fowler's model can best be appreciated as a multi-factorial model, given that its construct of faith is so broad as to include dimensions associated with the cognitive stage notions of Piaget, Kohlberg's moral development stage formulations, Erikson's, Loevinger's, and Levinson's concepts of identity development and developmental crisis, the development of perspective-taking as articulated by Selman, and self-development as proposed by Kegan (Fowler, 1981; Tamminen & Nurmi, 1995; Day & Youngman, in press).

Oser's concern has been with the construct of *religious judgment* development. Essential in Oser's theory are the interpretation of the human being's relation to Ultimate Being (God) and the action of the Ultimate Being in human life. As a person interprets the experiences of his or her life, discusses them or prays, as he or she studies religious texts and takes part in the life of a religious community, he/she actualizes the system of rules that concern his/her relationship to the Ultimate Being (Oser & Gmünder, 1991). This relation appears in verbal form in a *religious judgment* which is "some kind of cognitive pattern of religious knowing of reality" (Oser & Reich, 1990, p. 283; Day & Youngman, in press).

Central to attempts to understand Oser's perspective is the notion of religious *deep structure* or *mother structure* or *underlying structure*, terms which Oser borrows directly from Piaget (Oser & Gmünder, 1991). This structural notion lies at the heart of Oser's theory and its adaptations by Reich, and places the theory squarely in the Piagetian paradigm. Oser argues that this deep structure is a *universal* feature of *religious* cognition, present at every point across the lifespan, in all cultures, and irrespective of religious affiliation. Indeed both avowed atheists and agnostics are held by Oser, Gmünder, Reich and various ones of their colleagues, to be concerned with fundamentally religious questions of relationship to ultimate being and purposes in their lives and in the life of the world, and to think about such questions in ways which cannot be reduced to other constructs or forms of cognition (Oser & Gmünder, 1991; Reich, 1997; Day & Youngman, in press).

Critical to both models are the notions of stage and sequence as they are known in the work of Piaget and Kohlberg, though Fowler's adaptation of stage constructs and theory, and the breadth of his concept of faith offers a more fluid, and some would say, less precise, construct than does that of religious judgment in Oser's scheme. This distinction between the two theories has inclined some (see Power, 1991) to view Fowler's perspective as a *soft stage* theory and to consider Oser's model as coming closer to a *hard stage* model and the Piagetian criteria one would employ to assess such models, namely those criteria having to do with reversibility, invariant sequence in the stage-structured transformation of understanding, and hierarchy. Fowler's model allows greater movement across the various sequences of development envisaged in his multi-factorial model than does Oser's, which is more insistent on the linearity of development and on a fixed end-point as its most favorable, or mature, destination (see also Day, in press; Day & Naedts, 1995, 1999; Streib, 1991; Day & Youngman, in press). Both Fowler and Oser's theories are best understood as *stage theories* which envisage human development, and, in this case, religious development, as moving along a trajectory of mostly invariant sequences of stage transformations from less mature to more mature, and, in particular, from lesser to greater degrees and appropriations of individual autonomy (Day & Youngman, in press).

Fowler envisages a move from the heteronomous stage of '*intuitive-projective faith*', in which one is funded with long-lasting images and impressions of protective and menacing presence or powers in one's sphere of being, which are in turn given shape in the form of stories, gestures, and symbols, pregnant with emotion and dominated by the function of imagination, to 'universalizing faith' which, dependent as it is on earlier stages of increasing individuality and autonomy and a critical capacity to stand outside one's group, tradition, and symbol system, involves movement beyond polarities inherent in any given system and is characterized by detached, yet compassionate action, of continuity with the power of being/God, in a world conceived of as moving toward fulfillment in justice and love (Fowler, 1981). As in Kohlberg's notions of moral development, and Piaget's models of the development of logical reasoning, higher stages are regarded as more adequate both because of the relative complexity they represent, and because of the adaptive value they offer, given the real nature of the world (Day & Youngman, in press).

A hierarchical view to religious development is likewise apparent in the work of Oser and his associates, and perhaps more so, because it expresses a more strict concern with cognition, and both less worry about and less interest in other variables (affective and life-historical, which Fowler endeavors to take into account) in the religious experience of the subject. Oser would have us understand that development occurs when subjects move in their religious judgment from an orientation of religious heteronomy which he denotes as deus ex machina in which God is understood as all-powerful, active and relatively capricious, acting as he (sic) would with relatively little regard for human will or action, toward the most favored endpoint of an orientation to religious *autonomy and intersubjectivity* and a feeling of *universal and unconditional religiosity*. As in Fowler's model, the sense of solidarity and continuity achieved with the ultimate is according to Oser something which can occur only after the subject has passed through a stage of *absolute autonomy* and, customarily, a rejection of religious and all other 'external' authority. Like Fowler's model, Oser's assumes that higher is necessarily better on the grounds of adequacy which Piaget first asserted. Higher stages are at once more sophisticated and thus represent a greater differentiation of human cognitive capacity, and they come closer to representing the world as it is. As one moves upwards in the scheme, whether in Fowler's model or in Oser's, one moves increasingly toward an approximation of the world as it really is (see Fowler, 1981; Oser & Gmünder, 1991; Piaget, 1965; Day & Youngman, in press).

Both Fowler and Oser argue that development occurs *within* a subject through a trajectory of *stages* which represent movement from *lower to higher* structures of cognition that increasingly move the subject toward greater *rational sophistication* and congruence of *approximation* with things as they really are. Researchers grasp an understanding of the subject's *level* of development through interview and/or questionnaire strategies in which the subject's language is taken to be *representative* of *private constructions* guided by *internally held deep structures* of distinctively religious cognition.

There is a broad consensus among developmental psychologists that in the neo-Piagetian paradigm both models represent, Fowler and Oser have moved questions concerning religious development to a place of accepted importance. Furthermore, as Tamminen and Nurmi (1995) observe, their models have provoked considerable empirical research concerning religious development in adulthood and in the entire life span. They have, in addition, detailed programs of intervention, which have served educators interested in promoting the developmental endpoints envisioned in their models (Day & Youngman, in press).

There is some consensus as well that both Fowler's and Oser's models are flawed with considerable theoretical and methodological problems. To date, critiques of these models within the developmental literature have focused chiefly on the 'relatively unsatisfactory' nature of undergirding empirical evidence (Tamminen & Nurmi, 1995, p. 302; Wulff, 1997), the lack of longitudinal data to support their inherent developmental claims, and the lack of cross-cultural evidence to support claims of universality which rely, in turn, so heavily on 20th century theological models of personhood and human relations with the 'Ultimate' or 'God'. Despite recent and long-awaited evidence drawn from a longitudinal study (Di Loreto & Oser, 1996), and the development of questionnaires at Louvain for the empirical study of religious judgment (Day & Naedts, 1995, 1999), Tamminen and Nurmi's observation that "the existing measurements and descriptions are in many cases still relatively inaccurate or artificial" (1995, p. 302) would seem entirely pertinent to our aims in this chapter (see also Day, in press; Day & Youngman, in press).

Constructivist Assumptions and Research. A Critical Appraisal

Several problems plague the constructivist venture in the psychology of moral and religious development. (For a fuller treatment of several of these critiques, see also Day, in press).

The first of these problems can be illustrated on the basis of the research with hundreds of adolescent and young adult subjects whom we have studied over the course of some years at Louvain. With the help of these subjects we have tested the relationship between moral judgment levels and religious judgment levels assumed in the constructivist literature (Day & Naedts, 1995, 1999). Both Fowler and Oser argue moral development must precede religious development, because religious or faith reasoning by definition includes matters moral. Problematically, such a relationship has as yet to be demonstrated in the cognitive-developmental literature itself, because findings are highly contradictory and based on such small numbers of subjects as to warrant no certain conclusion (for reviews of the same see Day & Naedts, 1995, 1999). Employing the Socio-Moral Reflection

Measure pioneered by John Gibbs and his associates (1992) and a standardized measure of religious judgment, which we devised at Louvain (with the aid of Helmut Reich and John Gibbs), we sought to correct this deficit in the literature. Two of our findings are particularly interesting in light of constructivist claims. First, in our sample of several hundred subjects carefully controlled for age, educational status, and cultural background, moral judgment scores are so significantly similar to religious judgment scores that we are unable to conclude that religious judgment is distinct, at all, from moral judgment. We were thus led to conclude that religious judgment, as Oser has conceived of it, (and, we believe, faith reasoning as Fowler has put it), may be little more than elaborations in religious language of the same cognitive constructs otherwise considered statements of moral judgment. Second, it appears clear to us that many subjects who produce religious language when responding to religious judgment would not be likely to use such language to describe their thinking apart from the frame imposed by the questionnaire. The supposedly universal character of religious judgment, or faith reasoning, proposed by Oser and Fowler emerges in our research as little more than an artifact of research methodology.

As we have elsewhere observed (Day & Naedts, 1995, 1999), the very notion of deep structures of religious thought or preoccupation with meaning in faith, may be as much a by-product of those who produced the concepts as of anything verifiable on empirical grounds. However disappointing it may be to certain psychologists of religion, plenty of people are simply not concerned with the issues religious developmentalists assume to be our abiding human preoccupations. Religious deep structures do not on our view lurk everywhere just beneath the surface of ordinary discourse, and religious categories are not provably the stuff everyone's meaning-making processes.

It is curious in this light that both Fowler and Oser hold to their notions of stage and sequence and to their universal applicability, particularly when significant numbers of Kohlbergian researchers have concluded that the highest stages (5 and 6) of moral reasoning do *not* meet the criteria of stages in the Piagetian or Kohlbergian senses of them (see e.g. Gibbs et al., 1992). Why when these same stages serve as the basis for both Fowler's and Oser's conceptions of faith and religious judgment development, these same stages have not been called into question on grounds of Piagetian criteria, in light of this research, we hardly understand. Research in the near-domains

of formal and post-formal reasoning shows that employment of cognitive skill is highly context shaped and context-specific (see e.g. Dumont,
1999). We assume the same to be true of religious reasoning.

A second problem inherent to the constructivist case is neatly illustrated in the work of Carol Gilligan and colleagues (see e.g. Gilligan,
1982; Gilligan, Ward, & Taylor, 1988; Gilligan, Brown, & Rogers,
1990). At a critical moment in the development of the Kohlbergian
project, Gilligan invited researchers to consider the notion that moral
reasoning was not univocal, but specific to cultural context, and particularly the context of gender. She insisted at *least two voices, of justice
and of care*, ought to be taken into account. Demonstrating this notion in a series of studies on men and women in real-life problem-
solving situations, she undid the Kohlbergian construct that moral
development could be understood in terms of the structural transformations in a particular voice (justice reasoning) and described how
voice (justice or care) was particular to the kinds of problems at
hand, and the kinds of scenarios in which subjects were permitted
to speak. Gilligan's work asserting the existence of voices both of
justice and of care in moral reasoning has engendered a debate of
considerable proportions. For the purposes of this chapter it would
seem pertinent to point out that Gilligan's claims as to the existence
of more than one moral voice have been born out by a number of
other researchers (Brown, 1999; Brown & Gilligan, 1991; Lyons 1983;
Day, in press).

In somewhat parallel fashion, my colleagues and I have sought to
understand whether we might find such diversity of religious voice
in studies of adolescent and young adult accounts of moral and religious experience. Our findings demonstrate differences between boys
and girls, men and women, between muslim and roman catholic
young people, and between students in technical and professional
high schools contrasted with students in university-preparatory schools
(see Day, in press; Day & Naedts, 1995, 1997, 1999; Day & Youngman, in press). Fowler and Oser treat such differences either as nonexistent or as insignificant in comparison with the importance of deep
structure and stage hierarchy, ignoring the rich diversity of religious
language as it centers in social context and individual life history.
We find such neglect perturbing, at once untenable on empirical
grounds, and regrettable for its lack for attention to cultural and
individual differences.

A third problem in the constructivist account can usefully be studied drawing from research on cognitive style and its relationship to religious constructs. Dirk Hutsebaut and his associates have operationalised notions of religious cognitive orientation in terms of classical dimensions in research on cognitive style, and have measured the potential relationships between cognitive style and supposed religious developmental level of subjects. Hutsebaut has convincingly shown that cognitive style when operationalised to account for religious content, is in important ways *independent* of supposed developmental level. Cognitive styles may blend in the same subject depending on the time and issue in question, and do not necessarily follow developmental logic in their application. Thus Hutsebaut and colleagues conclude that what developmentalists hold to be hierarchical may be more a matter of personal style and factors of social and historical context than of the subject's relative cognitive sophistication and capacity for 'advanced' reasoning in moral and religious domains (Desimpelaere, et al., 1999; Day, in press; Hutsebaut, 1996, 1997a, b).

Heinz Streib's work, in ways complementary to Hutsebaut's, demonstrates the relevance of *cognitive style* to our discussion. As part of a larger study of processes involved in the joining and leaving of fundamentalist groups in Germany, Streib (1991, 1997) shows how language which might be interpreted by developmentalists in terms of stage and structure may equally well be understood as a communicative pragmatic. Taking a narrative turn that pays close attention to the life stories of his subjects, as well as their accounts of joining and leaving fundamentalist groups, Streib finds subjects employ the language that suits their employment in their narratives of joining or leaving. These subjects employ language thoughtfully, carefully, deliberately, so as to create a coherent picture of self, to justify their conduct, and to persuade their listeners that what they are saying is both sensible and wise. Analysis of these narratives in terms of developmental assumptions would be problematic in two ways. First, subjects speak at more than one developmental level at a time, and how they appear developmentally is more a function of how they wish to be heard than "how they are". It is more useful, Streib concludes, to view religious language in terms of style and communicational aim, than in terms of developmental level or deep structure. Both Hutsebaut and Streib underscore the highly social character of

language, as well as the mistaken priority developmental analysis
would give to pinning down subjects' places on ladders of developmental hierarchy (see also Day, in press).

To this point we have seen how the constructivist case for universal, invariant, and irreversible stages in religious development leaves
much to be desired. On grounds of internal consistency, empirical
verifiability, and the breadth and depth of religious experience which
we might wish to better appreciate, the cognitive-developmental
project appears at once conceptually misbegotten and empirically
weak. Reducing religious experience to the supposed deep structure of religious logic (which as we have seen, has been shown to be
of questionable value on both epistemological grounds and grounds
of empirical testing) and hierarchies of relative developmental sophistication might seem, on other grounds an objectionable endeavor.

Are there alternatives to the constructivist canon and whence do
they come? Does the notion of religious development remain an
enticing one, and if so, is it warranted on scientific grounds?

From Epistemic Subjects to Dialogical Selves: A Constructionist Shift

We begin our exploration of such questions in appraising the work
of those who were initially drawn to the developmental enterprise
as it was embodied in Kohlberg's work, and who, within the developmental frame Kohlberg had outlined, reinterpreted the kinds of
mind-action relationships which were inherent to the same. The work
of Habermas is instructive in this regard. Concerned with communication and social justice, Habermas began a conversation with
Kohlberg which lasted for some years. Habermas found in Kohlberg's
work a courageous facing of moral problems and philosophical issues
in psychology, and was intrigued by what he first took to be the
thoroughly interactionist contours of Kohlberg's approach to moral
psychology (see e.g. Habermas 1983a). Along the way, though,
Habermas (see e.g. 1979, 1983b; see also McCarthy 1982) argued
that cognitive-developmental theorists had not yet convincingly shown
that their internalist descriptions of structural transformation were
aptly directed to individuals as epistemic subjects. Habermas proposed an alternative conception to what he regarded as finally too
limited, too confined to the individual, and too much tied to a
metapsychology of supposedly internal structure and cognitive states

which could neither be adequately described nor empirically proven. Shifting to the communicative networks in which the kinds of moral problems the structuralists were concerned with were at issue, Habermas proposed that researchers turn their attention to *the socius* as the locus of moral action, and proposed that certain kinds of rules and communicative strategies, which he believed could be taught, would if applied likely produce the kinds of results (relatively more just solutions, relatively more sophisticated resources for constructing them) which the constructivists described as desirable outcomes of moral development and moral education.

Whether the strategies Habermas proposed are to be commended is a matter of considerable debate within both the philosophical and psychological literatures where matters of moral problem-solving are concerned (Gergen's own remarks in his 1999 book are instructive in this regard). What seems pertinent for the purposes of this chapter is that Habermas thus moved the focus of attention from the epistemic subject to *the discursive framework of interpersonal relationships.*

Were we to imagine that such a shift were inviting, we would, I think, be inclined to a different appreciation of what is going on when we interview subjects about religious experience, or about religious elements in their lived experience more broadly, and we might conceive of religious development in different terms. We would find it intriguing, at least, to think of subjects as *dialogical,* and we would think about how *relationships* as much as individuals, develop. We would question both the frames and aims of development. The constructivist notion of fundamentally separate selves communicating in language that neatly represents internally held notions or which would allow us to map internally located cognitive states would appear fragile, and unhelpful. The notion of ever increasing cognitive sophistication in an ever more autonomous subject, liberated from the constraints of social determination, as the aim of religious development, would seem to us both shallow, and wrong. We would have before us a horizon of developmental hope which would acknowledge our ongoing construction in relationship, we would prize relationship as the nexus of development, and we would privilege relational upbuilding in community as an aim of developmental work. We would need concepts which would help us appreciate how deeply interwoven what we call thinking is to processes of social enculturation, and we would be in search of a vocabulary which would permit us to better imagine how religious language comes to be seen as useful, even critical, to social conviviality, and how in some cases it comes to be understood as the very opposite of that. It is here where we turn our attention to notions of *narrative*, of *dialogical appropriation, ideological becoming* and *authorship*, and of *supplementation* and *joint action* in order to make this constructionist shift.

Narrative

Let us begin with the deceptively simple observation that when people talk, they do so, at least in part, in story form. When in psychological research, in clinical or pastoral work, the persons with whom we speak respond to questions we pose, regardless of our assumptions at the start as to what should qualify as a satisfying answer to our questions in a narrative way: they insist what they need to say requires a *story*, that apart from narrative their words make no sense: narrative as the key to the meaning they make in their explanations, *narrative as* what provides the power to illustrate the points they want to make; narrative as the tie that binds together the cognitive, affective, and connative dimensions of experience; narrative as the time-marker demonstrating the importance of past, present, and future in their accounts. Narrative is thus, however it is to be interpreted, a key element in the data we have at our disposal in developmental research. In embarking on this emphasis on narrative, we take a further step toward a constructionist attitude to religious experience and development.

Gergen calls narratives "forms of intelligibility that furnish accounts of events across time. Individual actions . . . gain their significance from the way in which they are embedded within the narrative" (1994, p. 224). Gergen suggests a well-formed or intelligible narrative generally meets certain criteria: (a) it has an established, valued, endpoint; (b) the events recounted are relevant to and serve the endpoint; (c) the events are temporally ordered; (d) its characters have a continuous and coherent identity across time; (e) its events are causally linked and serve as an explanation for the outcome; and (f) it has a beginning and an end. (Gergen 1994, p. 224.)

One author whose work demonstrates the utility of narrative in domains pertinent to those of this book is Ruard Ganzevoort, who's scholarly work in narrative and the psychology of religion has roots in his studies of religion and coping (Ganzevoort, 1998a; 1998b). His

work demonstrates how attention to narrative may help us to understand Gergen's insights into narrative as a discursive activity that
goes beyond representation to reconstruction of the self. In Ganzevoort's
dissertation work on narrative and coping and their implications for
pastoral theology, the subjects he studied coped more or less successfully with various stressful situations in life according to the efficacy
of their narrative strategies. Religious elements in these strategies
were more, or less, important in reducing symptoms of post-trau-
matic stress, according to their relative coherence with the narrative
emplotment subjects gave to them. Similarly, studying men in recovery from sexual abuse, Ganzevoort charts the relationship between
narrative structure, personal theology, world view, and healing processes
and outcomes: as his subjects adopt different strategies for structuring, through narrative, their accounts of abuse, so the god images
of which they speak change in character. For Ganzevoort, narratives
are intertwined with coping not only because through narrative elaboration symptoms subside, but also because it is through narrative
that the kind of re-imagination of self correlated with healing processes
takes place. Narrative is not only, then, about accounting for what
has been, but refiguring the self that is to be. In light of Ganzevoort's
contribution we may observe that the gods who will be believable,
useful, admissible, change according to the narrative reconstruction
of self in which the subject is engaged, and the communities of discourse in which stories about the self are rendered legitimate or
excluded from consideration (Ganzevoort, 1998a, b).

   Fowler himself devotes some attention to narrative in the autobiographical reconstructions of his subjects, but shares with Oser
et al., as he does with Kohlberg, a reductionist hermeneutic of reading narrative texts in an overwhelming concern with the hunt for
stage and structural features of subjects' discourse. Such readings
exclude the richness of context and time and emotion narrative brings
to life, and remain confined in a representationalist view to language
which would appear all too confining. The researcher's task in the
structuralist campaign is to parse through the debris of narrative
elements to the real stuff of those features of speech which can be
interpreted in terms of stage and structure, to ferret out the treasure and leave the dross behind. Moreover, this hunt affects the process
of the interview itself, sending the clear message to the interviewee
that she will be heard if and when her voice conforms to the confines
of the strucuralist canon, and that the rest of what she might say

may just as well be left out. The text is thus reduced both in the
reading of it, and in the making of it, to what is supposedly of universal importance, and much of what the subject insists upon is lost
(Day, in press).

A serious attention to narrative, as we have seen, augurs for a
critical re-examination of mind-language-action relationships in our
understandings of the human subject. In so doing we open new vistas for thinking about development as a concept in the sychology of
religion, and entertain new options for the application of such psychology in pastoral theology.

Not "What" but "To Whom": Religious Language as Performative

We might begin with what I have called the *moral audience*, or *religious audience*, insisting that moral action and religious behavior are
functions of the audiences to which they are played just as moral
and religious stories are functions of the audiences to which they are
told. We human beings act only in those ways we can imagine later
on accounting for to another person, and the resources for such
accounting come only from the narrative strategies available to us
in the communicative networks of which we are part. Thus in making a decision, we rehearse what it might be like to explain ourselves, in retrospect, to another. Our action is a function of the
stories we can imagine telling about it, both our conduct and our
speech are shared constructions (Day 1991). Thus, my efforts to
explain religious elements of my experience to you are not only
efforts at mapping, or describing, but also efforts at finding my place
with you, situating myself with you, finding ways to build, or alter,
my relationship with you. What you permit, by virtue of the discursive communities of which we are members, plays a large role
in shaping what I can imagine saying, what I may what, structurally,
it is possible to say, and what I will appear to "want" to say. Indeed
the discursive world(s) of which we are part will determine the contours of what sorts of exchanges we can have about anything at all.

This point may be illustrated in recent research in which I and
some of my students at Louvain devised interview strategies which
incorporated the notion of the research participant as a shifting, discursive, self, whose description of experience will vary according to
the kind of audience to which s/he speaks. When we asked our sub-

jects to describe a moral dilemma they had faced, or to speak about how religious elements figured in moral decisions, or asked for their own definitions of religious experience, religious dilemmas, and religious decisions, we noted differences according to gender, religious affiliation, and social class (as alluded to earlier). We also, though, noted remarkable differences when we prompted shifts in the "spoken to" parts of our subjects' accounts. Consider the following shift. When we said "Okay, now, I'd like you to imagine that your best friend (or mother, or teacher, or clergy person) had asked you that same question. Could you tell me how you'd answer them?", our subjects most often replied in ways quite different from those in which they had done previously.

Consider the case of an adolescent girl responding to a young woman researcher. The two have just had an exchange in which the adolescent subject has talked in some detail about a moral dilemma and about religious elements that have figured in its resolution. When the researcher asks how the same girl would address herself to her best friend, instead of to a researcher, the girl responds:

> Maybe you won't like me saying so but I think it would actually change a lot. I would talk about the whole thing, in a way, differently. I might begin at a different point, with a different emotion, or even different people in the problem. I mean, I don't know you. You are nice and everything, but well, you aren't one of my friends and you come from the University and I don't know if I will see you again. With my friend, I would talk more about, say, the details of what I would or wouldn't do with a boy. That would be kind of different because I would feel more comfortable talking with her about that. I already have an idea of how she will respond or what would make sense to her, for example, which I didn't have with you when we started talking.

She continues:

> Besides, girls have a different way of talking, or maybe I should say girls of my age, we have a different language between us from how I talk with you. So what I would say and how I would say that would change.

In another such situation, an adolescent boy said:

> Well, even with my best friend I'm not sure I would have told him some of what I just told you. Because with you it is kind of like a new place we are making, because I don't really know you. So I'm not just telling you how something happened. I'm telling you about a self that is actually happening, or growing or something like that, in

> this conversation right here with you. It's not just that I'm reporting
> something that already did happen. I am rethinking who I was then,
> in talking with you about it now, and imagining how I would like it
> to be, or how I would have liked it to be, then. I'm even thinking
> I'm not sure I want this to be our last discussion because what I am
> saying is maybe, well, something I would like to find myself saying
> more of. If you're not there I'm not sure I would be able to be that,
> or I mean, say that.

Both subjects tell us, in effect, that what they produce as "account"
or "representation" is an artifact of the discursive conventions of
which they are part. What they recount to us is a function of what
they take to be the narrative possibilities of the frame we embody.
What they would say to someone else would likely shift according
to the modification of frame which would follow. Such shifts in narrative frame change accounts of what happened, when, and to whom,
and modify what is said in terms of prospective being. In speaking
to us, our subjects not only furnish accounts of what has happened,
or what might have happened, who they were or might have been,
but explore the alternative selves they might become according to
the narrative opportunities we together with them construct.

As I have elsewhere tried to demonstrate, religious language is as
much a performative as it is an informative genre of human conduct. In speaking we work not only to map or describe, but also to
enact relationship according to what we understand to be the the-
atre of possibilities in which we are situated. The chief medium
through which we do this is language, not as factotum of an epistemic researcher who is recounting what s/he has constructed as
meaningful, but rather language as the groundwork from which our
understanding of possible meanings is formed. We speak in order to
have relationship. What we can say is ordained within the structures
of discursive possibility furnished by language and social convention. Different partners in dialogue will evoke different possibilities of
being according to the relative flexibility or restriction of exploration,
through language, they offer us (Day, 1991a, 1991b, 1993, 1998,
1999a, 1999b, 1999c; Day & Tappan, 1995, 1996).

Though it falls for now outside the framework of our research, it
is useful to point to prayer as a form of religious language which
has a clearly performative character. Prayer may of course tell someone about something but prayer also envisages, requests, pleads,
demands there is a sense in which the believer is taught in praying
personal transformation will occur.

As we build a constructionist frame, we seek a developmental model which would respect these points of departure: dialogical self-hood, narrative, and the performative character of language.

Development in a Constructionist Frame: Where Might We Go?

If we conclude that the constructivist paradigm is wanting in its definitions of developmental endpoints, descriptions of developmental processes, and methods of studying religious and other facets of human development, what alternatives have we? What authors, frameworks, models, and methods, would help us to better understand this discursive subject, this dialogical self in development, and how might we make the shift to a focus that would more adequately attend to relationships and discourse elements as key features in developmental processes and projects?

Like our constructivist colleagues in the field of religious development, we are interested in those processes by which human action becomes, for a given person and for her community, meaningful. We have already observed that we find the constructivist account of meaning-making unsatisfying, but have yet to say how meaning *develops* from a constructionist point of view. Our concern with narrative has already suggested that meaning is temporal, that is, it is at once local to particular speech contexts, and something which makes sense only when it can be spoken of in terms of plot, character, more or less favorable endpoints, and time. We have furthermore observed, with Streib, Ganzevoort, and contributors to our own research, that religious meanings change in function of the kinds of self-narratives we weave. Religious ritual, gesture, symbol, language, and terms, change according to the relative significance they have in the ongoing negotiation of relationship in which we talk ourselves into being.

Clearly, we find ourselves, with Gergen, "... principally concerned with explicating the processes by which people come to describe, explain, or otherwise account for the world (including themselves) in which they live ... Social constructionism views discourse about the world not as a reflection or map of the world but as an artifact of communal interchange". (Gergen, 1985, p. 266; see also Gergen, 1991, 1993, 1994; Gergen & Gergen, 1986.) Two sets of authors seem to us particularly helpful as we voice this concern and seek to enfranchise it in the developmental psychology of religion. We find Gergen's notion of *supplementation* particularly intriguing in

this light. We return to Gergen, and two of his colleagues, John
Shotter and Sheila McNamee, to begin, then consider the work of
Mikhail Bakhtin and some of our work within the frame he proposes, to take a new look at religious development. Supplementation,
according to Gergen (1994), is

> . . . the reciprocal process in which one person supplements or responds
> to another person's utterances or actions. The *potential* (Gergen's empha-
> sis) for meaning in the dyad develops through the supplementation
> process. The response may be one word or an expanded conversation.
> Each person of the dyad is immersed in a range of other relationships—
> previous, present, and future—and the multiple contexts of those rela-
> tionships influence the supplementations and meanings developed within
> the dyad. And conversely, the influence of the supplementation within
> the dyad carries over (or has the potential to carry over) to outside the
> dyad as part of an expanding reciprocal process. Thus, meanings are
> not permanently fixed but are continuously influenced, constructed, and
> reconstructed, over time (Anderson, 1997, p. 42).

As Anderson (1997) points out, Shotter's notion of *joint action* is similar to Gergen's concept of supplementation. Shotter (1993) describes
joint action as the way in which people mutually and reciprocally
negotiate sustainable conversation and associated contexts of meaning, allowing at once for constantly accumulating richness and appearance of continuity and order, and for creative re-interpretation of
categories and styles so that new meanings and competencies can
emerge: "All actions by human beings involved with others in a
social group in this fashion are dialogically or responsively linked in
some way, both to previous, already executed actions and to antici-
pated, next possible actions" (Shotter, 1984, pp. 52–53).

These concepts are useful because they describe ways in which
we can think of development as belonging both to the sphere of the
person and of the socius, the network of relationships of which s/he
is part. What we might hope to help persons to develop is the capacity to form, maintain, and enhance relationship through the kinds
of conversational competence which contribute to relationships going
on and becoming increasingly inclusive of becoming, themselves,
resources for their communities. Relationships are seen to develop,
on these grounds, when they are able to sustain the wellbeing of the
partners involved, and at the same time contribute to the welfare of
the communities of which they are part.

Likewise, McNamee (1999), writing with Gergen, outlines ways in
which concepts such as *responsability* can be considered in a con-

structionist frame. Rather than viewing responsability as an internally held attitude or disposition, or as is often done as the characteristic of a group through its handling of affairs to which it applies itself, McNamee views responsability as a kind of ongoing construction of responsivity, a kind of ongoing dialogic in which an ever-increasing number of parties is given voice and allowed room to influence events. Common to the projects of these scholars is an implicit notion that development involves increasing *communicative competence* within *relationships* and *networks of communicative contingency* (emphasis mine). What develops is not meaning, as something which stands apart from relationship within individuals, but the communicative capacities of persons in relationships. It is the continual emergence of meaningful *elaboration* of relationship which grows, or doesn't. It is the potential for supplementation (Gergen), joint action (Shotter), and responsability (McNamee) which grows, or stagnates.

Like Gergen, Shotter, and McNamee, Mikail Bakhtin is concerned with speech acts and their consequences in the development of mental processes. Influenced by the work of Vygotsky, Bakhtin argues that the human psyche is semiotically and linguistically mediated, and that it originates in the context of social relationships and social interaction (see also Wertsch 1991). Bakhtin is especially useful in this regard because unlike Vygotsky, who depends on a model of "internalization" to explain development in psychological processes, describing a move whereby external relations between persons become internal relations within the human psyche, Bakhtin avoids such a split between internal and external upon which Vygotsky's account relies.

Bakhtin views the self as a social construction, the differentiation of which occurs through linguistic processes. For Bakhtin the person comes to view herself *as* a self insofar as she is counted on to *speak* in her own *voice*, and to *answer* to others, to become part of the dialogues of which her world is composed, to respond when spoken to, to offer moves which will incline others to speak, to participate in the making of the world through her place in the way it is linguistically constructed and shaped. For Bakhtin what develops is *authorship* competencies. The person has to actively participate in the shaping of her world through language (Day & Youngman, in press). How does *authorship* develop? According to Bakhtin:

> It becomes one's own only when the speaker populates it with his own intention, his own accent, when he appropriates the word, adapting it to his own semantic and expressive intention. Prior to this moment of

appropriation the word does not exist in a neutral and impersonal language (it is not, after all, out of a dictionary that a speaker gets his words!), but rather it exists in other people's mouths, in other people's contexts, serving other people's intentions. It is from there that one must take the word, and make it one's own ... Language is not a neutral medium that passes freely and easily into the private property of the speaker's intentions; it is populated—overpopulated—with the intentions of others. Expropriating it, forcing it to submit to one's own intentions and accents, is a difficult and complicated process (Bakhtin, 1981, pp. 293–294; see also Bakhtin, 1986, 1990; Day & Tappan, 1996).

For Bakhtin, development in authorship is a kind of *ideological becoming* (Bakhtin, 1981, p. 341). Bakhtin observes that "one's own discourse and one's own voice, although born of another or dynamically stimulated by another" may come to be "liberated" from their overpopulation by another's voice, meanings, and authorities. It becomes the ground for answerability, something for which one assumes responsability, one becomes more or less able to act with weight and authority in the contexts in which one speaks, and to contribute to their possibilities for enhancing relationship.

Bakhtin's notions of maturity, like those of Gergen, Shotter, and McNamee, call to mind the work of Mark Tappan (e.g. 1992, 1999), who has done much to bring Bakhtin's work into the mainstream of developmental psychology. With them, we speak of a kind of development that is fully situated on the borderline of self and other, a kind of communicative competency and communicational balancing, which is at once concerned with the maintenance of interpersonal functioning and with personal differentiation. Such differentiation includes increasing abilities to contribute through "communicative return" to the group. In speaking of relationships, contexts, and discursive selves in development, we would privilege relational competence as a desirable goal of developmental processes: the capacity to engage in dialogue, the emergence of conversational skill so as to sustain connection, the capacity to speak with authority while allowing increasing room for the participation of others as partners in discourse. The developing person would "be the kind of speaker whose voice would invite rather than exclude, value rather than denigrate, prize rather than punish, further rather than retard" (Day & Youngman, in press), the participation of other voices in her communicative world. The definition of a person's relative development would include how it feels for other people to know her, work with her, interact with her, make love with her, speak to and be spoken

to by her. In such a view, obviously, competence is as much interpersonal as it is individual, something which happens between and
among persons rather than within them. Meanings are not internally
held but mutually elaborated.

Religious Development and Pastoral Theology

Constructivist canons in the application of developmental theory and
research to pastoral theology conceive of pastoral care for religious
development. The task of the pastoral theologian is to identify the
developmental position of his client or parishioner and help that
person to move toward more mature religious judgment or faith
activity. Stage, structure, hierarchy, disequilibrium in the service
of development: these Piagetian notions are applied in faith and religious development practices toward the enhancement of personal
autonomy and sophistication, ever more differentiated and adequate
understanding and supposedly related action. We have already made
clear our reluctance to embrace such a program, and outlined the
reasons for our hesitation.

How might a constructionist notion of religious development look,
and what difference might it make to the pastoral theologian?

First, a constructionist view to religious development might take
seriously the narrative features of psychological functioning we have
ever so briefly introduced and alluded to here, and in at least three
ways: (a) the person would be viewed as a potential author of narratives; someone with stories to tell; (b) the work of pastoral "intervention" would be sensitive to the power of narrative in religious
tradition in the accomplishment of its aims, and (c) pastoral counseling and care would be enhanced by the understanding that its
activity consists in the negotiation of mutual meanings through joint
or corporate story-making (See also Ganzevoort, 1998; Streib, 1997).

Second, a constructionist view might claim no privileged understanding of persons' "interiors". We would admit that what we have
access to is not "internal" to anyone or anything, but instead written on the slippery surfaces of ourselves in interaction. What we
have access to is behavior, and much of that is speech. We could
make no allusions or attributions of internal states (personalities, souls,
wills, intentions and the like would vanish from view) but rather use
richly the surfaces at our disposal. Pastoral work would steer clear

of intrusive and invasive suppositions as to the character of the "inner recesses" of persons. Clients and parishioners would instead be invited to explore how the languages they use affect their place with those who matter to them: God(s), others, what they take to be them "selves".

Third, a constructionist view might underscore the performative character of language. The pastor's questions would shift from a search for causes or explanations or deep structures to a concern with consequences. Not "where does that come from" or "why do you suppose you see God that way" but "When you talk about God that way, where does it take you? How does that affect your relationships? Imagine you were to talk to God differently? Who might you want to be? What would you say if you wanted to accomplish?"

Fourth, a constructionist take on religious development might bring the notion of audience more fully into view. Not talking about, but talking to, would become the focus of pastoral work. So the pastor might say "When you talk that way about yourself, whom do you imagine being there? Who is it you're talking to there? When you talk to yourself that way, whose voice is it you imagine answering you? What does it sound like when that other voice speaks? Now imagine another voice responded. What would it sound like? There where you're talking about what feels like God's answer to you, can you give that answer a voice? Is there any other way in which you might imagine God answering you?"

Fifth, a constructionist turn in viewing religious development might embrace a certain humility as to its epistemological status. We would accept that knowledge is communal, knowledge is culture-bound, knowledge is a fluid, ongoing, process. We would not know what the proper outcome of a client or parishioner's development would be, and would accept our not knowing about it.

Sixth, a constructionist view might endeavor to underscore that meanings are local, and that meanings evolve according to context, contingency, communicative capacity, and whether or not a person is enfranchised as a legitimate author in those places where questions of meaning will be elaborated. Pastors would pretend to no privileged position as to the meaning the client or parishioner "ought" to derive, but would instead be concerned with how to encourage the person's full participation in the networks where meanings in religious community are made.

Seventh, pastoral work in the service of religious education might take some cues from the shift we have suggested. In the classical constructivist paradigm, the task of the religious educator is that of helping individuals to move from one developmental point to another through the transformation of internally held stage structures, mapped through the speech of the student. We have already stated our reservations as to the conceptual adequacy of such a view, preferring to view mind-language-action relationships differently. We would displace the traditional emphasis on education as inculcation, or constructivist emphasis on movement toward increasing sophistication and autonomy, with an accent on those skills which contribute to the building of relationship and which expand, through discussion, the relational resources of the communities of which the student is part. Instead of being concerned with rote repetition of received truths, or the logical adequacy of a student's personal arguments, we would want to explore ways of evaluating whether and how groups (from dyads to larger groups) build, and sustain, relationship in the midst of conflict and dissonance. With Gergen (1993), we would want to explore pastoral responses to the notion that *belief* might be conceived of as a relational resource, and to better understand how it happens that in some lives talk of belief contributes to the building and sustaining and enhancing of relationship, whereas in some lives, or in some domains, talk of belief works as a kind of destructive conversational convention, obstructing rather than permitting or opening to dialogue. The fundamental notion privileged here is that ongoing dialogue, inclusive of a broad array of conversational possibilities permits creative problem-solving in a way that atomic sophistication and sparring does not. Pastoral work in the various domains upon which we have touched would make use of the "constructionist" insights and concepts we have offered in order to better understand how religious belief as a social construct contributes to human welfare, and how to reduce the deleterious consequences it has sometimes had in the inverse sense.

Concluding Prospects

In this chapter I have tried to build a case for considering constructionist alternatives to canonical constructivist paradigms of religious development, and have made a sketchy attempt to imagine how such alternatives might affect pastoral work, often conceived as an adventure in applied development. Though limited in scope, I hope these words will contribute to the ongoing work of psychologists, religious educators, and those persons of various religious traditions who conceive of their mission in developmental terms.

References

Anderson, H. (1997). *Conversation, language, and possibilities: A postmodern approach to therapy.* New York: Basic Books.
Bakhtin, M. (1981). *The dialogic imagination* (M. Holquist, Ed., C. Emerson & M. Holquist, Trans.). Austin: University of Texas Press.
—— (1986). *Speech genres and other late essays* (C. Emerson & M. Holquist, Eds., V. McGee, Trans.). Austin: University of Texas Press.
—— (1990). *Art and answerability* (M. Holquist & V. Liapunov, Eds. and Trans.). Austin: University of Texas Press.
Brown, L. (1999). Adolescent girls' development. In R. Mosher, D. Youngman, & J. Day (Eds.), *Human development across the life span: Educational and psychological applications.* Westport, Ct.: Praeger.
Brown, L., & Gilligan, C. (1991). Listening for voice in narratives of relationship. In Mark Tappan & Martin Packer (Eds.), *Narrative and storytelling. Implications for understanding moral development* (New directions for child development, No. 54). San Francisco: Jossey-Bass.
Day, J. (1991a). The moral audience: On the narrative mediation of moral 'judgment' and moral 'action'. In Mark Tappan & Martin Packer (Eds.), *Narrative and storytelling. Implications for understanding moral development* (New directions for child development, No. 54). San Francisco: Jossey-Bass.
—— (1991b). Role-taking reconsidered: Narrative and cognitive-developmental interpretations of moral growth. *The Journal of Moral Education, 20,* 305–317.
—— (1993). Speaking of belief: Language, performance, and narrative in the psychology of religion. *The International Journal for the Psychology of Religion 3* (4), 213–230.
—— (1994). Narratives of "belief" and "unbelief" in young adult accounts of religious experience and moral development. In D. Hutsebaut & J. Corveleyn (Eds.), *Belief and unbelief: Psychological perspectives.* Amsterdam: Rodopi
—— (1998). Verhalen, identiteiten, god(en): Narratieve bemiddeling en religieus discours [Narrative mediation and religious discourse]. In R.R. Ganzevoort (Ed.), *De praxis als verhaal: Narrativiteit en praktische theologie* [The praxis as narrative. Narrativity and practical theology]. Kampen, Netherlands: Uitgeverij Kok.
—— (1999a). Exemplary sierrans: Moral influences. In Mosher, R., Connor, D., Kalliel, K., Day, J., Yakota, N., Porter, M. & Whiteley, J., *Moral action in young adulthood.* National Resource Center for the First-Year Experience and Students in Transition: University of South Carolina Press.
—— (1999b). The primacy of relationship: A meditation on education, faith, and the dialogical self. In J. Conroy (Ed.), *Catholic education: Inside out-outside in.* Dublin: Veritas.
—— (1999c). Das Gute wissen—das Gute tun: Narrationen über Urteil und Handeln in den moralischen Entscheidungen junger Erwachsener. In D. Garz, F. Oser, & W. Althof (Eds.), *Moralisches Urteil und Handeln* [Moral judgement and action]. Frankfurt am Main: Suhrkamp Verlag.
—— (2000). *The social construction of morality: Archives of contemporary psychology: Voices in social constructionism.* Los Angeles: Master's Work Video Productions.
—— (in press). From structuralism to eternity? Re-imagining the psychology of religious development after the cognitive-developmental paradigm. *The International Journal for the Psychology of Religion.*

Day, J., & Naedts, M. (1995). Convergence and conflict in the development of moral judgment and religious judgment. *Journal of Education, 177* (2), 1–30.
—— (1997). A reader's guide for interpreting texts of religious experience: A hermeneutical approach. In J.A. Belzen (Ed.), *Hermeneutical approaches in the psychology of religion* (pp. 173–194). Amsterdam: Rodopi.
—— (1999). Religious development. In R. Mosher, D. Youngman, & J. Day (Eds.), *Human development across the lifespan: Educational and Psychological Applications.* Westport: Praeger Publishing.
Day, J., & Tappan, M. (1995). Identity, voice, and the psycho/dialogical: perspectives from moral psychology. *American Psychologist, 50* (1), 47–49.
—— (1996). The narrative approach to moral development: From the epistemic subject to dialogical selves. *Human Development, 39* (2), 67–82.
Day, J., & Youngman, D. (in press). Discursive practices and their interpretation in the psychology of religious development. From constructivist canons to constructionist alternatives. *Handbook of Adult Development.* New York: Plenum
Desimpelaere, P., Sulas, F., Duriez, B., & Hutsebaut, D. (1999). Psycho-epistemological styles and religious beliefs. *International Journal for the Psychology of Religion, 9* (2), 125–137.
Di Loreto, O., & Oser, F. (1996). Entwicklung des religiösen Urteils und religiöse Selbstwirksamkeitsüberzeugung. Eine Langsschnittstudie [Development of religious judgement and religious convictions about self-effectiveness. A longitudinal study]. In F. Oser, & H. Reich (Hrsgs.), *Eingebettet ins Menschsein. Beispiel Religion,* [Integral to humanity. Example: religion]. Lengerich, Germany: Pabst Science Publishers.
Dumont, V. (1999). Pensée postformelle et jugement réflexif. Unpublished doctoral dissertation. Université catholique de Louvain, Louvain-la-Neuve.
Fowler, J. (1981). *Stages of faith. The psychology of human development and the quest for meaning.* San Francisco: Harper & Row.
—— (1996). *Faithful change. The personal and public challenges of postmodern life.* Nashville: Abingdon.
Fowler, J., Nipkow, K & Schweizer, F. (Eds.). (1991). *Stages of faith and religious development.* New York: Crossroad.
Ganzevoort, R. (Ed). (1998a). *De praxis als verhaal: narrativiteit en praktische theologie* [The praxis as narrative. Narrativity and practical theology]. Kampen, Netherlands: Uitgeverij Kok.
—— (1998b). De praxis als verhaal: Introductie op een narratief perspectief. In R. Ganzevoort (Ed.), *De praxis als verhaal: narrativiteit en praktische theologie* [The praxis as narrative. Narrativity and practical theology]. Kampen, Netherlands: Uitgeverij Kok.
Gergen, K. (1982). *Toward transformation in social knowledge.* New York: Springer-Verlag.
—— (1985). The social constructionist movement in modern psychology. *American Psychologist, 40,* 266–275.
—— (1991). *The saturated self.* Cambridge, Ma: Harvard University Press.
—— (1993). Belief as relational resource. *International Journal for the Psychology of Religion, 3* (4), 231–235.
—— (1994). *Realities and relationships: Soundings in social construction.* Cambridge, Ma: Harvard University Press.
—— (1999). *An invitation to social construction.* London: Sage Publications.
Gergen, K., & Gergen, M. (1986). Narrative form and the construction of psychological science. In Th. Sarbin (Ed.), *Narrative psychology: The storied nature of human conduct.* New York: Praeger.
Gibbs, J., Basinger, K., & Fuller, S. (1992). *Measuring the development of socio-moral reflection. The socio-moral reflection measure revised.* Hillsdale, NJ: Erlbaum.
Gilligan, C. (1982). *In a different voice: Psychological theory and women's development.* Cambridge: Harvard University Press.

Gilligan, C., Brown, L., & Rogers, A. (1990). Psyche embedded: A place for body, relationships, and culture in personality theory. In A.I. Rabin, R. Zucker, R. Emmons, & S. Frank (Eds.), *Studying persons and lives*. New York: Springer.

Gilligan, C., Ward, J., & Taylor, J. (Eds.). (1988). *Mapping the moral domain: A contribution of women's thinking to psychological theory and education*. Cambridge: Harvard University Press.

Habermas, J. (1979). *Communication and the evolution of society* (Thomas. McCarthy, Trans.). Boston: Beacon Press.

—— (1983a). *Moralbewußtsein und kommunikatives Handeln* [Moral consciousness and communicative action]. Frankfurt: Suhrkamp.

—— (1983b). Interpretive social science vs. hermeneuticism. In N. Haan, R. Bellah, P. Rabinow, & W. Sullivan (Eds.), *Social science as moral inquiry*. New York: Columbia University Press.

Hutsebaut, D. (1996). Post-critical belief: A new approach to the religious attitude problem. *Journal of Empirical Theology, 9* (2), 48–66.

—— (1997a). Identity statuses, ego-integration, God representation and religious cognitive styles. *Journal of Empirical Theology, 10* (1), 39–54.

—— (1997b). *Structure of religious attitude in function of socialization pattern*. Paper presented at the 6th European Symposium for Psychologists of Religion, Barcelona.

Kohlberg, L. (1969). Stage and sequence: The cognitive-developmental approach to socialization. In D. Goslin (Ed.), *Handbook of socialization theory and research*. Chicago: Rand McNally.

—— (1981). *Essays on moral development, Vol. I: The philosophy of moral development*. San Francisco: Harper & Row.

—— (1984). *Essays on moral development, Vol. II: The psychology of moral development*. San Francisco: Harper & Row.

Lyons, N. (1983). Two perspectives: On self, relationships, and morality. *Harvard Educational Review, 53*, 125–145.

McCarthy, Th. (1982). Rationality and relativism: Habermas's "overcoming" of hermeneutics. In J. Thompson & D. Held (Eds.), *Habermas: Critical debates*. Cambridge: The MIT Press.

Oser, F., & Reich, H. (1990). Moral judgement, religious judgement, worldview and logical thought. A review of their relationship, Part 1. *British Journal of Religious Education, 12* (2), 94–101.

Oser, F., & Gmünder, P. (1991). *Religious judgement. A developmental approach*. Birmingham, Alabama: Religious Education Press.

Piaget, J. (1965). *The moral judgment of the child*. New York: The Free Press. (Original work published 1932)

Power, C. (1991). Hard versus soft stages of faith and religious development. In J. Fowler, K. Nipkow, & F. Schweitzer (Eds.), *Stages of faith and religious development: Implications for church, education, and society*. New York: Crossroad.

Reich, H. (1997). Integrating differing theories: The case of religious development. In B. Spilka, & D. McIntosh (Eds.), *The psychology of religion. Theoretical approaches* (pp. 105–113). New York: Westview Press.

Reich, H., Oser, F., & Scarlett, W. (1996). Spiritual and religious development: Transcendence and transformations of the self. In H. Reich, F. Oser, & G. Scarlett (Eds.), *Psychological studies on spiritual and religious development: Being Human: The case of religion, Vol. 2*. Lengerich, Germany: Pabst Science Publishers.

Shotter, J. (1984). *Social accountability and selfhood*. Oxford: Blackwell.

—— (1993). *Conversational realities: Constructing life through language*. London: Sage.

Streib, H. (1991). *Hermeneutics of metaphor, symbol, and narrative in faith development theory*. Frankfurt/M.: Peter Lang.

—— (1997). Religion als Stilfrage. Zur Revision struktureller Differenzierung von Religion im Blick auf die Analyse der pluralistisch-religiösen Lage der Gegenwart. *Archiv für Religionspsychologie, 22*, 48–69.

Tamminen, K., & Nurmi, K.E. (1995). Developmental theory and religious experience. In R. Hood Jr. (Ed.), *Handbook of religious experience.* Birmingham, Alabama: Religious Education Press.

Tappan, M. (1992). Texts and contexts: Language, culture, and the development of moral functioning. In L.T. Winegar & J. Valsiner (Eds.), *Children's development within social contexts: Metatheoretical, theoretical, and methodological issues.* Hillsdale, NJ: Lawrence Erlbaum.

—— (1999). Moral development in a postmodern world. In R. Mosher, D. Youngman & J. Day (Eds.), *Human development across the life span: educational and psychological applications.* Westport, Ct.: Praeger Publishing.

Wertsch, J. (1991). *Voices of the mind: A sociocultural approach to mediated action.* Cambridge: Harvard University Press.

Wulff, D. (1997). *Psychology of religion. Classic and contemporary approaches* (2nd ed.). New York: John Wiley.

PART TWO

THEOLOGICAL CONTRIBUTIONS

LOSING THE SELF, FINDING THE SELF: POSTMODERN THEOLOGY AND SOCIAL CONSTRUCTION

Mark I. Wallace

> *Whoever wants to save his life will lose it, but whoever loses his life for my sake will save it (Luke 9:24).*

> *The past guarantees nothing. If we wish to maintain our traditions in a world of rapid global change, we confront the everyday task of sustaining intelligibility. That is, we must carry out the forms of relationship, and the generation of rationality within these relationships, that will enable these traditions to remain sensible. It has been continuously necessary, for example, to rewrite or reconstruct Christianity in order to give it vitality in today's world.* Kenneth Gergen, Invitation to Social Construction, *49*

Introduction

One of the most intriguing koans of Jesus' ministry is his claim that whenever a person desires to save her life she will lose it and, conversely, that only when she is willing to lose her life will she be able to save it. Only when one forfeits the self can one discover genuine selfhood; the journey to the true self begins by first abandoning one's assumptions about selfhood. Unless one empties oneself and leaves behind the quest for self-certainty one cannot truly find oneself beyond the traditional notions of the subject that provide false security and comfort. This carefully crafted contradiction of Jesus' rhetoric is at the heart of a newly emerging vision of theology that plumbs the depths of the rich biblical images of self-emptying and self-giving as the keys to understanding authentic selfhood.

In this essay I will analyze the collapse of the received notions of the stable self in recent thought and then move toward a freshly innovative model of the self founded on biblical notions of solicitude for the other person. I use Paul Ricoeur to argue that the biblical texts construe the project of selfhood in terms of following the dictates of one's conscience to take responsibility for the neighbor— even at great cost to oneself. In biblical parlance, the individual only becomes a self by allowing the divine Other to "summon" or "call" it to its responsibilities for the human other. The morally awakened conscience is the first step toward meaningful subjectivity. In order to prepare the ground for this analysis of selfhood-through-conscience, I begin with a discussion of the Heideggerian-inspired move in contemporary theology away from metaphysical foundations toward a postmodern, constructionist understanding of its subject matter. Along with a side glance at Buddhism, I will use here Kenneth Gergen's thesis concerning the social construction of reality and the intersubjective, relational self to articulate the constructionist move in recent religious thought. Gergen's work will foreground my subsequent proposal for the scriptural ideal of the self-divesting subject (in the manner of Ricoeur) who discovers itself through losing itself in and with and for the other.

Theology Beyond Metaphysics?

Historically, Western thought about God and the self has been grounded on metaphysical foundations. Classical expressions of this tradition are Aristotle's and Aquinas's arguments that the human experience of contingent selfhood proves the existence of God as a necessary being, an unmoved mover, who is the necessary source and end of all particular beings. In Thomistic metaphysics, for example, God's being (*ens*) is God's existence (*esse*)—God's essence is to-be—whereas other beings exist not in themselves but only by virtue of their participation in God (Aquinas: 1.Q.3.art.4). The reality of contingent existence, therefore, leads one backward in a chain of iron logic to self-subsistent Being-itself as the non-contingent source of all dependent beings. This type of speculative reasoning grounds the long-held desire of historic philosophical theology to develop a metaphysically rooted system of beliefs with enough certitude to be considered a science. Unless and until theology becomes grounded on universal truths, so the argument goes, it runs the risk of remaining mired in the parochial origins of the early faith communities that gave rise to primitive theological reflection in the first place.

As the natural sciences have been able to secure foundational knowledge about the order and predictability of physical objects, so philosophical theology, historically understood, sought to specify the transcendental conditions for the possibility of every form of being and existence, including the being and existence of God. The dream of philosophical theology, therefore, has always been the ideal of metaphysics, that is, "inquiry beyond or over beings which claims to recover them as such and as a whole for our grasp" (Heidegger, 1977, p. 109). In Western culture, the various practitioners of metaphysical theology have hoped to articulate a body of intuitive beliefs about God, self, and world that are incorrigibly self-evident. The denial of these certain beliefs would so fundamentally alter the received understandings of reality with which we all operate that these beliefs cannot be seriously questioned. Insofar as the task of metaphysics is to explicate the conditions constitutive of being as such, theology, "properly understood," is the highest form of metaphysics because it interrogates the nature of the one strictly necessary being, God, who is the source and end of all other beings, including humankind.

This metaphysical tradition continues into the present. For many contemporary Christian theologians and philosophers of religion, belief in God should have the same intellectual status as other incorrigible, self-evident truths. Many of the primary exponents of normative theology today maintain that the problem of theology is that it has not adequately patterned its efforts after the models of its counterparts in philosophy and science. They argue that the iteration of the right conceptual system for establishing the cognitive claims of Christianity has gone begging and that without an adequate intellectual undercarriage the faith of the church will retreat into the twilight world of fideism untouched by the light of reason and argument.

Alfred North Whitehead, for example, laments that while Christianity "has always been a religion seeking a metaphysic" it has suffered from "the fact that it has no clear-cut separation from the crude fancies of the older tribal religions" (Whitehead, 1926, p. 50). Whitehead argues that if Christianity is to achieve the status of an authoritative, universal system of coherent beliefs, it must divorce itself from the intense experiences characteristic of its erstwhile tribal origins in antiquity and adopt a body of formal truths concerning the conditions for understanding the nature of reality. "Religion requires a metaphysical backing; for its authority is endangered by the intensity of the emotions which it generates. Such emotions are evidence of some vivid experience; but they are a very poor guarantee of its correct interpretation" (Whitehead, 1926, p. 81).

The called-for reliance of theology on metaphysical presuppositions raises a number of questions, however, for a theology that seeks primary fidelity to the biblical witness. Should theology seek to ground its proposals on a metaphysical foundation, or should it abandon its quest for such foundations? Even if theology chooses the latter, can it do so? Can theology and metaphysics be disentangled so easily? As Heidegger asks, can theology "overcome" or "step back" beyond "ontotheology"—the philosophical fusion of Greek philosophy and biblical notions of God—by asserting its independence from any and all metaphysical influences (Heidegger, 1969, pp. 42–76)? Or, as Derrida insists, "if one does not have to philosophize, one still has to philosophize"—in other words, even when one seeks to think outside the question of being, all thought, nevertheless, must circulate within a metaphysical economy (Derrida, 1978, p. 152)? Even if theology could insure its autonomy from the question of being, should it do so? Will theology not slide into tribalism and privatism unless it allows itself to be disciplined by ontotheology? Or does the practice of theology under the horizon of being threaten to undermine the novelty and heterogeneity that is distinctive of all modes of authentic religious life and discourse?

To use God-language, does God need the openings that a metaphysical vocabulary can provide? Or are the openings proffered by such vocabularies in fact foreclosings of the presence of the Other who transgresses all categories and concepts? Given the historic elision of God and Being, how is the divine life to be understood in a contemporary setting? Is God a metaphysically certain *existent* within common human experience, or is God the unknowable (but not unspeakable) *Other* who is absolutely free of all metaphysical delimitations? Is God the necessary Being, the *ens realissimum*, who is knowable as the supreme origin of our beings, or is God, as the one who is *not-being* but still *is*, the violation of all categories and determinations? Is God best understood as Being-itself who renders all derivative existence possible, or is God a reality anterior to and beyond all determinations (metaphysical or otherwise)?

In my mind, Heidegger is right that the question of Being in theology has saddled Christianity with a philosopher's God, the metaphysically certain God of supreme causality who mechanically functions as the cosmological ground and unity of all beings in the world. When God is relegated to the part of a place-holder in a chain of cosmic causality, theology becomes captive to ontotheological assumptions that limit God to the role of highest existent, *ens a se*, pure actuality, being-itself, and *prima causa*—a distant, frozen, and abstract deity who, as "the god of philosophy," is such that one "can neither pray nor sacrifice to this god. Before the *causa sui*, man can neither fall to his knees in awe nor can he play music and dance before this god" (Heidegger, 1969, p. 72). Using Heidegger's formulation, it is critical for theology that it engage in "god-less thinking which must abandon the god of philosophy" in order to approach the God of biblical faith (Heidegger, 1969, p. 72). In this model, God, in short, is not the *Being* known within the horizon of metaphysics, but the *occasion* for fostering new modes of scripturally nuanced existence that are no longer founded on the metaphysical securities of Western thought.

Theology in a Postmodern, Constructionist Context

My contention is that theology becomes a vital undertaking when it avoids the temptation to ground its enterprise on a philosophical foundation and returns instead to its living wellspring—the founding stories and images of biblical faith—as the source for its vision of human transformation in a fragmented world. Theology today is best served by returning to its roots in the biblical narratives and cutting its moorings to the ontotheological tradition of understanding God as supreme cause and ultimate Being. This metaphysical tradition is sterile and fruitless because it has imparted to modern religious life and thought a distant and unfeeling deity, an apathetic unmoved mover, who can be neither feared nor loved, pleaded with nor danced to, blasphemed nor glorified. Such a God cannot be wrestled with and struggled against, as was the God of Jacob at the river Jabbok in Genesis; feared in terror, as was the God of Moses at the burning bush in Exodus; railed against in anger and bitterness, as was the God of many of the protagonists of biblical wisdom literature, such as David and Solomon and Job; petitioned in blood, as was the God of Jesus in Gethsemane in the Gospels; nor loved and worshipped, as was the God of Stephen, when, upon being stoned to death by an angry mob in Acts, Stephen raised his eyes to heaven and said, "Lord, receive my spirit and do not hold this sin against them."

While recognizing that the ontotheological tradition has no resonance with the rich and variegated portraits of God within the biblical heritage, we may remain anxious that without the public security of an all-encompassing philosophical substructure, theology will lose

its standing in academe and the wider culture and sink back into
the netherworlds of privatism and tribalism. But this worry about
the universal versus private status of theology presupposes a sterile
binary distinction that obscures a hidden middle path beyond the
impasse generated by this false opposition. As an alternative to understanding theology in either universal, philosophical terms or private,
sectarian terms, my proposal is for a *postmodern theology with an emancipatory intent* that uses a variety of tools borrowed from critical social
theory for recovering from the biblical sources models for human
transformation in a broken world.

Postmodern theology emphasizes both intellectual rigor and creative fidelity to the textual origins of Christian faith. On the one
hand, it abides by communal norms of argument and rationality in
order to articulate a body of beliefs that can withstand critical scrutiny
and possible refutation; in so doing, however, it refuses to be held
hostage to any philosophical assumptions (metaphysical or otherwise)
that will blunt its move toward understanding the complexity of its
subject matter, the mystery we call God. On the other hand, postmodern theology seeks rhetorical resonance to its documentary sources
in order to construct a full-bodied vision of the divine life that can
engender vitality and well being; in so doing, however, a biblically
sonorous theology is vigilant in resisting the sectarian temptation to
limit theology to the role of defending biblical or church orthodoxy.
Eschewing both philosophical limits and ecclesial conformity, postmodern theology seeks creative and, at times, subversive fidelity to
the biblical and historical traditions that can fund visions of libera-
tion and change for a world in crisis.

Postmodern theology is akin to other similar movements in contemporary thought. On one level, it bears affinities with postmodern architecture, which eclectically uses historical quotation in order
to bring together materials, motifs, and styles from the past into a
new urban design (cf. Harvey, 1990, pp. 66–98). Like postmodern
architecture, it is an exercise in pastiche. It is a self-consciously *constructive* enterprise that selects from previous works thought forms and
vocabulary that can be usefully recombined and refashioned in an
idiom expressive of the hopes and desires of our age.[1] On another

---

[1] As a constructive discipline, postmodern theology is methodologically parallel
to Jeffrey Stout's notion of *bricolage* in contemporary moral philosophy. Quoting
Claude Lévi-Strauss, Stout writes that *bricolage* is the process whereby a *bricoleur* con-

level, however, postmodern theology goes beyond historical quotation and stylistic pastiche with its explicit commitment to enabling
transformative praxis. Postmodern theology utilizes a wide variety of
historical styles and motifs in order to craft a new theological framework that can productively engage the critical challenges of our time.

The constructionist project of Kenneth Gergen is a valuable resource
for developing the type of emancipatory theology imagined in this
essay. Gergen's central insight is that truth and rationality are constructed within social groups. Our assumptions about "'the nature
of things" or "what the world is really like" are not a result of individual minds having reliable sense impressions of hard facts, but a
product of shared experiences and tacit assumptions generated over
time by particular communities. For Gergen,

> knowledge is derived from value-interested conceptual standpoints rather
> than accurate mappings of the facts of nature. . . . In contrast to the
> empiricist position . . . the locus of knowledge [is] not in the minds of
> single individuals, but in the collectivity. It is not the internal processes
> of the individual that generate what is taken for knowledge, but a
> social process of communication. It is within the process of social inter-
> change that rationality is generated. . . . *Interpersonal* colloquy is neces-
> sary to determine "the nature of things" (Gergen, 1982, p. 207).

The world does not communicate its essential nature unadulterated
to the keen empirical observer. The world is not a mind-independent
reality yielding self-subsistent facts available to the neutral spectator.
On the contrary, while not denying the reality of the world "out
there," constructionists such as Gergen contend that the world only
has meaning and value based on the culturally embedded "in here"
conceptual schemas particular social groups rely on to organize the
data of experience.[2]

---

structs original artifacts (be they physical or conceptual constructs) based on the
contingent resources and arbitrary materials at hand. The *bricoleur* takes the assorted
odds and ends at her disposal and fashions them into a useful product; the random tools and elements at hand are the raw materials for the construction of the
new project envisioned by the *bricoleur*. Postmodern theology is a *bricolage* activity
wherein the theorist cobbles together a framework for conversation between ancient
source materials and contemporary realities and problems (Stout, 1988, pp. 71–81).

[2] A wide number of contemporary thinkers—including Richard Rorty, William
Cronin, Jeffrey Stout, Judith Butler, Stuart Hall, Cornel West, Sandra Harding,
and Thomas Kuhn—agree with Gergen's constructionist thesis that all modes of
understanding the world are products of intersubjective agreements about what does
and does not count as reality. Ludwig Wittgenstein is the progenitor of the constructivist position that inherited frames of reference constitute what a culturally situated

The recognition that all forms of inquiry are relative to inter-communal assumptions frees contemporary theology to reimagine God, self, and world through a very particular retrieval of the fecund imagery within the biblical texts that gave rise to Christian traditions in the first place. Theology can avoid, therefore, the hoary task of trying to ground its enterprise on the security of a metaphysical foundation in the hopes that such a foundation can provide a universally secure, God's Eye perspective on the whole of human experience. With the realization, as Gergen writes, that "[n]othing exists for us—as an intelligible world of objects and persons—until there are relationships" (Gergen, 1999, p. 48), and, that with attention to new patterns of relationship, "constructionism offers a bold invitation to transform social life, to build new futures" (Gergen, 1999, p. 49), theology is then freed to pay renewed attention to those potentially revolutionary patterns of relationship narrated within the biblical witness as models for human becoming. In a constructionist framework, appeals to timeless ontotheological notions of "God as Being," "eternal truth," or "the human being as such," are supplanted by close biblical readings of how particular persons transformatively interacted with one another to realize truth and goodness within their specific, historical social settings.

In the constructionist framework, theology, as a situated discourse rather than a philosophical system, is liberated to enter fully the public square of competing ideologies and thereby offer its scripturally rich visions of reality without relying on the pseudo-protection of metaphysics to "trump" the competitor thought-systems that surround it. Theology, then, becomes essentially an activity in rhetoric and persuasion, a highly imaginative exercise in the art of engaging conversation and communication with people and communities from all walks of life. It is no longer an in-house discipline only for the benefit of true believers but now a form of dialogical engagement with the wider culture that offers the biblical ideal of service to others along with, for example, radical environmentalism or new age psychology or genetic engineering as a paradigm for capturing the hearts and

---

subject understands to be the nature of things. Rationality is always generated and sustained within the "world views," "language games," or "forms of life" shared by persons in particular social relationships. Epistemology, in short, is a relational rather than an individual task, according to Wittgenstein. Whether in religion or psychology or science or literary criticism, claims about meaning and truth only make sense against the background of the received beliefs that allow such claims to be made and rendered intelligible in the first place (cf. Wiggenstein, 1953; 1969).

imaginations of persons committed to social change. As a type of communicative praxis, the potentially revolutionary intent of theological rhetoric becomes a player to be reckoned with in the marketplace of competing mores and worldviews.

Of course, without the bulwark of ontotheology, it may appear that postmodern theology is just one more solipsistic minority voice in the cacophony of viewpoints that vie for the loyalty of contemporary persons. This is a serious concern for many traditional theologians. Many religious thinkers suffer from acute legitimation anxiety and fear that unless theology grounds itself on a universal, metaphysical vocabulary it will continue to lose ground to other perspectives and further find that its once vaunted status as "queen of the sciences" is in terminal jeopardy. Many religious leaders are intimidated by diversity and rely on universal appeals to Truth or Nature to protect their threatened role in the wider society. For example, recent Protestant and Roman Catholic denunciations of gay and lesbian persons as unfit for church leadership roles generally depend on centuries-old theological assumptions about behavior that is deemed to be "contrary to nature." Heterosexist religious leaders are threatened by multiple perspectives on truth, goodness, and human nature; in a pluralistic world, they use "taken-for-granted" theological categories about "facts of nature" to shore up the shaky foundations of what they deem to be "biblical faith and morality."

Nevertheless, a vibrant and robust biblical identity need not feel threatened by ideological differences and social change but instead can learn to embrace diversity and polyvocity as opportunities for new growth. Still, the nagging questions remain—namely, are assertions about meaning and truth possible in such an environment? Gergen maintains that social constructionism does not disallow claims about the real and the good, but emphasizes rather that such claims always emerge within a contingent and historically located tradition that must appeal to its own intercommunal norms and warrants for the plausibility of the claims it advances. "The generation of good reasons, good evidence and good values is always *from within a tradition*; already accepted are certain constructions of the real and the good, and implicit rejections of alternatives" (Gergen, 1999, p. 50). Furthermore, constructionism enables us to be self-reflexive about competing constructions of value; it encourages a multi-positioned, cross-cultural awareness about the wide web of working assumptions that support the fragile relations within the global village that is our common postmodern reality.

For constructionists such considerations lead to a celebration of *reflexivity*, that is, the attempt to place one's premises into question, to suspend the "obvious," to listen to alternative framings of reality, and to grapple with the comparative outcomes of multiple standpoints. . . . This kind of critical reflection is not necessarily a prelude to rejecting our major traditions. It is simply to recognize them as traditions—historically and culturally situated (Gergen, 1999, p. 50).

Thus, far from being a beachhead for pernicious relativism, constructionism in theology permits serious, reflective dialogue with time-honored traditions, including the biblical traditions, that have engaged many persons' hearts and minds for generations. It encourages critics and practioners alike to be honest and self-critical about the healing power *as well as* the destructive underside of these ancient revealed texts and beliefs. Theology and social construction share, therefore, a deep affinity. Both modes of inquiry are committed to preserving the health and vitality of living traditions without insulating these traditions from serious scrutiny, vigorous criticism, and, at times, wholesale reconstruction. From this angle, the project of Gergen et alia is not a threat to the integrity of religious faith and tradition—though ontotheological and fundamentalist religious thinkers might think so—but an exercise in social scientific hygiene that helps theology purge itself of its desire for metaphysical or ahistorical security in a pluralistic, postmodern world.

Selfhood Without Foundations

In postmodern culture, the insight into the relational character of human rationality entails further the awareness that the self is a social construct. This constructionist thesis is a formidable challenge to the regnant model of selfhood in the West. Ancient and modern thought begins with the assumption that there is an immutable, interior entity called the "self" which has direct access to the visible world of objects through its powers of mental perception. An entitative noumenal self lies at the center of every human being. Correspondingly, the task of true selfhood is to discover this permanent, core self as the indubitable ground for knowledge of the world. We are all free, independent, rational "monads" who have direct access to a self-evident, empirically-given body of facts that can be used as a reliable foundation for understanding all reality.

In the current context, however, the assumption that there is a universal core "self" or "mind" that can provide ready access to the world of hard facts has been abandoned. "There is and can be no transcendental mind; on the contrary postmodernists claim that what we call the mind or reason is only an effect of discourse. There are no immediate or indubitable features of mental life. Sense data, ideas, intentions, or perceptions are already preconstituted" (Flax, 1990, p. 35). Since there is little evidence for the reality of a permanent mental substratum underlying the subject, the ideal of the fixed, supreme self of Western thought has been humbled, if not extinguished altogether. In postmodernism, the self is a *relay* for the exchange of conflicting discourses, not a stable *site* for processing raw sense data or intuiting timeless truths. The self is a dynamic within social flow patterns wherein it must craft and script its own identity in its regular commerce with the cultures and languages it inhabits. The self subsists in a complex web of discourses and relationships and is continually challenged to remake itself in this web without the benefit of any epistemic foundations upon which to ground this creative process. Here the person as "self" does not *discover* herself by *uncovering* an occult substratum at the core of her being. Rather, the person as "self" *creates* herself by *inventing and reinventing* herself in her daily interactions with the discursive practices and exercises of social knowledge within which all journeys to subjectivity are formed.

Gergen consistently makes the point that the self is a social construct, a product of its various relationships, not a preexisting interior reality. The "I" of self-identity rises into consciousness already nourished by the fertile soil of social relations that makes possible identity formation in the first place. "If it is not individual 'I's who create relationships, but relationships that create the sense of 'I,' then 'I' cease to be the center of success or failure, the one who is evaluated well or poorly, and so on. Rather, 'I' am just an I by virtue of playing a particular part in a relationship" (Gergen, 1991, p. 157). Consciousness does not begin with Cartesian independence from all external influences but a deep awareness of how one's very capacity for articulating an understanding of selfhood is constituted by the founding plausibility structures and forms of life that define one's communal heritage. "We can replace the Cartesian dictum *cogito ergo sum* with *communicamus ergo sum*, for without coordinated acts of communication, there is simply no 'I' to be articulated" (Gergen, 1991,

p. 242).[3] Pulsing toward full selfhood does not commence with the philosophical hubris that the subject is an autonomous ego but with one's inmost understanding of how one enters consciousness and communicative competence always already formed by one's inherited social matrix.

A wide variety of different global religious traditions offer an understanding of selfhood that is similar to the constructionist position. Briefly, let me highlight this emphasis in one particular tradition: the central tenet of historic Buddhism that there is no-self (*anatta*). Buddhism challenges the conventional belief in an entitative noumenal ego by promulgating the idea that all things, including the individual self, are essentially empty and impermanent. The idea of the self is a "construct" or "artifice" of human societies that functions to provide false security in a world of radical flux and change. According to Buddhism, we cannot face the hard reality that everything is passing away and so we attach ourselves to the mistaken belief in a permanent, substantial self that will somehow perdure through time amidst the rapid changes that is our fate as human beings. Classical Buddhism maintains that we all want to "believe that some part of us, perhaps a soul or some other kind of invisible and interior stuff, will endure even after our body dies and begins to decay. It is probably our attachment to a notion of our own individual, independent, and substantial self, something the Indians called the *atman*, that is our deepest, most pernicious attachment" (LaFleur, 1988, p. 81). In Buddhism, the self interdependently "arises" out of the social milieu within which all persons perform their lives as social subjects; there is no self independent of the cultural contexts that make up our common lot.

According to Buddhism, much of the spiritual and psychological suffering we experience stems from our attachment to the belief in an *atman* or a self that underlies all reality. Our obsession with the notion that being is permanent—and our corresponding unwillingness to face the reality of the impermanence of becoming as the defining characteristic of the human condition—keeps us mired in the illusory hope that we can escape the flux and vicissitudes of life

---

[3] Gergen's generally positive understanding of the social self is in stark contrast to other social theorists (for example, René Girard and David Riesman) who argue that group formation of the self is an oppressive and conflictual force that denies to individual persons any sense of identity outside of the group. (For an appreciation and critique of Girard's position, see Wallace, 1996.)

on a fragile and evolving planet. Provocatively, the move in constructionist and Buddhist thought toward emptying the self of its pretensions to permanence and immutability is a move made today in Christian theology as well. I turn now to this move toward radical self-emptying within recent Christian thought in the penultimate section of my essay.

Performing the Displaced Self in Benevolent Relations with Others

To this point, I have argued for a postmodern theology that seeks to disentangle itself from ontotheology in dialogue with the constructionist insight into the social production of knowledge. I have also taken up the constructionist notion of the empty self and briefly sounded its connections with the Buddhist teaching of *anatta*. In what follows, I will turn to a central emphasis in Paul Ricoeur's thought—the role of conscience in mediating the relationship between self and other—in order to articulate a constructionist theological vision that understands self-formation, ironically, as self-divestment.

Ricoeur's project in moral and religious thought begins with an analysis of the "wounded cogito" after the demise of the supreme, rational subject of modern philosophy. For Ricoeur, the self is permanently "other" to itself because, contrary to Descartes's metaphysics and in a manner similar to constructionism, the self is not an independent subject, in full possession of itself, that perdures over time. But while the self is not a fixed entity, according to Ricoeur, it does not follow that the human person is simply a biological organism with no original capacity for genuine selfhood. Some anticogito thinkers contend that insofar as there is no entitative core self, then the subject is nothing more than the sum total of its physical processes. Certain analytic philosophers (for example, Derik Parfit), who also criticize Cartesian metaphysics, argue that the subject is reducible (without remainder) to its brain states and bodily functions. Ricoeur rejects both of these essentialist options—the metaphysical and physicalist—through a tripartite analysis of the phenomenon of passivity or alterity within selfhood (Ricoeur, 1992, pp. 1–39, 125–29, 297–356). My self—as neither a permanently stable entity nor purely biochemical phenomenon—cobbles together its identity by experiencing the "otherness" of my own body, the dissymmetry between myself and the other person in front of me, and, finally, and most importantly for my analysis, the originary phenomenon of being called by

the voice of *conscience*—a voice both proximate and exterior to me—
that summons me to my obligations and responsibilities.

What does Ricoeur mean by the term "conscience"? Conscience,
Ricoeur writes, is

> the voice . . . addressed to me from the depths of myself. . . . the *forum*
> of the colloquy of the self with itself. . . . We need, I think, to pre-
> serve within the metaphor of the voice the idea of a unique passivity,
> both internal and superior to me. . . . In this sense, conscience is noth-
> ing other than the attestation by which a self affects itself. . . . The
> point is that human being has no mastery over the inner, intimate
> certitude of existing as a self; this is something that comes to us, that
> comes upon us, like a gift, a grace, that is not at our disposal. This
> non-mastery of a voice that is more heard than spoken leaves intact
> the question of its origin. . . . The strangeness of the voice [of con-
> science] is no less than that of the flesh or that of other human beings.
> (Ricoeur, 1996, pp. 453–55)

In the depths of one's interiority, the subject is enjoined to live well
with oneself and for others. The colloquy of the self with itself—the
phenomenon of being enjoined—occurs in the place where the self
appropriates for itself the demand of the other upon it. Conscience,
then, is the forum for the summoning of the self to its social obligations.

In his theological writings, Ricoeur identifies the origins of conscience in the voice of God—a voice that enjoins the hearer to care
for oneself and attend to the needs of others. Conscience as the
inner chamber where the divine mandate is heard and understood;
in the interior voice of obligation, each person is called by God to
exercise responsibility for oneself and the other. Indeed, conscience
is now valorized as the inalienable contact point between the Word
of God and human beings; it is the forum where divine forgiveness,
care for oneself, and solicitude for others intersect. "Conscience is
thus the anthropological presupposition without which 'justification
by faith' would remain an event marked by radical extrinsicness. In
this sense, conscience becomes the organ of the reception of the
Kerygma, in a perspective that remains profoundly Pauline" (Ricoeur,
1995, p. 272). Without conscience, the divine voice that summons
the self to its responsibilities falls on deaf ears. In Ricoeur's earlier
writings, the *productive imagination's* capacity to interpret symbolic language played the role of a sort of *praeparatio evangelica* for the reception of the divine word (Ricoeur, 1967). While not denying this
previous emphasis, the focus is now on the subject's *moral* capacity

for an internal dialogue with itself that makes possible the hearing and understanding of God's voice in the life of the listening subject.

Ricoeur's analysis of conscience reflects the life-long impact of Emmanuel Levinas on his thought. As does Levinas, Ricoeur argues that the biblical scriptures consistently press onto the reader the obligation to appropriate God's demand—a demand definitively represented by the biblical prophets—to take responsibility for the welfare of the other. Conscience is the site of intersection between selfhood and otherness, the place where my ethical ownness "within" and the commanding voice of the other "without" indwell one another, according to Ricoeur (Ricoeur, 1992, p. 341; cf. Levinas, 1991, pp. 112–114). Alongside Levinas's exposition of Jewish ethics, Ricoeur maintains that the ideal of the morally commissioned self is the determinant model for selfhood in the scriptural texts. The Jewish and Christian ideal of the called self, therefore, is the central thrust of the biblical witness: to perform the task of selfhood is to heed the call of obligation for the other; one becomes a true self by refusing to secure oneself in isolation from others but rather by pouring oneself into a life of love and service toward the other. I have no self—I am not an "I"—without the other awakening me to my responsibility for her welfare. In exegeting the Abrahamic/Mosaic response "here I am," Ricoeur writes, "I see, for my part, in this figure of a 'summoned subject' a paradigm that the Christian community, following the Jewish community, could make use of to interpret itself" (Ricoeur, 1995, p. 267). Ricoeur's position regarding the mandated subject is analogous to Levinas's, who writes that "[t]he religious discourse that precedes all religious discourse is not dialogue. It is the 'here I am' said to a neighbor to whom I am given over, by which I announce peace, that is, my responsibility for the other" (Levinas, 1989, p. 184). Self-identity is constituted by the gesture of other-regard. By divesting myself of myself in response to my social obligation for the other, I perform my identity as a self willing to risk my personal security for the sake of my neighbor's welfare.

Conclusion

My concern in this essay has been to reposition contemporary religious thought away from the sirens of ontotheology toward an ethically engaged postmodern theology in dialogue with social construction.

First and foremost, such a theology privileges being roused by one's conscience in response to the needs of the other. As a religious thinker, what makes the constructionist thesis particularly interesting to me is its concern with the liberating potential of performing self-hood through social interactions. Thus, my underlying question in this paper has been, How can the dialogue with social construction enable the practice of religion to be a voice to reckoned with in a contemporary world where the concern for enriched and transformed relations with self and other is paramount? This concern with praxis shifts the focus away from understanding religion primarily in terms of dogmatic agreement or ritual observance toward a revitalized notion of religion as lived, intersubjective spirituality with an eman-cipatory intent. Ongoing interreligious conversations between Christian, Jewish, and Buddhist sources and thinkers (among others) regarding the moral aims of lived spirituality is critical in this contemporary dialogue. In response to this dialogue, Christian theology is empow-ered to recover its biblical beginnings and the summons therein to find the self by loving God and neighbor above all else. This ideal of self—discovery through self-loss is the *summum bonum* of all religious life and thought and should be the center of the dialogue between contemporary theology and social construction.

But while the dialogue between social construction and theology is very promising, this dialogue is also fraught with difficulties and potential areas of sharp disagreement. I have highlighted in this essay the constructionist celebration of social relationship as critical to reen-visioning the role of conscience in grounding the task of self-emp-tying personhood within Christianity. My thesis is that since we are all social beings, it is only through our conscience-driven ethical rela-tions in and with the other that true subjectivity is realized. But the introduction of the role of conscience into the discipline of selfhood raises a thorny issue for constructionism, namely, Can conscience communicate to the self a mode of other-directed care that funda-mentally calls into question *all* of the social relations and commu-nal norms within which the self is embedded? If, as constructionism claims, there is no "self" or "mind"—and, by implication, "con-science"—apart from the social world, then what role, if any, can an individual's distinctive moral convictions play in calling that indi-vidual to perform actions that undermine the beliefs and values of one's cultural milieu?

The problem with social construction, in other words, is a certain tone deafness to the importance of *alterity* in the formation of selfhood. If subjectivity is reducible to culture, is there any place for the sometimes unique and distinctively "other" voice of "the good within" to tear apart the fabric of one's social relations in an effort to work out the meaning and truth of one's *ownmost, radically individualistic, and oftentimes antisocial sense of the good*? Is not conscience often the voice of a profound sense of social unrelatedness—of the *totaliter aliter*—that allows persons to press beyond the limited confines and orthodoxies of their communal groups in order to realize new expressions of truth and goodness? The consistent emphasis in social construction on the relational interdependence of all life and thought seems unable to account for the visionary excesses of the distinctive individual whose praxis appears independent from, and a comprehensive challenge to her lived surroundings.

The life and work of Dietrich Bonhoeffer is a troubling counterexample to the constructionist emphasis on selfhood as a social predicate. Bonhoeffer was a Lutheran pastor and theologian whose active resistance to the Nazis—culminating in his participation in the conspiracy to assassinate Hitler in 1944—eventually led to his execution in the Flossenbürg concentration camp in 1945. It is ironic, however, that precisely at the time in which Bonhoeffer was plotting to overthrow the rule of the National Socialists in Germany, he was *also* imploring the readers of his work in theological ethics to avoid any "apocalyptic diabolization of government"—for while concrete acts of disobedience to government are occasionally licit, no regular and systemic disobedience of government is permissible, no matter how anti-democratic and anti-God the ruling powers have become (Bonhoeffer, 1956, pp. 339–353). The irony is that while Bonhoeffer is arguing his theological apologetic for "government as a social good" he is also actively plotting to overthrow his particular government as hopelessly evil and corrupt. Bonhoeffer was well aware of this conflict. He writes that in order to listen to and heed one's conscience—under the tutelage of the Gospel message—it is sometimes necessary to abrogate the social compact and "bear guilt for the sake of charity" (Bonhoeffer, 1956, p. 245). In fidelity to conscience, one may find oneself running the risk of violating social values and incurring personal guilt in pursuit of the responsible action in service to the neighbor. At times, therefore, one must do the *wrong thing* in order to pursue a *higher good*. Given his theology of the divine right of government, Bonhoeffer, in living out the dictates of his conscience to join the conspiracy to kill Hitler, set aside society's most sacred moral code, the right to life, by becoming a murderer and disobeying the commandment of the decalogue, "Thou shalt not kill." In becoming a killer, Bonhoeffer undermined the social world within which he lived and thought and had his very existence.

The redolence of Durkheimian functionalism wafts about social construction, rendering religious beliefs a product of social groups instead of understanding such beliefs as frontal, prophetic challenges to culturally embedded belief systems. In functionalism, religion *confirms* rather than *undermines* the social whole. Using Bonhoeffer, then, my criticism here of social construction is its relative lack of awareness of the special—sometimes antisocial—role of the unassimable voice of conscience for hyperethical persons who risk everything to be faithful to their inner voice. From a theological perspective, social construction needs to be broadened by a deeper appreciation of the abyssal otherness and antinomic chaos that lies at the heart of all expressions of transgressive moral activity.

This caveat notwithstanding, I have argued that social construction is an important resource for assisting the theological recovery of biblical stories of self-giving as a transformative paradigm for integrated subjectivity in and with the other. In spite of the tension noted here, the dialogue between social construction and theology has the potential to bear much fruit. Through this dialogue one can sense the haunting beauty of Jesus' ironic claim that unless one loses oneself one cannot find oneself. By allowing oneself to be appropriated by the ethical possibilities projected by the biblical texts, the task of becoming a full self is most adequately performed. In this gesture, a person's spiritual practice becomes her destiny as a moral subject: by taking the risk of becoming assimilated into the strange universe of the biblical texts, one makes good on the wager that a scripturally refigured self is the crown of a life well lived.

References

Aquinas, Th. (916–37). *Summa Theologica*. New York: Benziger Bros.
Bonhoeffer, D. (1956). *Ethics* (Trans. Neville Horton Smith) (Ed. Eberhard Bethge). New York: Macmillan.
Derrida, J. (1978). Violence and Metaphysics. In: *Writing and Difference* (pp. 79–153). (Trans. Allan Bass). Chicago: University of Chicago Press.
Flax, J. (1990). *Thinking Fragments: Psychoanalysis, Feminism, and Postmodernism in the Contemporary West*. Berkeley: University of California Press.
Gergen, K.J. (1982). *Toward a Transformation in Social Knowledge*. New York: Springer-Verlag.

—— (1991). *The Saturated Self: Dilemmas of Identity in Contemporary Life*. New York: Basic Books.
—— (1999). *An Invitation to Social Construction*. London: Sage Publications.
Harvey, D. (1990). *The Condition of Postmodernity*. Cambridge, Mass.: Blackwell.
Heidegger, M. (1969). The Onto-theo-logical Constitution of Metaphysics." In: Heidegger, M., *Identity and Difference* (Trans. Joan Stamburgh) (pp. 42–76). New York: Harper and Row.
—— (1977). What is Metaphysics? In: Heidegger, M., *Basic Writings* (Trans. David Ferrell Krell) (pp. 95–112). New York: Harper and Row.
LaFleur, W.R. (1988). *Buddhism: A Cultural Perspective*. Englewood Cliffs, NJ: Prentice-Hall.
Levinas, E. (1989). God and Philosophy (Trans. Richard A. Cohen & Alphonso Lingis). In: Hand, S. (Ed.). *The Levinas Reader* (pp. 166–189). Oxford: Blackwell.
—— (1991). *Otherwise than Being or Beyond Essence* (Trans. Alphonso Lingis). Boston: Kluwer.
Ricoeur, P. (1967). *The Symbolism of Evil* (Trans. Emerson Buchanan). Boston: Beacon Press.
—— (1977). *The Rule of Metaphor: Multi-Disciplinary Studies of the Creation of Meaning in Language* (Trans. Robert Czerny with Kathleen McLaughlin and John Costello). Toronto: University of Toronto Press.
—— (1991). Narrative Identity. *Philosophy Today*, 35, 73–81.
—— (1992). *Oneself as Another* (Trans. Kathleen Blamey). Chicago: University of Chicago Press.
—— (1995). The Summoned Subject in the School of the Narratives of the Prophetic Vocation. In: Ricoeur, P., *Figuring the Sacred: Religion, Narrative, and Imagination* (Trans. David Pellauer and ed. Mark I. Wallace) (pp. 262–275). Minneapolis: Fortress Press.
—— (1996). From Metaphysics to Moral Philosophy." *Philosophy Today*, 40, 443–58.
Stout, J. (1988). *Ethics After Babel: The Languages of Morals and Their Discontents*. Boston: Beacon Press.
Wallace, M.I. (1996). *Fragments of the Spirit: Nature, Violence, and the Renewal of Creation*. New York: Continuum.
Whitehead, A.N. (1926). *Religion in the Making*. New York: Macmillan.
Wittgenstein, L. (1969). *On Certainty* (Trans. Denis Paul and G.E.M. Anscombe) (Eds. G.E.M. Anscombe and G.H. Von Wright). New York: Harper and Row.
—— (1953). *Philosophical Investigations* (Trans. G.E.M. Anscombe) (3rd ed.). New York: Macmillan.

ULTIMATE MEANING AS SILENCE:
THE MONOLOGIC AND POLYPHONIC AUTHOR-GOD IN RELIGIOUS COMMUNICATION

Chris A.M. Hermans

1. *Introduction*

There are many disputes about religious communication in our time. One of the current debates concerns how we describe God. How can we talk about God? How can mere words express something, which is beyond comprehension? How do words express the otherness of God (Smith, 2000; Sarot & Markus, 2000). The topic of this chapter is not to discuss the truth and meaning of God-talk (see Wallace and Immink, in this volume), but to examine the way religious people construct their life 'coram Deo'. God is not just a meaning, next to other meanings, but the ultimate, final meaning in their life. That is why Augustine says God knows him better than he knows himself (Smith, 2000). Within religious communication, people express this ultimate meaning. They sing, praise, preach, and narrate what their life means in the face of God. Therefore, the focus of this chapter will be on the anthropologic side of religious communication instead of the 'theistic side'.

There are many debates regarding the anthropologic side of religious communication. One debate relates to the process of secularization; specifically, the individualistic trend that works within the process of secularization (Dobbelaere, 1999). People want to decide autonomously what they believe and how to express their faith. However, is communication primarily an individual process of meaning making? Here social constructionism is useful because it stresses a communal process in the creation of meaning. In doing so, one must go beyond the dominant individualism present in society, while preserving the influence of the subject in the creation of meaning (see section 2.1).

A second debate relates to the plurality of religions in our society (Knitter, 1995). In constructing the religious meaning of their life, people are confronted with other religious viewpoints, each expressing different ideas and feelings. Religious communication is challenged not so much by the otherness of God (see above), but by the separateness of other people, each expressing different religious viewpoints. Here social constructionism is useful because it stresses the transformative power of dialogue. By doing so, it opens a dialogue between differing religious voices within society (see section 2.2).

However, the main topic of this chapter concerns the idea that truth in religious communication is relative to meaning within a certain tradition, place and time and form of life. According to Wittgenstein, 'forms of life' as human activities that have a social structure recognizable to others in society. This debate grows out of the postmodern idea that meaning cannot be fixed because words are constantly being re-contextualized (Chatelion-Counet, 1998, pp. 46–52). Although we agree with the idea of communal creation of meaning and the transformative power of dialogue (see above), we assert that the loss of an ultimate meaning is highly problematic for religious communication. This chapter begins with the epistemology underlying the inter-subjective conception on communication in social constructionism (section 2). After referring to some viewpoints of communication that are useful in debates regarding religious communication (see section 3), we address the concept of religious communication (section 4). This analysis is based heavily on the work of Bakhtin. Bakhtin is one author which Gergen grounds his own inter-subjective theory of communication. We will outline the differences between Bakhtin and Gergen. We also have focused on Bakhtin for a second reason. Bakhtin explicitly reflects on God as the author of the text of a person's life, as is characteristic for religious communication. The chapter ends with a discussion about religious communication based on our analysis of Bakhtin and Gergen (section 5). We discuss questions about empirical research on religious communication, and evaluate the idea of ultimate meaning as silence from a theological point of view.

2. *Epistemological Assumptions of Social Constructivism*

Epistemology investigates the nature and origin of knowledge. How do people know reality? Do we know reality 'as it is'? To what extent do we know reality? In his discussion of the epistemological orientation of social constructionism, Gergen distinguishes two intellectual traditions. The first is the exogenic perspective. The second one is the endogenic perspective (Gergen, 1985, p. 268).

According to Gergen, the exogenic perspective sees knowledge of reality as a pawn of nature. Knowledge is a mirror of reality; in other words, it is true knowledge if it reflects the world 'as it is'. Knowledge of reality is derived from experience. Induction is the method in which knowledge is built from experience. Within the field of philosophy, empiricism justifies the view of the mind as a mirror of experience. This tradition can be traced back to Aristotle, and to the Enlightenment thinkers Locke, Bacon, Hume, Mill and others (Gergen, 1999, p. 10).

The endogenic perspective locates the origin of knowledge in processes endemic to human beings. 'Humans harbor inherent tendencies, it is said, to think, categorize, or process information, and it is these tendencies (rather than features of the world itself) that are of paramount importance in fashioning knowledge' (Gergen, 1998, p. 269). The endogenic perspective forms the metatheoretical basis of different schools of thought. For rationalists, from Platonic philosophy to contemporary cognitive psychology, mental processes within the individual play a critical role in fashioning knowledge. We do not know the world directly. Concepts such as time, number or causality cannot be derived solely from observation. According to Kant, people are born with certain innate ideas to help them understand the world. The same principle underscores the view of contemporary cognitive psychology. 'The world does not produce our concepts; rather our concepts help us organize the world in various ways' (Gergen, 1999, p. 11).

Gergen points to the contradiction between the exogenic and endogenic perspectives that is reflective of the object-subject scheme dominant in Western thinking. In Western philosophy, the origins of human knowledge has been explained using both a exogenic and endogenic epistemological perspective. Both perspectives can be criticized (see Gergen, 1999, pp. 10–11). However, the basic problem lies within the scheme itself. By starting with the dualism between subject and object, one is left with the problem of how to get past the gulf that divides them. Based on this dualistic approach, one cannot investigate the nature and origin of knowledge. Gergen finds a new epistemological basis for understanding of the world in a subject-subject scheme. Reality is social construction through discourse. We create our world through language.

What is the basis of intersubjective epistemology? There are four working assumptions of social constructionism (Gergen, 1999, pp. 47–50).

1. 'The terms by which we understand our world and our self are neither required nor demanded by "what there is" (o.c., p. 47). According to the correspondence theory of language, language is not a picture of an independent world. Gergen disagrees, stating that there are many unsolved problems within the correspondence theory. For example, there is no well-defined explanation of how words correspond to experienced realities. In other words, 'how can we accurately convey our private experience to others—report accurately on what we feel or see?' (o.c., p. 20). It is not possible to depict the world using specific words. One of the assumptions of social constructionism is that what we have learned about ourselves and the world can be false. We can use language to construct another world. 'Our account of the world is not demanded by "what there is"' (o.c., p. 47).

2. 'Our modes of description, explanation and/or representation are derived from relationship' (o.c., p. 48). Instead of a correspondence theory of language, social constructionism favors a theory of language games (cfr. Wittgenstein). A word is like a pawn in a chess game. Only within the game does this piece of wood have meaning. Outside the game it means nothing (o.c., p. 34). Each word's meaning is grounded in its use in language. This concept breaks with an individualistic tendency within Western thinking.

> The individual mind (thought, experience) does not thus originate meaning, create language, or discover the nature of the world. Meanings are born of coordinations among persons—agreements, negotiations, affirmations. From this standpoint, relationships stand prior to all that is intelligible (Gergen, 1999, p. 48).

3. A third assumption of social constructionism is that our future is fashioned as we describe, explain or otherwise represent it. Whereas, the second assumption stated that language usage is bound within relationships, this assumption addresses the idea, that 'relationships are bound within broader patterns of practice—rituals, traditions, "forms of life"' (o.c., p. 48). Gergen refers to Wittgenstein, who has embedded language games into broader patterns of actions and objects which he calls "forms of life". Without forms of life words have no meaning; however, the reverse is also true. As with the pawn in a game of chess, which loses its meaning outside the game, without words, there are no forms of life. 'Language, in this sense, is not a mirror

of life, it is the doing of life itself' (o.c., p. 35). Language is a major ingredient in the world of action; it is essential to our social life.

4. The last working assumption of social constructionism is the idea, that 'reflection on our forms of understanding is vital to our future well-being' (Gergen, 1999, p. 49). According to Gergen, there are two challenges for social constructionism, first to sustain valued traditions and second, to create new futures. From a constructionist viewpoint, the ability to generate good judgement and values always comes from within a tradition. But at the same time, our judgements are blind to alternatives outside our tradition. That is why reflexivity is crucial to our future well-being. Reflexivity is 'the attempt to place one's premises into question, to suspend the "obvious", to listen to alternative framings of reality, and to grapple with the comparative outcomes of multiple standpoints' (Gergen, 1999, p. 50). Critical reflexivity is an opening to dialogue that leads to common ground between people. Is this common ground the 'ultimate truth'? No, there is no final answer according social constructionism. In other words, there is no end to dialogue (Gergen, 1999, p. 228).

The implications of this intersubjective epistemology for religious communication are discussed at the end of this chapter. Here, we will question whether Gergen really discusses matters of truth or if the question of truth is resolved into questions of meaning. First, there is a complex philosophical debate between the relationship between of subject, words (text) and object (see Chatelion Counet, 1995, pp. 93–137; 1998, pp. 12–41). Although we do not want to debate this, we must make Gergen's position clear. Gergen often discusses presumptions of ultimate or absolute truth. Matters of truth decide our understanding of reality. Is what we say about reality an adequate description of it? As mentioned above, Gergen disagrees with the subject-object model and the corresponding concept of truth connected with it. Within his subject-subject scheme, Gergen is interested in how people understand one another and create meaning within relationships. Social reality plays a role in connection with language games (see above). According to Gergen, when we say something is the truth, we defend a way of life. Within language games, truth is 'a way of talking or writing that achieves its validity within a local form of life' (o.c., p. 38). There is no ultimate Truth. No authority can claim the Truth, nor can a critic challenge

a form of life claiming "the truly true". All truth claims are bound
to traditions, networks or relationships. We must also abandon concern 'with the hidden reservoirs of motivation or ideological bias said
to be lurking behind people's words. (. . .) Rather our attention moves
to the forms of life that are favored (or destroyed) by various ways
of putting things' (o.c., p. 38). By speaking in one set of terms as
opposed to another, we favor certain kinds of people, institutions or
ways of life and at the same time suppressing other interpretations.
Social reality plays an important role in the construction of language
meaning. This is one of the strengths of social constructionism because
people are connected to each other in concrete forms of life. Gergen
is not concerned whether words correspond with certain forms of
life. What is 'out there' has different meanings. Gergen does not
address whether forms of life are true or false. The forms of life by
which we are connected, back up the meaning of our words. Gergen
defines truth as equivalent to meaning. This is an important point
necessary for a correct understanding of social constructionism as
developed by Gergen. We will not discuss further how Gergen treats
the epistemological question of truth. The remainder of this chap
ter focuses on meaning in religious communication.

3. *Communication*

As noted in the introduction, the theory of social constructionism is
useful in the current debates about religious communication. The
understanding of communication within social constructionism challenges the individualistic trend in the construction of meaning. Change
of meaning is also a central focus of social constructionism in addition to construction of meaning. Within the communal construction
of meaning there is responsiveness for otherness, which makes transformation of meaning possible. Both characteristics are useful in the
debate about religious communication in secularization and religious
pluralism. The focus of this section will be in these characteristics
of communication. Specific religious aspect of religious communication (namely the possibility to express ultimate meaning) is the subject of next section.

3.1   *Meaning in Relationships*

The dominant view in Western society is that of the self-contained individual. According to Gergen, this viewpoint is problematic because of its consequences.

> When the self is the essential atom of society, we find invitations to isolation, distrust, narcissism, and competition; we find relationships reduced to inessential artifice and our freedoms threatened; and we find an obtuse simplification of our ills (Gergen, 1999, p. 122).

In order to solve this dominant individualism, we must transcend the binary logic behind it, namely self/other, inner/outer, individual/society and other binary distinctions. Binary logic implies the principle of exclusion: 'A is not B'. There can be influences from A on B, or from B on A, but A and B exist separately. They are entities in themselves. For A, the relationship to B is something, something added to its own identity. It is not something that is constitutive for A.

The problem with this theory is that meaning exists within each individual mind. However, 'if meaning was preeminently an individual matter, we should be unable to communicate' (Gergen, 1994, p. 27). If individuality is the starting point in the construction of meaning, we are left with a dichotomy between self and others (society) that cannot be resolved. Social constructionism reframes this theory of the acquisition of meaning by not using the individual as its starting point.

> Rather than commencing with individual subjectivity and working toward an account of human understanding through language, we may begin our analysis at the level of the human relationship as it generated both language and understanding (Gergen, 1994, p. 27).

Primacy exists not in the individual, but in patterns of relationships and their embedded meaning that preexist the individual. Understanding is generated by participation in a system of language or signs common to a given culture. When we participate in the meaning system of a community, we are initiated into a process of signification. Social constructionism replaces the Cartesian dictum '*Cogito ergo sum*' ('I think, therefore I am') with '*Communicamus ergo sum*' ('We relate, therefore I am') (Gergen, 1999, p. 221). Or, in Bakhtinian terms: 'To be means to communicate' (quotation in: Gergen, 1999, p. 131).

Gergen utilizes Bakhtin's concept of 'utterance' to ground meaning in relationships. When we communicate, we draw from an enormous

and diverse selection of words. But the utterance contains not only
fragments from a diverse heritage, but also additional meaning because
of the present context and the intonation used. Language is a system of abstract grammatical categories, but also a tool for people to
understand themselves and others. The utterance belongs to this second category. Bakhtin approaches language within the model (or
metaphor) of thirdness, i.e. an utterance, a response and a dialogue
between them (Holquist, 1990, p. 38). An utterance has an internal
dialogue in it (Bakhtin, 1980, p. 38). Words in a spoken conversation are oriented towards a future answer. Each utterance provokes
an answer, anticipates it and structures itself in its direction. According
to Bakhtin, understanding is activated not by the speaker, who says
the message but by the listener, who recieves and responds to the
message. This 'primacy of understanding' prepares the ground for
active and engaged understanding. 'In the actual life of speech, every
concrete act of understanding is active: it assimilates the word to be
understood into its own conceptual system filled with specific objects
and emotional expressions, and is indissoluble merged with the
response, with a motivated agreement or disagreement' (Bakhtin,
1900, p. 283). There are no words which are not a part of a relationship. Words are directed to someone and come from someone.
According to Bakhtin, 'addressivity' is the concept that utterances
constantly have a response.

> Addressivity is *expressivity*; what we usually call life is not a mysterious
> vitalistic force, but an activity, the dialogue between events addressed
> to me in the particular place I occupy in existence, and my expres-
> sion of a *response* to such events from that unique place (Holquist, 1990,
> p. 49).

Gergen draws two conclusions from the idea that meaning of utterances is generated in a dialogic relationship. First, 'there is no meaning that is not derived from relationship itself. Second, we find that
the ability of the individual to mean anything—to be rational or
sensible—is owing to relationship. (. . .) Self and other are locked in
the generation of meaning' (Gergen, 1990, p. 131). For example, if
a person says 'I love you'. This utterance frames the relationship as
one kind of connection and not another. However, if a slightly
different expression, such as 'I think you're nice' is used, it does not
signify the same kind of relationship as 'I love you'. When we communicate, we perform an action within a relationship. This is why
Gergen states, that utterances serve a performative action. 'I love

you' is not an expression of a private state but a public action. We do not own our emotions or thoughts, as much as we perform them within a relationship. The origin of every utterance (or performance) lies in past relationships, and at the same time carries the stamp of the relationship we are moving into. 'Thus, when I perform I am carrying a history of relationships, manifesting them, expressing them' (Gergen, 1990, p. 133).

This relational model of the construction of meaning can be useful in the current debate on individualization and privatization of religion. We will not elaborate on this debate on individualization and religion (for an overview, see Dobbelaere, 2000, pp. 236–243). We agree with Luckman who states that:

> The new, basically de-institutionalized, *privatized* social form of religion seemed to be relying primarily on an open market of diffuse, syncretistic packages of meaning, typically connected to low levels of transcendence and produced in a partly of fully commercialized cultic milieu (Luckman, 1996, p. 73).

At the same time, religious meaning cannot originate from the individual constructing his or her own 'sacred canopy'. Here, social constructionism is useful because it stresses a communal process in the construction of meaning. We need the other ('outsidedness') to construct meaning. With this in mind, social constructionism can contribute to the debate about religious communication in a secularized and individualized society. It is useful to go beyond an idea of a solipsistic creation of meaning, while preserving the influence of the subject in the creation of meaning.

3.2 *Transformative Dialogue*

In addition to the creation of meaning, social constructionism also focuses on change of meaning. Dialogue is not just an exchange of views. However, the challenge of dialogue is to become a transformative medium. Why? Language is essentially a differentiating medium with words separating out what is named and unnamed. If something is a loving action, then we exclude other actions as unloving at the same time. Gergen calls this the binary logic of language. Unfortunately, the consequence of binary logic is that our utterances create otherness and conflict. Each time consensus is created around what is 'real and good'; classes of what is 'undesirable and bad' are under construction.

> Wherever there are tendencies toward unity, cohesion, brotherhood, commitment, solidarity, or community; so is alterity—or otherness— under production. And it is here that seeds of conflict are sewn (Gergen, 1990, p. 149).

Otherness does not necessary lead to conflict. It only leads to conflict when differences are fixed. 'Any fixed standard or requirement will always remove the privilege of meaningful participation from some person or group. Further, by solidifying such standards or requirements, we diminish the possibility of new alternatives' (Gergen, 1990, p. 151). According to Gergen, this process of fixation is predominates in a modernistic worldview, where rationality and objective realities are presumed. For example, by fixing 'the problem', we establish limits in which dialogue must proceed. By defining the problem, other things are excluded as being not relevant. By setting limits on love, other actions are excluded. By establishing limits, 'we diminish the possibilities for the mutual construction of the real' (Gergen, 1990, p. 152). This conflict is intensified by the dominant individualism in Western society. When dialogue is viewed as a relationship between separate, autonomous individuals, 'the other will always be alien, unknown, and fundamentally untrustworthy' in spite of temporary agreements (see Gergen, 1999, p. 152).

Gergen outlines five components of transformative dialogue.

The first step is a move away from individual blame to a more relationally responsible language. 'If all that we take to be true and good has its origin in relationships, and specifically the process of jointly constructing meaning, then there is reason for us all to honor— to be responsible to—relationships of meaning making themselves' (Gergen 1999, pp. 156–157). One must search for a means to sustain the processes of communication in which meaning is never fixed, but is continuously growing and changing.

Second, within each communicative exchange, both the speaker and listener must understand each other. The self needs others to construct selfhood.[1] Storytelling is an important tool used to reach this understanding. According to Gergen, stories are easier to understand than abstract arguments. Stories also engage the audience bet-

---

[1] The term that Bakhtin uses for this is 'outsidedness'. We refer to this because it plays a key role in the next section on religious communication. Outsidedness is a translation of the term '*exotopy*', which is literally 'finding oneself outside' (Todorov, 1984, p. 99). In the simplest sense, one can say 'I get myself from the other'. The

ter than abstract ideas. A personal story generates acceptance instead of resistance.

Third, it is important for the speaker to gain a sense of the listener's affirmation within the dialogue. 'Because meaning is born in relationship an individual's expression doesn't acquire full significance until supplemented' (Gergen, 1999, p. 159). Each utterance seeks a response from the listener in order to receive its meaning. According to Gergen, meaning is not located in actions, but within the action-supplement conjunction or in the coordination that is achieved between the speaker and listener. Affirmation is necessary to tell if the other has truly understood. If the words 'I love you' are met with loud laughing, it is likely the recipient does not share that assertion.

Fourth, 'if we are to generate meaning together we must develop smooth and reiterative patterns of interchange' (Gergen, 1999, p. 160). Meaning making is essentially coordinated action. Co-constitution occurs when our actions contain an element of the actions of others. For example, sharing a pipe around a circle, before addressing a question, is a powerful means of connecting people. Similarly, people often have heated discussions while having dinner together.

The fifth component is a shift in dialogue toward self-reflexivity. 'Self-reflection is made possible because we are polyvocal. We participate in many relationships (. . .) and we carry with us a myriad traces of these relationships. In effect we can speak with many voices' (Gergen, 1999, p. 162). When we speak, we only give 'voice' to one of these voices while suppressing others. According to Gergen, we move toward transformative dialogue if these suppressed voices are located and brought out while discussing differences. Fixed boundaries are shifted depending on the 'voice' we use. According to Gergen, these five conversational moves open the way for more

---

only way to construct the self is from the outside. 'In order to be perceived as a whole, as something finished, a person of object must be shaped in the time/space categories of the other, and that is possible only when the person of object is perceived from the position of outsidedness' (Holquist, 1990, p. 31). We see others as whole, or as Bakhtin refers to as a 'consummated biography'. We know their beginning and their end. But we cannot do the same thing from the position of 'I-for-myself'. The self's own time is constantly open, a flux of sheer becoming. We can author ourselves only from the position of *outsidedness*. From this outside position, we create the stories of our lives. Only from the position of the other, can we see our beginning and our end.

mutual appreciation, reducing the exclusion of others. However, none of these components join together the real or the good.

> Needed are what might be called *imaginary moments* in the dialogue in which participants join visions of a reality not yet realized by either. These imaginary moments not only sow the seeds for mutual building, but also shift the orientation of the participants from combat to cooperation (Gergen, 1999, p. 163).

Metaphors and narratives have this imaginary power to create new realities. They can create space within relationships that transcend fixed meanings.

This transformative concept of dialogue is useful in the debate on interreligious dialogue. One of the most challenging questions in this debate is how to find a starting point where dialogue can be developed. How is it possible to define themes or content of dialogue without favoring a certain religion or philosophy of life? This would not be necessary if there were 'universalia', or 'Grundbereiche' (basic topics) of human existence, or if there was consensus on what the anthropological constants or basic needs are (Van der Ven, 2000, p. 41). However, the only consensus among scholars is that there are no universal basic topics. Within a dialogue, a person favors one point of view above others. If meanings were fixed, dialogue would end. The five conversational moves of transformative dialogue are aimed at breaking this fixation of meaning. Gergen wants to avoid the opposition and conflict characteristic in binary logic, by the inclusion of otherness in the construction of meaning. His stress on meaning-making as a coordinated action is also useful in the current debate on interreligious dialogue (Knitter, 1995). Inter-religious dialogue must be grounded on joint action by adherents of different religions and not on the theoretical debate about beliefs and ideas (see Hermans, 2000). This is especially vital for people who are marginalized by society.

4. *Religious Communication*

In addition to the horizontal dimension in religious communication, or the communal creation of meaning, there is a vertical dimension in religious communication. This vertical dimension defines religious communication. Gergen does not address this aspect of religious communication. We refer to Bakhtin clarify this debate. We choose Bakhtin because he shares some basic assumptions about communication with Gergen. For example, they share the idea that the creation of meaning is a never-ending process, which is based on the dialogic relationship between an utterance and response. They also share the theory that meaning is related to the social language of a particular group or community to which a speaker belongs. However, Bakhtin does not exclude the possibility of an ultimate meaning. Nevertheless, he does struggle with the question of how to justify the dialogical process of the construction of meaning against the possibility of an ultimate meaning.

In this section, the concept of authoring is first described. An understanding of authoring is necessary in order to grasp religious communication from Bakhtin's perspective. Next, two models present in the work of Bakhtin are outlined, each offering a different perspective on religious communication. Both models share the central metaphors of 'God as author' and 'man as hero'. In religious communication, we construct our lives by saying, 'God is the author of the text of my life'. In Bakhtin's framework, every text has a subject or author (speaker, writer). According to Bakhtin, there are various kinds of authors available. We will differentiate between the monologic and polyphonic author, referring to God as the monologic author-God or the polyphonic author-God.

4.1 *Authoring*

If we express something or talk with someone, we choose language to express ourselves. 'Consciousness finds itself inevitably facing the necessity of *having to choose a language*' (Bakhtin, 1981, p. 295—italics in the original). The words used reflect the voice of a social group. A speaker expresses himself or herself *through* language. When speaking with a personal voice, we speak simultaneously with a collective voice (Hermans & Kempen, 1995, p. 108). We cannot distance ourselves from language. By producing unique utterances, speakers always use social languages, and these social languages shape what they say individually (Wertsch, 1991, p. 95). This idea parallels Gergen's viewpoint on social constructionism. Meaning is grounded in the tradition that people belong to and the forms of life in which they live.

Authoring is the process of choosing one's own voice (Bakhtin, 1973, p. 47). Different degrees of authority are allocated to the voices or discourses of others. These discourses are either 'authoritative' or 'internally persuasive' (Bakhtin, 1981, p. 342).

According to Bakhtin, examples of authoritative discourse are: religious dogmas, political doctrines, moral values; the word of a father, acknowledged scientific truth, or a currently fashionable book. 'The authoritative word demands that we acknowledge it; (...) it binds us, quite independent of any power it might have to persuade us internally; we encounter it with an authority already fused to it. The authoritative word is located in a distanced zone, organically connected with a past that is felt to be hierarchically higher. (...) It is a prior discourse. It is therefore not a question of choosing it from other possible discourses that are its equal' (Bakhtin, 1981, p. 342). What happens when meaning is constructed based on authoritative discourse? Authoritative discourse demands unconditional allegiance. It does allow free appropriation or assimilation of words that add meaning to our lives. Authoritative discourse is either completely affirmed or rejected. It is bound to its authority (i.e. a political party, an institution, a church, or a person). A rejection of an 'authoritative discourse' implies rejection of the authority that is intrinsically linked with it. 'Reciting by heart' is the pedagogical method connected with 'authoritative discourse' (Bakhtin, 1981, p. 341).

The second type of discourse is 'internally persuasive discourse'. Internally persuasive discourse is constantly evolving. It is the process of applying old words to new contexts. This process of appropriation and assimilation is not simply interpreting someone else's word. According to Bakhtin, 'we can take [a word] into new contexts, attach to it new material, put it in a new situation in order to wrest new answers from it, new insights into its meaning and even wrest from it new words of it own (since another's discourse, if productive gives birth to a new word from using response)' (Bakhtin, 1981, pp. 346–347). Although an internally persuasive word is half-ours and half-someone else's, it is wound together with our own word through assimilation. 'Its creativity and productiveness consist precisely in the fact that such a word awakens new and independent words, that it organizes masses or our word from within, and does not remain in an isolated and static condition' (Bakhtin, 1981, p. 345).

This distinction between authoritative and internally persuasive discourse is important when viewing if and how religious communication leads to an ultimate meaning. Within authoritative discourse, an external authority (God) decides the ultimate meaning of life. There is little debate against the concept of ultimate meaning in religious communication. However, questions arise when looking at the amount of influence a person has in the construction of meaning in their life? Are people only passive recipients of ultimate meaning? No. Individuals play an essential role in the construction of meaning in internally persuasive discourse. A person assimilates a voice in his or her own context. But is this still ultimate meaning? Acquiring a voice is a process, a never-ending struggle by people to construct the meaning of their life. There are different, even conflicting interpretations, about the meaning of each person's life. The question remains, how can there be an ultimate meaning within the polyphony of meaning?

4.2   *The Monologic Author-God*

Within religious communication, God is the voice that gives ultimate meaning to our lives. To interpret religious communication, Bakhtin uses the author-hero model of artistic creativity. Authors mould and shape their heroes by using their own creativity. The author decides the fate of the hero; what the victories are, where the battles are fought, when the hero dies. An aesthetic event is accomplished only when there are two emerging consciousnesses. 'If there is only one unitary and unique participant, there can be no aesthetic event' (Bakhtin, 1990, p. 22). There is no art, if there is no otherness. The author is not the same as the hero. The author and hero must be inter-related but they do not live at the same level.

> When the hero and the author coincide or when they find themselves standing either next to one another in the face of a value they share or against one another as antagonists, the aesthetic event ends and an *ethical* event begins (polemical tract, manifesto, speech of accusation or of praise and gratitude, invective, confession as a self-accounting, etc.). When there is no hero at all, not even in a potential form, then we have to do with an event that is *cognitive* (treatise, article, lecture). And, finally when the other consciousness is the encompassing consciousness of God, a *religious* event takes place (prayer, worship, ritual). (Bakhtin, 1990, p. 22).

As mentioned above (section 2.1), in order to understand ourselves, we need the other. We must step outside the ongoing process of experience (or as Bakhtin says: the flux of becoming) to construct the meaning of our life. Using the model of the monologic author, outsidedness is extreme. The level where the author and hero exist are radically different. Bakhtin uses the term *transgredience* when referring to this extreme outsidedness. Transgredience is often used in litera-ture, when a work is 'perceived and depicted from one and the same authorial position. There is no point at which the author's field of vision intersects or collides dialogically with the hero's field of vision and attitudes. The author's word does not experience resistance from the hero's potential word, which would interpret the same phenomena 'from the point of view of its own truth" (Bakhtin, 1973, p. 58). When using the monologic author model, transgredience becomes the metaphor for Gods' transcendence and corresponding omniscience (Coates, 1998, p. 43). People are incapable of seeing their life as a whole. God is the author who consummates a person's whole life. By doing so, the author-God saves the 'I-for-myself' from being undefined.

The frameworks of speech communication and finalization are use-ful in explaining the monologic author-God. Finalization is when the helpless "hero" is lifted up by the authoritative author-God. Finalization gives form to an unfinished character. '*Character* is the name we give to that form of the author-hero interrelationship which actualizes the task of producing the whole of the hero as a determinate personal-ity' (Bakhtin, 1990, p. 174). The hero is in a constant state of growth, with no beginning and no end. A hero does not add up their life and say 'this is all of me—there is *nothing more* anywhere else or in anything else; I already exist *in full*' (Bakhtin, 1990, p. 127). Heroes need ultimate meaning, but it is impossible to obtain alone.

> In the deepest part of myself, I live by eternal faith and hope in the constant possibility of the inner miracle of a new birth. I cannot, axiologically, fit my whole life into time—I cannot justify it and consummate it in full within the dimension of time. A temporally consummated life is a life without hope from the standpoint of the meaning that keeps it in motion. From within itself, such a life is hope-less; it is only from outside that a cherishing justification may be bestowed upon it (Bakhtin, 1990, p. 127).

The last word of the hero lacks perfection. The hero must surren-der to the mercy of the author-God, in order to obtain ultimate meaning in their life. Finalization by the author-God is redemption or justification. God is not the voice of conscience or the purity of penitent self-denial of anything given within ourselves. He is not the one into whose hands we fear to fall. Characteristic reactions of the author-God are 'kindness', namely tenderness, forbearance, merci-fulness, and loving admiration.

'God is now the heavenly father who is over me and can be merciful to me and justify me where I, from within myself, cannot be merciful to myself and cannot justify myself in principle, as long as I remain pure for myself. What I must be for the other, God is for me' (Bakhtin, 1990, p. 56).

Inherent in the relationship between the monologic author-God and the hero-man is an imbalance in power. The author-God views the hero as inferior. Their relationship is asymmetric. 'The monologic author retains complete control over his heroes; they are always the objects of representation and tools in the hands of their creator, who uses them essentially for the expression of his or her own 'truth', or point of view on the world' (Coates, 1998, p. 85). In the end, there is only the truth of the author.

Bakhtin cites power as one of the barriers to communication. According to Coates, Bakhtin deals with the issue of power under the rubric of the benign dictatorship. This is based on the model of the Creator's relationship to his Creation: 'the power of the author will never be abused because aesthetic activity is always motivated by self-sacrificial love' (Coates, 1998, p. 87). However, there is no balance between the monologic author-God and the hero. Only the author-God knows the real happiness of the hero. Happiness is more important than freedom in the monologic author-God model.

4.3   *The Polyphonic Author-God*

A second model of God in religious communication is the model of the polyphonic author-God. This model is best understood in the context of conflicting voices (or in Bakhtin's terminology, 'social heteroglossia'). Bakhtin refers to language mixing that takes place when referring to any object. During communication, we enter into a dialogue between people on a certain topic, whatever the topic may be.

> Only the mythical Adam, who approached a virginal and as yet verbally unqualified world with the first word, could really have escaped from the start to finish this dialogic inter-orientation with the alien word that occurs in the object (Bakhtin, 1980, p. 279).

When voices conflict (social heteroglossia), the author is no longer able to speak with authority. The polyphonic author-God cannot stand outside the life of the hero and complete it by giving that life form and content. There are two characteristics of the polyphonic

author-God. First, he renounces control over his heroes, then he
allows them to seek and express their own meaning, which is not
inferior to the meaning of their creator (see Coates, 1998, p. 86).
The polyphonic author-God does not stand in a transgredient position towards the hero. Although he remains on the outside, the
author does not utilize information not visible to the hero. For
Bakhtin, Dostojevsky exemplifies that kind of author.

> From the first to the final pages of his artistic work he was guided
> by the principle: never use for objectifying or finalizing another's con-
> sciousness anything that might be inaccessible to that consciousness,
> that might lie outside its field of vision (Bakhtin, quotation in Coates,
> 1998, p. 88).

In this model of the polyphonic author-God, the playing field has
leveled. Although the role of this author differs from that of the
monologic author-God, his position has not changed. As author, God
remains in a position of 'outsidedness'. Without this position, it is
impossible to construct a 'whole' in dialogic communication. The
polyphonic author still needs to have 'consciousness of consciousness'
in order to depict the self-consciousness of the hero. However, polyphonic author-God does not speak on behalf of the hero. The hero
has a right to self-definition, however hopeless it is, and also a right
to wrestle with the meaning of life, however difficult it is. 'The hero
is by nature unable to give himself any kind of aesthetic form, since
he lacks access to a comprehensive perspective on himself form which
he might form a credible judgement' (Coates, 1998, p. 88). In this
matter, we refer back to Bakhtin's central concept of dialogue, which
interprets life as the event of becoming. The meaning of life is
still to come. In the process of becoming, there is always the next
moment, which reveals only a part of the meaning of the present
action. The hero must live with profound incompleteness and frag-
mentation. There is no escape, other than to except this as a human
condition.

According to Coates, freedom is more important than happiness
in the polyphonic author model. The author-God respects the freedom of his creation, rather than guaranteeing that the hero is blessed
or justified (Coates, 1998, p. 89). Bakhtin has not found an easy
explanation for the hero's freedom within the polyphonic model. If
there is only heroic freedom, how can the author design the life of
the hero? Is it possible for heroic freedom to coexist with heroic cre-

atedness? Can authorial freedom coexist with authorial constraint?
Bakhtin gives one answer regarding authorial constraints.

> Firstly, the hero is said to pre-exits the work in some way (the cre-
> ative act 'reveals what is already present in the object').(. . .) Secondly,
> the artist's concept of the kind of hero he wants, once he begins to
> put it into practice, reveals a logic of his own which he is obliged to
> follow (Coates, 1998, p. 91).

This answer does not solve the problem of the coexistence of heroic
freedom with the creative initiative of the author in designing the
hero's life. The question remains; how can one save 'outsidedness'
for the polyphonic author without falling back to transgredience?

According to Coates, Bakhtin searches for a model of polyphonic
authorship, which vacillates between the poles of design versus dialogue, or transcendence versus immanence. If these poles are stretched
to their extreme, there is no freedom left for the hero. If dialogue
and immanence are stretched to their end, it leads to the death of
the polyphonic author. How can the polyphonic author exist in a
dialogic universe where the author participates together with the hero
in creating the meaning of his or her life? Here, Coates introduces
the metaphor of the silenced author. In speech born out of silence,
the author does not participate in the power struggle usually present in speech within the context of social heteroglossia. Within each
communicative act, a power struggle exists. For example, when we
give voice to our belief in God, we exclude a disbelief in God. We
need to occupy an ideological center. This is necessary to establish
ourselves in discourse in order to carve out our unique place. Meaning
not embodied is only an empty possibility. If we do not occupy an
ideological center, we are lost in time and space. In order to give
value to our life, we must to search for our own authorial voice.

In one of Bakhtin's latest works, he refers to Christ as the model
of silence in Dostojevsky's book 'The brothers Karamazov'. In this
book, there is a story of Christ returning to earth. It is a lengthy
monologue by the Grand Inquisitor, explaining the policy of the
church after the resurrection of Christ. The Grand Inquisitor is the
opposite of Christ. He represents all that is problematic in discourse.
He is an image of the monologic voice, dominating all others, even
using lies to manipulate. Christ is silent, remaining silent during the
discourse by the Grand Inquisitor. Christ's only action is to kiss the
Grand Inquisitor at then end. For Bakhtin, this kiss is a model of

unuttered meaning (Bakhtin, 1986, p. 148). Christ does not have to assert his individuality, because he knows who he is. He does not have to find himself in the other. Christ represents a meaning of life that does not seek words to define itself. He is the model of self-assertion through self-denial. This form of authority aims at helping people toward self-understanding without imposing a definition on them. It is speech born out of silence 'which abstains from the projection of self, from any explicit ideology of its own, but seeks to help the other's word to greater clarity' (Coates, 1998, p. 120).

What does this mean for the polyphonic author-God? This author abstains completely from asserting their presence at the expense of the hero's right to self-assertion. This author is concealed within the polyphony of voices, which the hero casts out into the world. The silenced author is not embodied directly in meaning, but is known only indirectly.

As mentioned above, Bakhtin does not expel the author from the creative process. Bakhtin differentiates between the primary author and secondary author, connecting the metaphor of silence only to the primary author. The primary author is not created, but creating. Unfortunately, we have no image of this author. Bakhtin uses terms from 'Duns Scotus' to express the difference between the primary and secondary author.

> The primary (not created) and secondary author (the image of the author created by the primary author). The primary—*natura non creata quae creat*; the secondary author—*natura creata quae non creat*. The image of the hero—*natura creata quae non creat*. The primary author cannot be an image. (. . .) When we try to imagine the primary author figuratively, we ourselves are creating his image, that is, we ourselves become the primary author of the image. The creating image (i.e., the primary author) can never enter into any image that he has created (Bakhtin, 1986, p. 148).

When we make an image of the polyphonic author-God, we use the work the author has created to make an image of the creator. Caution is necessary because this can make the author-God part of the polyphony of voices. However, the primary author is beyond this struggle. Therefore, there is no immediate experience of the primary author that is hiding in the polyphony of voices.

Bakhtin points to the use of the liberating strategies, such as laughter and irony, which are used in order to reach the silence of the primary author-God. The hero reaches freedom through a denial of the sphere of necessity. Although the hero must not abstain from finding an authorial voice, he or she cannot cling to the embodiment of meaning as the absolute or ultimate meaning.

> 'The denial of (failure to understand) the sphere of necessity through which freedom must past (both on a historical an the individual-personal plane), is that intermediate sphere that lies between the Grand Inquisitor (with his state power, rhetoric, and authority) and Christ (with his silence and his kiss)' (Bakhtin, 1986, p. 151).

The polyphonic author uses different liberating strategies. The author must break the identification of absolute meaning in order to move beyond, into meaning found in silence. This silence does not equal the intermediate sphere of 'not-knowing', which is found in the field of liberating or subversive strategies. The author-God must withhold authority or use his authority to say that embodied meaning is not ultimate meaning. By doing so, the polyphonic author-God plays the role of the medieval fool who turns reality upside down.

> The word removed from life: the word of the idiot, the holy fool, the insane, the child, the dying person, and sometimes women. Delirium, dream, intuition (inspiration), unconsciousness, alogicality [alogism], involuntary behavior, epilepsy, and so forth (Bakhtin, 1986, p. 148).

As mentioned above, irony and laughter are among the subversive strategies used by the polyphonic author. Irony is speaking with reservations (Bakhtin, 1986, p. 132). By using irony, the polyphonic author starts to question meaning. Then, the embodied meaning, which the author thinks is the absolute, perhaps is not. In this way, irony can be liberating. According to Bakhtin, laughter can also free and unite us (Bakhtin, 1986, p. 135). Laughter is available to everyone, and not just for someone who identifies himself or herself with a certain voice. Laughter transcends power struggles, which are evident in most speech acts. Laughter transcends opposition, indignation and anger.

Laughter is also the great equalizer. One perspective on the meaning of life is no greater than another. It ends the dominance of one voice over another. The polyphonic author-God is concealed in the subversive strategies of irony and laughter in the interest of freedom and truth. By doing so, the polyphonic author-God allows the hero to be defined.Is this state of silence something that can be experienced in this life? Can the hero find the meaning of life that is beyond the conflicting voices of reality? Is this a living possibility or an allusion? According to Coates (1998, p. 122), this is possible. This state of silence can be achieved when authoritative discourse and internally persuasive discourse are united in a single word or utterance.

However, there are profound differences between both types as illustrated above. One can surrender gradually to an internally persuasive word, so it eventually become indistinguishable from one's own. On the other hand, authoritative discourse always remains alien to one's own word. Nevertheless, Bakhtin finds this unity between authoritative discourse and internally persuasive discourse present in Christ. Christ is an incarnated consciousness who commands ideological, persuasive authority. He represents an author-God who preserves the freedom of the hero within the world.

> For Bakhtin, as for Dostojevsky, Christ is the most convincing historical figure, the apotheosis of compelling historical truth, and those who have been persuaded by him are his truest representatives; they bring God down, as it were, into the world, where He can be encountered as an equal (Coates, 1998, p. 169).

Another term Bakhtin uses when explaining the incarnation of truth in the living hero is the concept of 'meeting'. Bakhtin refers to 'a meeting with a great human being, as something that determines, obligates, and unites—this is the highest moment of understanding' (Bakhtin, 1986, p. 142). Bakhtin has written frequently elsewhere in his works on meeting as a central chronotope in literature (Bakhtin, 1980, pp. 97–98). The 'meeting' is one of the oldest literary devices for structuring a plot. In a meeting, time and place must coincide, if not, there is no meeting. Meeting connects to the road. In religious narratives and rituals, meeting is a dominant motif. However, it remains unclear what Bakhtin means when he refers to 'meeting with a great human being' within the polyphonic model of the author-hero relationship.

5. *Discussion*

In this final section, two models of religious communication are first evaluated. This is done using an external criterion (i.e. how it fits in cultural context of Western society), and an internal criterion (i.e. the principle of dialogism, which characterizes social constructionism). Second, questions regarding research on religious communication are addressed. Finally, we return to the epistemological question asked at the beginning of this chapter. Is it possible for ultimate meaning to exist in religious communication without loosing the dialogue necessary for communication?

5.1   *Evaluation of the Models of Religious Communication*

Models of religious communication can be evaluated using both internal and external criteria. First, we use an external criterion, namely how these models fit into the cultural context of Western society.

Certainly, the answer to this question depends on how Western society is described. There is long debate as to which era we live in: pre-modern, modern, late-modern, or post-modern. This debate will not be repeated here (see Van der Ven, 2000). Indeed, these descriptions each describe an aspect of our complex society. In other words, society is complex because each of these processes is at work in Western society. Gergen (1999, p. 16) describes Western society as moving toward the postmodern. Yet, he cannot be identified with postmodern thinkers, such as the French authors, Lyotard and Derrida. The question remains: how do two models of religious communication fit into the context of Western society?

The monologic author-God model of religious communication, where God gives form to the life of the hero, fits better into a pre-modern context. In this model, religious communication must be placed within the dialogic relationship between people and God. Within this relationship, God envisions the life of a person and knowing the ultimate meaning of that life, bestows it on them. The sacred and authoritarian word is removed by its very nature from dialogue.

> Because of its sacrosanct, impenetrable boundaries, this word is inert, and it has limited possibilities of contacts and combinations. This is the word that retards and freezes thought. The word that demands reverent repetition and not further development, corrections, and additions (Bakhtin, 1986, p. 133).

In the end, there is only one absolute meaning, which is unknown, but given externally by the monological author-God. 'In the monological world *tertium non datur*: a thought is either confirmed or negated' (Bakhtin 1973, p. 64). This is why this model fits into a pre-modern context, where religion gives ultimate meaning to all aspects of daily life. In pre-modern society, religion is the all encompassing principle in life, on both societal and personal levels.

The polyphonic author-God model of religious communication is better suited to a post-modern context. One characteristic of postmodernism is polyvocality, a characteristic, which suits this model well (Gergen, 1999, p. 162v.). There is polyvocality stemming from

different religious traditions within Western society. On a personal
level, there can be polyvocality within the same person. The model
of the polyphonic author-God is a reaction to the social heteroglossia that is experienced in society. It seems, therefore, that both models live in different worlds, but, as mentioned above, these worlds
are part of our society.

Another way to evaluate the two models is by using an internal
criteria, namely the concept of dialogism. This concept is at heart
of Bakhtin and Gergen's works on social constructionism. The meaning of utterances is generated in a dialogic relationship. Meaning
cannot be derived without relationships but is found in the relationship between the self and the other. If the self is not part of a
relationship with another, there is no meaning. Here, Bakhtin introduces the model of 'thirdness'. Thirdness is an utterance, a response
and the relationship between them. Without the relationship between
the utterance and response, we are unsure of the meaning. It is lost
in the infinite possibilities. The same is true when explaining how
the self understands the meaning of life. It is only from another perspective that wholeness of our lives is constructed. 'I-for-myself' is
constantly being reinvented. At the same time, we cannot abstain
from speaking and give meaning to life. Bakhtin calls the process of
choosing a voice authoring. By selecting a voice, we personify its
meaning. However, this must be seen in the ongoing process of
speech communication. There is no first or last word. The selected
voice is given to us. Each word enters an ongoing, infinite dialogue,
in which the meaning is developed, changed, renewed or forgotten.
Dialogue is fundamental for human existence. We cannot escape it.

How can both models of religious communication be evaluated
using this dialogic criterion? The model in which the monological
author-God finalizes the life of hero-man has trouble fitting into this
criterion. Nevertheless, there are many characteristics in this model
that fit well into the concept of constructed meaning between God
and people. First, the relationship between God and humans must
be understood as a relationship between self and other. The self is
created, in part, because the other stands on the outside. In religious communication, the other is responsible for the process of
finalization, that is, the construction of the life of the self into a
whole. This model of the monologic author-God can go a long way
within a dialogic criterion; however, it comes up short. The reason
for this is because of the idea that God and man exist on a funda-

mentally different levels. The monological author-God sees pieces of the hero which are impossible for others to see. This is outsidedness to the extreme (or in Bakhtin's terminology 'transgredience'). In the world of the monological author-God, there is one, dominant voice, which brings an end to all dialogue. It is the voice of absolute truth. Here, other voices are polemically negated. In reality, it is impossible to represent them, because these voices must fit into the dominant voice. Therefore, an important question remains. If the voice of the hero is heard only by the monological author-God, in the end, is there only one word, the word of God?

According to Coates, Bakhtin saw this problem and looked for a way out in his writings. The polyphonic author-God addresses these concerns. The polyphonic author-God fits well into the dialogic criterion. The polyphonic author-God does not enter the polyphony of voices in order to silence them by speaking the ultimate word. Instead, the polyphonic author-God hides in the multitude of voices. God is only found in the silence beyond, where authoritative and internally persuasive words unite. Ultimate meaning is found in silence as unuttered truth.

Although we assert that the model of the polyphonic author-God fits very well into the criterion of dialogue, at the same time, we do not want to suggest that all theoretical problems are solved. One major problem is the author's function within the process of understanding. Does the author disappear into the polyphony of voices? The author exists only if there is ultimate meaning. Consequently, is there ultimate meaning if there is only meaning within dialogue? Does ultimate meaning imply an end to dialogue? We return to these questions at the end of this section when addressing the epistemological assumptions of social constructionism.

5.2 *Empirical Theological Research on Religious Communication*

Social constructionism has major repercussions on how we research religious communication. Here, we highlight some of these consequences.

1. One end result of social constructionism we must research is the process of the construction of reality as it happens within a relationship. For example, if a person says, 'I believe God prevented my baby from dying' we must frame this in the context of a dialogue. Another example where the construction of meaning in a dialogue

is important is the situation where a man and wife talk together about their grief, or in another case, when a father or mother talks to an older brother or sister that has been miraculously 'saved'. It is something different to send a questionnaire to people, asking if they belief God can prevent a child from dying, than to research the social construction between people inside a relationship. We are not saying that it is useless to research people's belief systems in a questionnaire format. What we must realize however, is that by doing this, we reduce reality to what was previously given and ready-made. According to Bakhtin, this type of research is so common, because it is easier to do.

> It is much easier to study the *given* in what is created (for example, language, ready-made and general elements of world view, reflected phenomena of reality, and so forth) than to study what is *created* (Bakhtin, 1986, p. 120).

Interviewing people about their religious communication, then recording the way they construct meaning in relationships with others in the same sociocultural situation, is a different research setting. In an interview, a person constructs meaning within the relationship of the interview. This differs from the situation in which a grieving man and wife talk alone about their beliefs.

What about a situation where no one else is present, for example when a person prays at bedtime? Or when a person quietly meditates? Or when hermit lives alone in the dessert? Is there still construction of meaning within a relationship? Yes. Each person has a relationship with a deity. They pray to their God. Even if it is a prayer of despair, like in the psalms of personal complaint, in which a person complains that they are unable to find God, there remains a relationship, a relationship between the person and an absent God.

Empirical research about the relationship between God and people cannot be done directly. However, we can research the voices used in religious communication, a voice uttered within speech communication. Voice has a communicative structure contained in it (see Wertsch, 1990). When I select a voice (i.e. a certain prayer of a community), other people speak to me. Each voice is uttered from somewhere, and each utterance finds a response someplace in the future. A silent prayer is like the construction of meaning before an imagined audience. In order to research this, we must find methods where the individual can give insight into this process (i.e. methods of self-reflection where a person makes a reconstruction of this dialogical process before an imagined public).

2. Another important point is the use of the models of the monological author-God and the polyphonic author-God as a heuristic device for empirical research into religious communication. There is an abundance of empirical research in which images of God are investigated (see for example, Hutsebaut & Verhoeven, 1991; Van der Ven, 1998). The two models of Bakhtin should not be understood as different images of God, but as variations of religious communication. These models offer different constructions regarding the framework of religious communication. The first model must be understood against the background of authoritative discourse. The second model implies a merging of authoritative and internally persuasive discourse. It is important to note that Bakhtin developed these models from a Christian background. Research is necessary to find out if these models also can give insight into religious communication in other world religions.

3. The third point is that utterances must be interpreted as a part of speech communication. According to Bakhtin, because language is at its very basis, a dialogue, an utterance is always directed at response. A response is guaranteed because of the finalized wholeness of the utterance. One of the factors determining wholeness is the use of typical compositional and generic forms of finalization. Bakhtin calls them 'speech genres'. Speech genres differ between religious traditions, within traditions, and between contexts and differing groups of people. An understanding of speech genres enables people to understand what others say within each communicative act. Gergen refers to 'scenarios' in dialogue. 'In what sort of scenarios do assertions of religious belief function to bring people into accord, and in what relational patterns do they operate divisively?' (Gergen, 1993, p. 234). We do not compare Bakhtin's 'speech genre' and Gergen's concept of 'scenario' here. Our main point is that at the core of research into religious communication, we should look for speech genres used in the dialogic construction of meaning in all aspects of religious studies. For example, in research about prayer, we can also examine differing speech genres. In the study of religious education, research can be done juxtaposing the different speech genres pupils use when speaking to others from their own tradition compared to when speaking to others from a different tradition.

Another aspect for study is to examine the type of speech genres used by the ministry during funerals? Are there differences between the speech genres of the public gathered for the funeral compared to the public gathered for some other function?

4. A last point regards the context of Western society on these models. Perhaps one of the greatest challenges of religion in Western society is to find a response to post-modernism (Tracy, 1991; 1994; Chatelion Counet, 1998; Boeve, 1999). The theistic tradition within Christianity does fit well into this post-modern context. To be brief, one of the unsolved problems within theism is how to accept the freedom of man. What is even more important, is that little is known about religious communication within the context of post-modernity. Although the monologic author-God stands clearly within the theistic tradition, there is little research into the polyphonic model (Coates, 1998, p. 84). Therefore, we propose that empirical research into the polyphonic author-God model is put at the center of our research agenda.

Research into this model should examine how people construct meaning within relationships beyond the struggle of voices. Within social heteroglossia, people defend embodied truth as absolute truth. Within the polyphony of voices, there are dominant voices, using their power to silence others. According to Bakhtin, absolute meaning is found in silence as unuttered truth. Freedom is found after breaking the identification of embodied truth as the absolute truth. Within this process of de-identification, people can use liberating or subversive strategies, such as laughter. Within the Bakhtin's framework, research should be directed to contexts where polyphonic author-God is revealed.

First, there are times when people use subversive strategies in religious communication. An example is when there are work groups within a parish focused on a societal problem, such as poverty. Another example is a liturgy where a person plays the role of the fool who turns reality upside down. A last example is at a religious festival where people from different religions are invited (see also Gergen, 1999). These are all contexts where voices of people, that are normally excluded from speaking, can be heard.

Second, one can think about contexts of silence as unuttered truth. For example, people talk to a loved one on their deathbed about their life. In this context, two people are able to reconcile by coming to a loving understanding even while acknowledging that their views are irreconcilable.

5.3   Ultimate Meaning as Silence

In discussing the epistemological assumptions of social constructionism, we questioned Gergen's idea that there is no truth claim that can justify itself. A truth claim is only one position in a dialogic process, not the end of it. If it is examined in terms of the construction of meaning: 'there is only my meaning, your meaning and, if there is mutual understanding, then there is perhaps a shared meaning; but there is no ultimate meaning. A correct understanding of Gergen shows that his battle is with every absolute truth claim that ends the dialogical process in the construction of meaning. We agree with Gergen and opt for a transformative notion of communication (see section 3.2). However, we disagree with Gergen, when he asserts that dialogism and ultimate meaning mutually exclude another. This is not necessarily true. This would imply a non-objectifying (Smith, 2000), non-possessive (Witvliet, 1999) or non-violent (Pannikar, 1979) concept of ultimate meaning. We elaborate on this below, but will first return to the models of Bakhtin.

In the model of the polyphonic author-God, religious communication attempts to save the dialogic process without loosing the author and their authority to construct the hero's whole life. If there is no author-God, constructing the whole of our life, we would live an open-ended life. Everything could have another meaning or even no meaning in the end. Bakhtin wants to combine a dialogical construction of meaning with ultimate meaning. By loosing the dialogical principle, we loose our freedom. If the possibility of ultimate meaning is lost, the authority of God as transcendent author is lost. Both principles must stand together. In the end, Bakhtin's own model of the monological author-God does not meet his outlined principles of dialogue (see section 5.2). Indeed, this is what Bakhtin tries to construct in the model of the polyphonic author-God. The core premise of this model is that if the dialogue is brought to its end point, this ultimate end is silence. This is not a new position within the struggle of voices within social heteroglossia. In particular, ultimate dialogicity is not a new position either, but a new voice within the polyphony of voices. Bakhtin refers to it as unuttered truth, silence. It is a truth that does not need to enter as an utterance into the dialogic construction of meaning because it is the ultimate meaning. If it is uttered, it enters again the battle of voices around our lives. This is why the polyphonic author-God is the silent author, or the primary author who is creating but not created. This ultimate meaning that is born out of silence is at the same time outside man, but also inside. This is why Bakhtin speaks of a unity between authoritative discourse (spoken by the author-God) and internally persuasive discourse (experienced by the hero as his own internal truth).

With this said, what about the fact that life is a struggle for meaning; and that sometimes it is difficult to see any meaning at all. What about people who are already dead and forgotten before they die? Does this limiting situation break the conceptual connection between dialogism and ultimate meaning? Bakhtin says no. It is exactly the dialogical openness of everyday life and the presence of every utterance that helps us to reach the meaning of life in the future (how far it may be).

> At any moment in the development of the dialogue there are immense, boundless masses of forgotten contextual meanings, but at certain moments of the dialogue's subsequent development along the way they are recalled and invigorated in renewed form (in a new context). Nothing is absolutely death: every meaning will have its homecoming festival (Bakhtin, 1986, p. 170).

Bakhtin's use of the term 'festival' reminds us of the liberating strategy as an intermediate sphere to silence. Ultimate meaning does not equal the denial of meaning or the experience of not-knowing. Sometimes, it is necessary to go through these experiences in order to reach ultimate meaning. According to Bakhtin, the polyphonic author-God uses liberating or subversive strategies to withhold his authority. Nonetheless, this particular embodied meaning or lack of meaning is not ultimate meaning.

From a theological viewpoint, this combination of liberating strategies and the (mystical) silence found beyond, is at the heart of the current debate about God in post-modern times. For example, David Tracy stresses within post-modern theology a conjunction of prophetic and mystic trajectories (Tracy, 1991, p. 263). 'Genuine postmodernity begins not in ennui but in ethical resistance' (Tracy, 1994, p. 108). Differences which are not accounted for in the dominant culture and the grand modern narratives are the focus of this ethical resistance. The postmodern turn to 'the other' has influenced a renewed stress on the shattering otherness of God. 'Revelation is the event-gift of the other's self-manifestation. Revelation disrupts the continuities, the similarities, the communalities of modern religion' (Tracy, 1994, p. 109).

Perhaps, it is no surprise to see that the metaphor of silence plays an important role in the current theological debate about negative or apophatic theology. For theologians who think about God from the philosophic frame of reference of Derrida, the metaphor of silence is used to refer to the end of predication (Caputo, 1998; Chatelion Counet, 1998). Predication captures in concepts, what is transcendent, or at least incommensurate with the order of predication. From another frame of reference (namely non-dualistic thinking), Panikkar comes to the same conclusion when conceiving a non-objectifying way to speak about God. When we understand something, we assimilate it, and thus change the object of our thinking. If we think something through, it becomes totally an object of our thinking. 'A tree, for instance, simply stops our thinking at a certain point. It possesses an enclosure forbidden to or rather impenetrable to our thinking' (Panikkar, 1979, p. 225). To be 'thought-proof' is the criterion of reality. We can only be touched by the otherness of reality (or God) when it offers resistance to thinking. That is why there is a big difference, according to Pannikar, 'between an idea of God, which has infinite possibilities, and a real God who stops and silences our thinking' (Panikkar, 1979, p. 225).

Whether or not silence is an adequate metaphor to speak about God as the ultimate meaning of life, is a complex debate within theology. Some scholars think that praise, not silence, is the adequate manner to talk about God.

> Thus, it is possible to speak about God, but in the mode of *praise*, as a non-objectifying, not-positivistic mode of conceptualization which does not reduce God to a concept, but rather employs language in such a way that respects Gods transcendence and *refers* the listener to experience the thing itself (Smith, 2000, p. 79).

Others suggest that the impossibility to speak about God within mystic theology does not lead to silence but to the use of many words. From a Christian point of view, one needs to experiment with language in order to stretch it to its limits. We must go beyond denials (God is not x.) and analogies (God is like x.) (Sarot & Markus, 2000, p. 156). This is not elaborated on here, however.

We hope we have shown that the model of the polyphonic Author-God is an interesting and useful perspective in this debate. This model combines the dialogicity of the subject-subject model of speaking with the expression of ultimate meaning as silence (or unuttered truth). If it succeeds fully in this combination, is a matter of further debate.

References

Bakhtin, M. (1973). *Problems of Dostojevski's Poetics.* Ann Arbor: Ardis.
—— (1981). *The Dialogic Imagination. Four Essays.* Austin: Un. of Texas Press.
—— (1986). *Speech Genres and Other Late Essays.* Austin: Un. of Texas Press.
—— (1990). *Art and Answerability. Early philosophical essays.* Austin: Un. of Texas Press.
—— (1993). *Toward a Philosophy of the Act.* Austin: Un. of Texas Press.
Boeve, L. (1999). Postmoderne politieke theologie? Johann Baptist Metz in gesprek met het actuele kritische bewustzijn [Postmodern political theory? Johann Baptist Metz in conversation with the modern critical mind]. *Tijdschrift voor Theologie* 39(3), 244–264.
Caputo, J. (1998). God Is Wholly Other—Almost: *Différance* and the Hyperbolic Alterity of God. In: O. Summerell (ed.). *The Otherness of God* (pp. 190–205). Charlottesville: Un. Press of Virginia.
Chatelion Counet, P. (1998). *Over God zwijgen. Postmodern bijbellezen* [Not speaking about God. Postmodern Reading of the Bible]. Zoetermeer: Meinema.
Contee, R. (1000). *Christianity in Postmodern. God and the textual author.* Cambridge: Cambridge U.P.
Dobbelaere, K. (1999). Towards an Integrated Perspective of the Processes Related to the Descriptive Concept of Secularization. *Sociology of Religion* 60(3), 229–247.
Gergen, K.J. & M.M. Gergen (1988). Narrative and the Self as Relationship. In: L. Berkowitz (ed.). *Advances in Experimental Social Psychology* (pp. 28–51). New York: Academic.
Gergen, K.J. (1993). Belief as relational resource. *The international journal for the psychology of religion* 3(4), 231–235.
—— (1994). The Communal Creation of Meaning. In: W.F. Overton & D.S. Palermo (eds.). *The nature and Ontogenesis of Meaning* (pp. 19–39). Hillsdale N.J.: Lawrence Erlbaum.
—— (1995). *Social Construction and the Transformation of Identity Politics.* Paper for New School for Social Research Symposium. April 7, 1995.
—— (1999). *An invitation to social constructionism.* London: Sage.
Hermans, C.A.M. (2000). The other in dialogue. Interreligious communication from a sociocultural perspective. In: Ziebertz, H.-G., Schweitzer, F., Häring, H. & Browning, D. (Eds.). *The human image of God* (pp. 285–309). Leiden: Brill.
Hermans, H.J.M., & Kempen, H.J.G. (1995). Body, mind and culture: The dialogical nature of mediated action. *Culture and Psychology* 1, 103–114.
Holquist, M. (1990). *Dialogism: Bakhtin and his world.* London: Routledge.
Hutsebaut, D. & Verhoeven, D. (1991). The Adolescents' Representation of God from Age 12 to 18. *Journal of Empirical Theology* 4(1), 59–72.
Knitter, P.F. (1995). *One earth many religions: multifaith dialogue and global responsibility.* Maryknoll: Orbis Books.
Luckman, Th. (1996). The Privatization of Religion and Morality. In: Heelas, P., Lash, M. & Morris, P. (eds.). *De-traditionalization: Critical reflections on authority and identity at a time of uncertainty* (pp. 72–86). Cambridge Mass.: Blackwell Publishers.

Nistelrooy, A. van (1999). *Collectief organiseren. Een sociaal-constructionistisch onderzoek naar het werken met grote groepen* [Organizing collectively. Social constructivistic research on working with large groups]. Utrecht: Lemma.

Panikkar, R. (1979). The myth of pluralism: The tower of Babel—A meditation on non-violence. *Cross Currents*, 197–230.

Sarot, M. & Markus, A. (2000). Denken aan Wie ons ontsnapt. Rationele theologie en de transcendentie van God [The One who escapes our thinking. Rational theology and Gods' transcendence]. *Nederlands Theologisch Tijdschrift*, 54, 145–157.

Smith, J.K.A. (2000). Between predication and silence. Augustine on how (not) to speak of God. *The Heytrop Journal* 41(1), 66–86.

Schwandt, Th.A. (1994). Constructivist, Interpretivist Approaches to Human Inquiry. In: Denzin, N.K. & Lincoln, Y.S. (Eds.). *Handbook of qualitative research* (pp. 118–137). London: Sage.

Tracy, D. (1991). The hermeneutics of naming God. *Irish theological Quarterly* 57, 253–264.

——— (1994). Theology and the many faces of modernity. *Theology Today* 51, 104–114.

Todorov, T. (1984). *Mikhail Bakhtin: The dialogical principle*. Minneapolis: University of Minneapolis.

Ven, J.A. van der (1998). *God Reinvented. A Theological Search in Texts and Tables*. Leiden: Brill.

——— (2000). Multiculturalism in Education. Politics of Recognition. *International Journal of Education and Religion* 1(1), 19–46.

Wertsch, J.V. (1991). *Voices of the mind: A sociocultural approach to mediated action*. London: Harvester Wheatsheaf.

HUMAN DISCOURSE AND THE ACT OF PREACHING

Gerrit Immink

Introduction

Do human activities like *speaking, knowing, believing* and *experiencing* pre-suppose the existence of an individual human mind, or do they require a so-called "interior life"? In *An Invitation to Social Construction*, Kenneth Gergen argues that these activities must be understood in terms of social relationships. In his view, psychological discourse is not constituted by a so-called individual mental state, it rather arises from performative acts within relationships (Gergen, 1999, p. 133). Consequently, one of his main theses is that relatedness precedes individuality. There is, however, a second thesis lurking in the back-ground. Once being is apprehended as *relational being*, his next step is to argue that relational being must be understood as *socially constructed being*. Human discourse is a matter of performative action—that is action-in-relationship—and furthermore it is socially and culturally embedded. Ultimately, according to Gergen, the so-called psychological or philosophical categories receive their meaning from *social conventions*. So it turns out that the psychological is fashioned out of the social. Concepts that refer to a so-called mental state owe their meaning to social life and historical development, and ulti-mately we—as human beings—construct and re-construct meaning and truth in a continuously ongoing process of social relationships.

From the perspective of theology, his analysis is quite challenging. After all, in religion in general—and may be in Christianity in par-ticular—relationship is a key concept. Consider for example the chris-tian idea of creation. That notion not only expresses that there once was a beginning, or that history will be completed. It points rather to distinctness and otherness. Being created in the image of God presumes that distinctness and relation are fundamental categories in the human condition. The human self does not exist in solitari-ness; we are essentially related to other people, to our environment and to God. Many religious practices, for example, worship, pas-toral and diaconal care, disclose a pattern of relationship. Religion itself is a personal communing with God, a personal encounter which takes place in faith. The encounter between God and humankind, albeit conceptualized in different theological models, is a matter of relationship and reciprocity. One could even argue that apparently contradictory theological paradigms nonetheless agree on the fundamental insight that relationship is most basic. Schleiermacher's antropological paradigm cannot be understood without notions such as "Geist" and "Gemeinschaft" (Schlenke, 1999). On the other side of the theological spectrum: Barth's incarnational doctrine of God and man united in Jesus Christ must primarily be understood as an enactment of identity: the human and the divine revealing themselves in one act of reconciliation. And Emil Brunner's *Wahrheit als Begegnung* testifies that religion is relational. Notions such as covenant and community characterize the Christian religion. Human beings do not realize their subjectivity in solitariness; they act as *responsible* creatures. If there is a human self, then it develops in a concrete, active and responsible encounter.

It would not be correct, however, to agree with Gergen on the basis of a theological concept of relational being. Of course there are similarities between Gergen's social constructionism and some aspects of the Christian faith. Mainly his emphasis on relationship coincides to some extent with a Christian understanding of life. And, further, from a christian perspective the dominant individualism in the Western tradition has been criticized more than once. However, social constructionism is a theory to account for *human discourse* in terms of relationships. Gergen proposes an interpretation of human discourse that rejects both the independent existence of the psychological world of the self and the independent existence of the material world "out there". As a matter of fact he opposes any dualist ontology (Gergen, 1999, p. 8). According to Gergen, the mind is neither an autonomous realm, nor a mirror to nature.

Practical theology deals with the practice of faith in the human condition. Consequently, practical theologians reflect on faith as a human act and, further, on communicative processes which generate and cultivate faith. These processes are peformed by human discourse. So practical theology, most of all theological disciplines, deals with human discourse.

In this article I will first deal with Gergen's social constructionism and argue that human discourse should not only be understood in terms of performative action, but that it is as much a matter of *illocutionary* action. From that perspective I will argue that the social or institutional dimension of language has a *normative* import and that it is not merely a matter of choice and convention. Further I will argue that illocutionary action requires some form of *metaphysical realism*, and that, consequently, there are limits to human constructionism and convention. In the second part of my article I will turn to human discourse in the act of preaching. First, I will describe three specific features of preaching as a communicative act. Then I turn to two main models in homiletical discourse and I will argue that in succesful communication the *noetic* act precedes the performative act. Finally I will deal with the praxis of preaching.

Human Discourse

As human beings we perform all kinds of activities in which we relate to other people and to the world around us. We make promises, we ask questions, we make assertions—and we do so by performing speech acts. Furthermore, we act intentionally, we make decisions, we exhibit feelings, we show emotion, we express attitudes. And, as human beings, we acquire knowledge: we form beliefs about the world, about ourselves and about other people. So when we consider human discourse, we run into activities such as: intentional action, speech, noetic functioning and (moral) reasoning. The question now is: how do we interpret these human activities? Do they presuppose something like an individual human mind? And if so, how is this mental realm related to the external world? Let us first consider Gergen's view on the so-called mental acts and our human perception of an external world.

The human mind. Gergen argues that the older traditions, which construe human consciousness from the perspective of a first person or a third person account, are in trouble. Neither phenomenology with its emphasis on the private approach to inner life (introspection), nor behaviorism which understands consciousness from the perspective of behavior which is observed in other persons, are adequate theories. Gergen shows some affinity with Mead's idea that mental phenomena should not be comprehended as structures or attributes of the mind, rather as relations between the organism and its environment. He expands this theory, however, in such a way that the relation is understood as a *social construction*. So Gergen rejects the idea that the human self is an isolated individual mind and he

broadens the term "relation" in such a way that the human self is
situated in social life. 'I want to propose a relational view on self-
conception', so he says, 'one that views self-conception not as an
individual's personal and private cognitive structure but as *discourse*
about the self—the performance of languages available in the public sphere. I replace the traditional concern with conceptual categories (self-concepts, schemas, self-esteem), with the self as a narration
rendered intelligible within ongoing relationships.' (Gergen, 1994,
p. 185) Since the preoccupation with the isolated individual mental
process has, according to Gergen, been quite unsuccessful, social constructionism is seen as a welcome paradigm shift in discursive development. The basic idea is that not the individual but *relationship* forms
the fundamental unit of social and mental life (Gergen, 1994, p. 253).
For the constructionist '. . . relatedness precedes individuality. The
constructionist challenge, then, is to fashion a reality of relatedness,
linguistic intelligibilities, and associated practices that offer new potential for cultural life.' (Gergen, 1994, p. 214)

Gergen is not saying that, in addition to the individual, there is
relatedness. In that case relationship would be a byproduct of independent individual selves. Nor is he saying that the individual self
is only realized through participation in the whole. His claim is much
stronger: the relation has priority over the related subjects. And, further, relations are carried out in human interaction: in the act of
people encountering each other. The vocabulary of mental life is so
to say "parasitical upon" the acts of human discourse. Mental concepts are "entia per alio", they don't presuppose the existence of a
so-called human mind, rather they are a byproduct in a theory on
human interaction. As far as I see it, the idea of human interaction
as a performative act plays the first fiddle in Gergen's theoretical
framework. And, further, the meaning of a performative act originates in its historical and cultural situation. Consequently, the human
self is not understood as an independent centre of consciousness, nor
as a subject who has all kinds of mental capacities; rather, the human
self is unfolded as a social artifact.

The realm of the world. We observed that Gergen criticizes the existence of an independent human self. Let us suppose for a moment
that it is redundant to accept the existence of an independent human
mind. We just stick to the acts of discourse. Nonetheless, discourse-
analysis suggests that we—as human beings—have the ability to relate
to the natural world around us. I know that my car is in front of

the house, I am aware of the trees in the garden, I know that some of our children have gone to bed now. Hence the fact *that my car is in front of the house* stands in a certain relation to my knowing activity. But if there is no independent human self who does the *knowing* and *perceiving*, wouldn't then the world around us stay mute? Gergen, I suppose, refuses to interpret this relation in terms of a *subject* of consciousness and an *object* of thought. In his version of constructionism he rejects on the one hand the presupposition of the individual human mind and, on the other hand, the existence of an independent ontological realm. Not that Gergen denies the existence of a natural world (mountains, stars, animals and comfortable houses). His point is that we don't have access to that reality-as-it-is. Constructionism is *ontologically mute*, so he suggests. Once we attempt to articulate "what there is", so he says, we enter the world of discourse. The idea is: once we have access, it is necessarily constructed. This way Gergen disconnects human discourse from the world around us. I can specify that at two places in his theory of discourse. He rejects for example the referential aspects of language (1), and he pays little attention to the illocutionary forces of speech-acts (2). His focus is that in any discourse the process of construction commences, and that process is ". . . inextricably woven into processes of social interchange and into history and culture (Gergen, 1994, p. 72). 'The adequacy of any word or arrangement of words to "capture reality as it is" is a matter of local convention.' (Gergen, 1994, p. 73) Gergen's view is that we don't grasp the world as it is; rather, the reality which we apprehend in human discourse, is constituted by human convention. We could construe it differently. So there is no objective world, at least we cannot apprehend it as an objective world. And there is no truth, because things are true by convention. '. . . constructionism doesn't try to rule on what is or is not fundamentally real. Whatever is, simply is. However, the moment we begin to articulate what there is—what is truly or objectively the case— we enter a world of discourse—and thus a tradition, a way of life, and a set of value preferences. Even to ask whether there is a real world "out there" is already to presume the Western metaphysics of dualism . . .' (Gergen, 1999, p. 222) Consequently, meaning is, according to Gergen, continuously negotiable.

What did we observe so far? In our knowledge we do not apprehend an objective world and in our language we don't represent what truly is the case. Further, there is no mental state located in the individual mind where the external world is re-presented either. Although our vocabulary seems to suggest a psychological mental realm, there is not such an interior world. How then to understand human discourse? Human discourse is a performative act in the inter-human encounter, and this performance is essentially *relational*. So utterances like *I love you* are understood from a *performative* perspective. When we use these words, we are performing an action within a relationship. 'Even statements of fact . . . are performances in a social group . . .' (Gergen, 1999, p. 132)

So Gergen maintains three important principles: (1) psychological discourse is performative and (2) performative actions are always relationally embedded.

> . . . treating psychological discourse as performative and embedding performances within relationships, we are now positioned to see the entire vocabulary of the mind as constituted by and within relationship. There is no creation of an independent mind through social relationships, as in the earlier accounts. We don't have to worry about how the social world gains entry into the subjective world of the individual. Rather, from the present standpoint there is no independent territory called "mind" that demands attention. There is action, and action is constituted within and gains its intelligibility through relationship. (Gergen, 1999, p. 133)

And (3) the whole phenomenal world receives its basic structure from convention. The understanding of ourselves and of the world is a social artifact, a product of historically and culturally situated interchanges among people.' (Gergen, 1994, p. 49) Meaning and truth arise in the context of ongoing relationships. They result from the "human coordination of action" and are dependent upon the "vicissitudes of social process" (Gergen, 1994, p. 51) So human discourse is not an act in which we accomplish a correlation between minds and states-of-affairs or processes, it rather is that very act of performing relationships.

Truth claims are not about referential worlds or interior impulses, they rather inhere in the pragmatics of human action. 'The value of psychological discourse lies not in its capacity to reflect truth but in its capacity to carry out relationships.' (Gergen, 1994, p. 71) The point is how do truthclaims '. . . function, in which rituals are they essential, what activities are facilitated and what impeded, who is harmed and who gains by such claims?' (Gergen, 1994, p. 53) Criteria for truth and meaning depend on patterns of cultural life.

Perhaps one hears some critcism in my analysis of Gergen's theoretical framework. Indeed, I do think that constructionism pushes some principles too far. Let me mention two main points. (1) Human discourse presupposes cognitive capacities of a human mind and a link between these human faculties and the ontological realm. (2) Human discourse is not simply a matter of convention and construction. It is as much a matter of acquiring rights and responsibilities.

Conventions or Rights and Responsibilities?

Is human discourse ultimately a matter of convention? Let us for a moment focus on those speech acts which seem to imply some sort of social convention. Gergen uses the example of a greeting ceremony. The act of greeting receives meaning from a joint action (Gergen, 1999, p. 146). There is no meaning in the heads of the individuals and there is no causal link between my handshake and your re-action; it is rather a relation of convention. 'If you smile and greet me warmly, your actions have no necessary effect on my behaviour. However, by dint of custom, I will return the greeting . . .' (Gergen, 1993, p. 234) So under certain cultural and historical conditions, a specific act is *conventionally followed* by expressions of positive regard. Hence meaning is located in the way in which *we go on together*, it is an *emergent property of coordinated action.* (Gergen, 1999, p. 145)

Is human discourse indeed such a cultural or social ritual? Some speech acts, as Searle has pointed out, presuppose *human institutions.* They are dependent upon rules, conventions, social practices. It is only given the institution of marriage that certain forms of behaviour constitute Mr. Smith marrying Miss Jones. By means of the utterance "guilty", someone may be send to prison. There is, indeed, no causal or ontological connection between someone's uttering "guilty" and someone else's going to prison. It depends on rules that apply, and the acceptance of these rules by the relevant parties involved. Indeed, speech acts, as a way of human beings interacting with each other, cannot be understood in a model of exerting causal influence over someone. But should we then on the basis of "rules" and "social practice" jump to notions like convention and construction? According to Wolterstorff, these speech acts present us with another, profoundly different, phenomenon: that of acquiring rights and responsibilities and of doing so in accord with, or in violation of, obligations.' (Wolterstorff, 1995, p. 93) The relevant issue in terms of rules is not that they could have been otherwise, on the contrary, the decisive point is whether or not I take *responsibility for their holding* (Alston, p. 43) What is at stake is not the putative origin of these rules in social convention, but the *normative stance* we take in human discourse. Proper discourse is embedded in normative conditions. Of course we might learn these conditions in social practice. Nonetheless, the appropriate thing is to act responsibly. That's what we learned. As Wolterstorff says: 'To institute an arrangement for the performance of speech actions is to institute a way of acquiring rights and responsibilities.' (Wolterstorff, p. 84)

Gergen elaborates the idea of a social practice in terms of a convention, and further in terms of choice and construction. Meaning, so he says, is continuously negotiable and the meaning of a specific sentence borders on the infinite (Gergen, 1999, p. 236). Some philosophers of language, on the other hand, have argued that the idea of convention is not really appropriate in these matters. According to Russell and Alston, conscious decisions and deliberately adopted conventions have very little part to play in the meaning of language. Alston: '. . . semantic change seems to be largely an unconscious affair, a matter of habits getting established without anyone or any group trying to establish them.' (Alston, p. 57). The term "language game" emphasizes the fact that the participants in a discourse conform themselves to specific rules. When I participate in a game, let's say tennis, then I observe specific rules. These rules count and I take responsibility for their holding (Alston, p. 43). So the social and institutional dimension of human discourse certainly has a *normative* import. When the jury uses the word "guilty" in court, it could have the effect that someone else is sent to prison. Why? Because normative conditions have been attached to that utterance. The jury is not expressing her inner self, but takes up a normative stance in the public domain. Indeed, contexts matter. Suppose I utter the word "fire". The illocutionary force of that utterance is situation-specific: when my house is on fire, it hopefully will activate the fire-department. But in case I am the commander of an army, the soldiers will understand that they have to fire their guns. Hence, I would say that the participants in human discourse accept certain rules and act accordingly. Speech acts are indeed embedded in a system of habits. That system implies rules which regulate our social behaviour. When we participate in human discourse, we accept our responsibility for some rules which are implied in that specific type of discourse. If, for example, we are promising without intending or asserting without believing, and we do so systematically, we undermine the system. In the long run, our act of "promising" will be meaningless.

Gergen, however, explains the social practice in a different way. 'We continue to appreciate the multiple constructions that are possible in a given situation, the incapacity of the referent to determine the choice of construction, the principled undecidability of meaning in any given situation, and the power of linguistic conventions to compel our descriptions and understandings.' (Gergen, 1999, p. 42) This quotation seems to suggest that the meaning in a specific act of discourse is limitless. I would like to question that thesis. First, the referent of a term limits our choice of construction. I will turn to that issue in the next section. Secondly, the meaning of a sentence in a given situation is partly limited by the intention of the author *as expressed in that sentence*.

Language and Metaphysical Realism in Human Discourse

In Gergen's analysis, human discourse is interpreted mainly as a *per-locutionary* act. I would like to present another aspect of human discourse: the *illocutionary* act. According to Searle and Austin, these illocutionary acts have to be distinguished from the utterance as such and from perlocutionary acts. This illucutionary dimension is an essential constituent of human discourse. As a matter of fact, speaker and hearer exchange noetic or propositional content (the illocutionary force of a sentence) and I think that this exchange is the very heart of speech and communication. Apparently human beings are designed in such a way that they can entertain meaning and propositional content before and after the discourse event; while, during the act of discourse, that content is transferred from the speaker to the listener. Yet, if illocutionary actions are neither identical with the utterance of a sentence, nor with their perlocutionary effect, what then are they like? If thoughts, wishes, promises, commands and the like, are neither identical with utterances, nor with inscriptions or brainprocesses, how should we understand them? Are mental representation and social construction the only alternatives?

According to *metaphysical realism*, the noetic content is neither an idea in the mind, nor a physical reality. They are what Frege once called *ideal objects*. They can be identified and reidentified by different individuals at different times as being one and the same. In modern analytical philosophy, they are labeled as abstract entities: multiply exemplifiable objects, like properties, propositions, actions, relations, numbers (Immink, 1987, p. 40). Properties and the like are neither mere words nor utterances, nor mental states or thoughts, but objects *sui generis*. These entities exist in their own right and must be distinguished from concrete things like trees, human beings, and the like. But, at the same time, these abstract entities can be apprehended by human beings. Here the metaphysical assumption is that what we entertain, when we think, are abstract entities. And these abstract entities have being independently of the human mind. The mind may discover them, but cannot create them. So metaphysical realism holds that the mind conforms to reality and that the reality even of properties is independent of the human mind. The idea that properties are founded in linguistic activities or that they are merely mental is rejected: properties are not mind-made. At this point I cannot go in further detail now, but it may be clear that realism offers an alternative to the empiricist tradition of mental representation. Philosophers like Frege, Russell, Carnap and many modern analytical philosophers like Alston, Chisholm, Plantinga, Wolterstorff and many others reason along these lines (Plantinga, 1974 and 1993; Chisholm, 1977; Wolterstorff, 1995).

How do these philosophers understand truth? The truth of a sentence is the *propositional content of the illocutionary act*. Hence a proposition is true, if and only if it obtains, and false if and only if it does not obtain. (Chisholm, p. 88) Consequently, language is not understood as a picture of reality, but the proposition expressed by a sentence is true or false. Consider the simple subject predicate uttering "Tom is ill". That sentence expresses a proposition, and the proposition predicates a property of a certain subject, namely the property of being ill. So the proposition singles out a given subject and says something about it: that he is ill. As a result the proposition is true or false: true if the subject it is about has the property it predicates of that subject, false otherwise (Plantinga, 1993, p. 117). Consequenlty, truth is not dependent upon our linguistic behavior as such.

So far this is my argument: (1) the *illocutionary force of speech* is a constitutive mark of human communication, and (2) the content of the illocutionary act is *noetic* or *propositional*. Once we express it, both the speaker and the addressee, when they are in the appropriate circumstances, do conceive or apprehend the propositional content. Hence we do communicate thoughts and feelings and the like; we can understand and transmit them. That is, in discourse I do not grasp the depth of your soul, but I understand your intention, or feeling, or thought as-it-is-expressed in that utterance (be it linguistic or other). There is a third point: (3) since discourse is about something, we make a link with reality. As Ricoeur observed, '. . . discourse implies the possibility of distinguishing between *what* is said by the sentence as a whole and by the words which compose it on the one hand, and *that about which* something is said on the other. To speak is to say something about something . . .' (Ricoeur, 1981, p. 167). Hence illocutionary acts have a *noetic* and *designative* content.

In my view the illocutionary dimension of human discourse presupposes that human beings have *noetic functions*. Whether we call it *mind* or not, these functions facilitate human discourse. One major question remains: how do these noetic faculties operate? Do they represent some sort of mental state or do they reflect an external realm?

The Enlightenment tradition—in it's Kantian form—presented a third option: reality shows a *phenomenal input*, but the human mind perceives it *under concepts*. The structuring is on our side, but we cannot do this without the appearance of reality. There is, so to speak, a mental receptivity and a mental activity. Reality produces a phenomenal input on us (we are appeared to in a certain way) and the human mind is capable of mental representations by means of an active conceptualization of these appearances. Receptivity consists in inputs produced by reality and the creativity consists in the conceptually interpretation of this sensory input. In its Kantian form conceptualization—and thus knowledge—is a structural feature of our human condition (Wolterstorff, 1997, p. 11). Appearances are always appearances in space and time; but space and time are not characteristics of reality. So human awareness is always an awareness structured by concepts and, further, our knowledge is always conceptual. The basic thesis in its Kantian form is that reality is structured by our human conceptual activity. Were there no persons engaging in conceptualization, there would be no structured world. We cannot say anything about the world-as-such. What we think of reality is already conceptualized reality. Objectivity and truth are products of human conceptualization. Well, in some respects Gergen follows this line of thinking. Only, conceptualization is substituted for convention: the phenomenal world is a conventional world.

Metaphysical realists understand it somewhat differently. They reject the idea of mental representation as an intermedium between object and concept. According to realism, objects have properties and properties are the kind of things our human mind grasps. Hence, properties '. . . are at one and the same time entities that we grasp and entities that external objects possess. They are links.' (Wolterstorff, 1997, p. 22) It is a capacity of the human mind to perform this kind of action: to conceive reality. Hence the human mind conforms to reality and the reality even of properties is independent of the human mind. What then about concepts? They are not construed as mental states, but also as links between mind and reality. A concept of, say Socrates, is a *set of properties* we *believe* that person to have (Immink, 1987, p. 179). A concept is a set of properties grasped by the human mind. Our concepts don't necessarily cover all the properties of Socrates: it is a subset of the properties he actually has. Accordingly, it makes sense to distinguish between the *concept* of Socrates and the *referent* of the term "Socrates". They are not identical. Which means that concepts do apply to reality. At this point, further inquiry is needed; but I cannot go in detail at this moment. I mention two aspects: (1) How to deal with the process of concept-formation and abstraction? Are there significant differences between empirical concepts, logical concepts, relational concepts and psychological concepts? (Geach, 1971). (2) Concepts also have a subjective aspect: can we say that one knows a concept when one knows how to use it properly in human discourse? I leave these questions now for what they are. I think the matter of realism is very important in theistic discourse. Realists in theology hold that in religious discourse we do refer to God and, further, our concepts indeed do apply to God (Immink, 1992, p. 133). Theologians who think along the lines of mental representation in a Kantian model, mostly use the category of *limitexperience* and argue that God is beyond the reach of our human noetic faculties (Tracy, 1996, p. 93).

Back to Gergen. According to his version of social constructionism we are not determined by "what there is". '. . . we must suppose that everything we have learned about our world and about ourselves—that gravity holds us to the earth, people cannot fly like birds, cancer kills, or that punishment deters bad behavior—could be otherwise. There is nothing about "what there is" that demands these particular accounts; we could use our language to construct alternative worlds in which there is no gravity or cancer, or in which persons and birds are equivalent, and punishment adored.' (Gergen, 1999, p. 47) According to Gergen, we are not locked within any convention of understanding.

From the perspective of metaphysical realism, however, there are a few restrictions. I agree that we can think of alternative situations. Many things could have been different. For many facts and rules we can construe alternatives. These alternatives could have been actual (Plantinga, 1974). But not so for what is *logically impossible*. Could it be that *2 + 2 = 4* be false? Or that *whatever is red is colored* be false? Could these propositions be otherwise or could we by convention make them otherwise? Of course we can *use* these propositions in different contexts, but that's not the issue. Further, some things are *ontologically impossible*. Could persons and birds be equivalent? I don't think so. There are a few characteristics which are *essential* to being a person. For example, *being-a-human-being, having consciousness, having the ability to act intentionaly*, and the like. Of course we can disagree on the properties of this set, but could it be that a living creature, lacking this set of properties, could be called a person? I don't think so. It is ontologically impossible. And further, the construction of an alternative world is also *morally* limited, because it could make mute the truth of violent facts.

Preaching as a Communicative Act

Preaching is a communicative act and as such an act of human discourse. From the perspective of communicative action preaching is, because of its complexity, a most interesting phenomenon. Let me mention three aspects.

1. The act of preaching is a face-to-face dialogue between the preacher and the congregation, it is an utterance in *a dialogue situation*. The discourser addresses an audience, and the addressees have the chance to respond. Maybe not in a direct way, for the congregation is mostly not responding during the act of praching. However, during the preparation and after the delivery of the sermon, there is an actual dialogue between the minister and the congregation. According to Henning Luther right from the beginning there is a relation with the addressee (Luther, 1983, p. 226). Preachers have the intention to interact with the experiences, questions and beliefs of the congregation. And Zerfaß observes that the act of preaching can be considered as an intervention (Zerfaß, 1992, p. 14). Recently Lucy Rose argued in favor of a conversational approach to preaching. The preacher and the congregation, so she argues, gather symbolically at a round table without head or foot. The language used by

the preacher is 'able to invite to the sermonic round table the experiences, thoughts, and wagers of all those present and even of those
absent' (Rose, p. 6).

2. In the act of preaching the preacher deals with a written text. I
do not mean the manuscript of the sermon, rather the biblical text.
It is what Ricoeur called the *distanciated text* situation. The preacher
intends to interpret the biblical text on behalf of the congregation.
So preacher and congregation are engaged in an act of reading and
interpretation. This act of discourse is logically distinct from the act
of discourse mentioned above, although it is performed in one and
the same act of preaching. It is important to note that theories which
deal with textual meaning shape our understanding of the preaching event. In the circles of historical criticism the meaning of the
text is tied up with the author's intention. Modern literary criticism,
however, advocates a somewhat different approach: the meaning of
a text is *in* a text. So the emphasis is not on the (historical author),
but on the literary work itself (Barton, p. 50). The text has a certain autonomy, and that implies that the meaning of a text is not
found in its origin, instead in its *performance*. So the meaning is not
found in the intention of the author; rather, in the interaction with
the hearer/reader. Most preachers feel the tension of these two positions. Preachers intend to do justice to the text of the bible, but they
also realize that preaching is a performative act. Besides, wasn't the
bible text right from the beginning a text to convince or to change
people? Craddock says, 'In biblical studies, the historical disciplines
have looked upon the texts as a *result* of certain events and interactions, while the preacher looks upon the text as the *cause*, the gen-
erator, of events and interactions.' (Craddock, p. 113) And Long
argues that preachers have to do justice to the literary forms of the
bible and he notices that 'the rhetorical dynamics . . . are likely to
take place in *front of* the texts, that is, *between* text and reader' (Long,
1989, p. 24). So the literary form is not simply an ornament. 'Texts
are not packages containing ideas; they are means of communication. When we ask ourselves what a text means, we are not searching for the *idea* of the text. We are trying to discover its total impact
upon a reader—and everything about a text works together to create that impact.' (Long, 1989, p. 12)

3. Preaching as an act of discourse also has a theological component: it is understood as an act of *divine discourse*. Preaching has an
apostolic dimension; it is an authoritative and effective word that
evokes faith and hope. In preaching, Christ's redemptive work is

presented and mediated to us. This divine discourse is re-constructed in different ways. On the one hand, there is a mildly sacramental view. 'Preaching is', according to Mary Catherine Hilkert, 'the art of naming grace' (Hilkert, p. 44). She unfolds preaching as sacramental imagination. 'The art of preaching . . . has to do with declaring the presence of the transcendent God within the limits of human experience.' (Hilkert, p. 193) On the other hand, in the Protestant tradition divine discourse is understood in a slightly different way. There is a sacramental remnant in the second Helvetic Confession: the preaching of the Word of God *is* the Word of God. This "is", however, is understood in a more *pneumatological* way. Effective preaching depends on the inward testimony of the Spirit and the faithful reception of the hearer. When preaching is faithful to Scripture, then, according to Calvin, it also borrows the status "Word of God". The phrase "Word of God" means that which is spoken by God; not simply in its first giving but in its every repetition. It does not somehow become weakened by repetition. The encounter between God and man, however, is not *caused* by the human act of discourse. The preacher is not captive of the divine presence. Especially in the Calvinistic tradition preaching is understood as a catechetical *instruction* of faith, rather than a sacramental encounter.

In both traditions, however, there is some sort of double-agency: in the act of human discourse God is performing his act of discourse. Human utterances are the medium of God's discourse. According to Wolterstorff it is very well possible to construct models for a double agency discourse, for example deputized discourse or appropriated discourse. (Wolterstorff, 1995, pp. 37–57)

These three factors demonstrate that the act of preaching is an act of human discourse ánd that, from a theological perspective, human discourse somehow mediates divine discourse. Likewise it turns out that preaching is a performative action: the dialogue between minister and congregation aims at a re-enactment of understanding, experience and action. Hence preaching definitely is a relational act, but should we construe it as an act of performing relationships? More precise, should we interpret this act as a social construct? In order to develop a better insight in the issues involved I will shortly explore some models of homiletical discourse. These models show that key notions from theories of human discourse—for example the function of the human mind in discourse or the reference to an 'outward realm'—do indeed mingle with the theological perspectives of the models.

Models of Homiletical Discourse

The expressive-symbolic model. There is a long tradition, modelled and reinforced by the Enlightenment tradition, that preaching has a predominently *expressive* character. The idea is that in a communicative act one is expressing his/her inner state. In preaching, so Schleiermacher observed, we re-present our religious consciousness. In order to avoid the negative pitfalls of Enlightenment rationality, Schleiermacher claimed that faith does not belong to the realm of reason, neither to that of morality. Faith, so he suggests, is a genuine and direct movement of our consciousness, it is a feeling of absolute dependence. Religion is an awareness and a taste of the Ultimate. In preaching we communicate our religious awareness in the form of a mental expression (*Mitteilung des zum Gedanken gewordenen frommen Selbstbewußtseins.* Schleiermacher, p. 108). According to Schleiermacher, we are urged to such an expression by the overwhelming experience of faith, and besides it is truly human to express oneself. So preaching is a communicative act in which we express what we have experienced and in doing so we re-present it for other people. In this model the preacher is considered to be a 'religious personality' (Niebergall) who represents faith-consciousness.

In recent homiletical models we can still find similar movements. In his *Homiletic. Moves and Structures* David Buttrick argues that preaching '. . . mediates some structured understanding in consciousness to a congregation.' (Buttrick, p. 320) He speaks of structures of consciousness and he holds that preaching presents and evokes fields of understanding. Although, according to Buttrick, preaching as self-expression places too much burden on self and on religious affections, he nonetheless holds that religious language is bound up with deep levels of human experience. Expressive models have been popular in periods when romanticism has been at odds with rationalism, as for example in conversionist and pietist traditions, and in the liberal tradition where religious language received a symbolic explanation (Buttrick, p. 178).

Kerygmatic models. In this model the personality of the preacher is deemphasized and the corebusiness of preaching has nothing to do with our human consciousness. So preaching is not expressive. According to Barth the key-image for the preacher is the herald: 'proclamation is human language in and through which God himself speaks, like a king through the mouth of his herald . . .' (Long,

1986, p. 25). Hence discourse reveals a dialectic structure: in the discourse of *human performance* (preaching) we meet the *divine action*. And the first and principal locus of divine performance (or: divine discourse) is the event of Jesus Christ. In the heyday of dialectical theology, Thurneysen vehemently argued that preaching as a communicative act is never the communication of human experiences, be they pious or not. Instead, preaching is about God, that is, about his salvific *acts in history*. The emphasis is on God's saving activity in the world, and not on our human religious experience. The herald model underlines that personal experience, or personal opinion, or colorful anecdote are not truly important in the act of preaching (Long, 1986, p. 27). Instead, the divine—human encounter in Jesus Christ has to be re-presented and actualized. Preaching has to serve the Word of God: that is Jesus Christ as the *act* of God. And for that reason preaching is the exposition of Scripture. Consequently, our subjective experience or subjective interpretation is deemphasized in the act of preaching. Preaching is rather *sacramental*: it is a human speech-act through which God's salvific action is re-presented. Not in the sense that we can domesticate God, but rather that God can make it such that the Christ event is performed in our midst. Preaching is a kerygmatic event, not an expression of human consciousness.

In the kerygmatic model the performative element is emphasized. As Bartow argues ' . . . if the divine self-disclosure in Jesus Christ is the primary locus of performative action for practical theology, it is imperative that we attend to that self-disclosure with all the varied means appropriate to it.' [. . .] 'The Word of God is face to face, oral-aural situated, and suasory discourse . . . it is not a dead letter. . . . It is an event of actio divina (God's selfperformance, if you will). It is in fact God's human speech.' (Bartow, p. 3) In this approach the gospel is primarily understood as an *event*, the event of the divine self-performance. And that self-performance is enacted again in preaching. In the *homo performans* we meet the divine action (Bartow, p. 60). Preachers are not referring to the imaginations of their hearts, they testify to the divine self-performance. So the language has not primarily an expressive function, rather a relational and reality-depicting character. What does it evoke? Not merely knowledge or emotion, rather human action brought about by the enactment of God's self-disclosure in preaching.

A comparable critique on our individual experience as normative for preaching is presented by the Yale school of theology. Hans Frei, in his postliberal reconstruction of narrative theology, rejects the presuppositions of the Enlightenment and Existentialist traditions by denying that the individual self and his or her experience constitute the criterion of meaning. According to Frei, the uniqueness and particularity of Jesus Christ cannot be reduced to categories of human experience. Claims about God are not identical with claims about the experience of human beings. When we observe Christ primarily in human experience, then we lose 'the unique, unsubstitutable identity of Jesus as the ascriptive subject of his own predicates' (Campbell, p. 142). So there is an "extratextual" reality that activates and regenerates us: God's saving presence in and for the world. That event is proclaimed in preaching.

It turns out that models of preaching to some extent mingle with theories of human discourse. Experiential-expressive and expressive-symbolic models exhibit some affinity with models in discourse which emphasize the representational and creative activity of the human mind. Kerygmatic models deemphasize the role of the human mind and highlight the *event* of the Christian religion: God's-salfivic-action-in-the-world. Here, the communication of faith is primarily a matter of divine performative action and not a matter of mental representation or interpretation.

Preaching as a speech-act aims among other things at change of lives, comfort, understanding, freedom, readiness to act responsibly and socially. Although homiletical models do describe this perlocutionary force and effect in different ways, it nonetheless is a common characteristic of the models we described. Expressive models intend to enliven the religious consciousness of the community; or, as Schleiermacher put it, to edify the hearer. Kerygmatic models intend to evoke the new reality of God's salvific presence: a presence that changes us and our world fundamentally. What differs, however, is the understanding and construction of the *illocutionary* force of speech-acts. It is precisely this *illocutionary force* that matters in the act of communication. For, in order to be effective, a speech-act must be understood. Grasping the meaning of an utterance is a prerequisite for a possible reaction or answer on the part of the addressee. I agree with Gergen that someone's speaking and another's response are not related in a causal way. Behavioristic theories fall short in their analysis of human communication; because they ignore

the rather complicated process that lies between speaking and responding. Gergen's social constructionism, on the other hand, also fails.
We already observed that Gergen, because of his critique of the idea
that meaning is a mental state or a psychological phenomenon, is
in favor of the view that meaning is a social construction. However,
does his solution do justice to the act of communication? I don't
think so. In a dialogical situation, the illocutionary force of an utterance—namely, that *what is said*—is (under certain conditions) understood by the addressee. When a person speaks intentionally, he/she
utters a well-formed sentence, while the recipient understands its
meaning in a *noetic* act. That act of comprehending and understanding pertains to the illocutionairy force of that utterance. We
note, however, that the noetic act as such is rather complex and
composed of many constituents. Let me give some of the items. In
the first place, the noetic act depends for example on my cognitive
faculties working properly in an appropriate environment (Plantinga,
1993, pp. 4–11). Secondly, the noetic act is a conventional act in
so far as speaker and addressee take for granted that some rules
apply in the given context. Since preaching is part of the worship
of the church, it takes for example for granted that the the ministry
of the Word of God brings about that God's salvific presence is
mediated. So, if we insist on the word "convention", it has, among
other things, to do with common background-beliefs and with a normative stance within a given context. Thirdly, we already observed
that the noetic act as a component of the act of communication precedes the perlocutionairy act, and that the noectic act pertains to
the illocutionairy force. However, the illocutionairy force is not identical with some mental state or with a state of consciousness. Rather,
it is the intention-as-expressed-in-the-illocution. In order to grasp the
speaker's intention in my noetic act, I do not investigate the speaker's
innermost self, I rather comprehend the illocutionairy force of the
sentence expressed by the speaker. And the speaker, if he wants to
communicate, must take into account which interpretations we are
likely to put on his words (Wolterstorff, 1995, p. 199). Illocutions
also have a propositional content. A speaker may refer to an object-
in-the-world, for example to a person, a tree, a color, a number,
and he may predicate properties of these objects. In my noetic act,
I understand the propositional content of the utterance and I may
also have an opinion about the truth-value of the propostion. I could

disagree with the speaker and say that the proposition is false, because the object referred to docs not have the property which the speaker ascribes to that object.

My conclusion is that Gergen underestimates the role of the illocutionary force of language in communication. Consequently, he cannot do justice to the role of the noetic act in human discourse. In human communication, this noetic act has to do with that-what-is-said; it is not necessarily tied up with states of consciousness. From this perspective, I think that the expressive-symbolic model of homiletical discourse is somewhat one-sided. When we consider the illocutionary force in terms of the *noetic* and *designative* content, discourse is not primarily an art of mental re-presentation. Religious language does not depict our internal life, but names the many facets of the divine—human encounter. In discourse we express the realm of faith, and that includes the realm of the divine—human encounter.

The Praxis of Preaching

Finally, I turn to the praxis of preaching. I use the material of five Easter Sunday sermons delivered in one of the middle-sized cities in The Netherlands in 1997. During that time I analysed the sermons from the perspective of the *Missio Dei* (Immink, 1999, pp. 116–135). I focussed mainly on the use of God-language in those sermons. How do preachers speak about God? Do they depict him as an acting God, as a centre of consciousness, or is "God" a symbol for a more inclusive reality or process? Further I dealt with the question of how God's-Presence-in-the-world really makes a difference in our human condition.

Now I will deal with the relation between the illocutionary and perlocutionary act in two of these sermons. My tentative hypothesis is that the performative act is shaped to a great extent by the illocutionary force of the sermon. Consequently, what the sermon evokes and creates depends to a great deal on the *noetic framework* of the congregation (including both speaker and hearer). I will confine myself to two sermons. In sermon I, the preacher links the Old Testament reading of the Exodus with the resurrection of Jesus. The preacher of sermon II just refers to the Gospel narrative. It turns out that both sermons intend to evoke hope and to create a new perspective. At first sight, what the ministers intend to achieve is not so different, although the way in which they proceed is quite divergent.

I will illustrate that by analysing their interpretation of Easter.

Sermon I. Jesus' resurrection is represented as an irresistible power of God. It is a dynamic power that brings life. The preacher depicts it as a force of vitality, a bud of life. Although she describes that power as a mystery, it is nonetheless associated with a set of ordinary images. These images express a certain contrast: night—morning; the darkness of the night—the light of the day; sleepless nights—the relief of the morning; the labour of birth—the life of a new child. The contrast, however, is a contrast of daily experience. We know what nights of worry are and how it feels to wait for the first bird that sings in the morning. The shift from night to early morning turns out to function as a continuous theme in the sermon. *'The night has been heavy, the darkness thicker than ever. But now the morning has come. The night is over, the morning dawns . . .'.* Ample treatment is given of how a child finds its way from the womb into the world through a narrow channel. This same power, she argues, moves the gospel of the resurrection. This life cannot be stopped, the stone is simply rolled away by an angel. The preacher hardly focusses on Jesus' resurrection as such. She structures her sermon in such a way that her images evoke a world in which the potency towards life is a key element. Easter is associated with the creative divine energy of which we already have some experience.

Sermon II. *'At Easter people search for Jesus . . .'.* The women search for a dead Jesus, for a precious memory, but finally they meet the risen Lord. Although the language of experience is rather dominant in the sermon, it does not diminish the concentration on Jesus as an active person, as a source of action. Jesus is characterized as a speaking person: He addresses Mary. The preacher: *'When someone calls your name, when someone knows you through and through—he cannot be dead and buried.'* However, the preacher also uses the word of Jesus "Do not hold on to me" to depict the otherness of Jesus. He is ahead of us, on the way to the other side. Distance and nearness play an important role in the sermon. He is our brother (because he died for us), but he is also ahead of us to the father. According to the preacher, there is also an awakening within us. We are witnesses of the same word and consequently something arises in us: a longing for God.

Both preachers refer to a new world which becomes manifest in the resurrection of Jesus Christ. In sermon (I) the preacher starts from images we are familiar with and tries hard to project a world where the power of resurrection fits. The preacher of sermon (II) does depict Jesus Christ as a *distinctive reality*, but nonetheless as a reality that is presented to us in our experience. However, it is not a movement from within, but towards us.

We observed that sermons intend to achieve something, they evoke change in the hearers. Preachers not simply tell a story or discuss a theme; they make demands upon the hearer (Long, 1989, p. 86). In a broad sense, these sermons concur in their performative force: they evoke hope and create a new perspective. However, on closer investigation, it turns out that the sort of action and trust which is evoked is rather dissimilar. The trust and comfort of sermon (I) are dynamic and powerful in accordance with the description of the dynamic power of life. *'There is a seed in you, a bud . . .'*, deep down in our soul is a hidden power and God reaches out to that soul and activates us. Further, the new perspective created by the Easter gospel is a life in freedom. There is, she says, an intimate connection between the gospel of the resurrection of Jesus and the "resurrection of women all over the world". It is impossible that one half of humanity would stay behind and she accuses those who use to gospel for the oppression of women. The performative force of sermon (II) is somewhat different. Since Jesus is ahead of us, and since he suffered with us and conquered death, we can trust God. Hence, fear not, we belong to God. The preacher intends to sustain. The language he is using expresses some sort of confidence and reassurance: coming home, longing for, being found, trust, fatherhood. . . . There is considerable emphasis on the fact that we live now in a new relation with God: (a) we experience a new world beyond the empirical world, (b) we found again a trustworthy father, (c) we experience a new longing for God.

Preaching as an act of human discourse is definitely a perlocutionary act. What it evokes or achieves on the part of the hearer, however, stands in relation to the illocutionary act. The illocutionary act can be understood as a *link* between the intention of the speaker and the noetic apprehension of the hearer. These sermons show that the intended perlocutionary act is related to the frame of reference of the preacher (and the community of faith). Is that frame of reference socially constructed? If we assume that preachers represent the community in which they speak, it is most likely that they share some basic beliefs. A succesful preacher will find words to adjust to the people in the pew. We might call this the social-cultural context (Engemann, 1993). Different contexts indeed call for different speech acts. Preachers act in communities of faith which disclose specific belief-systems. However, this does not necessarily imply that the belief-system as such is a social construction.

References

Alston, William P. (1964). *Philosophy of Language.* Englewood Cliffs: Prentice-Hall.
Barton, John (1996). *Reading the Old Testament. Method in Biblical Study.* London: Darton, Longman & Todd.
Bartow, Charles L. (1997). *God's Human Speech. A Practical Theology of Proclamation.* Grand Rapids: Eerdmans.
Buttrick, David (1987). *Homiletic. Moves and Structures.* London: SCM Press.
Campbell, Charles L. (1997). *Preaching Jesus. New directions for homiletics in Hans Frei's postliberal theology.* Grand Rapids: Eerdmans.
Chisholm, Roderick (1977). *Theory of Knowledge.* Englewood Cliffs: Prentice Hall.
Craddock, Fred B., (1985). *Preaching.* Nashville: Abingdon Press.
Engemann, Wilfried (1993) *Semiotische Homiletik. Prämissen—Analysen—Konsequenzen* [Homiletics: A Semiotic Approach. Principles—Analyses—Consequences]. Tübingen: Francke Verlag.
Geach, Peter (1971). *Mental Acts. Their Content and their Objects,* London: Routledge & Kegan Paul.
Gergen, Kenneth (1993). Belief as Relational Resource, *The International Journal for the Psychology of Religion,* 3 (4), 231–243.
—— (1994). *Realities and Relationships. Soundings in social construction,* Cambridge/London: Harvard University Press.
—— (1999). *An Invitation to Social Construction,* London/Thousand Oaks: Sage.
Hilkert, Mary Catherine (1997). *Naming Grace. Preaching and the Sacramental Imagination,* New York: Continuum.
Immink, F.G. (1987). *Divine Simplicity,* Kampen: Kok.
—— (1992). Theism and Christian Worship. In: Gijsbert van den Brink, Luco J. van den Brom, Marcel Sarot (eds.), *Christian Faith and Philosophical Theology* (pp. 116–136), Kampen: Kok.
—— (1999). Missio Dei in Preaching: God Language and Human Receptivity. In: Tsuneaki Kato (Ed.), *Preaching as God's Mission* (pp. 116–135). Tokyo: Kyo Bun Kwan.
Long, Thomas G. (1989). *The Witness of Preaching,* Louisville: John Knox Press.
—— (1989). *Preaching and the Literary Forms of the Bible.* Philadelphia: Fortress Press.
Luther, Henning (1983). Predigt als Handlung (Preaching as action). *Zeitschrift für Theologie und Kirche* (80), 223–243.
Plantinga, Alvin (1974). *The Nature of Necessity.* Oxford: Clarendon Press.
—— (1993). *Warrant and Proper Function.* New York/Oxford: Oxford University Press
Ricoeur, Paul (1981). *Hermeneutics and the Human Sciences.* Cambridge: Cambridge University Press.
Rose, Lucy Atkinson (1997). *Sharing the Word. Preaching the Roundtable Church.* Louisville: John Knox Press.
Schleiermacher, Friedrich (1993). *Kurze Darstellung des Theologischen Studiums zum Behuf einleitender Vorlesungen* [Brief Outline of the Study of Theology in function of Introductory Lectures]. (critical edition by Heinrich Scholz). Darmstadt: Wissenschaftliche Buchgesellschaft.
Schlenke, Dorothee (1999). *Geist und Gemeinschaft. Die systematische Bedeutung der Pneumatologie für Friedrich Schleiermachers Theorie der christlichen Frömmigkeit* [Spirit and Community.

The Meaning of Pneumatology in Schleiermacher's Theory of Christian piety].
    Berlin/New York: Walter de Gruyter.
Wolterstorff, Nicholas (1995). *Divine Discourse. Philosophical reflections on the claim that
    Gods speaks.* Cambridge: Cambridge University Press.
—— (1997). *Is it possible to talk about God?* unpublished paper.
Zerfaß, Rolf (1992). *Grundkurs Predigt. Textpredigt 2* [Homiletical Instruction: Textual
    Preaching 2]. Düsseldorf: Patmos Verlag.

SOCIAL CONSTRUCTIONISM AND RELIGIOUS EDUCATION: TOWARDS A NEW DIALOGUE

FRIEDRICH SCHWEITZER

1. *Introduction*

Ever since the publication of the now famous book by Peter Berger and Thomas Luckmann (Berger/Luckmann, 1971, first edition 1966), the idea of the "social construction of reality" has received at least some attention in the field of religious education. Yet to my knowledge, this attention has never been developed into a more focused concern with the core concepts of social constructionism. For religious education, the "classic" from this school of thinking now is the "Heretical Imperative" (Berger, 1979) and not the epistemological and methodological approach offered in the "Social Construction of Reality".

In terms of the family of approaches which focus on the construction of reality and which are described by Kenneth Gergen (1999, p. 60), it is certainly not his *social constructionism* which has been of prime influence in the field of religious education. Instead, the psychological *constructivism* in the tradition of Jean Piaget has played this leading role, especially in its application to religion by developmentalists like James Fowler (Fowler, 1981) and Fritz Oser (Oser/Gmünder, 1984). This is also true for my own work which, at least in some respects, is strongly influenced by constructivist ideas (Schweitzer, 1987, 1996, Fowler/Nipkow/Schweitzer, 1991, Schweitzer et al., 1995).

Yet with the more recent changes in society and culture which have been described as religious pluralization and as the transition to a multicultural and multireligious society, it has become obvious that religious education has to go beyond psychological models which do not take account of the cultural and historical or societal influences on learning, communication and development. As the processes of pluralization and individualization still seem to continue to exert a more and more powerful influence on the religious landscape, religious education must face up to the plurality (Nipkow, 1998) which now is as operative within religious communities as it is between different religions and worldviews—at the level of society or at the level even of the global culture to which theories of globalization now refer (Beck, 1997).

In this situation, religious educators like myself are looking for theoretical tools which may help them to identify the tasks and challenges of religious education in a multicultural and multireligious society. This will also be the main perspective for the present chapter: What may (Christian) religious education profit from including the perspective of social constructionism? Consequently, my aim in the following will not be to do justice to social constructionism in itself or in terms of social science discussions. Rather, my evaluations and discussions will all be related to religious education—for the sake of a new dialogue between social constructionism and religious education.

For practical reasons I will limit my considerations to the "*Invitation to Social Construction*" published by Gergen in 1999. And since this book does not include religion with the fields which are to be discussed, it seems necessary to start out with some clarifications on how I see social constructionism in relationship to religion and theology.

2. *Social Constructionism and Religion*

Given the general hesitancy among many traditional hard core (social) scientists to include anything religious in their work and to limit their interest in religion—at best—to what is seen as the neutral and objective study of religion, it may not be surprising that Gergen (1999) does not address the relationship between social constructionism and religion. The *Invitation* does not seem to include those working in the field of religion. Yet from my point of view, a different understanding of the relationship between social constructionism and religion is also possible. There are many parallels which may be seen between some of Gergens's core interests and the topics which have played an important role in theological discourse over the last two or three decades. It may be helpful to point out some of these parallels.

In the first place, I consider social constructionism's central concern with the construction of *meaning* a characteristic which makes this way of thinking a close neighbor of theology. Rather than just being interested in what commonly is called a hard fact, the focus of this approach is on what may also be seen as the object of theology: meaning as experienced and constructed by individuals or

communities. To be sure, this parallel between social constructionism and theology is not really developed in Gergen's *Invitation* in that
this book does not include the effort to clearly distinguish between
different types or levels within the social construction of meaning.
So again there is no special reference to, say, overarching meaning
systems etc. Still, the understanding of reality offered in this book,
clearly goes beyond all attempts of limiting reality or knowledge to
that which is empirical and measurable. In this sense, we may consider constructionism a neighbor of theology or religious education.

Next to this basic interest in the dependence of reality on different
perspectives and interpretations, social constructionism's interest, and
appreciation, of *tradition, narrative*, and *metaphor* must be mentioned
(Gergen, 1999, p. 50, p. 64, p. 68). These are topics which have
also played a major role in recent theological discussions including
religious education—among others in the context of so-called narrative theology (Metz, 1973, Wacker, 1977) and of Biblical interpretation, especially with reference to the parables in the New
Testament (Ricoeur/Jüngel, 1974, Weder, 1978, Noppen, 1988). It
seems fair to say that both, social constructionism as well as theology or religious education, pursue a similar interest, at least in this
respect. They advocate the need for a new appreciation of tradition,
narrative, and metaphor vis-a-vis the dominating influence of the
culture of science and of factual knowledge which may be put down
in propositional statements.

Another parallel between social constructionism and religious education or theology may be identified in the emphasis which is given
to the *relational character of the self* (Gergen, 1999, pp. 116ff.). This understanding clearly corresponds to the views of Christian anthropology
as developed, for example, by Wolfhart Pannenberg (1983). Since
this question deserves special attention, I will come back to this
understanding in a later section.

Other parallels which I just want to mention here without taking
them up in more detail, might be found in the role of *community* or
in the value which is attributed to *dialogue* (Gergen 1999, pp. 33ff.,
pp. 142ff.)—again topics of theological or religious interest (Buber, 1973,
Hauerwas, 1981). What I have not mentioned so far, is the understanding of *truth* which Gergen maintains throughout his book. While
some of his claims concerning the relationship between truth and
tradition again sound close to theology, the general tendency to (completely?) subordinate truth to the social, will not be acceptable to

many theologians. In order to explore this issue more closely at least for the context of religious education, I will not take it up in this section but will also come back to it at a later point.

Summarizing these initial observations, it seems important to repeat that it is surprising that all these parallels between social constructionism and theology or religious education so far have not lead to any cooperation or even conversation between these fields. So in this sense, I consider the present volume an important beginning of a dialogue which may enrich practical theology no less than social constructionism.

3. *The Social and Cultural Basis of the Self*

As stated in the beginning of this paper, the contemporary situation which is often referred to as multicultural and multireligious society, has created a new need for religious education to go beyond psychological considerations and to ask about the social and cultural basis of the self which is to be supported in its development. This need arises from two problems related to the accounts of the self on which religious education has come to base its work as far as social scientific theories are concerned. The first problem is related to the *descriptive account* mostly of psychological theories which treat the social and cultural environment in an abstract manner. Even if I do not agree with Gergen's critical view that constructivism limits its understanding to the individual mind—a view which does not take account of the relationship between "organism" and "environment" which is constitutive for all Piagetian theories—constructivist theories have indeed, at least for the most part, failed to offer a substantial understanding of contemporary culture. Interestingly enough, where constructivists like for example Robert Kegan (1994) have tried to do so, constructivism has turned out to be quite helpful and enlightening in social and cultural analysis. Yet it is easy to see that social constructionism includes a clear thrust towards social and cultural analysis from the beginning (although surprisingly little of this kind of analysis is actually contained in Gergen's *Invitation*).

The second problem with what has become almost the standard model of the self in the social sciences and in social theory, is the *normative understanding* maintained by influential theorists like Jürgen Habermas (1981). As I have critically discussed elsewhere in some more detail (Schweitzer, 1999), this model sees no ultimate place for religion once the self has reached true autonomy. In this view, religion may have to play a role within the early stages of the development of self or identity which, at these stages, are based on myths and on belonging to particular communities like a religious group or body, church or synagogue. Yet once the ideal of postconventional identity is achieved, all cultural, social, or religious roots which may not be universalized, have to become subordinate to the principle of ideal discourse and of universal norms. Consequently, in this view, religion cannot play any decisive role at this highest level of self or identity which is referred to as "postconventional".

Naturally, religious educators like myself (cf. Schweitzer, 2000) have been looking for alternative accounts of the self. New impulses have come from social theorists like Charles Taylor (1989) who is often considered a mild communitarian, or from Paul Ricoeur's (1992) account of the role of narrative in the formation of self, or from the feminist philosophy of Seyla Benhabib (1992) with her attempt of "situating the self". In many ways, social constructionism may be seen as another important source for developing more adequate and contextual understandings of the self—understandings which include social relationships, culture, and society not only for the early stages of the life cycle but also for their visions of maturity and completion.

I have already pointed out that the emphasis on the relational character of the self (Gergen, 1999, pp. 116ff.) may be seen as a parallel between social constructionism and religious education or theology (Pannenberg, 1983). Gergen's critique of individualistic understandings of the self could also be based on theological arguments pertaining to the relational view of the human being, for example, in the theology of creation (cf. Welker, 1995). Even more specifically, the appreciation of performative speech acts, of collective remembering, and of their constitutive meaning for the self may find full theological support (Jüngel, 1977, Metz, 1977).

It would be interesting to continue this discussion by focussing on what has been called the postmodern self—a topic which Gergen also has addressed in earlier publications. In this respect, one of the central questions to be addressed is how the unity of the self which traditionally is seen as a presupposition of healthy development and of successful identity formation, may be accounted for by social constructionism in terms of its strictly relational views. Yet the focus of the present volume is not the self. Rather, it is on religious communication to which we will turn now.

4. *Intercultural and Interreligious Communication and Learning*

How is social constructionism related to religious communication and learning in the context of intercultural and interreligious learning?

First of all, social constructionism is helpful in that it highlights the challenge of communicating accross the boundaries between different denominations and different religious communities. If meaning is intimately bound to communities and to their traditions, communication with others who do not belong to one's own community and who do not share one's own tradition, is a major challenge.

However, the close ties between meaning and social relationships which is emphasized so strongly by social constructionism, also have a flip side which may indicate how the challenge of interreligious communication can be approached in religious education. Taking social constructionism as our starting point we may assume that building up relationships between different religious groups and between their individual members, creating a social context in which they will be able to be together and to work together, is the decisive presupposition for interreligious dialogue. In other words, social constructionism cautions us not to confine our educational approaches only to content or to norms and values which are to be taught. Rather, it makes us think of what relationships may be created in order to have a social basis for interreligious communication and learning.

Yet there also are possible objections. In some sense, this kind of approach seems to be exactly what many people in (German) education who advocate religious education classes with students from different denominational and religious backgrounds rather than with the traditional denominational groups, actually have in mind: Bring the students from different cultural and religious backgrounds together and have them work and study together in the same classroom. And it is expected that the shared social context which is thus created, will serve as an effective basis for intercultural and interreligious communication and that it also will work towards tolerance, mutual respect, and even appreciation of the other (for this discussion see Lott, 1992). Yet while it is certainly true that children and adolescents should be in contact with others who come from a different cultural and religious background in order to make being together and living together in one and the same society possible, the assumption that social contact will by itself lead to intercultural and interreligious understanding, may not be very realistic.

Especially with interreligious communication, more intentionally thematic approaches which go beyond being together, are necessary. Among others, this is due to the role of religion in contemporary western societies. As has been observed by many sociologists of culture and religion, religion has become not only pluralized—an effect which is the starting point for thinking about the need for interreligious communication—but religion has also become individualized and privatized. In this context, privatization means that religion is left to the discretion of each individual person and that it is often excluded from communication in public. And the public from which religion is removed, may even be extended to the conversations within the family so that religious topics become more and more related only to inner feelings and to conversations of the individual person exclusively with himself or herself.

In this kind of situation, building up social relationships between children and adolescents will obviously not automatically do the job of effectively establishing interreligious communication. Consequently, we have to again ask what social constructionism may contribute to the task of interreligious learning. With this question in mind, let us turn to Gergen's considerations of dialogue.

It is interesting for religious education to see how seriously the problem of "alterity" is taken by social constructionism: "all world constructing relations create a devalued exterior—a realm that is *not us*, not what we believe, not true, not good". So the major challenge is identified as proceeding "in such a way that ever emerging conflict does not yield aggression, oppression, or genocide" (Gergen, 1999, pp. 148f.). This is where Gergen sees the place of dialogue—not in the sense of an abstract discourse ethics but of what he calls "*transformative dialogue*".

This kind of dialogue is described in ways which could be applied immediately to interreligious learning, thus defining this type of learning as a sensitive encounter between two or more people from different backgrounds yet with a general openness for the other. The following elements which I have taken from Gergen (1999, pp. 158ff.) and which I render in my own paraphrase, may also characterize successful interreligious communication:

– story telling as a way of expressing oneself which is easy to understand
– active affirmation of the other in the process of listening

– "coordinating discourse" which carefully works towards comprehending each other
– self-reflexivity as openness for questioning one's own position
– finding/creating new views together.

No doubt—such principles are helpful in any kind of constructive
dialogue. It is no surprise that most of these principles have also
found their place in psychological models of successful conversation,
of course with less emphasis on epistemology than in social constructionism. Nevertheless, for religious education in a multireligious
situation—and specifically in working with children and adolescents—
two important aspects are missing in this model of dialogue. The
first has to do with *childhood* or *adolescence*: Is it enough to speak about
dialogue or do we need special references to children or adolescents?
The second aspect concerns the question of *truth* about which more
needs to be said in the context of religious communication than
social constructionism might be willing to offer. In the remainder of
this chapter I will focus on these two questions.

5. *Education and the Child: Constructionism versus Constructivism?*

As mentioned before, Gergen sees strong tensions between his social
constructionism and the *constructivist* approaches which are closer to the
psychology of human development. I do not want to examine here
the adequacy of his objections to constructivism which he considers
as limited to the individual and to the individual mind (Gergen,
1999, p. 237)—a view which, as stated before, could certainly be
challenged. Yet rather than focussing on the conflict between the
different camps of interpreters of true construction, I am interested
in the question if social constructionism is sufficient for religious education and, conversely, what religious education would lose if it was
to side only with social constructionism.

   One of my main interests in constructivism (Schweitzer, 1987,
1992) has always been its strength in pointing out the differences
between adults and children. Especially the early Piaget of the 1920s
and 1930s made the point that children have their own ways of
making sense of the world and that the worst thing psychology can
do is to render the logic of children's thinking in terms of immatu-
rity, deficiency, or even deviation. Actually, his critique of this kind
of psychology and of its looking down upon children's psychological
capacities was the decisive reason for Piaget to break away from the

psychology in which he had been trained (Piaget, 1976). Consequently, he had to search for a new way of understanding children's world-views—a way which would take their particular perspective seriously.

It is unfortunate that, in part, Piaget himself and, in any case, many of his followers later adopted the idea of developmental "progress" to such a degree that the early Piaget's interest in faithfully rendering the perspective of the child (a psychology "from below"), has almost been lost. Yet making good educational use of constructivism does not mean limiting oneself to the individual mind at the expense of social interaction, and neither does it mean to only hurry the child towards ever higher stages of development.

Maybe even more for religious education than for education in general, it is important to insist that the weight and dignity of the religious tradition is not emphasized in such a way that there is no more space for the children's ways of working with this tradition by changing it and by assimilating it to their own worldviews, to their own needs, hopes, and longings. Within Christian education, revelation has often been understood to imply that the knowledge to be passed on to the next generation may never be changed, especially not by education or by undue adaptation to the child. There is a long history of religious education trying to work against such objectivist views of religious transmission (cf. Schweitzer, 1992). What does this mean for the relationship between constructionism, education, and the child?

Recently, research on childhood has moved into the direction of social constructionism (cf. Honig et al. 1999). Childhood itself is then seen as a social construction, not as a psychological or even biological state. So one might object to my understanding of constructivism that it naively holds on to a dated view of children. Yet as an educator I am still hesitant to give up insisting on the children's right of having their own ways of making sense of the world. While we certainly have to be critical of ourselves by asking what—distorting or oppressive—constructions of the child we may be producing or at least be working with, this kind of self-criticism may itself become contradictory. And this is certainly the case if it is to mean that we can just forget about the special character of children from the beginning.

As opposed to constructivism, Gergen's *Invitation* does not make reference to different ages or stages in the human life cycle. The ideas, however, which Gergen sets forth in the short section on education (Gergen, 1999, pp. 179ff.) are quite in line with what we need in religious education: collaborative classrooms and the development of "multiple voices, forms of expression, or ways of putting things" (ibid., p. 183). But in my understanding, such an approach to religious education might be greatly strengthened by including the insights of constructivism. Moreover, the insights of constructivism might be needed if we are to support the education Gergen speaks for.

Why do we need constructivism? Educationally, Gergen's statement that "there is no truth beyond community" (ibid., p. 180), is highly ambivalent. It *may* mean that education must be aware of the social and communal nature of all learning and that teachers should strive for building up social and communal structures in all learning settings by being involved, consciously and intentionally, in processes of "coconstituting" (Gergen, 1999, p. 160). Probably, this is what Gergen actually has in mind. Yet his statement might also be taken to imply that all (religious) knowledge and insight is intrinsically bound to an existing (religious) community and that the acquisition of such knowledge and insight is only possible by becoming socialized (or catechized) into this community. In religious education, this understanding is not only an abstract possibility. Under the impression of George Lindbeck's (1984) cultural linguistic interpretation of theology and Christian faith, religious educators have actually tended towards a neo-catechetical approach to religious education (for a critical appraisal see Lachmann, 1998). The result of this tendency is a type of religious education which breaks with the basic understanding of modern religious education by not longer accepting the central role of the learning person as an active subject—a subject which may never be turned into a passive object of inculcation.

My point is not that I consider Gergen himself as prone to neo-catechetical approaches. Yet his theory of social constructionism may not offer the grounds for religious education to defend itself against such a turn. In this regard, again constructivism may have to make an indispensable contribution and should not be replaced by social constructionism. In my own understanding, there is no need to choose: Why should it not be possible to combine both approaches—a social constructionism which is open for the insights of constructivism, and a constructivism which is more intentional in respect of society and culture? For religious education in any case, this kind of combination seems more promising than turning either towards social constructionism or towards constructivism in order to make it its sole ally.

6. *The Social Nature of Truth and the True Nature of the Social—Why "Co-constituting" is Necessary but not Sufficient for Religious Communication*

It is a well-known characteristic of religions that they include claims to truth—often to absolute truth. In our contemporary situation, such claims raise many questions, among others concerning the potentially totalitarian consequences which may result from absolute truth claims, and concerning the possibly conflictual relationship between competing truth claims maintained by different religions or worldviews. Consequently, the question of truth is of special importance for religious education as well as for interreligious communication in a multireligious society. How does social constructionism approach this issue, and how may social constructionism's views be put to use by a religious education which is concerned about truth?

Again, as stated in the first section of this chapter, there are interesting parallels between theology and social constructionism in this respect. Gergen's attempt to widen our understanding of truth beyond the reference to "facts" which is often connected to science, clearly is in line with the interpretive work of theology. It is one of the central concerns of contemporary theological work to show how a narrow modern notion of truth and rationality in science has not much to do with the Biblical understanding of truth. Often it is suggested (cf. Meyer, 1991) to translate the Biblical references to truth in a different way—not with "truth" but rather with "faithfulness", "trustworthiness", "loyalty", etc. In any case, the Biblical or theological terms are not on the same level with the scientific notion of truth. Nor can they be taken to mean a more naive or preliminary understanding of truth (that which has not yet been explained, etc.). Rather, they mean a *different kind* of truth altogether in that they refer, at the cosmic level, to an understanding of the whole or, at the existential level, to the meaning of personal life (Härle, 1995). The religious question is not how we may give a most accurate account of facts in the sense of science but how we may live and what our lives may be entrusted to.

Without going into the details here of a theological understanding of truth we may say that an adequate understanding of truth requires a notion of truth which does justice to its various uses, meanings, and contextual references. But although Gergen is interested in widening the understanding of truth, there is not much effort to address different conceptual meanings of truth in Gergen's *Invitation*.

But this is not a general shortcoming of social constructionism. The work of Berger and Luckmann (1971) indicates that social constructionism can be quite aware of the different kinds of truth claims as well as of the different functions such claims have to play in individual and social life. Most notably, their concept of "symbolic universes" has been attractive to many students of religion. Social constructionism as described in Gergen's *Invitation*, needs to be broadened in order to include a more sophisticated understanding of truth and meaning, especially if it is to be of interest to religious education.

Another point concerns the relationship between the foundational role of social relationships on the one hand and of truth and tradition on the other. In Gergen's *Invitation*, there seems to be some ambivalence. One the one hand, he maintains that "meaning is an *emergent property of coordinated action*" (p. 145); on the other hand, he states that, "most frequently", coordination is "specified within a tradition" (p. 147). The first statement can be taken to mean that social relationships are the absolute basis of all meaning and truth, the second statement may imply a circular interplay between social relationships and tradition. The first understanding would not be acceptable to Christian theology in that it seems to imply a temporal or even ontological priority of social relationships. The second understanding which sees a strong connection between meaning, truth, and social relationships, comes closer to a theological understanding of religious community.

While it makes sense theologically that meaning is never without social relationships, theology also must hold on to the possibility that meaning *creates* community and *sponsors* social relationships. For theology, the church is formed through social relationships but it also is *creatura verbi*—a creation of the Word. This emphasis of the creative power of meaning and truth does not necessarily contradict social constructionism. Yet it includes an important objection to all foundationalist understandings of social relationships. Possibly, it may be taken as an incentive for social constructionism to include a more serious reference to the circular and reciprocal interplay between social relationships and truth or tradition.

7. Conclusion

At the end of this chapter, it seems helpful to summarize some of the above considerations on the relationship between social constructionism and religious education. Throughout my discussions of this approach, important parallels between social constructionism and religious education or theology could be discovered. This speaks for a new dialogue between these fields which may have more in common than has been known up to now. Social constructionism may be of help for religious education in the context of multicultural and multireligious society and of the interreligious communication which is needed in this situation. At the same time, the dialogue with religious education could challenge social constructionism to be more explicit about religion. This would include the further refinement of its notions of truth, meaning, narrative, etc.

Finally, as important as social constructionism may be—or become—for religious education, it should never be seen as its sole ally or social scientific basis. As we have seen from the example of constructivism, religious education may not just simply choose one approach over the other. Rather, religious education must remain a multi-perspective endeavor.

References

Beck, U. (1997). *Was ist Globalisierung? Irrtümer des Globalismus—Antworten auf Globalisierung* [What is Globalization? Errors of Globalism—Responses to Globalization]. Frankfurt/M.: Suhrkamp.

Benhabib, S. (1992). *Situating the Self: Gender, Community and Postmodernism in Contemporary Ethics.* Cambridge: Polity Pr.

Berger, P.L. (1979). *The Heretical Imperative: Contemporary Possibilities of Religious Affirmation.* Garden City: Doubleday.

Berger, P.L./Luckmann, T. (1971). *The Social Construction of Reality: A Treatise in the Sociology of Knowledge.* Harmondsworth: Penguin.

Buber, M. (1973). *Das dialogische Prinzip* [The Dialogical Principle]. Heidelberg: Lambert Schneider.

Fowler, J.W. (1981). *Stages of Faith: The Psychology of Human Development and the Quest for Meaning.* San Francisco: Harper & Row.

Fowler, J.W./Nipkow, K.E./Schweitzer, F. (Eds.) (1991). *Stages of Faith and Religious Development: Implications for Church, Education, and Society.* New York: Crossroad.

Gergen, K.J. (1999). *An Invitation to Social Construction.* London/Thousand Oaks/Delhi: Sage.

Habermas, J. (1981). *Theorie des kommunikativen Handelns* [Theory of Communicative Action]. Frankfurt/M.: Suhrkamp.

Härle, W. (1995). *Dogmatik* [Dogmatics]. Berlin/New York: W. de Gruyter.

Hauerwas, S. (1981). *A Community of Character: Toward a Constructive Christian Social Ethic*. Notre Dame: Univ. of Notre Dame.

Honig, M.-S., Lange, A. & Leu, H.R. (Eds.) (1999). *Aus der Perspektive von Kindern? Zur Methodologie der Kindheitsforschung* [From the Perspective of Children? On the Methodology of Research on Childhood]. Weinheim: Juventa.

Jüngel, E. (1977). *Gott als Geheimnis der Welt. Zur Begründung der Theologie des Gekreuzigten im Streit zwischen Theismus und Atheismus* [God as the Secret of the World. Foundations of the Theology of the Crucified in the Debate Between Theism and Atheism]. Tübingen: Mohr.

Kegan, R. (1994). *In Over Our Heads: The Mental Demands of Modern Life*. Cambridge/London: Harvard Univ.

Lachmann, R. (1998). Systematische Theologie auf dem religionspädagogischen Prüfstand [Evaluating Systematic Theology from the Perspective of Religious Education]. In: Ritter, W. & Rothgangel, M. (Eds.). *Religionspädagogik und Theologie. Enzyklopädische Aspekte* [Religious Education and Theology. Encyclopedic Aspects] (pp. 36–49). Stuttgart: Kohlhammer.

Lott, J. (Ed.) (1992). *Religion—warum und wozu in der Schule* [Religion—Why and for What Aim in School]. Weinheim: Deutscher Studien Verlag.

Lindbeck, G.A. (1984). *The Nature of Doctrine: Religion and Theology in a Post-Liberal Age*. Philadelphia: Westminster.

Metz, J.B. (1973). Kleine Apologie des Erzählens [In Defense of Story Telling]. *Concilium* 9, 334–341.

—— (1977). *Glaube in Geschichte und Gesellschaft. Studien zu einer praktischen Fundamentaltheologie* [Faith in History and Society. Studies towards a Practical Fundamental Theology]. Mainz: M. Grünewald.

Meyer, I. (1991). Wahrheit/Gewißheit—Aus biblisch-theologischer Sicht [Truth/Certainty. From a Biblical-Theological Point of View]. In: P. Eicher (Ed.). *Neues Handbuch theologischer Grundbegriffe* [New Handbook of Basic Theological Terms]. *(Vol. 5)* (pp. 241–249). München: Kösel.

Nipkow, K.E. (1998). *Bildung in einer pluralen Welt* [Education in a Plural World]. *(Vol. 2): Religionspädagogik im Pluralismus* [Religious Education and Pluralism]. Gütersloh: Gütersloher.

Noppen, J.-P. van (1988). *Erinnern, um Neues zu sagen. Die Bedeutung der Metapher für die religiöse Sprache* [Remembering for the Sake of the New. The Meaning of Metaphor for Religious Language]. Frankfurt/M.: Athenäum.

Oser, F. & Gmünder, P. (1984). *Der Mensch—Stufen seiner religiösen Entwicklung. Ein strukturgenetischer Ansatz* [The Human Being—Stages of Religious Development. A Cognitive-Developmental Approach]. Zürich: Benziger.

Pannenberg, W. (1983). *Anthropologie in theologischer Perspektive* [Anthropology in Theological Perspective]. Göttingen: Vandenhoeck & Ruprecht.

Piaget, J. (1976). Autobiographie [Autobiography]. In: *Jean Piaget—Werk und Wirkung* [Jean Piaget—His Works and Their Effects] (pp. 15–59). München: Kindler.

Ricoeur, P. (1992). *Oneself as Another*. Chicago: Univ. of Chicago.

Ricoeur, P. & Jüngel, E. (1974). *Metapher. Zur Hermeneutik religiöser Sprache* [Metaphor. On the Hermeneutics of Religious Language]. (Evangelische Theologie—Sonderheft). München: Kaiser.

Schweitzer, F. (1987). *Lebensgeschichte und Religion. Religiöse Entwicklung und Erziehung im Kindes- und Jugendalter* [Life History and Religion. Religious Development and Education in Childhood and Adolescence]. München: Kaiser.

—— (1992). *Die Religion des Kindes. Zur Problemgeschichte einer religionspädagogischen Grundfrage* [The Religion of the Child. Tracing the History of a Foundational Problem of Religious Education]. Gütersloh: Gütersloher.

—— (1996). *Die Suche nach eigenem Glauben. Einführung in die Religionspädagogik des Jugendalters* [In Search of a Faith of One's Own. Introduction to Religious Education in Adolescence]. Gütersloh: Gütersloher.

—— (1999). Autonomie ohne Religion—Religion ohne Autonomie? Religiöse Autonomie in strukturgenetischer Sicht [Autonomy Without Religion—Religion Without Autonomy? Religious Autonomy in Cognitive-Developmental Perspective]. In: Althof, W., Baeriswyl, F. & Reich, H.H. (Eds.). *Autonomie und Entwicklung* [Autonomy and Development] (pp. 301–328). Freiburg: Universitätsverlag.

—— (2000). A Stronger Case for Religion: Perspectives on Multicultural Education and on Religiously Affiliated Schools. *International Journal of Education and Religion*, 1 (1), 47–63.

Schweitzer, F., Nipkow, K.E. & Faust-Siehl, G. & Krupka, B. (1995). *Religionsunterricht und Entwicklungspsychologie. Elementarisierung in der Praxis* [Religious Education and Developmental Psychology. The Praxis of Elementarization]. Gütersloh: Gütersloher.

Taylor, C. (1989). *Sources of the Self: The Making of the Modern Identity*. Cambridge: Harvard Univ.

Wacker, B. (1977). *Narrative Theologie?* [Narrative Theology]. München: Kösel.

Weder, H. (1978). *Die Gleichnisse Jesu als Metaphern. Traditions- und Redaktionsgeschichtliche Analysen und Interpretationen* [The Parables of Jesus as Metaphors. Analyses and Interpretations of the History of Tradition and Composition]. Göttingen: Vandenhoeck & Ruprecht.

Welker, M. (1995). *Schöpfung und Wirklichkeit* [Creation and Reality]. Neukirchen/Vluyn: Neukirchener.

ORGANISING AND CHANGING THE CHURCH

Aad de Jong

Gergen's social constructionist approach to psychosocial phenomena devotes some attention to organisational issues (e.g. Gergen, 1996; 1997; 1999, pp. 175–179). From the point of view of practical theology that opens up interesting perspectives on church construction and, more particularly, on organisational issues affecting churches. To what extent could such an approach help us to progress beyond developments that have taken place in this field in recent decades? In looking for a (critical) answer to this question I was greatly inspired by J.R. Searle's recent publications on the construction of social reality (see Searle, 1990; 1995; 1999). There Searle offers an explanation of institutional phenomena which also applies to organisations. An intriguing aspect is the subtle distinction he makes between "social construction of reality" and "construction of social reality". Partly for this reason, I propose focusing in this article on a more specific question: to what extent does our (study of) church construction take the social constructionist approach further, against the background of Searle's analyses of institutional phenomena?

To this end I first outline the evolution of (the study of) church construction over the past few decades and its relation to a social constructionist approach (section 1). I then try to make the most balanced assessment I can of a possible constructionist approach to the organisational aspects of church construction: what positive aspects are there that warrant more detailed attention, and in which respects does such an approach need amplification or correction (section 2)? Following from this, I try to indicate how Searle's insights into church construction could help to overcome the shortcomings of a social constructionist approach to church construction. I illustrate this with three concrete examples: power sharing in episcopal appointments in the Catholic Church, attempts at resolving conflicts in the Dutch ecclesiastic province of the Roman Catholic Church by means of a process of dialogue, and the quest for responsible reorganisation of parishes in parish councils (section 3). The article concludes with a critical application of Gergen's organisational approach to the relation between local churches and the "global church". This is because

Gergen's ideas on global corporations strike me as the most inspiring part of his constructionist theory of organisation.

1. *From* Societas Perfecta *to Social Construction*

First, then, we consider how a possible constructionist approach could
relate to recent developments in the field of church construction and
practical-theological reflection in this regard.

1.1 *Fifty Years of (Study of) Church Construction*

To my mind these developments are best understood as a reaction
to the church order and church organisation that obtained in the
first half of the 20th century. In Catholicism this was characterised
by the notion that the church possessed an "objective", preconceived
and fixed hierarchical, closed and uniform structure formalised in
the codex. In Protestantism, too—even though many churches applied
a synodal church structure—the church was consistently organised
in terms and on the basis of its formal ecclesiastic offices. Y. Spiegel
(1060) describes the church as a bureaucratic organisation. Within
it, church life was largely governed by formalism and, more especially, by collectivism and heteronomy. In reaction to this, the main
trend in subsequent developments in church construction and organisation has been marked by a striving for greater individual autonomy, expressed in appeals for a "church from below", a church that
is open to change and in which plurality is increasingly regarded as
enriching rather than threatening.

   In the latter half of the 20th century this evolution proceeded
globally in three phases, applicable to the full spectrum of pastoral
work, catechesis and practical theology. These phases were sequen-
tial in the sense that certain approaches predominated in each phase.
But to some extent they also cut across each other. Thus prominent
representatives of the first and second phases are still active today,
while as far back as the early 1960s one finds people pioneering
views that belong more properly to the third phase. Hence one could
speak of three emphases or trends in the present-day evolution of
(the study of) church construction.

For and About People

The first trend relates closely to, and should be understood in terms of, what may be called the anthropological turn in the religious and ecclesiastic spheres, and certainly in practical theology as well, in the 1950s and 1960s. The focus shifted from the objective doctrine and structure of the church (the faith) to believers as human beings, and more particularly as subjects. In addition people strongly opposed any kind of formalism and sought to direct more attention to substantive aspects of their faith.

For the approach to the organisational aspects of the church this anthropological swing meant that the church as a community, and certainly its organisational facets, were considered to be subordinate and subservient to religious people and human faith. Consequently less attention was paid to the organisation and structure of the church as an entity and the accent was on the people that constituted it, on their lives and religious experience. (See Hiltner, 1958; Arnold *et al.*, 1964–1969; Firet, 1968.)

More concretely, this approach meant that church leadership became more conscious of the people in the church. In the Roman Catholic Church, for instance, this is very evident in a reduced emphasis on holy orders and the rise of unordained pastoral workers. This was accompanied by a shift away from all people churches and the concomitant structures to voluntary churches.

In the Current Societal Context

The late 1960s and early 1970s saw growing criticism of this approach, or at any rate of this conception of the anthropological turn. It was considered to focus too much on the individual and the church itself, and to show too little concern for the broad societal context and developments in society. Such criticism gave rise to a new trend in church life and practical theology, with a strong emphasis on the relationship between people and their environment (both societal and ecclesiastic). In addition there was keen theological awareness of a need for a contemporary reinterpretation of both the Bible and the Christian tradition, whose relevance for modern people was increasingly experienced as problematic. In short, the anthropological turn made way for, or was amplified by, contextual broadening.

For church construction, and more specifically for its organisational aspects, this implied greater emphasis on church organisation—instead of an exclusive or preponderant accent on its human elements—especially in relation to social developments, in the form of democratisation, a striving for functionality and openness. Scholars of church construction started speaking about the church as an open system (Weverbergh, 1985; Pasveer, 1992), with explicit attention to the maintenance of its identity (Van Kessel, 1989).

In practical terms this was a period when basic communities were formed, leading to overt strain between the institutional church and its members, but which also saw a breakthrough in the phenomena of parish councils, greater lay participation and incorporation of voluntary workers, and concomitant training (pastoral schools, training courses, etc.).

Exploring Feasible Avenues
But in the course of the 1980s even this contextual broadening came to be seen as inadequate. It was still too much confined to Christianity, too little concerned with secularisation and the plurality of world-views and far too idealistic. As a result practical theology generally, and (the study of) church construction in particular, entered a third phase. Although not easy to pin down, this phase has a marked mystagogic slant, a preference for empirical research and, in a sense, a pragmatic orientation.

For the approach to church construction and organisational development in churches this has brought a more realistic adaptation to, and acceptance of, the existing organisational structure, as well as greater attention to questions of meaning within this structure.

In practical activities the emphasis shifted to "building with (ecclesiastic) images" (Weverberg, 1992), encouraging participation (Sonnberger, 1996), forms of self-direction and what is known as communicative self-examination. The main difference from the second phase was that the prime focus was no longer the relation between organisation and environment but rather the relation between the theory and practice, between ideal and reality.

An overview of this evolution reveals a kind of radicalisation of the striving for autonomy and growing emphasis on self-determination, at any rate in theory. The primary concern is with the autonomy of individual human beings and how ecclesiastic organisations can serve that autonomy. There was also a striving for autonomy of the various organisational entities within the church, and for the church's autonomy in relation to other social organisations. In Catholic Church practice the striving for the autonomy of church members is proving increasingly difficult to reconcile with the church's hierarchical structure. This has coincided with a kind of restorative counter movement, giving rise to great internal tensions which, after the unworkable polarisation of the second phase, people are currently trying to scale down.

There also seems to be a kind of inherent contradiction in this whole evolution. In a sense the three phases may all be seen as variants or radicalisations of the anthropological turn and the concomitant striving for the autonomy of individual believers that started in the first phase. But the individual autonomy of believers is manifestly difficult to accommodate with the organisation of a collective. Viewed superficially, at any rate, a striving for autonomy necessarily entails a weakening of collectivity and organisational ties. And this has been substantiated, inasmuch as the organisational perspective in mainstream practical theology has been largely superseded in recent decades by a focus on communication and personal identity.

1.2   A Social Constructionist Approach

How does a social constructionist approach relate to this evolution? For a clear grasp of this relationship we shall review the key premises of social constructionism as a whole. We then outline the application of these premises in organisational science. Finally we look at the relation between the premises and their application to the evolution we have outlined above.

We Create What Exists

The most fundamental, crucial premise of social constructionism is the "ontological" notion that no objective reality exists independently of the human mind and that the whole of reality is a human construction. Constructionism is primarily a reaction against the realist, objectifying approach to phenomena, more specifically the notion that knowledge is a kind of representation of an objective reality.

But to avoid the pitfalls of subjectivism, solipsism and individualism Gergen stresses that these phenomena are not reducible to products of purely subjective thoughts and feelings, which he claims is what happens in what he calls a romantic approach to organisations. He believes that this problem can be resolved by viewing phenomena as social constructions, that is, as originating from interpersonal relations.

In the process of social construction, he maintains, linguistic interactions play a vital role. Here he proceeds from the premise that all
language is performative in the sense that it creates reality. This view
of Gergen's is strongly influenced, not only by Wittgenstein and especially Austin, but also by Bakhtin's concept of dialogue, more specifically
his advocacy of heteroglossia and polyvocality.

Organising is a Human Activity
In Gergen's own work in organisation science he opposes both what
he calls a romantic approach which puts the accent exclusively on
the individual human mind (e.g. human resource theories), and a
rationalist approach which focuses on the efficiency of a (mechanis-
tically understood) whole. Instead, Gergen argues, organisations should
be viewed as cultural systems which generate symbolic worlds and
make activities possible. This can be done by using different metaphors.
Thus managers should try to "see" organisations in diverse ways and
communicate the most fruitful view.

To Gergen organisational change plays a major role in this overall process. In his view it happens mainly through changes of perspective. That is why he so strongly advocates (permitting, even
promoting) heteroglossia, internal criticism, listening closely to minority views, et cetera (see Gergen, 1996).

He works out this approach more concretely under three points. The
first is the issue of power and power sharing in organisations. Here
he stresses that power is a matter of interdependence and social coordination. The second point is conflict in organisations and how to
deal with it. Actually he is very positive in his general view of conflict,
regarding it mainly as a source of creative innovation in organisations. The third point is what he calls 'future search' for instance in
the reorganisation of industries or associations. Here he advocates
maximum participation by all parties in the evaluation process (see
Gergen, 1999, pp. 175–199).

Only from Ourselves
When we relate this approach to organisational issues to the evolution of (the study of) church construction in recent decades as
described above, we find that it is in part a kind of radicalisation
of the anthropological swing—in that organisations are explicitly
regarded as human products—but that it also goes one step further:
it strongly emphasises that they are products of social interactions.

We can elaborate on the first point as follows. The anthropological turn in the church and (practical) theology was an early reaction against the objectification of faith and the church and strongly accentuated the person as a subject. The same trend underlies social constructionism. There have also been practical theologians and scholars of church construction who maintained that no reality exists independently of the human mind. But to my knowledge nobody has hitherto gone so far as to posit that all reality is reducible to human constructions, hence to what people make of it. Such a view attests a highly optimistic view of human capability. At all events, it is extremely radical.

Gergen's assumption that organisations are not the doing of individual humans but are constructions arising from social interactions to some extent parallels the second phase of the evolution we have described, when it was heavily emphasised that church people lived in a social environment as well. But again Gergen goes further. Firstly, his primary concern is not about possible negative environmental influences on individuals. He adopts a far more positive view of society and social relations. In this respect he belongs more properly to the third phase. More importantly, he does not see society and organisations as a pre-existent reality which offers scope for individual persons. Instead he maintains that reality is actually constructed in social relations and the processes occurring within them. In this way Gergen's constructionist approach seems to overcome the striving for individual autonomy which has characterised the entire evolution of practical theology, also in the field of church construction, in recent times.

This means that constructionism provides greater scope for changing organisations, namely by changing the meaning that people assign to organisations and the intersubjective relations within them.

2. Our Conceptions and What Already Exists

The question now arises: what value does such an approach to organisations and organisational change have for us? What are its strong points which merit application and refinement in the field of (the study of) church construction? And what are its weaknesses which require amplification or even correction?

2.1   *Valuable Intuitions*

I discern mainly three positive points that are useful for church construction and merit application.

Created by People

The first point has to do with the notion that social phenomena exist as organisations solely by virtue of the fact that people agree that they exist. They owe their existence to the value people ascribe to them. In this sense it implies that social reality is a human construction (see Searle, 1995). This in no way contradicts or detracts from the confession of Christian believers that the church is also the work of God and has a divine order, at any rate not if it is also acknowledged that God works through human agents, especially at a social level. Hence another advantage of Gergen's approach is that he focuses strongly on attribution of meaning as a factor in organisational issues. A further implication is that it is advisable to pay close attention to people's conceptions of organisations, hence their conceptions of the church as well.

In the same context Gergen rightly points out the possibilities for changing meaning. At this level, indeed, nothing is fixed for ever and we differ fundamentally from the physical order or nature. Hence I consider Gergen's idea of reconceptualising organisations from different angles, for instance that of women, to be extremely useful.

The same applies to his notion that there can and must be a multiplicity of meanings and perspectives existing side by side, and that organisational problems can often be resolved by introducing fresh approaches. Such a plurality of paradigms strikes me as equally salutary for the organisational aspects of church construction.

In Relations with Others

A second, related and extremely positive point in Gergen's approach is his recognition of the social character of the construction process. The fact is that social phenomena are never purely individual products, even though some individuals are usually more influential than others. Organisations and organisational change always arise from interactions between people. Thus Gergen rightly points out that power is a matter of social interdependence. People have power partly because, and for as long as, they are given it by others. The power wielded by institutions, too, is not independent of ascription by individual people. This also applies to the ecclesiastic hierarchy of the Catholic Church.

Another appealing point is the rider that Gergen adds here, namely that everybody in the organisation should participate maximally in discussion—in any event, that nobody should be excluded. This needs to happen far more often in churches. Equally pertinent is his insistence that there should be ample opportunity for minority viewpoints to be heard and that heteroglossia and polyvocality should be promoted. Churches would do well to heed this injunction.

The same applies to the levelling of the distinction between inside and outside, between organisation and social environment. Constant exchange and integration of the organisation with the world at large are beneficial to both. This is in fact the merit of the appeal for an open church, for an aggiornamento, et cetera.

By Means of Language
Finally, in the context of the social character of the construction process, Gergen rightly points out the importance of intersubjective exchange, specifically by means of dialogue and language. When it comes to episcopal appointments or meetings to combine two parishes, for example, language is the medium used—and not merely in order to describe facts but also in part to create those facts. The symbolising aspect of language is indeed essential for the construction and change of organisations. Hence Gergen is quite right when he says that there does not first have to be an identity before meaningful dialogue is possible, but that identity originates and develops through dialogue. This applies to both individuals and organisations, including churches.

This means that it is vitally important for those involved in organisational development to pay close attention to the meaning of the terms that are used, especially when introducing changes which require the modification of meanings.

Hence Gergen is equally right in calling attention to the history of the organisation. That history reveals the meanings that have been assigned to the organisation in the past and thus clarifies what exactly is being changed.

2.2 *Not Real Enough*

Nonetheless Gergen's approach also has some fundamental shortcomings which, in my view, need to be augmented or even corrected. Fundamentally it is not real enough and does not take sufficient cognizance of institutional facts. If we confine ourselves to those points which relate directly to, or have implications for, the organisational aspects of social constructionism—more specifically as applicable to church construction—it boils down to three main issues.

Reductions of Language

The first issue has to do with Gergen's conception of communication in language. Here three reductions play a crucial role.

Firstly, Gergen reduces all speech acts and their components to predicates that form part of assertions. Thus he denies that answers could have a referential, hence identifying function in the sense that they could refer to an existing, "objective" reality. Indeed, he reduces meaning to predication. According to Searle (1969, 122) this is one of the most obdurate errors in the history of Western philosophy. In addition Gergen tacitly assumes that speech acts articulate a slant, a perception, a perspective. True, Gergen nowhere denies that people can also use language to offer directives, ask questions, make promises and express feelings. But the examples he cites are in fact limited to speech acts which communicate beliefs, recollections or observations. And when he expounds the meaning of assertions, he usually tries to show that they are not really expressive of physical states but are merely ascriptions of conceptions; moreover, he explicitly disregards the semantic rule that they necessarily raise the truth question.

Secondly, Gergen reduces illocutionary acts to perlocutionary acts, more particularly to persuasive perlocutions. Yet there is an important difference between the two. Illocutionary acts like questions, promises, affirmations and warnings are effective because they are performed and understood according to meaning rules that apply to them. The effectiveness of perlocutionary acts such as persuading, scaring or comforting someone, although performed by means of illocutionary acts, depends on many other factors, for instance the psychological biography of the listeners, their free will, et cetera (Searle, 1969, pp. 25 and 46). Because Gergen fails to distinguish between the two, he arbitrarily treats all judgments, for instance, as attempts at persuading people, and all logic as rhetoric.

Both the aforementioned reductions probably stem from a more fundamental reduction, namely the reduction of meaning to the use of language—more particularly people's use of language to persuade others to adopt a particular view (of reality?) (see Searle, 1969, pp. 146f.).

Insufficient Cognizance of Facts

A second objection to Gergen's constructionist approach, which to some extent also underlies the reductions of language described above, concerns his conception of social phenomena, particularly institutional facts and how they come about or are modified.

This conception is based on a reduction of collective action to individual action plus shared ideas (see Searle, 1990, p. 404). Here Gergen in effect disregards the distinctive, irreducible nature of collective activities as the realisation of individuals' collective intentions. This will be dealt with in more detail in section 3.

In addition Gergen reduces the assignment of status functions to causation by a particular slant or manner of perception. In so doing he overlooks the teleological character of functions, the fact that functions are assigned as a means to realise intentions (see Searle, 1995, pp. 37–43).

Thirdly, Gergen fallaciously reduces all rules and conventions to regulative rules, thus ignoring the existence and importance of constitutive rules in an institutional context (see Searle, 1995, 27–29).

Intentionality Reduced to Intersubjectivity

But the mot important and most fundamental objection to this constructionist approach is that subject-object relations are reduced to subject-subject relations.

This is partly because the ontological distinction between subjectivity and objectivity is confused with, and reduced to, an epistemological distinction between the two; in effect ontological conclusions are drawn from epistemological analyses. This is a fallacy, since the answer to the question of *how* we know something does not answer the question of *what* it is that we know (see Searle, 1995, pp. 8–12)

The main implication of this reduction is that truth is reduced to meaning, more specifically the meaning of convictions and assertions. That this is fallacious is immediately apparent when one considers that in that case people could never be mistaken—which is hardly plausible.

All this means that a constructionist approach on Gergen's lines takes insufficient cognizance of the existing institutional facts of and within organisations. When it comes to church construction it inevitably leads to unrealistic speculations which are not sufficiently directed to what already exists, and to the realisation of ideas and ideals.

3. Building on Existing Institutions

Hence the question arises: how can these shortcomings be overcome, for instance by using Searle's analyses of social and, more particularly, institutional facts? And what practical implications would that have for issues of power, conflict and reorganisation in churches?

3.1   The Construction of Social Reality

Following Searle, three issues strike me as particularly important: (1) The construction of social reality is a matter of collective action, (2) in which status functions are assigned to people and things, (3) this being done in accordance with constitutive rules. Let us examine these three aspects more closely with reference to organisational issues in the sphere of church construction.

Organising as Collective Action
What do we mean when we say that organising is a matter of collective action and that organisations are the result of collective activities?

   Like all other activities, collective activities are realisations of intentions. A characteristic of intentions, hence of plans and prior intentions, is that they link reality with mind (the reverse applies to cognitive intentionality, where mind is linked with reality) and that the realisation of such intentions are caused by the mind (in the case of cognitive orientations truth is caused by reality). Hence intentions cannot be reduced to convictions or other cognitive intentionality like recollections or observations (see Searle, 1983, p. 88 and pp. 170–172).

   The fact that we are dealing with collective intentions and activities does not mean that these are the intentions of groups. Intentions are always those of individual people. They are called collective only because they pertain not just to the activities of the individuals concerned but to activities performed in conjunction with others, and their accomplishment cannot be reduced to individual contributions. Structurally, therefore, collective intentions are made up of both individual and collective components, in a relationship of means to ends (see Searle, 1986). Applied to organising as a collective activity, it means that it is always a matter of individual contributions to the realisation of goals that cannot be achieved by people working on their own.

   There is a further proviso. People can only have collective intentions and can only perform collective activities in a context where the attitude among participants is sufficiently cooperative, where there is a certain sense of "us" and where people have adequate social and communicative skills (see Searle, 1986, pp. 413–415). From the perspective of church construction this strikes me as a crucial insight to augment a social constructionist approach.

Assignment of Status Functions
There is a further issue. When it comes to institutional facts regarding organisations, these are facts that result from a highly specific kind of collective activity: the assignment of status functions. What does that entail?

In the first place it is a matter of functions, for instance that a building serves as a church or that a person is assigned leadership of a congregation or parish. These are not intrinsic attributes of the things or people but are linked to the spectators or consumers. Such functions cannot be reduced to relations of cause and effect, but presuppose a relationship of means to ends within the framework of a set of values and goals (see Searle, 1995, pp. 13–43).

Secondly, we are speaking of a special kind of function, namely a status function. These are functions that things or people have not simply because of their physical or natural attributes but because of "cultural" characteristics, tasks or roles which people attribute to them. Thus someone in an organisation may be given the status of boss, or someone in a church may acquire the status of priest (see Searle, 1995, pp. 40–43 and pp. 95–112).

Thirdly, such status functions are often conferred by means of what are known as performative speech acts. These are speech acts in which speakers or listeners explicitly state what speech act they are performing, for instance, "I herewith promise that . . .". Consider also appointments and judicial declarations (see Searle, 1989; 1995, pp. 54–55).

Constitutive Rules
Status functions operate as constitutive rules with a basic structure of "X acts as Y in C", where X is the thing or person to whom the status function is assigned; Y is the function assigned; and C is the context in which the thing or person is assigned that status function. Of course, whether or not this rule is in fact constitutive will depend on the consensus and recognition of a particular community (see Searle, 1995, pp. 43–48).

Given such consensus and recognition, these rules not only regulate the behaviour of the people concerned and those with whom they associate. They also constitute the activities which they regulate. This implies that they make certain activities possible. A person who is assigned the status function of chairperson can, by virtue of that function, open a meeting. And an ecclesiastic judge can annul a marriage.

As a result the states of affairs called into being by constitutive rules are objective institutional facts and, as such, unalterable. If one wants to change them, one has to change the rules. And because the rules are constitutive, changing them is much more difficult than a constructionist approach may lead one to suspect.

3.2   *Episcopal Appointments, Dialogue Process and/or Merging of Parishes*

To demonstrate more concretely how Searle's approach can augment and correct a constructionist approach to church construction, I offer three examples, arising from Gergen's views in his publications on organisations and organisation science. The first has to do with power, in this case at the macrolevel of the "global church". The second reflects conflict management, the focus being the mesolevel of an ecclesiastic province. And the third has to do with what Gergen calls "future search", here conducted at the microlevel of parishes.

Sharing the Power of Appointment

Our first example is of power sharing in the Catholic Church, focusing on the appointment of bishops. At present the position is that the unrestricted right to appoint bishops belongs to the pope. "Medieval canonists legitimised this development with the concept of papal plenary power'. The first Vatican Council defined this as supreme and direct judicial power over all churches, pastors and believers, jointly and severally" (Huizing & Walf, 1980, p. 5; our translation).

A constructionist approach to this issue would undoubtedly entail advocating extensive procedures to ensure maximum participation by interested parties (and outsiders), in the course of which it hardly matters whether an appointment is actually made or who is eventually appointed. The proposal in itself is not new. There have been other appeals to consider granting God's people more say in the choice of bishops, also on theological grounds (see Granfield, 1980).

This undoubtedly has appealing facets. But anybody familiar with developments in Catholic Church organisation will know what far-reaching implications episcopal appointments can have and how difficult it is to influence these effectively (see Ellis, 1980). An application of Searle's analysis of institutional facts makes that perfectly understandable.

That does not detract from the fact that one can work towards changes at this level on the basis of Searle's ideas. But it then becomes apparent that really effective change can only be accomplished if the constitutive rules governing Episcopal appointments are amended, maybe even the status function of bishop is changed. And everybody knows that in order to effect such changes merely sharing a different view of the episcopate will not suffice. Effective change in this regard can only be achieved through collective action.

And that takes a lot of staying power . . .

Taking on Conflict in Dialogue
The second example relates to conflict management in church organisations. Here I focus on the dialogue process in the Catholic Church in the Netherlands. Gergen would probably applaud this method of making headway.

But experience has taught that to date such dialogue has not accomplished a single real change in church organisation. On the basis of what was said above one may reasonably expect that it will not do so in future either, unless the dialogue partners collectively implement different status functions. "For dialogue really to be dialogue between people they have to accept each other fully as human beings. The question is whether the report of the commission [instituted by bishops to get the dialogue process going—*A de Jong*] proceeds from this fundamental premise. It does mention taking seriously the expertise of academics, people of note in society, journalists. But the poor, the vulnerable, the helpless, those who possess no kind of power whatever, they have to 'experience the care of the church', have to be well looked after. In the report they have nothing to say that could be of any importance to a church. They remain the obscure corner, the underside of church and society" (Van Munster, 1995, pp. 21–22; our translation). In fact, it is still very much a question whether people occupying top positions but who, from the church's point of view, still have only lay status will ultimately have any say in changing church organisation. For to do so requires more than just sharing convictions: it entails introducing real changes in the constitutive rules that govern church activities.

But the existing institutions of the church are tenacious . . .

Consultation about Reorganisation

The third example concerns reorganisation in the church, particularly when congregations or parishes can no longer survive on their own and have to be combined or merged.

Parish councils and other consultative bodies in churches can exchange views about what they would like; what clinches the matter is the decision of those who have been assigned the status function of taking such decisions. And if church members want something else there is not much point in disputing the decision; it would be a matter of devising new rules for competence, for this is what determines real change in church organisation. Clear proof of this is the current magnification of the scale of pastoral units—in effect, the combination of parishes in the diocese of Roermond in Southern Netherlands, in which I am actively involved at present. Parish councils may voice their preferences about the form the mergers should take, but their counsel is in no way binding and affects only secondary issues of form. The deliberations of these councils have so far been largely a waste of time and highly frustrating, since they appear to have little or no impact on the decisions taken.

Only if the powers and actual clout of these consultative bodies were to be enhanced structurally would there be any point in collaborating. Hence the first essential step would be to work at effecting these improvements, both from the bottom up and from the top down, but especially in communication with each other—that is, if there are still people who can summon the patience to do so....

4. *Local Church and "Global Church"*

In this article so far I have been highly critical of constructionism, particularly of the applicability of organisations' constructionist approaches to problems of church construction. In this final section I shall naturally be no less critical, although I should like to conclude the article on as "constructive" a note as possible. From the angle of church construction I find the article "Technologies of representation in the global corporation" (1996) by Gergen and Whitney most intriguing. It deals with multinationals, more specifically with power relations between central top management and local establishments. The cardinal thesis is that the top may well exercise far less influence on the base than some people fear, and that these very multinationals may well develop into polyphonous organisations. The thesis is intriguing, since it immediately raises the question: to what extent does it apply to a multinational like the Catholic Church? And this is precisely the question to which I want to find as constructive an answer as possible in this concluding section.

4.1   *Power and Polyphony in Multinationals*

What exactly does Gergen's and Whitney's approach to global corporations entail?

Is there a Danger of Colonisation?

According to Gergen people often think—and fear—that multinational organisations have a destructive impact on local cultures. Because of their expansionism they are seen as a threat to the lifestyles, value systems, ideals and political autonomy of every culture they penetrate. The same applies to global non-profit organisations committed to combatting famine, improving health or preventing a nuclear war. Hence there is growing concern about colonisation by all these kinds of multinationals. They are thought to assimilate others and inculcate in people from different cultures their alien beliefs, values and practices. Their by-products, such as provision of goods, information dissemination, advertising and various services, are said to undermine indigenous cultures and traditions. They simply are not democratically based, permit no open communication and do not meet the needs of the various "publics" such as the family, the school and the state. Hence they are said to colonise the perceptions, attitudes and activities of these "audiences".

Gergen's main focus is the functioning of the official representations of these organisations. By this he means their discursive, sometimes graphic objectifications such as policy plans and annual reports, which sometimes in no way refer to anything that actually exists, so that one could speak of "underdetermination". In social exchange processes these presentations can be implemented in various ways, or not implemented at all. Self-representations from the top, such as policy plans, organisational schemes, annual reports and training manuals are meant to promote organisational goal achievement. They are essential sources to impart meaning within the organisation's culture. As such they operate in two ways. Firstly, they seek to establish a local ontology: this is our organisation. Secondly, they present a code of values: this is how we should behave. Hence they represent both the *is* and the *ought* of organisational life, and therefore entail illocutionary imperatives. Thus they stipulate how the various ranks in the organisation should relate to each other and how they should behave towards each other. They lay down standards of honour etcetera. Creating such meaning is in fact necessary for the proper functioning of the organisation. But the flip side is that people will internalise the rules of conduct imposed by this "juridico-discursive" power. In this way the organisational process in a sense shackles itself. This applies very much to globalising organisations. The greater the power of leadership to organise life beyond its organisational goals, the greater its power to change its environment.

There are variations of these communication practices, which operate differently. It depends very much on the context in which the communication partners relate to each other. In face-to-face organisations it occurs through dialogic representation. There the boss has disciplinary power through direct description. It occurs in a particular context. Its author is a specific individual and it is directed to a specific person. It is accompanied by nonverbal signs. Personal history plays a role in it. Direct feedback is possible, hence it is much more differentiated. All this is ideal for the exercise of disciplinary power. Large organisations, on the other hand, have to resort to written representations, for here working with printed media is cheaper and the representations can be disseminated faster. Graphic representations like organigrams are also rhetorically more forceful than discursive expositions. In these the pyramid metaphor is popular. In larger, more complex organisations the metaphor of communication lines in a telephone network is more apposite. But if the organisation grows even larger, as happens with global expansion, it has to revert to the dialogic form of communication, albeit in a different way from that of face-to-face organisations. The media through which dialogue is conducted are now electronic: e-mail, fax and especially the telephone. Substantively the dialogue becomes much more abstract. Although general goals may be defined, for instance, no practical methods of achieving them are spelled out since these may differ from one practical situation to the next. Usually dialogue is confined to clarifying general values which are declared valid for the organisation. Often physical representations like buildings make way for human relations. In practice this is accompanied by loss of power on the part of the centre.

Five factors are particularly important in this process. Firstly, the context of the representation changes. Actually it largely disappears, so that the words may have less meaning. They remain abstract particularly when general values are defined. Secondly, it is not at all clear who the actual author of a representation is. Often it is anonymous. Usually nobody can explain precisely what is meant by these pronouncements. Besides, the status of the author is unclear: is it a boss or an equal, hence how cogent is the directive? Thirdly, and directly related to this, the speech acts concerned become much less forceful. Is the report simply an open-ended suggestion or a mandatory order? Fourthly, the identity of the recipient, too, becomes ambiguous. Is it intended for me and, if so, in what capacity and to what extent or in what way? In the fifth place, the recipients have much less say. Their sensitivities are not taken into account. There is no differentiation and no feedback, which greatly increases the chances of resistance or, at any rate, of misconstruction.

This development has two major consequences. Firstly, it greatly complicates control from the top and promotes resistance to it at the bottom. Local representatives get lost in a hermeneutic jungle, even though the centre may have a panoptic surveillance system. After all, the data for such surveillance are "mediated", and hence manipulated, in situ. There is still a local process of constructing reality. At the same time all this promotes self-organisation at the local level and a feeling of "us" as opposed to "them". Through face-to-face relations representations can be contextualized at this level; here it is clear who the authors are and what the illocutionary acts imply; also, the identity and personal input of the recipients are available. As a result the communication is action-specific, thus magnifying the chances of resistance.

In view of all this Gergen believes that there is a need for a new approach—and a corresponding new metaphor—which is suitable for the transition to electronic dialogue and which can in fact ensure the fulfillment of organisational functions without strict centralised control. This would entail an approach and a metaphor which make it possible to put local languages in a mutually beneficial relationship with the centralized powers, so that the entire concept of organisational efficacy remains continuously negotiable. Such an approach already features in new organisational theories, for instance when the metaphor of language is used in preference to that of the telephone network. Gergen himself prefers the literary metaphor of the polyphonous author, which he borrows from Bakhtin and in which dialogue is focal. In a polyphonous organisation monologue is replaced by dialogue between the voices of the constituent cultures and sub-cultures. The language of the system makes way for that of the sys-tase. There is no central voice around which order is established, but rather a patchwork of linguistic pragmatics. This means that there is a collective praxis in ongoing process. Here Gergen discerns parallels with chaos theory. It also permits unity of a higher order.

Gergen maintains that an institutional gap will have to be bridged if there is to be any change of this nature. This can be done by broadening the dialogue to include other sciences that are moving in the same direction, and by invoking experience with a similar approach. But the cardinal requirement is still the actual process of polyphonous dialogue, that is interactive exchange rather than crys-tallised representation. Hence this is not a reversion to face-to-face interactions but an appeal for myriad capillary dialogues between top and bottom, inside and outside.

4.2 *"Holy See" and "Ordinary Parish"*

How applicable is this approach to churches like the Catholic Church? After all, from the point of view of participation it would be very nice if it were to apply there as well (see Nichols, 1997). It would certainly remove unnecessary fears—maybe even unjustified suspi-ciousness—of Rome and thus have a moderating influence. And it would undoubtedly help to reduce the skepticism of local religious communities as expressed in such comments as, "we have no say in things anyway", thus inspiring greater fervor to have a hand in influencing the larger whole. So the question is to what extent and under what conditions it in fact applies or could be made to apply to that church.

Any skepticism in this regard is perfectly warranted if we con-sider, for instance, how after the first Vatican Council in 1870 tele-graphy helped to make Rome a mighty center of power, thus enabling it to suppress the legitimate diversity of local churches (see Hebbleth-waite, 1987). But what strikes me as more fundamental is that the applicability of Gergen's approach is still restricted today by its dis-regard of institutional facts and their role in church organisation. In the Catholic Church certainly a centuries-old process of function assignment has resulted in an organisational structure—and culture!—which can manifestly not be changed in its entirety, but where a great deal more has to happen than just dialogic communication between top and bottom if any essential changes are to be made. Besides, the church is a normative rather than a utilitarian institution, an institution, moreover, whose norms derive not merely from its (operational) goals and universal principles of humaneness, rationality and the like. Churches profess to derive their norms and values from divine revelation and it is no coincidence that those at the top of the Catholic Church so frequently invoke "divine justice". Religious legitimation of norms and the exercise of leadership makes change "from below" far more complicated than in other multinationals. But surely the most crucial problem is that the top brass in the Catholic Church tend to be highly defensive and conservative about the existing order, with the concomitant control of submission to rules, whereas the top management of multinationals are intent on innovation and stimulating creative entrepreneurship (see Van Nieuwenhuis, 1995). You cannot change that simply by replacing monologic communication with dialogue, quite apart from the question of the actual readiness for dialogue both at the top and at the grassroots (see Schavan, 1994; Fürst, 1997).

That is not to say that Gergen's approach is totally inapplicable to the Roman Catholic Church. It offers at least some ideas which even "religious multinationals" would do well to apply. First there is his notion of linking language and its meaning with a practical context. This in itself is by no means new in the religious sphere. All of hermeneutic and contextual theology is in fact just one great endeavour to take this link seriously. And all discussions about inculturation of the Christian faith and the church revolve around the question of exactly how that link is to be forged. But I know of no publications which have pursued this issue to the organisational problems of power relations between top and bottom in the Roman Catholic Church. All I would like to add to Gergen's approach to this issue is that the problem of context affects not just the meaning of "self-representations", imperatives from the centre and language and signs generally, but also and especially the fulfilment of language, the implementation of imperatives and the truth value of representations. That goes a step further than Gergen and complicates the inculturation problem even more. For then it is not sufficient for words merely to have meaning in diverse cultural contexts. There is the further question of the extent to which the context permits their actualisation.

Two other aspects of Gergen's approach are also promising. The first is his appeal for polyphony, particularly inasmuch as it is in effect an appeal for pluralism and diversity. The second is his notion of "capillary communication", in the sense of reciprocal communication between top and bottom or centre and periphery. The latter is far too rare in the Catholic Church and may well solve many problems. However, it would require better structural provisions. Communication between Dutch Catholics and the Holy See, for instance, still proceeds step by step, hence is filtered and predominantly top-down. Still, this problem is easier to deal with than that of pluralism. The top and the centre are still a long way from recognising the positive value of pluralism in the church. The striving for unity dominates absolutely. Nonetheless I agree with Gergen that in the long term pluralism is a more fruitful option for organisations, hence for the church as well, than what one might call "interrelated diversity".

But Gergen fails to mention the cardinal condition for real change of church organisation in this direction. That is willingness on the part of both those at the centre and people in local churches to participate and contribute to collective activities that transcend their immediate circle and its interests. What is required from practical theologians is to cultivate participatory attitudes and skills, in the sense that "ordinary parishioners and church members" will want to and be able to join in reflection on, and discussion of, things which they want to and could achieve, in cooperation with other local churches and under the guidance of higher managerial organs in the Roman Catholic Church, including the Holy See. Of course, this would only make sense inasmuch as these higher managerial organs genuinely wish to involve themselves with the desires, ideas and activities of people at the grassroots. To date experience in this regard has not been encouraging. Still, Gergen's constructionist approach challenges practical theologians to look for practical improvements, which will at least do away with every form of solipsism and complacency about the status quo.

References

Arnold, F.X., Rahner, K., Schurr, V. & Weber, L.M. (Eds.) (1964–1969). *Handbuch der Pastoraltheologie. Praktische theologie der Kirche in ihrer Gegenwart I–V* [Handbook of Pastoral Theology. Practical theology of the church today]. Freiburg: Herder.

Brants, A. (red.) (1995). *Samenspraak en tegenspraak. Beschouwingen bij gelegenheid van de studiedag dialoog op 28 april 1995 in het Universitair Centrum voor Theologie en Pastoraat te Heerlen* [Dialogue and contradiction. Reflections on the occasion of the conference about dialogue on 28 april 1995 in the University for Theology and Pastoral Care in Heerlen]. Heerlen: UTP.

Fürst, G. (Ed.) (1997). *Dialog als Selbstvollzug der Kirche?* [Dialogue as self-realization of the church?]. Freiburg: Herder.

Gergen, K.J. & Whitney, D. (1996). Technologies of Representation in the Global Corporation: Power and Polyphony. In: Boje, D.M. *et al.* (Ed.), *Postmodern Management and Organization Theory* (pp. 331–357). Thousand Oaks: Sage.

Gergen, K.J. & Tatchenkerry, T.J. (1997). Organizational science in a postmodern context. In: *Journal of Applied Behavioral Science,* 32, pp. 356–377.

Gergen, K.J. (1999). *An Invitation to Social Construction.* Londo: Sage.

Gerwen, G. van (1988). Over organisatie en management in de kerk [About Organization and Management in the Church]. *Tijdschrift voor theologie* 28 (4), 371–392.

Granfield, P. (1980). De sensus fidelium bij de bisschopskeuze [The sensus fidelium at the choices of bishops]. *Concilium* 1980 (7), 37–43.

Greinacher, N. (1965), Soziologische und organisatorische Aspekte einer diözesanen kirchlichen Strategie [Sociological and Organizational Aspects of a Diocesan Ecclesial Strategy]. *Lebendige Seelsorge,* 16 (4), 124–128.

Hiltner, S. (1958). *Preface to Pastoral Theology.* Nashville: Abingdon Press.

Kessel, R. van (1989). *Zes kruiken water. Enkele theologische bijdragen voor kerkopbouw* [Six pitchers with water. Some theological contributions for developing the church]. Hilversum: Gooi & Sticht.

Munster, H. van (1995). Dialoog en de vergeethoek [Dialogue and oblivion]. In: Brants, A. (Ed.) *Samenspraak en tegenspraak.* Heerlen: UTP.

Nichols, T.L. (1997). *That All May Be One. Hierarchy and Participation in the Church.* Collegeville Minnesota: The Liturgical Press.

Nieuwenhuis, F. (1995). *Monseigneurs en managers. De Kerk van Rome en de Shell vergeleken.* [Monsignors and managers. The church of Rome and Shell compared]. Rotterdam: Ad. Donker.

Pasveer, J. (1992). *De gemeente tussen openheid en identiteit. Een open systeemtheorie als model voor de gemeente ten dienste van haar opbouw* [The Congregation between openness and identity. An open system theory as model for the congregation for the use of her development]. Gorinchem: Narratio.

Schavan, A. (Ed.) (1994). *Dialog statt Dialogverweigerung. Impulse für eine zukunftsfähige Kirche* [Dialogue instead of refusal of dialogue. Impulses for a church of the future]. Kevelaer.

Searle, J.R. (1969). *Speech Acts. An Essay in the Philosophy of Language.* London-New York: Cambridge University Press.

Searle, J.R. (1983). *Intentionality. An Essay in the Philosophy of Mind.* London: Cambridge University Press.

—— (1986). Meaning, Communication and Representation. In: Grandy, R.E. & Warner, R. (Eds.), *Philosophical Grounds of Rationality. Intentions, Categories, Ends* (pp. 209–226). Oxford: Clarendon Press.

—— (1989), How Performatives Work. *Linguistic and Philosophy* 12, 535–558.

—— (1990), Collective Intentions and Actions. In: Cohen, P.R. *et al.* (Eds.), *Intentions in Communication* (pp. 401–415). Cambridge Mass.: Bradford Books, MIT Press.

—— (1995). *The Construction of Social Reality*. New York: The Free Press.

—— (1999). *Mind, Language and Society. Doing Philosophy in the Real World*. London: Weidenfeld & Nicholson.

Sonnberger, K. (1996). *Die Leitung der Pfarrgemeinde. Eine empirisch-theologische Studie unter niederländischen und deutschen Katholiken* [The leadership of the parish. An empirical-theological study on Dutch and German Catholics]. Kampen: Kok.

Spiegel, Y. (1969). *Kirche als bürokratische Organisation* [The Church as a Bureaucratic organization]. München.

Weverbergh, R. (1985). Missionaire kerk als open systeem [Missionary church as an open system]. In: J.A. van der Ven (Ed.). *Toekomst voor de kerk? Studies voor Frans Haarsma* [Future for the church? Studies for Frans Haarsma] (pp. 227–239). Kampen: Kok.

—— (1992). *Bouwen met beelden. Onderzoek naar theorie en praktijk van kerkopbouw* [Building with images. Research about the theory and praxis of the development of churches]. Baarn: Gooi & Sticht.

PERSONAL RELIGION

Hans Schilderman

Introduction

The title of this chapter, 'Personal Religion', refers to the fact that people's identities differ when it comes to religion. It suggests, moreover, that religion is practised or 'made' either by or for persons. At the same time it indicates the nature of human beings, since it seems incongruous to speak of non-personal or impersonal religion. In contrast to its opposite, 'public religion', the term 'personal religion' emphasises individual activity as contributing to or even creating religious identity. This construction activity as a denotation of religious identity represents a challenge to the commonly used term 'soul'. Rooted in Greek philosophy and Christianity, the soul has always been a key concept in religious identity. It refers to such diverse notions as the essence of human individuality, the immortal aspect of the self, a communication channel with God, and the locus of morality; at the same time it indicates a difference from body and material form. These metaphysical denotations and connotations of soul are challenged by social constructionism. Social constructionism is characterised by the idea that our reality is socially constructed. Not only outward phenomena are socially constructed, but also inward notions such as self, emotions, person and identity.[1] Is the soul—the God-given and God-bound origin of human beings—a social construction too? From the perspective of social constructionism, the answer to this question is likely to be affirmative. If religious identity is to be understood as a social activity, what are the consequences for personal religion? And what are the consequences of this approach for our understanding of pastoral care?

---

[1] The indiscriminate application and extension of social constructionism can and must be questioned. One cannot deny that it is hardly possible to think of something that is not socially constructed, as expressed in the rhetorical title of Ian Hacking's book '*The social construction of what?*'. From a critical rationalist point of view this kind of theory is open to charges of self-immunisation, a conceptual shelter against falsification.

In this chapter I will take on the challenge implied in these questions. In doing so I do not disclaim or disregard traditional concepts of religious identity, but will merely explore the usefulness of a new paradigm. I do not profess to offer more than a preliminary examination of the type of problems, concepts, processes and challenges that are implicit in a study of religious identity and pastoral care in a social constructionist perspective. Nonetheless I hope to show that personal religion can be understood as individual appropriation of definitions of ultimate reality by employing rhetorical language and invoking persuasive processes within a social network of meaning. To clarify this, I will first sketch one aspect of modernity that entails a basic problem of personal religion, namely religious individualism. This phenomenon results from a tendency to rely less on religious intermediaries and to foster moral appreciation of religious authenticity. The emerging emphasis on personal, authentic religious expression raises the question of how religious identity should be understood. This is examined in the second section of this chapter by applying Rom Harré's concept of personal identity to religion. People's personal understanding of their religious identity is interpreted as personal religion. To illustrate this notion, and to demonstrate how it can be explored, I then describe three cases of personal religion, based on a pastoral care method known as spiritual inquiry. In the final section, by way of evaluation, I deal with some objections to the notion of personal religion and to the incorporation of the concept of persuasion in pastoral care.

Religious Individualism

We live in societies that offer a host of opportunities to express personal values and lifestyles, each with its own persuasive appeal to the individual. These alluring opportunities for self-expression are found in every domain of modern society. For instance, individualism is firmly rooted in democracy, the consensus orientation of which presupposes individual independence as influenced by coercive strategies.[2] But politics is not the only source; economic and technologi-

---

[2] To the French political scientist Alexis de Tocqueville, democracy offers equalised conditions for expressing individualism. While individual independence may be considered a dangerous opponent of religion, the adaptation to, and incorporation of, values based on individuality and equality cause religion to thrive on individualism (De Tocqueville, 1972, pp. 26–28).

cal developments, too, have encouraged individualism. Economically, evolving markets have turned individuals into self-conscious loci of commercial choice, agents for contracts and patients for liability. The technological revolution has opened up opportunities for travel, communication and interaction, stimulating individual exploration of the world without the scrutiny of social control. In modern society individualism is also becoming a dominant characteristic in the religious realm and some of its roots actually have a long religious history. I will touch on a few characteristics of religious individualism and comment on them briefly from a moral angle.

What are the characteristics of religious individualism? In his monograph on individualism, Lukes (1973, pp. 45–78) offers some answers to this question. First of all, individualism stresses human dignity. This is not just a modern characteristic. Ever since its inception Christianity has advocated human dignity by acknowledging the supreme worth of the individual under the sovereign will of God. Autonomy is a second characteristic, stressed by the Reformation's tendency to consider the solitary individual as being ultimately responsible to God alone. Another feature is the notion of privacy, with its ancient roots in the notion of an intimate self, the soul: the religiously enshrined locus of personal identity set apart from the public realm. Privacy has been emphasised, for instance, by the spiritual and mystical traditions of Christianity, which contributed to the notion that any access to God springs from the intimacy of the self. The Renaissance and Romantic traditions stressed a fourth characteristic: self-development. This referred to the need to cultivate the self and thus presupposed ultimate self-regulatory values within the person. The last characteristic is abstract individuality, the parallel of Bellah's notion of ontological individualism. It presents individuals as independent of social context, and society merely as a set of arrangements that correspond with personal requirements. These notions of individualism: human dignity, autonomy, privacy, self-development and abstraction have implications for the religious context in which personal identity is embedded. Like other social domains, religion cannot escape the consequences of individualism. Thus we can define religious individualism as 'the view that the individual believer does not need intermediaries, that he has the primary responsibility for his own spiritual destiny, that he has the right and the duty to come to his own relationship with his God in his own way and by his own effort' (Lukes, 1973, p. 94). This definition of religious individualism attaches great importance to spiritual equality and religious self-scrutiny. Though these notions may be more explicit in Reformed thinking than in Roman Catholicism, the basic idea is that of a growing religious *Wahlverwandschaft* between God and individual human beings.

There is another aspect of religious individualism that may easily be overlooked. This happens when definitions of individualism are introduced into ethical discourse and are treated as moral notions. Not uncommonly, authors contrast individualism with social engagement. The growing emphasis on the individual comes to be understood as egocentrism that will ultimately lead to social anomy. Other authors disagree with this view. Capps, for instance, criticises the concept of individualism in an analysis of the American discussion of Bellah's *Habits of the Heart* (Bellah *et al.*, 1985; Gelpi, 1989; cf. Lasch, 1979). Capps's criticism is directed against the myopic ideology that regards community orientation as the reverse of individualism. According to him, setting up social orientation as the antithesis of individualism reveals a failure to understand the changing conditions for social bonds and incurs a risk of undermining the moral resources of personal autonomy, of obscuring personality constraints and of promoting narcissistic dependence on institutions (Capps & Fenn, 1992, p. 6, p. 13; Capps, 1993). Charles Taylor also holds a more balanced view of individualism. According to him, individualism is one of the malaises of our time, since it dissociates a personal achievement orientation from the moral horizons that have always constituted identity (Taylor, 1992). But, far from repudiating individualism on grounds of narcissism or hedonism, Taylor recognises the moral idea in individualism, which he calls 'authenticity'. Whereas formerly the moral source was considered to be God or some inner notion of the good, nowadays we expect to derive well-being from a favoured disclosure of our original self.[3] Though it can hardly be denied that this individualism promotes some kind of relativism, the notion of authenticity also demands a dialogical conception of identity, which acknowledges that our ties with others constitute us and that we do not coincide with the arbitrariness of our personal desires. In asserting personal free will we must presuppose significant values, which transcend the notion of self-choice, and which moreover appeal

---

[3] This by no means excludes the religious roots of individualism, as Taylor explains in his interpretation of the Reformist theology of ordinary life (Taylor, 1989, pp. 211–233).

to others to recognise our identity and are realised in interaction
with others on a basis of fairness and love. From such a perspective, narcissism, social atomism or instrumental reasoning may be
categorised as dysfunctions of authenticity, maladjusted to the social
tissue in which authenticity has its natural pith. Taylor makes another
point, one that strikes me as relevant when we apply his concept of
authenticity to religion. This is his notion of the altered understanding
of art (Taylor, 1989, pp. 490–493; 1992, pp. 62–69). Like art, religious faith can no longer be defined mainly as imitation ('mimesis'),
in the sense of following rules, methods and precepts for imagination. Like art, faith seems to be developing into something valuable
in its own right, and is not adequately understood as a means of
fostering or satisfying an institutionally fixed ideal, be it aesthetic or
moral. If there is some truth in the idea that we construct our own
identity, this implies an awareness that we create instead of merely
imitate. What is decisive is not the ideal of expertise in following
blueprints, but the ideal of appropriating uniqueness. As a moral
notion, authenticity relates not to the matter but to the manner of
appropriation. The assertiveness of an 'I' who appropriates is not
necessarily inimical to the efforts of others or the orientation to the
common good. In Taylor's view, the moral principle is the public
interpretation of personal sensibility aimed at authenticity.

The aspect of modernity outlined here does not picture the soul
as a metaphysical attribute of personal identity but as an 'intrigued
identity', curious to trace its origin within itself and simultaneously
rhetorically demonstrating this quest to its public. This idea of identity as ('identifying') activity may be understood as a persuasive
attempt to integrate personal and social assent. Viewed thus, the soul
is not a mute object of pastoral care but its own pastoral subject,
stating its claim to genuine religious self-interpretation. Or, in perhaps more familiar terms: the soul manifests itself in confession,
invoking shared convictions while declaring its personal religion.

Religious Identity

If religion is increasingly characterised by individualism, and if religion in modern times has to be understood as a personal assertion
of authenticity, what is meant by the religious identity of a person?
I will try to answer this question from a social constructionist

perspective by exploring the notion of identity as persuasive activity and religion as a cultural framework for this activity.

From a social constructionist point of view, the question of what identity is must be understood in relation to the rhetorical function of language, without which identity construction would be impossible. The question of who we are is not so much a matter of fact as of rhetoric to establish what is real in the light of social controversy. It is not that facts are distorted because of specific convictions, but that factual accounts are artefacts of actions in which the credibility of the speaker is at stake (Potter, 1996, pp. 106–108). This rhetorical function of language facilitates the persuasive processes in which personal identity is socially constructed. In this context Rom Harré developed a theory of selfhood, partly relying on Vygotsky's theory of thought and language. Harré understands the quest for identity as an ambivalent effort to acquire both a social identity (an honoured status in the social order) and a personal identity (a unique biographical profile). Not satisfied with the Cartesian inner-outer opposition and its analogy with the subjective-objective distinction, Harré (1983, pp. 41–46) offers a more comprehensive notion of identity by distinguishing between various dimensions of identity. A first dimension is the addressed public to whom one displays one's psychological attributes. This dimension ranges from private display entailing personal and private purposes, to public display entailing general, open performances. For instance, one may ponder one's faith privately or test it by professing it before a church audience. A second dimension is the possession of, and control over, psychological attributes. This dimension varies from individual realisation that calls for personal validation, to collective realisation that refers to social authority. For instance, in one's religious life one may rely on personal religious experience or on the norms of a religious community.[4] Harré locates the two dimensions at right angles to each other, resulting in a model of four quadrants that represents a conceptual space for interpreting stories of personal identity.

---

[4] The dimensional model can be extended at will. In fact, Harré includes a third dimension—orthogonal on the previous two—namely that of active versus passive agency, depending on whether one is an agent exercising power or a patient suffering liability.

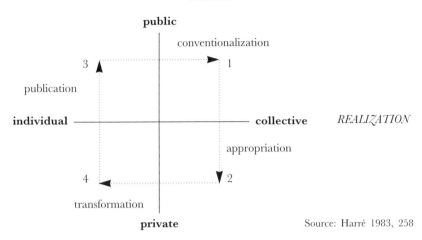

Source: Harré 1983, 258

By describing the transitions between the quadrants of this dimensional model, Harré elucidates his notion of the social construction of personal identity. In the public/collective quadrant 'theories of persons' are available that can be appropriated by metaphorically comparing these models for identity with one's own experience (from quadrant 1 to quadrant 2). As private interpretations, these theories are transformed into an inner sense of identity: the self (from quadrant 2 to quadrant 3). Subsequently, this identity has to be made public in adequate metaphors that permit social recognition in concurrence with other identities (from quadrant 3 to quadrant 4). Finally, the (successful) identities may in their turn function as models for identity, which of course presupposes that they have been conventionalised into new theories of persons (from quadrant 4 to quadrant 1) (Harré, 1983, pp. 41–46; Murray, 1989, pp. 179–181). Thus identity is a process of appropriating selfhood from available models of personhood by transforming it into a sense of self that is published and to some extent socially consented to via conventions. 'We learn to conceive of ourselves as personal beings by the appropriation of the concept of social being from our public-collective activities for the purposes of organising our experience as the mental life of a self-conscious agent' (Harré, 1983, p. 108).

   In Harré's dimensional model, selfhood depends on language in a twofold way. In the public-private dimension language is an instrument

of representation that locates contents on a spatio-temporal continuum of awareness. In the individual-collective dimension language is
an instrument of action that makes it possible to act adequately from
the changing contents of awareness. The formal unity of these aspects
of identity construction is vouchsafed by the belief structure of personal identity. This belief structure is implied in language, which
unites a centre of consciousness (knower) in the midst of represented
psychological attributes with a source of action (actor) in the midst
of a life history. It is this rhetoric which establishes the person both
as a practical entity, enabling him or her to act in accordance with
available social models, and as an empirical entity: the sense of idiosyncratic singularity that is expressed in autobiography. The narrative offers a local theory of who we are: concordant and discordant
voices settle before a specific public, at a particular moment and to
some extent, the disturbing issues about who we are, where we come
from, where we are going to, who we should be, what we should
avoid, and so on. These core questions of identity are not merely
our personal make-up as displayed in daily interaction; they are the
threads that weave us into the web of social life

Since language is constitutive for our identity, the rhetorical structure of identity has to be understood in terms of the interactive linguistic networks of our culture: the shape of our collective consciousness
and intentionality (Searle, 1995, p. 228). It is in this sense that Harré's
dimensions of identity construction are applicable in a religious context. Thus the dimension of public versus private display has to do
with the interaction between a religious audience and a person's religious attributes. The dimension of individual versus collective realisation, again, concerns the question of how a person's religious
attributes are effectuated in religious contexts. Proceeding clockwise
through the quadrants of the dimensions, the social construction of
religious identity becomes apparent. Depending on culturally available models of religious identity, a person appropriates religious attributes by comparing them metaphorically with his or her own experience.
Depending on the success of this appropriation of religion, religion
can be transformed into the self, an inner sense of how reality should
be understood and assessed religiously. Depending on the perceived
salience of this religious self, religious attributes can be expressed or
practised in a recognisable and attractive religious profile. This, in
turn, may serve as a valuated cultural model of religious identity.
The application of Harré's dimensions is not merely an adaptation

of the identity construction process to specific cultural—that is, religious—content. The notion of culture has a more direct significance. Culture may be understood as a framework of, and for, self-theories: narratives that facilitate both reflexive cognition (self-knowledge) and reflexive action (self-mastery) which are necessary for identity to be constructed. A culture's tradition contains beliefs about ourselves— for instance that we are God-believers—in the setting of a moral order in which these beliefs have to be realised. This applies to both the public-private dimension, in which self-knowledge aims at moral honour, and the individual-social dimension, in which self-mastery aims at moral will. Cultural narratives facilitate identity projects: those socially accepted beliefs that encourage uniqueness within a moral order (Harré, 1983, pp. 256–284).

Can religion be understood as a cultural institution for such identity projects? This question can be answered affirmatively in the sense that religion offers a moral order, or various moral orders, in which moral honour can be attained on the basis of the role models that a religious tradition offers for developing self-knowledge. Also, practising the moral codes implied in religion can develop a moral will. But religion offers a more distinctive persuasive characteristic for identity construction if we consider Geertz's well-known definition. Geertz (1993, p. 90) defines religion as 'a system of symbols which acts to establish powerful, pervasive, and long-lasting moods and motivations in men by formulating conceptions of a general order of existence and clothing these conceptions with such an aura of factuality that the moods and motivations seem uniquely realistic'. Interpreted in Harré's social constructionist perspective, religion does not represent its implicit moral orders as goals to be achieved, but as realities that are reaching out, breaking through or even being realised at that very moment. Religion offers cognitive clarity about an order behind seeming chaos by presenting convictions symbolically as realised states of affairs. It clothes everyday life with envisaged alternatives. The construction seems to be a representation of reality but actually offers motives to realise this reality. This fluid transition that religious symbols facilitate from a factual to a normative or a metaphysical reality in fact expresses and evokes religion. Religious symbols integrate human beings' lived life-ethos by summing up the quality of life, the moral and aesthetic styles and comprehensive insights. The use of metaphors promotes a rhetorical application of personal identity construction to shared, collective and ultimate aims.[5] If we apply Geertz's definition of religion to Harré's notion of cultural identity projects, the social construction of religious identity demands self-knowledge and self-mastery with regard to the following activities. Firstly, specify and apply attitudes of a general order of existence in the face of imminent chaos. Secondly, draw the meaning of the symbols that these attitudes evoke into reality. Thirdly, clarify the moods created by the symbols and attitudes. Fourthly, turn the motivations which the attitudes give rise to into practical consequences of action. Fifthly, ritualise these attitudes.

Religious identity evokes the ultimate significance of a culture's life-ethos, as expressed in ideal moral, aesthetic, emotional and intellectual models for the social construction of personal identity. Thus the social construction of religious identity depends on the persuasive processes that are activated by presenting an envisaged ultimate reality as a realised notion. Personal religion is the interpreted and narrated result of these persuasive processes.

Inquiry Into Personal Religion

I have tried to show how persuasion is implicit in the construction of religious identity. The next question is: what is the result of this construction process? How is personal religion shaped by this construction activity? I shall answer this question pragmatically by demonstrating a method that clarifies and validates personal religion. I illustrate this method by describing three cases of personal religion in the context of religious individualism.

One way of clarifying and validating the construction of religious identity is the method of spiritual inquiry. It is an application of the self-confrontation method, which is based on the valuation theory developed by Hubert Hermans. Personal religion can be interpreted as a self-narrative describing the process of constructing religious identity. The person symbolises appropriated experiences of religious identity in what are known as 'valuations'. These valuations are arranged in a valuation system that is narrated in the form of a plot.[6] The self-confrontation method presents an inventory of these

---

[5] In a later publication Geertz (2000, pp. 167–186) warns against an overly individualistic approach to questions of religious identity by drawing attention to developing faith communities of religiously assertive social actors which become axes around which the struggle for power swirls.

[6] There are good reasons to interpret valuation theory in terms of a social con-

symbols in a conversation in which a helper (therapist) challenges a person (client) to specify and validate the various valuations. The helper's role in the interaction is to confront this identity with inconsistencies, lacunae or delusions. The construction of personal identity is not a solipsistic activity but a process based on social interaction, guided by the principle of mutual competence: that of the helper as an identity researcher, and that of the person as an experiential expert on his or her own identity. The self-confrontation method assesses personal identity by means of a questionnaire that elicits the person's focal religious concerns. The result is a set of sentences that express the person's valuation system or indicate his or her personal religion. The valuations are tested against a list of affects to determine their emotional significance. The affects vary in an evaluative dimension of positive and negative feelings, and a motivational dimension of self-related feelings reflecting self-enhancement, as opposed to other-related feelings reflecting desire for contact with others.

Over the years valuation theory has been applied to a variety of religious identity issues.[7] In spiritual inquiry self-confrontation is employed as a pastoral care method aimed at clarifying personal religion. There are several ways of doing this.[8] The biographical procedure of spiritual inquiry resembles the standard valuation research procedure. It raises questions about the person's relationship with religion by incorporating the term 'spirituality' into the guiding questions that are commonly used. 'Spirituality' here connotes the activity of appropriating religious identity. The term is also chosen to avoid any possible aversion to more conventional expressions (religion, faith) which may link religious identity too directly with a specific creed or church. The biographical questionnaire contains

---

structionist paradigm. I will not elaborate on this here; mainly because the complex notion of the dialogical self demands more attention than I can give it here (Hermans, Kempen & Van Loon, 1992; Hermans, Rijks & Kempen, 1993; Hermans & Kempen, 1993; Hermans & Hermans-Jansen, 1995, pp. 101–111; 187–188).

[7] Hermans (1989), for instance, explicitly presents valuation theory as a theory of meaning construction and the self-confrontation method as a method for studying personal meaning. He also stresses the function of God imagery in relation to lifespan and moral development, the quest for meaning, ultimate recognition or ultimate value (Hermans & Hermans-Jansen, 1995, pp. 215–220; 109). The self-confrontation method has been applied to religious faith in various empirical studies, both in theology (Van Knippenberg, 1987; Putman, 1998) and in psychology of religion (Gerritsen, 1984).

[8] For instance, based on Glock's distinction with regard to personal religious commitment, I designed self-confrontation questionnaires to assess belief, practice, insight, experience, affects and consequences.

items that elicit valuations of past, present and future spirituality; spiritual unity and opposition; spiritual activity, enjoyment and relations with society; and spiritual emotions. The usual procedure is as follows. In a session lasting several hours the person's religious identity is discussed, in the course of which the results are described or symbolised in personal valuations. Afterwards the person relates his or her spiritual valuations to an affect matrix and the pastor uses basic statistical analyses to determine emotional balance (positive versus negative; self versus other) and affective covariance between valuations. Subsequently, in a second session, the results give rise to further exploration and validation of the spiritual valuations. Note that here, too, the construction of religious identity is based on mutual competence realised in social interaction: the pastor as the religious identity expert confronts the person as the experiential expert with muzzy, missing or delusive elements of his or her personal religion.

The procedure that I have described was followed in a campus ministry context, in which students were offered the opportunity to engage in spiritual inquiry to clarify their religious identity.[9] In the course of several years 56 spiritual inquiries were arranged, three of which are presented here by way of example.[10] I present these valuations as illustrations rather than as corroborations of personal religion.

One of the aims of the clarification of personal religion is to assess religious individualism. Let me give an example of religious individualism. Jonathan is a university student, a child from a broken marriage and concerned about his moral and religious identity.

Jonathan's case is illustrative of the religious individualism encountered in many other students who participated in the spiritual inquiries. Religion is a private concern. It is learnt (valuation 1) and reinforced (valuation 2) from childhood that 'imposed' or 'outward' religion should be avoided and that inner spiritual growth is preferable. If

---

[9] A Dutch campus ministry pastor, J Huysmans, offered the self-confrontation inquiry to Dutch university students in Nijmegen. In the course of several years he conducted 56 self-confrontation inquiries, some of which I present.

[10] The related scales contain several affects for each dimension: P(ositive), N(egative), S(elf) and O(ther). Each affect is scored on a scale ranging from 0 (not experienced at all) to 5 (experienced strongly). In this investigation the scores varied as follows: P (joy, satisfaction, enjoyment, unity, warmth, trust, safety, energy, inner calm, freedom): 0–50; N (powerlessness, fear, worry, anxiety, self-alienation, unhappiness, guilt, loneliness, anger and disappointment): 0–50; S (self-esteem, strength, self-confidence, pride): 0–20; and O (care, love, tenderness, intimacy): 0–20.

Valuation	S/O	P/N
1. When I was younger I learned from Sunday school that it is not good to impose spirituality. It should develop spontaneously within a person.	7,8	4,38
2. My parents taught me that the church is an outward phenomenon where personal feelings are of little importance.	6,5	343
6. My father's death raised doubts in my mind about whether there is a heaven where he now lives or will be forgiven.	5,17	25,36
8. I hope that there is a God who makes it clear that I have a destiny.	5,18	21,35
9. It's fine for me to learn lessons from difficult situations; however, it must not amount to bullying. God should let me live comfortably.	11,11	7,43
15. Sometimes, when I am alone, I feel intense happiness and these are moments when I feel I love myself.	20,15	32,11
20. Heavy churches, which impose a specific behaviour on people.	7,0	0,40
21. The Pharisees of today, the pope, the bishop, who know nothing about understanding and love but everything about church doctrine.	14,0	0,24
22. Sects that lock people up and cut them off from reality.	13,0	4,42
31. The meaning of my life is to learn from pain that comes my way, to live from a source of religious knowledge, and besides that simply to enjoy my life, be happy and give happiness to others.	16,17	21,35

we locate this individualism in Harré's dimensional model, it stresses private display and rejects public display, at least cognitively. However, Jonathan does not experience these valuations as positive. Looking back, he may even conclude that this individualism has caused loneliness, especially since the loss of his father (valuation 6). The religious autonomy he has gained may contribute to his ambivalence about his relationship with God, as it appears to have characteristics of a *fugit amor* experience characterised by a merging of dominant negative feelings with a desire for the other (valuation 8).[11] The learnt ban on religious public display may have made it difficult for Jonathan to appropriate the experience of God in moments of despair. Though life is hard for Jonathan, he expects God not to teach him the harsh way but to comfort him, as indeed happens when he is

[11] This notion of loss is also echoed in the 6th (r = .58) and 9th valuations (r = .50) and shows an intimate affective parallel between father and God as missing persons.

alone (valuations 9 and 15). Jonathan's religious individualism is also reflected in his opposition to organised religion that functions as an intermediary between God and human beings. These intermediaries actually stand between natural and artificial behaviour (valuation 20); between the good life and authority (valuation 21); between freedom and captivity (valuation 22).[12] Jonathan's emotional reaction has two characteristics: firstly, he registers a strong, dominant negative valuation and, secondly, he indicates feelings of self-enhancement, which express affective ascendancy of the self over desire for the other. If there is one criterion of the validity of personal religion, in Jonathan's view, it may well be an authentic life, accepting hardships and at the same time living an authentic, self-enhancing religious life, as it might prove beneficial to others (valuation 31).[13] The striving for authenticity runs a risk of being blocked in the processes of appropriation and transformation because of the structural ambivalence between private and public display, and the difficulty of integrating collective aspects of religion with a sense of religious individuality.

Religious identity is formed through a process of appropriation and transformation, in which private and public display is tested and collective and individual ways of control are tried. Barbara is a university student. Her valuations provide an interesting illustration of this formation process.

Ever since childhood Barbara's religious identity seems to have been characterised by a dynamics of internal versus external control. The metaphor of a puppet revealingly expresses her relationship with God as an entity controlling her life from the beginning (valuation 1). The image of a God who left her no opportunity for self-development illustrates the possibility of being locked up in a private display of religion. To transform this experience of God, Barbara needed to reappropriate God in a public setting. A church group proved to her that spiritual life could also appeal to her, bypassing religious convention as apparently represented by her father (valuations 2 and 19). But when she fell ill and started praying, she suddenly felt that someone was pulling the strings again (valuation 7).[14]

---

[12] The affective pattern of this resistance resembles that of his youth, if we note the significant positive correlations between valuations 1–2, 20–22 ($r > .48$).

[13] Jonathan's religious identity is marked by solitude, expressed in the hierarchy of affects in his inquiry which has loneliness at the top with a mean of 3.3.

[14] The emotional pattern shows a very high correlation with the first valuation ($R = .90$).

Valuation	S/O	P/N
1. Ever since I was a child God has held me in his hands like a puppet.	4,3	8,36
2. The youth group changed my attitude. Things were said in a way that touched me. Without Bible waffle.	11,7	28,10
3. The message of love was preached in church. I didn't manage it at home.	5,6	11,40
4. During a religion course I chose a photograph of birds flying away. I wanted to join them, heading for freedom. I was laughed at.	17,15	44,5
6. Music takes me into another world. For me it speaks. I find spirituality in it.	16,15	43,3
7. At a particular moment during my serious illness, I started praying. My independence was affected. It startled me.	0,3	2,46
9. (The isle of) Terschelling is my big love and refuge. Elysium perhaps. The dunes, the seagulls: I belong with them, I cannot live without them.	17,16	47,2
10. When I write I turn from chaos to calm. Writing is perhaps everything to me.	19,16	43,7
19. Papa is a hypocrite in his faith. He does not live by it, a Sunday Christian.	8,5	7,27
23. Although my boyfriend was not brought up religiously, I experience spiritual unity with him, so close are we.	17,18	45,6
24. With my mother, I also have spiritual solidarity. We stand together, have a close relationship.	10,15	31,14
25. *Jonathan Livingston Seagull* is my life book; I feel spiritually one with him.	20,15	44,2
29. For me, feelings of solidarity are connected with spirituality.	15,16	44,3
31. Death played a key role from my 18th to my 19th year. It fascinated me, attracted me.	6,7	29,18
32. Death now, I fear it more, because I appreciate life so much.	16,0	16,14

Barbara's cardinal concern seems to lie in the question: is there a private display of religion without an omnipotent God? The old images of religious identity seem inappropriate to express her personal religion. However, during a religious course she finds her own spiritual expression in the image of a bird that symbolises her identity in terms of freedom, solidarity and self-enhancement. It transforms her religious identity. Not the Bible but *Jonathan Livingston Seagull* becomes her 'life book'. Situations in which Barbara experiences togetherness constitute her spirituality and evoke a very similar affective pattern (valuations 4, 6, 9, 10, 23, 25, 29).[15] Her attraction

[15] The valuations cohere strongly (R = > .90). It also characterises her relationship with her mother (valuation 24; R = .61).

to seagulls seems to integrate the need for personal control (flying away) while also expressing the importance of solidarity (flying together) and freedom (flying above the Elysian fields). Her valuation system actually seems to contribute to self-enhancement.[16] Note that her attitude towards death has changed from seeing it as a more or less attractive escape to perceiving it as an unwanted contingency in life.[17] One has to admit that, from a conventional perspective, Barbara's spiritually cannot be called explicitly Christian. However, her valuations also demonstrate that traditional religious models can be dysfunctional to the acquisition of personal identity. Meanwhile, Barbara's seagull seems to be a sacred metaphor that symbolises her life-ethos as an envisaged reality that is worth living for. Barbara appears to have creative potential, a spiritual talent for personal religion when public religion fails.

In this chapter I have emphasised persuasion as a process underlying the construction of religious identity. I want to illustrate this with a last case, that of Mike. For Mike, his personal religion is of great importance in decision-making.

Faith is not simply transferred belief; it is an ongoing persuasive activity acquired from social interaction while simultaneously shaping and changing this interaction. Mike's first valuation reflects this very clearly. He appropriates his personal religion by discovering that his identity was at stake when he moved to a new home and by asserting the personal validity of his religion that had become obsolete. He had to persuade himself and others, although this caused an affective ambivalence that proved problematic even later in his life (valuations 1 and 17).[18] As a child, his faith was challenged again when a friend died (valuation 2). At a time when God seemed remote he experienced something of the supernatural with a psychic person who helped him restore his faith by suggesting that death is relative (valuation 3). This persuasion to think that God does exist, that there are grounds for justice, that death is not the end, reflects an active process of appropriation. It seems to have engendered a sense of personal responsibility for social justice.[19] It has transformed Mike's

---

[16] In the hierarchy of feelings the most frequent feelings are: energy (3.4), strength (3.3), self-esteem (3.1), self-confidence (3.1) and trust (3.0).

[17] The correlation of these valuations is zero.

[18] The valuations correlate positively: R = .59.

[19] Note a high positive correlation with hope, Mike's feeling of spirituality (valuation 29; R = .72).

Valuation	S/O	P/N
1. When we moved to a new home when I was 13, I had to defend and adapt my own religion.	11,3	21,29
2. When a friend was killed in an accident, my sense of God's justice and omnipotence vanished.	8,0	7,36
3. At the time when I felt that my faith was crumbling, I met a paranormally gifted person who talks with deceased relatives and Jesus and is clairvoyant. This gave me strength.	14,12	39,10
6. I hope that I can develop my spirituality in a way that in future I will be strong enough to resist temptation (such as elitist behaviour on account of wealth, pursuing wealth, loss of ideals).	18,7	34,20
7. My internship in Africa will maybe give me a goal and so shape my calling by God to work for justice among people.	14,10	26,12
8. In conversation with God I arrive at my own image of justice and I feel a vocation to work for this.	15,14	43,13
12. For me, enjoyment is only possible if it does not harm others; the most enjoyable things are things that prove to be good in the long run.	8,14	31,4
14. Talking to God while walking in a lonely wood (or elsewhere in nature) is to experience intense spiritual enjoyment.	17,16	40,13
15. The feeling of sharing spiritual views with others and conversations about this are also important for my sense of enjoyment.	17,18	37,3
16. I think a lot about ethical issues: 'did I do the right thing?'	10,5	12,35
17. I think a lot about the possibility of holding on to God in a world that usually thinks in terms of atheistic science.	8,0	9,34
26. Jesus image from 'Jesus Christ Superstar'.	17,14	38,18
29. Hope (= feeling of spirituality).	7,10	33,11
31: Aim: to show something of the kingdom, a just alternative to the world.	14,13	25,22

identity in the sense that he feels a personal urge to change his life to correspond with a new moral order. Mike accounts for this by seeing it as a vocation which he considers to be religious (valuation 8). Maybe the fact that the psychic person who helped restore his faith by 'talking to Jesus' also fostered his calling to strive for justice.[20] The painstaking scrutiny which is apparent in his pondering on moral issues (valuation 16), and which is still symbolised by the ambivalence that the metaphor of the kingdom evokes (valuation 31), seems to be transcended by a religious calling, which Mike experiences as joyful (valuations 8, 12 and 14). For Mike, spirituality is not an aim in itself but something to hope for. Actually Mike understands religious feeling as hope (valuation 29), as is also implied in

---

[20] Support for this is apparent in high positive correlations between valuations 3 and 26 (R = .70), and 3 and 8 (R = .74).

his wish to practise his religious vocation during his internship (val-uation 7). Meanwhile his spirituality strengthens his identity, as indi-cated by strong feelings of self-enhancement.[21] Mike's case illustrates that the rhetorical character of religious language can be experienced as faith and hope. Faith and hope are not so much an effect of per-suasion but may also represent its motives, conditions, means, aims, form and content.

Caring for Personal Religion

In this last section I shall comment briefly on opportunities to care for personal religion. These opportunities will have to be appropri-ated by taking on the challenges that the foregoing view of religious identity presents to various aspects of pastoral care. I will outline three of these challenges: religious individualism, religious instru-mentalism and religious relativism.

First, religious individualism presents a challenge to the established role of the pastor. In pastoral care the pastor's function and, by the same token, the church's objectives are defined as mediating reli-gious identity. This is evident, for instance, in the classical pastoral metaphors of the shepherd who leads the church, the teacher who offers doctrinal guidance, and the priest who mediates grace sacra-mentally. This dependence of care for religious identity on the inter-mediary role of the pastor tends to conflict with a growing religious individualism that questions the role of the pastor as an institutional representative of public religion. If modern people find solace in per-sonal religion and seem to be in charge of their own religious iden-tity, what is the point of the pastor's ecclesiastic services?

One answer to this question is to regard pastoral care as part of religion's persuasive function of promoting authentic selfhood. In such a view pastoral care would consist in stimulating people's capac-ity for religious exploration, harnessing their resources for religious development, and enhancing their religious problem-solving strate-gies.[22] This view can be applied to the debate between client-centred and mission-centred interpretations of pastoral care. Client-centred

---

[21] In Mike's hierarchy of affects, strength (3.2), energy (3.2), self-esteem (3.1) and trust (3.0) rank highest.

[22] Elsewhere I have interpreted these three aspects in a Jamesian framework as functions of spiritual guidance (Schilderman, 1998, 157–165).

interpretations of pastoral care emphasise a natural capacity for religious growth. This religious growth process is stimulated by salutary attitudes such as congruence, empathy and unconditional positive regard. Religious identity will flourish whenever the quality of religious communication is assured. Mission-centred interpretations of pastoral care emphasise the religious impetus and pastoral invocation of such things as revelation (kerygma), experience (Spirit) and pastoral activities (sacraments) as intrinsically valuable aims to pursue. Religious identity will flourish whenever religious core concerns are dealt with. In principle, both the client-centred and the mission-centred notions of pastoral care can be implemented in the context of religious individualism. But both may fail to value the necessary persuasive processes entailed by a social constructionist approach to religious identity. A client-centred approach to pastoral care may underestimate the persuasive effort needed to appropriate models of religious identity in personal selfhood. A mission-centred approach, on the other hand, may overestimate the persuasive effects of presented models of religious identity on personal selfhood. The point at issue is that the construction of religious identity must be understood neither as a person's solipsistic activity, nor as the outcome of a dyadic interaction between person and pastor, nor as an automatic process, but rather as a shared activation of the whole network of religious meaning that features in social interaction. Pastoral care can be seen as a persuasive function through which this network of meaning is explored, developed and applied to problems with the aim of attaining authentic religious selfhood.

Traditional key concepts of pastoral care in fact illustrate this. Let me cite the example of the classical definition of pastoral care by Clebsch and Jaekle. Following Hiltner's analysis, Clebsch and Jaekle (1975, pp. 32–66; Heitink, 1998, pp. 127–147) discern four pastoral aims in their anthology on the history of pastoral care: healing, sustaining, guiding and reconciling. Healing is interpreted as the effect of rituals that restore a person to wholeness. Rituals like anointing, devotional practices, exorcism and administration of sacraments may be seen as pastoral efforts to signify and incorporate the meaning of illness and health in the shared religious beliefs that make up personal religious identity. In this sense, it is not the priests or the rituals that persuade: it is the whole religious network supporting personal identity that is reappropriated and re-expressed. Thus, healing is experienced as a beneficial personal renewal of religious identity.

The second function described by these authors is sustaining, which is interpreted as support in suffering. It consists of four elements: preservation by limiting a specific loss; consolation by interpreting this loss in the context of the person's relationship with God; consolidation by harnessing the person's own resources to cope with the loss; and redemption by embracing the loss. Sustaining is based on the belief that in the experience of loss something is gained. The rhetorical effect of religious language in particular is that the reality of suffering is clothed in an aura of actual relief. Note that persuasion here is an act of compassion which expresses a shared authentic identity in the midst of (identity) loss. A third function of pastoral care is guidance. It orients the person facing problems with regard to lifestyle and world-view by applying the *sapientia perrennis* of religion to personal choice. Between listening and advising, guidance clarifies the relevance of faith to the vicissitudes of everyday life. Guidance may be considered a problem-oriented form of persuasion, strengthening religious identity when it is challenged by the contingencies that form its natural habitat, and establishing life praxis based on the better alternatives that faith offers. Reconciling is the last major characteristic of pastoral care described by Clebsch and Jaekle. It is defined as helping alienated persons to establish, consolidate or renew their relationship with God and their neighbour. In the mode of forgiveness, reconciliation actively demonstrates opportunities to leave behind old barriers and progress to reunion with God and with other people. In the mode of discipline, an admonition, correction, amendment or punishment is administered to guard against the temptations or evils that challenge faith. Reconciling is an attempt to accommodate the consequences of a person's actions in her or his religious identity by placing personal identity within the overarching framework of religious identity as ultimately expressed in the reality of God. These four functions of pastoral care can be interpreted as contributions to personal religion. Pastoral care makes use of the social networks in which religious selfhood is realised. It is realised, not by persuading somebody of something, but by putting into service ultimate definitions of reality, by employing implicit rhetorical language and by harnessing the persuasive processes in social interaction. This is one answer to the question of the pastor's role in religious individualism.

Secondly, religious instrumentalism challenges the function of the pastor. Religious instrumentalism is the theory that religious princi-

ples are tools or instruments for handling problems in a social environment, to be judged by their practical usefulness. Thus moral and
religious ends are transformed into means for a learning or growth
process.[23] Religion has as its instruments rhetorical language and persuasive processes, utilised in pastoral care with a view to authentic
religious selfhood. Does this view not reduce religion to a means to
some therapeutic end? This impression may be created if personal
religion is seen as a narrative reflecting a process of religious identity construction in which the pastor's task is merely to clarify, stimulate and guide. In the first place, there are good reasons to regard
therapy as a generic term for both pastoral care and psychotherapy.
The phrase 'therapy of the soul' reflects both an archaic notion of
pastoral care (*cura animarum*) and a modern denotation of psychotherapy
(Woolfolk, 1998). That therapy is a broad term encompassing both
psychotherapeutic and pastoral care is a point made by some authors,
with specific reference to the implied persuasive functions that make
therapy work.[24] In social constructionism therapy is seen as a discourse of authenticity. The therapist's competence does not lie in
the application of fixed diagnostic tools, but in assessing the client's
life story within the framework of a dialogue between client and
therapist (Anderson & Goolishian, 1992, pp. 34–37). This emphasis
on the instrumental function of narrative has prompted some social
constructionists to coin the term 'narrative utility' as a technique to
correct the individual's dysfunctions. This utility is not aimed at
reconstructing the world, nor does it refer to an internal model of
the self; it is understood as the actual performance of a narrative,
the illocutionary effects of which create, sustain or alter the client's
social reality. Referring to narrative utility, Gergen criticises its dependence on the commitment or belief structure of narratives in therapy because they suggest a 'true personal identity', leading to a kind

---

[23] For Dewey, who coined the term instrumentalism, this inquiry process aimed
at controlling experience had distinct religious significance.
[24] A theory that stresses this line of thought is that of Jerome Frank. Some decades
ago he developed a unified theory of suffering and healing that clarifies this persuasive function of therapy. Basically Frank understands the notion of identity from
the 'assumptive world', which is the set of beliefs that enables people to predict the
motives, behaviours and outcomes of (their) social interaction. The unhealthy state
is redefined as 'demoralisation', since it refers to the consequences of failed interaction with the world. Therapeutic success is a factor of mutual belief in healing
brought about by a myth that restores faith in one's own identity (Frank, 1973;
Van Kalmthout, 1991, pp. 83–86).

of rigidity that limits flexible construction of the world (Gergen & Kaye, 1992, pp. 175–183). Here Gergen seems to be overstating his case. The notion of suffering, curiously lacking from Gergen's argument, can be adequately interpreted as a violation of personal (and for that matter religious) identity. If personal identity presupposes ongoing identifying activity and if suffering can be understood as hampering this activity, therapy can very well be—and even must be—understood as an activity conducive to the persuasive dynamics of identity construction. In this sense, the naive criticism of instrumentalism in pastoral care has to be rejected.

But the criticism of religious instrumentalism goes further. The usual interpretation of persuasion is that it is a dyadic activity: the pastor influences a person with regard to religious attitudes. If religion indeed depends on rhetorical language, how do we account for the instrumental and strategic connotations of the concept of persuasion? The question is relevant in more than one respect. For one thing, it tempers the basic moral stance of authenticity in (religious) individualism that conflicts with the supposedly veiled intentions of persuasive praxis. Also, it jolts awake a type of religious missionary orientation of which proselytisation is the only or main goal and which misses the notion of appropriation that promotes religious identity. However, by viewing persuasion as a covert tactic, be it neurotic or political in nature, one misunderstands at least three things. Firstly, rhetorical language is much more deeply ingrained in everyday communication than its popular reference to successful oratory suggests. Ranging from highly personalised self-talk and the intimate strategies of family communication to the tools of social intercourse, marketing tactics and the conventions of public display, our reality is filled with beliefs, convictions and alluring attitudes. Rhetoric is readily overlooked and in many instances it strikes us as debatable only when reality is clearly at odds with the envisaged alternatives. A second oversight when branding persuasion instrumental or strategic is that persuasion is not a mere technique but a variable whose success depends on diverse aspects such as the situations in which it is applied, the motives fuelling it, the methods and techniques employed, the amount of pressure exerted, the aims pursued, and the effects. Opaqueness in any of these aspects of persuasive action can and must be discussed, but in doing so—as the notion of persuasion in fact implies—there is an appeal for induction, argument and choice. Though free will to persuade and be persuaded still depends on the communicative transparency of the various aspects of persuasion processes, this by no means implies that propaganda is its natural expression. Finally, the notion of persuasion implies de facto that we do not live in a transparent and stable world of controlled facts. The alternative to persuasion is not flawless access to reality through natural perception of the world. On the contrary, there is every reason to suppose that without persuasion our wishes, desires and fantasies may tend to reflect nonnegotiable characteristics of perception and behaviour. The principal argument is that persuasion puts the alterity of reality to the test by reflecting, not a world controlled by our actions, but one which prevents our actions from coinciding with the actuality that we stumble upon and which thus opens up our behavioural repertoire for innovation. As William James observed, we would believe much more if we only could. Hence the criticism of religious instrumentalism in pastoral care has to be put in the perspective of more basic assumptions regarding rhetorical language and persuasive processes in therapeutic or pastoral interaction.

Thirdly, religious relativism challenges the very core of pastoral care, namely its divine orientation. Religious relativists claim that there are no universal but only relative and variable religious truths depending on personal or social beliefs. In this view, changing or conflicting religious principles are equally true, so that there is no objective way of justifying any principle as valid for all people and all societies. This view is easily inferred from the social constructionist concept of religious identity that we have outlined. Personal religion, especially when understood as a result of rhetorical language and persuasive processes, may lead to religion for one's own convenience. In dealing with this issue, I want to point out first of all that, although the influence of institutionalised religion on personal identity should not be underestimated, a personally appropriated and expressed religion is above all an actuality. This does not apply only to the modern tendency towards *bricolage* which refers to eclecticism with its highly personalised religious styles. This tendency has probably always existed, though it may be underestimated because of the dominating influence of church monopolies and theological doctrines on the definition of religious reality. When we take up the challenge of religious relativism, we have to be aware of what is does not claim. The use of rhetorical language in religion and its persuasive appeal do not necessarily presuppose the absence of a

religious universal structure underlying these beliefs, nor do they pre-
clude criticism of such a belief structure. It also does not repudiate
the rationality implied in belief, nor does it necessarily rule out reference to underlying universal dispositions that facilitate valid interpretations for the justification of specific religious principles. So the
argument really affects the procedures through which we accept truths
as truths in religion.

Relativism is not necessarily presupposed in the social constructionist approach to religion outlined in this chapter. Does persuasive
religion presuppose that God is reduced to an illusory object, socially
constructed with the suspect objective of clarifying one's own identity? Or, to put it more bluntly, is God a social construction? The
question is relevant, since a person's religious identity and the personal identity of God are intrinsically linked, not merely as a perspective consequence of social constructionism, but basically as the
distinctive theistic characteristic of a personal God in the Abrahamic
religions of Judaism, Islam and Christianity. The pertinent question
is: when our core notions of identity, such as person, self and soul,
appear to be artefacts of social construction, is not a personal God
although transcending the intimacy of the self—likewise a human
creation? At first glance this question has to be answered affirmatively
in a social constructionist perspective: God is not a fact but an object
of persuasion. Even this supposition does not mean, however, that
the reality of God is questioned. For one thing, postulating God as
dependent on persuasion is not a judgment about the (un)reality of
the objects of belief.[25] In fact, persuasion must be understood as an
explicit invocation of the social understanding of these objects of
belief. Since any persuasive effort is rendered futile by premature
recognition that truths are relative and variable, explicit religious relativism has no credibility at all.

However, critical questioning of the justification of religious truths
is called for, since the truths themselves do not follow from persuasive processes. Here the notion of religious identity as the *trait de
union* between God and person must be taken up again. The point
is that the question about the reality of God cannot be answered
without answering the question about people's authenticity when they

---

[25] Even Freud's criticism of religion as illusory merely makes the point that religious beliefs depend on an affinity with wishes; illusions—in contrast to delusions—
are not necessarily at odds with reality (Freud, 1972, p. 65; 1980, pp. 110–113).

speak of God's reality. Our personal dependence on the reality of God entails the mediation of our imaginative capacities to grasp something of the unseen. This cannot simply be dismissed, for instance by invoking the biblical prohibition of making images of God. That prohibition is directed against idolatry, which is not necessarily, if at all, presupposed in attempts to express or to name God. The principal theological argument is quite the opposite: it holds that no finite expression can fully contain or refer to God, and thus confines human beings to the need for a right intention in signifying God.[26] This right intention comes very close to the notion of authenticity; alternatively, it can be criticised according to criteria of inauthenticity. An answer to the question of God's reality in objective truth claims misses the point that God's reality requires faith, as assessed in authentic judgments of taste. Such a judgment of taste requires personal answers in the ambivalent struggle between private and public display, individual and collective realisation of our religious identity.

In this struggle, God is a matter of faith, a better choice based on good reasons crucially linked with appreciation of ourselves, especially in the effort through which we appropriate and express shared beliefs in personal religion. Caring for this presents one of the basic challenges of pastoral ministry in modern times.

References

Anderson, H. & Goolishian, H. (1992). The Client is the Expert: a Not-Knowing Approach to Therapy. In: McNamee, S. & Gergen, K.J. (1992). *Therapy as Social Construction* (pp. 25–39). London: Sage Publications.

Bellah, R.N., Madsen, R., Sullivan, W.M., Swidler, A. & Tipton, S.M. (1985*). Habits of the Heart: Individualism and Commitment in American Life*. Berkeley: University of California Press.

Capps, D. (1993). The Depleted Self. Sin in a Narcissistic Age. Minneapolis: Fortress Press.

Capps, D. & Fenn, R.K. (Ed.) (1992). *Individualism Reconsidered: Readings bearing on the endangered self in modern society*. Princeton: Princeton Theological Seminary.

Clebsch, W.A. & Jaekle, C.R. (1975). Pastor*al Care in Historical Perspective*. New York: Jason Aronson.

Ester, P., Halman, L.; & Moor, R. de (Ed.) (1993). *The Individualizing Society. Value Change in Europe and North America*. Tilburg: Tilburg University Press.

---

[26] In classical theology the actual significance of understanding God is not implied in God images (*attribuere Deo*) but in perceptions that intend God (*tendere in Deum*). This does not mean that in naming God analogies cannot be used to express the mutual commitment of God and humans (Schillebeeckx, 1966, p. 213).

Frank, J.D. (1973). *Persuasion and Healing. A Comparative Study of Psychotherapy*. London: Oxford University Press.

Freud, S. (1972). *Das Unbehagen in der Kultur*. Frankfurt am Main: Fischer. (Translation: Civilization and its Discontents 1983. New York, Norton).

—— (1980). *Die Zukunft einer Illusion*. Frankfurt am Main: Fischer. (Translation: the Future of an Illusion, 1964. Garden City, NY: Doubleday).

Furnham, A. (1990). Commonsense Theories of Personality. In: Semin, G.R. & Gergen, K.J. (Eds.). *Everyday Understanding. Social and Scientific Implications* (pp. 176–203). London: Sage Publications.

Geertz, C. (1993). *The Interpretation of Cultures. Selected Essays*. London: Fontana Press.

—— (2000). *Available Light: Anthropological Reflections on Philosophical Topics*. Princeton: Princeton University Press.

Gelpi, D.L. (Ed.) (1989). *Beyond Individualism. Towards a Retrieval of Moral Discourse in America*. Notre Dame: University of Notre Dame Press.

Gergen, K.J. (1985). Social Constructionist Inquiry: Context and Implications. In: Gergen, K.J. & Davis, K.E. (Eds.). *The Social Construction of the Person* (pp. 3–18). New York: Springer-Verlag.

—— (1989). Warranting Voice and the Elaboration of the Self. In: Shotter, J. & Gergen, K.J. (Eds.). *Texts of Identity* (pp. 70–81). London: Sage Publications.

—— (1999). *An Invitation to Social Constructionism*. London: Sage Publications.

Gergen, K.J. & Kaye, J. (1992). Beyond Narrative in the Negotiation of Therapeutic Meaning. In: McNamee, S. & Gergen, K.J. (Eds.). *Therapy as Social Construction* (pp. 166–185). London: Sage Publications.

Gerritsen, A.J. (1984). *Religieuze ontwikkeling. Godsdienstpsychologisch onderzoek met behulp van de zelfconfrontatiemethode bij deelnemers aan een gebedspraktikum* [Religious Development. Research in psychology of Religion, using the Self Confrontation Method with participants of a prayer-retreat]. Lisse: Zwets en Zeitlinger.

Harré, R. (1983). *Personal Being. A Theory for Individual Psychology*. Oxford: Blackwell.

Heitink, G. (1998). *Pastorale zorg. Theologie, differentiatie, praktijk* [Pastoral care. Theology, differentiatie, practice]. Kampen: Kok.

Hermans, H.J.M. (1975). *Gaat de unieke persoon in de psychologie ten onder? De relatie tussen psycholoog en persoon vanuit het perspectief van een tweerichtingtheorie* [Does the unique person fade in psychology? The relationship of psychologist and person from the perspective of a bi-directional theory]. Amsterdam: Swets en Zeitlinger.

—— (1989). The Meaning of Life as an organized Process. *Psychotherapy*, 26 (1), pp. 11–22.

Hermans, H.J.M. & van Loon, R.J.P. (1991). The personal Meaning of Symbols. A Method of Investigation. *Journal of Religion and Health*, 30, 241–261.

Hermans, H.J.M., Kempen, H.J.G. & van Loon, R.J.P. van (1992). The Dialogical Self. Beyond Individualism and Rationalism. *American Psychologist*, 47 (1), 23–33.

Hermans, H.J.M. & Kempen, H.J.G. (1993). *The Dialogical Self: Meaning as Movement*. San Diego: Academic Press.

Hermans, H.J.M., Rijks, T.I. & Kempen, H.J.G. (1993). Imaginal Dialogues in the Self. Theory and Method. *Journal of Personality*, 61, 207–236.

Hermans, H.J.M. & Hermans-Jansen, E. (1995). *Self-narratives. The Construction of Meaning in Psychotherapy*. New York: Guilford Press.

Kalmthout, M. van (1991). *Psychotherapie. Het bos en de bomen* [Psychotherapy. The forest and the trees]. Amersfoort: Acco.

Knippenberg, M.P.J. van (1987). *Dood en religie. Een studie naar communicatief zelfonderzoek.* [Death and Religion. A study of communicative self-research]. Kampen: Kok.

Larson, C.U. (1992). *Persuasion. Reception and Responsibility* (6th edition). Belmont: Wadsworth Publishing Company.

Lasch, Chr. (1979). *The Culture of Narcissism: American Life in an Age of Diminishing Expectations*. New York: Warner Books.

Lukes, S. (1973). *Individualism. Key Concepts in the Social Sciences*. Oxford: Basil Blackwell.

Mulholland, J. (1994). *Handbook of Persuasive Tactics. A Practical Language Guide*. London: Routledge.

Murray, K. (1989). The Construction of Identity in the Narratives of Romance and Comedy. In: Shotter J. & Gergen, K.J. (1989). *Texts of Identity* (pp. 176–205). London: Sage Publications.

O'Keefe, D.J. (1990). *Persuasion. Theory and Research*. London: Sage Publications.

Peursen, C.A. van (1985). De opbouw van de wetenschap. Een inleiding in de wetenschapsleer. [The formation of science. An introduction into the philosophy of science]. Meppel: Boom.

Potter, J. (1996). *Representing Reality. Discourse, Rhetoric and Social Construction*. London: Sage Publications.

Putman, W. (1998). Godsbeelden en zelfverhaal. Een onderzoek met behulp van de waarderingstheorie en de Zelfconfrontatiemethode, naar de betekenis van persoonlijke godsbeelden [God-images and self-narrative. Research, using valuation theory and the Self Confrontation Method, into the meaning of personal god-images]. Tilburg: Tilburg University Press.

Ricoeur, P. (1992). *Oneself as Another*. Chicago: University of Chicago Press.

Schilderman, J.B.A.M. (1998). Guidelines for a Research Program. In: T. van Knippenberg (Ed.). *Between two languages. Spiritual Guidance and Communication of Christian Faith* (pp. 153–167). Tilburg: Tilburg University Press.

Schillebeeckx, E. (1966). *Wereld en Kerk. Theologische Peilingen 3* (Tilburg: Tilburg University Press. World and Church, 1982. London: Sheed and Ward). Bilthoven: Nelissen.

Searle, J.R. (1995). *The Construction of Social Reality*. London: Penguin Books.

Shavitt, S. & Brock, T.C. (Ed.) (1994). *Psychological Insights and Perspectives*. Boston: Allyn and Bacon.

Shotter, J. (1993). *Conversational Realities. Constructing Life through Language*. London: Sage Publications.

Stiff, J.B. (1994). *Persuasive Communication*. New York: The Guilford Press.

Taylor, C. (1989). *Sources of the Self. The Making of the Modern Identity*. Cambridge, Massachusetts: Harvard University Press.

—— (1992). *The ethics of Authenticity*. Cambridge M.: Harvard University Press.

Tocqueville, A. de (1972). *Democracy in America* (The Henry Reeve text as revised by Francis Bowen now further corrected and edited with introduction, editorial notes, and bibliographies by Philip Bradley). New York: Alfred A. Knopf.

Woolfolk, R.L. (1998). *The Cure of Souls. Science, Values, and Psychotherapy*. San Francisco: Jossey-Bass Publishers.

SOCIAL CONSTRUCTION OF MORAL IDENTITY IN VIEW OF A CONCRETE ETHICS

CHRIS A.M. HERMANS
JOOST DUPONT

1. *Moral Identity from a Social Constructionist Perspective*

There is no canonical set of theoretical presumptions of social constructionism. From a perspective of social constructionism, it is absurd to look for such a canonical set. We will describe some features of a social construction of moral identity, based on the work of Gergen (1985; 1991; 1998; 1999) and Day and Tappan (Day 1991, 1996; Day & Tappan, 1996). We will relate values and norms to religion in order to point to some specific insights and questions that a social constructionist conception of moral identity can raise (section 1.1). Afterwards we will refer the criticism of this social constructionist perspective on moral identity, especially from scholars within the Kohlbergian tradition (section 1.2).

1.1 *Social Construction of Moral Identity*

What characterizes a social construction of moral identity? We will not repeat what we have said above about a social construction of identity. We will focus on the characteristics of a *moral* identity, as it is constructed socially. We will draw on several authors who stand in the paradigm of social constructionism. They all share the idea that narratives play a central role in a social construction of moral identity. We will begin by considering Gergen's reflections on this storied nature of moral identity, and add some ideas, which have been advanced by other authors within this line of thinking. This is not a school of thought as, for example, the Kohlbergian tradition is. Putting these authors under the heading of social constructionism does not mean that there are no differences between them.

Gergen (1998, p. 195) clarifies the concept of the moral self in three points.

The first is the idea that narrative has a pragmatic function in cultural life. The meaning of language is derived from its social (or pragmatic) function in life. The same is true for narrative. A good story has to be understood in terms of the social function of the story (Gergen, 1998, p. 185). A key question is: 'Who is benefiting from this story in this situation?' The content and structure of a story is also influenced by the social context in which it is told. Within a social group a certain story serves as an ideal of a well-structured narrative. Research on testimonies in the courtroom shows that a story is to be believed truer, to the degree that it is closer to this 'ideal story' of the social group.

The second point is that narratives create values. Every story is directed towards a valued end (Gergen, 1998, p. 172). Everything that is happening is directed towards this end. According to Gergen, this valued end is influenced by the sociocultural context in which people tell their story. Some ends are valued within a social group, and others are not. By directing a story to this valued end, the narrator enters the realm of moral and political valuation (Gergen, 1998, p. 187).

Self-narratives are a way to identify and preserve values for the self, and a moral community. Human moral conduct cannot be considered apart from its emplotment in self-narratives. Through a story, a self is created that is responsible for his or her acting, and has moral integrity as an acting subject (Gergen, 1998, p. 195). At the same time, the basis for a moral community is created by these self-narratives. There are always other people included in a story, who are mutually responsible for one another within a community. These connections between the actions of persons create a moral community. In my narrative I confirm the valued end of others, and in their story the valued end of my actions is also confirmed. This inter-relatedness implies that if I question their narrative, I question the moral identity of other people. For example, if one questions the narrative of the Holocaust, one also denies the moral identity of Jews who have suffered in and from these events. Or to put it in a positive way: community begins, wherever we begin to understand the story of others (Gergen, 1998, p. 198). Community is constructed in the very process in which two of more people construct a story, understandable for them both, about what has happened. And whenever these shared stories become a part of the implicit horizon of understanding of a social group, they function as a guarantee of mutual solidarity.

Day (1991, 1996; also Day & Tappan, 1996) adds two things to the above idea of social construction of moral identity.

1. There are two different moral voices (justice & care) which represent different languages on values. Most persons, who tell their story, voice both 'voices' (see also Brown et al., 1989). These two voices or moral orientations are: justice and care.

> The justice voice reflects an absence of oppression or an ideal of equal-
> ity, reciprocity, and fairness between persons; the care voice reflects
> safeguards against disconnection of an ideal of a responsive relation-
> ship, of loving and being loved, listening and being listened to, and
> responding and being responded to (Tappan, 1993, p. 4).

The voices of justice (vs. inequality) and care (vs. oppression and abandonment) are universal human experiences. In some situations and for some persons, a certain voice is dominating. It is also pos-sible for there to be a shift in a history of events from one voice to another voice. Individuals are however 'polyphonic', that is, they can speak in the language of both voices of justice and care. According to Tappan, these voices are gender-related, not gender specific (Tappan, 1993, p. 6). Research into both voices, indicates that males are more frequently oriented toward justice than females, while females are more frequently oriented toward care than males. There is no indication in the research that both voices are gender-specific (Brown et al., 1989). Females use the voice of justice, and males use the voice of care. There is a polyphony of voices, and people shift in time from one voice to another voice (Tappan, 1993, p. 11).

2. Moral life is not just storied, but theatrical. Moral actions occur in relation to other persons-as-audience. If we want to understand the moral judgment and moral action of a person, we need to grasp the nature of the actor's relation to the audience(s) before whom she most centrally acts (Day & Tappan, 1996, p. 70). The meaning of moral actions is always decided within relationships (Day, 1991). Moral terms are seen as grammars effected to shape relationship(s), and applying only in the social world. A person is never simply speaking in order to express what is inside (such as beliefs, feelings of principles). A person is always speaking to—both to others and to the self. If one wants to understand what a person is saying, one has to be mindful of the audience the individual is addressing. The nature of this dialogical process between self and others is misunder-stood, if one understands the self as just being influenced by others,

or by taking the position of the other. Day and Tappan (1993, p. 73) quote Charles Taylor who says that: 'Human beings are constituted in conversation; and hence what gets internalized in the mature subject is not the reaction of others, but the whole conversation, with the interanimation of its voices.' The moral self arises in the midst of the struggle between different voices. It is impossible to strip the voice of the moral audience being addressed. A girl of fifteen years old will express her moral voice differently when speaking with her peer group than to her teachers. Or a professional in the health care system will express herself differently to another professional than to a patient. If one wants to understand the meaning of what a person says, one has to include the audience to which a person is speaking. According to Day and Tappan (1993, p. 70), moral development consists of the formation and transformation of moral audiences in the experience of moral actors. If we want a person to become a moral actor, we have to involve this person in a dialogue with others in order to construct a moral audience in this person. Through a process of internalization, this person will start to understand her moral actions in the context of this audience. If the moral audience consists of people that belong to a religious community, this should result in a connection between religion and values and norms in this person. The kind of connection depends on the conception of this connection within the tradition of this religious community. For example, there is a tradition within Christianity that interprets values and norms as derived from the Christian religion. This means that Christian ethics is a special ethics that leads to norms and values different form other ethical systems. This position is sometimes described as 'religious ethics' [in German: 'Glaubensethik'] (see Auer, 1977, pp. 30–32). There is also a tradition within Christianity that regards values and norms as a domain independent of religion. This position is described as 'autonomous ethics' [in German: 'autonome Moral']. Each of these traditions can be differentiated in sub-traditions (Schüller, 1976; Böckle, 1981). In the context of this chapter we will not elaborate on these different positions. From a social constructionist perspective, these differences can be interpreted as different moral audiences from which people construct their moral identity.

Tappan (1991; 1993) offers a *telos* for the moral development. He speaks about moral authorship as the aim of moral development. Authority implies responsibility and accountability (Tappan, 1991,

p. 7). Tappan clarifies this concept of 'authority' in two steps. To author a story is to construct the meaning of one's actions. In the same way as an author is responsible for the normative end of a story, a person is responsible for his or her action. There is an analogy between authoring and acting. There is also a second reason for why authorship is helpful in an analysis of human action. An author is not only the creator of his or her story, he or she is also responsible for it. 'As authors of our own lives, we are necessarily responsible and accountable for our thoughts, feelings, and actions in the world.' (Tappan, 1991, p. 11). Authority is inexorably connected to responsibility.

According to Tappan, this *telos* of moral authority is applicable to moral development across a variety of gender, racial, class, and cultural differences. The moral content of this authorship is connected with a particular perspective of the stories of a specific group or community. Whatever these stories are and what is valued in them, to become the author of one's life means to be responsible for one's acts. This process of becoming the author of one's life has to be placed within a relational and sociocultural context. A child begins by assimilating and internalizing the stories of others, and gradually the child's own voice emerges within the polyphony of voices within a situation. Tappan refers to a notion of Bakhtin, who differentiates between internally persuasive words and externally authoritative words (Tappan, 1991, p. 20). The second refers to telling one's story in the words of others. For example, a child explains why what she has done is right in the way her mother would. Through the words of the child, her mother is speaking. Internally persuasive refers to the process of telling one's story in one's own words. This does not imply an individualistic, isolated, "here-I-stand" autonomy. Even when such an authority and independence is achieved, this must still be understood within the context of dialogue and relationship.

The relationship of values and norms to religion complicates the process of development of moral authority. In the tradition of 'religious ethics' values and norms are to be accepted on the basis of Gods authority. According to Schüller (1976) there are two types in Catholic moral tradition. In the first type values and norms have a foundation in the aims of nature, in which God as Creator manifests his care for humankind. In the second type, the moral justification of certain values and norms is the prerogative of God, and cannot be given by humankind. The religious basis of values and norms in

a 'religious (i.e. Christian) ethics' puts them in the category of externally authoritative words. The authority of God can not be removed
from these values and norms without transforming them. Acting on
the basis of these norms and values will always be done bases on
the authority of God, and not on ones own authority. This is different
in the case of 'autonomous ethics'. God has created humankind as
moral autonomous beings (Böckle, 1991, p. 56). The destination of
a person in creation is to find their own moral autonomy in acting
towards others, nature and the self. In this latter tradition the goal
of moral development is the transformation of values and norms into
internally persuasive words. The difference between internally persuasive words and externally authoritative words within a social constructionist perspective on moral identity can help us clarify the way
people handle values and norms within religious communities.

1.2   *Criticism of the Social Constructionist Perspective*

Theorists, who stand within the Kohlbergian tradition, heavily criticize the constructionist perspective of moral identity. A special issue
of *Human Development* in 1996 was dedicated to the debate between
the constructionist[1] and Kohlbergian tradition (see Lourenco, 1996;
Lapsley, 1996 and Puka, 1996). These are the major points of criticism of the constructionist conception of the moral self?

The first is the absence of a moral criterionby which human actions
and ideas can be judged (Lourenco, 1996, pp. 85–87). Do we not
end in moral relativism and nihilism without a moral stance based
on universal moral principles? The social constructionists describe
how people come to moral authority. They have to accept every
moral narrative, because there is no moral stance to judge all the
different stories. There is no universal truth beyond local narratives.[2]

Secondly, from a constructionist perspective moral principles are
publicly shared in communicative practices and forms of discourse
(Lapsley, 1996, p. 103). There is nothing 'just in the head'; the moral

---

[1] In this special issue, they speak about narrative approaches instead of a constructionist approach. We think that it is possible to place Day and Tappan within
the constructionist tradition. They often refer to literature within the constructionist tradition (especially Gergen), but do not place themselves within social constructionism

[2] Not everybody agrees with this critique. According to Puka (1996, p. 109),
Lourenco is equating caring contextualism with relativism and nihilism.

self arises out of the narratives that people share. 'Moral narratives are theatrical in the sense that we rehearse our options and enact our intentions before an internalized audience of real or imagined individuals whose critical review gives shape to our moral performances' (Lapsley, 1996, p. 103). The problem is however, is my story true? Theatrical can be the equivalent of 'make-believe'. Is it really my story or just something that I have made up in order to reach the result that I desire in a specific situation? Is the narrative approach not running into problems it cannot solve, unless it finds a ground in a concept of rationality as the Kohlbergian approach did? According to Lourenco (1996, p. 93), this rationalist assumption in Kohlberg's theory is reflected in its emphasis on the logical criteria of integration, differentiation, equilibrium, reversibility, and universalizability that define the moral point of view. The level of moral reasoning is determined by the ability of individuals to use these logical criteria. This developing rationality can deal with the complexity of a situation, a complexity reflected in the polyphony of voices in a situation. In moral development *sensu Kohlberg*, one of the characteristics of moral development is an increasing capacity to recognize and cope with this complexity. The constructionist conception seems to lack such an aspect. The finding of one's own voice can even lead to a simplification of the situation. Complexity stands against simplicity, while relativism stands against objectivism.

Thirdly, social constructionism implies that different moral viewpoints cannot be compared because they operate within different narrative traditions. We are left with no arguments for why we should choose cooperative narratives in stead of opportunistic one's. We can see in everyday life within our society, that the narrative of caring is not rigid enough to break the oppression which exists on both a personal and an institutional level in our society (Puka, 1996, p. 109). The theory of Kohlberg, on the other hand, is more than just a methodology. It has its foundation in deontologic theories of morality (Kant, and Rawls).

A last point of criticism refers to the concept of care (and relates indirectly to the work of Gilligan and her colleagues). We will restrict ourselves to one element in this discussion. Day and Tappan distinguish to the voice of care from the voice of justice. The idea is that care is a distinct moral competence, related to a single moral voice. According to Puka (1996, p. 112; also Blum, 1992, p. 197) this poses an interpretive problem because the concept of care is interpreted differently in different situations. Is there just one voice of care, or a polyphony of voices of care? I suppose that Gergen would opt for the latter, instead of the first. But this brings us back the question of whether we should have a moral principle from which we can judge the actions and convictions of people. Is there moral criterion to be found within this multitude of voices?

The focus of social constructionism is on the psychological process of *how* persons construct their moral judgment. There is but little reflection on what a good moral judgment or moral action is. Only Tappan (1991) speaks about a *telos* in moral development, but has not elaborated this point from an ethical perspective. He refers to the process of ideological becoming but offers little reflection on the concept of morality implied in this process of becoming. By what moral principle could we judge people actions or judgments? Can there be a 'last' principle within a social constructionist perspective? Does everyone have his or her own 'principle' from which they tell his or her story?

2. *Different Types of Ethics*

The debate between the social constructionist theory on moral identity and moral development and the Kohlbergian tradition leaves us with the impression that the first is without a moral principle (or better, plagued by a plurality of moral principles), while the second has a firm moral ground in the deontologic ethics (Kant, Rawls). We want to challenge this formulation of the debate between the social constructionist and Kohlbergian tradition.[3] There is a difference between both theories, but we think that this difference goes back to different ethical traditions within Western moral philosophy. At the core of these traditions, there is a different moral criterion or moral principle.[4] In the next section we will first elaborate this idea

---

[3] This debate is often interpreted from the personal-impersonal framework (see Lourenco, 1996; Puka, 1996). There is a beautiful analysis by Blum (1993), in which he challenges this framework. Some moral actions are distinct from the pursuit of personal good and the demands of impersonal morality: such as direct caring on behalf of a fellow (communal) member, appeal on vocation, a specific relationship with a specific history.

[4] Principle is understood here in a broad sense, as the moral ground to judge some action or conception as good or not good. We do not restrict the term principle to the rational rules of moral judgement, as is characteristic for rational ethics.

of different types of ethics (section 2.1.). We will then go deeper into the moral criterion that is behind one type of ethics, namely a concrete ethics (section 2.2).

2.1 *Nearness and Distance*

The Belgian ethicist Johan Taels (1998) can provide us with a theoretical framework to interpret both the constructionist and Kohlbergian position. According to Taels, every ethical position requires a double movement between distance and nearness, or reflexivity and commitment. Without reflexivity and distance there can be no ethics. Reflexivity breaks the close proximity of 'self' and 'other'. A person is a moral being, because (s)he doesn't coincide with the natural and social space in which (s)he lives. As Nietzsche has said, humans are moral beings because they are a 'nicht fest-gestelltes Tier' (an non-determined animal) (Taels, 1998, p. 373). Human beings have themselves as task; they need to find an orientation towards themselves, the other and the world. Through the process of self-distancing, people can question what is right or wrong. According to Taels, it is possible to differentiate between three types of self-distancing, within (post)modern, Western society, namely a rational, an esthetic and a concrete conception. According to Taels, both aspects of distance and nearness, or reflection and commitment are necessary for an ethical position. However, there are a differences within these three different ethical theories in the amount of stress they place on these two aspects.

Within the rational tradition (for example Kantianism, utilitarianism) all the stress is on the reflective aspect. According to Kant, human nature is subject to influences of natural laws and motivated by needs and lust. There can only be a moral person if the human will is subjected to the laws of reason. With the help of reason people have to try to reach a maximum of transparency of their own deeds, and the actions of others. According to Kant, 'every reasonable being, as aim in itself, must regarding all the laws that it might be subjected to, at the same time consider himself as the maker of a general law'. How does this rational ethics deal with the aspects of distance and nearness? It is by reflectivity that the 'I' disconnects itself from the symbioses with the 'not-I', and creates an irreducible tension within existence between the 'I' and 'not-I', between the possible world and the actual world. Rational ethicists want to handle this division within human existence through distance, and to find the truly good by abstraction of the contingent reality. Within contingent reality, nothing is necessary and thus everything could be something different. However, the prescriptive rules for people to act upon should be universal: they should be the same for all people in the same circumstances.

The (post)modern esthetic tradition sees the esthetic experience as the true ethical ideal (see for example Richard Rorty, Zigmund Bauman). This is the ideal of self-creation and self-development. Persons do not have an archimedic center, but consist of a plurality of selves or quasi-selves. Human relations are fragmented and discontinuous. The estheticist believes passionately that the self is 'lord of the kingdom of possibilities'. Through a process of narrative recreation, people try to be the author of their ever-changing life story (Taels, 1998, p. 381). This ideal of self-creation is unmistakably based upon a grammar of self-distancing, but this is an esthetic grammar driven by the pathos of the possible. 'The esthetic pleasure is not immediately, but reflective: he takes joy not in reality as such but in the lucid dealing with reality, of their own control in creating a space without borders or obstacles' (Taels, 1998, p. 382). How does an esthetic ethic deal with the aspects of distance and nearness? Within the esthetic ethics one tries to resolve the existential split between possible and actual world by distancing from the embeddedness of the self in contingent reality. This distance creates a possibility for the narrative transformation of reality. Through imagination, the self creates meaning in the chaotic and contingent reality. Within esthetic ethics it is not the rational will but the creative imagination that is the instrument with which a person creates the moral good.

In concrete ethics, the process of self-distancing is realized through the involvement in the concrete, contingent reality in which people find themselves. A concrete ethics is, in the first place, a clarification of the paradox of existence between possibility and fact, between actuality as given and ideality as task. According to Taels, this kind of ethics is to be found in virtue ethics, hermeneutic and phenomenological ethics, and also an ethics of care (Taels, 1998, note 32). 'The concrete ethics is an ethic of nearness, that wants to put the demand of self-knowledge as concrete as possible in the life of this particular subject' (Taels, 1998, p. 383). The self reflects on the concrete relationships it is in, not with the aim to transcend this particularity, but of finding itself as a moral subject within these relationships. The self accepts the seriousness of the particularity of time and place in becoming a moral self. This is a deed of acceptance and affirmation of the situatedness of his or her concrete relationships. Only through a moral commitment to the appeal of this particular person or this situation, is the ethical meaning of reality revealed. It is through the other that the self receives its moral quality, as a self that is responsible for the other, or for the situation. Without the appeal of the other, there could be no moral self. Ethical responsibility is always first person responsibility: there is always someone responsible for something to somebody else.

We think that this typology can help us to put the discussion between the Kohlbergians and social constructionists in a different perspective. Perhaps one could say, that the Kohlbergian school of moral development feels more at home in a rational ethic, which puts more stress on distance and reflectivity than on nearness and commitment. Or more precisely, nearness and commitment is reached through distancing and reflection. However, it would be wrong to say that the Kohlbergian tradition is abstract, with little attention to motivation and commitment (see Day & Tappan, 1996). Both reflexivity and nearness are there, but there is a focus on reflexivity. The Kohlbergian tradition has a firm basis within rational ethics (Kant, Rawls). The question is whether a social constructionist perspective on moral identity could find a moral basis in one of the other types of ethics, namely an esthetic ethic or concrete ethic.

2.2 *The Problem of Otherness within an Esthetic Ethics*

A social constructionist perspective on moral identity can be connected to an esthetic ethic or to a concrete ethic. Most scholars within social constructionism see moral identity as created through narratives. Moral imagination is narrative imagination. The moral ideal is equivalent to the esthetic ideal of self-creation. This esthetic ideal is also a moral criterion, and perhaps even a universal principle in the sense that it is same for everyone in every situation. However, it is different from prescriptive rules like the Kantian categorical imperative, or the moral musical chairs of Rawls. The esthetic ethics is closer to a rational ethic than to a concrete ethic in the sense that the rational and esthetic ethics share the focus on distance and reflectivity. We think, that not many scholars within the social constructionist perspective perceive this resemblance with a rational ethics. However, we see a more fundamental problem in esthetic ethics. We can agree with esthetic ethics that "All reality is interpreted by the stories we tell", but this does not mean that one can tell any story. An esthetic ethics neglects the experience of passivity in the construction of moral identity. According to Paul Ricoeur (1992, p. 318) there are three restrictions for a narrative construction of moral identity: our bodily existence, the other (and his bodily existence) and our consciousness. Ricoeur calls this the triad of passivity, and hence of otherness (o.c.). The otherness is not added to selfhood, but the self attests to otherness as a constitutive part of the self. In this experience of passivity, it becomes clear that the self cannot tell any story imaginable.

Firstly, suppose that a health care worker constructs a story of a successful practitioner that is loved by all his patients. While telling this story, the practitioner feels a pain in his stomach or his heart beating fast. His body is resisting the story that he is telling. It is not the right story or at least not the complete story. Or consider the case of a physical therapist that wants to give manual therapy to a patient. In this treatment, the physical therapist is restricted by the possibilities of his body (i.e. the movement of his hands). This experience of passivity of our own body restricts the moral imagination of an esthetic ethics.

Secondly, other persons with their feelings, expectations, ideas and moral standards can resist the story that we tell. For example, a physical therapist can tell a story in which he has cured the patient of certain physical pains, but the other has to say whether the pain has diminished or not. The physical therapist cannot tell any story about the cure of the patient. The other, and especially what is foreign to the self, restricts the moral imagination of an esthetic ethics.

Thirdly, conscience can resist an arbitrary construction of narrative moral identity. The first aspect of conscience that Ricoeur points to is the force of suspicion (Ricoeur, 1992, p. 347). It is the experience of the physical therapist that asks him- or herself: 'Is it true that I have done a good job in this situation'. Are there facts, feelings, effects that resist this story of a good job? A second aspect is what Ricoeur calls 'listening to the voice of conscience' (Ricoeur, 1992, p. 351). It is a voice that speaks to a person prior to any action towards the other. This voice calls a person to live well with and for others in just institutions, and to esteem oneself as the bearer

of this wish (Ricoeur, 1992, p. 352). This appeal or vocation is experienced by the person as coming over him or her (and in this sense
is an experience of otherness), but is at the same time something
that is part of the self. For example, one could think of a physical
therapist confronted with the suffering of a patient. Technically speaking, the physical therapist has done all that he can to cure the
patient. From an institutional perspective, he is at the end of the
treatment. The patient should look for help somewhere else. But 'listening to the voice of his or her conscience' the physical therapist
does not want to break the relationship with this patient, and wants
to respond to the needs of the patient.

An esthetic ethic that focuses on moral imagination has problems
dealing with this experience of passivity or otherness. It neglects the
passivity, which is based on the otherness, that is an essential part
of the self (and thus for a narrative construction of moral identity).
We will see in the next paragraph that a concrete ethics can deal
better with this experience of passivity or otherness.

2.3   *The Subjective Irreducibility of the Other*

If one wanted to develop a social constructionist conception of moral
identity in connection with some form of concrete ethics what would
its moral criterion be? To be clear, it is also possible to connect
social constructionism with an esthetic ethics. In a sense this would
be even closer to the Kohlbergian tradition, because esthetic ethics
and rational ethics (Kant) both belong to an ethic of distance. We
choose the opposite road and search for a moral criterion in an ethic
of nearness. The reason for this is that an ethic of nearness is closer
to one of the characteristics of social constructionism, namely the
construction of meaning within relationships. We are looking for a
moral criterion that is implied in a dialogic construction of moral
identity. From a social constructionist perspective, ethics and sociality are seen as closely related to another.

This search leads us to a modern ethics of dialogue, such as offered
by Levinas and Bakhtin. Although there is a lot of difference between
these ethics, they seem to share a common moral principle, namely
the subjective irreducibility of the other as the groundless ground of
concrete ethics (Nealon, 1997; Gardiner, 1996). It is the moral ground
for dialogic relationships, which gives room both to alterity and to
proximity within every relationship. Dialogic intersubjectivity is

grounded in the response that the subject owes to the other in the
dialogue of 'sociality'. This response preserves the otherness of the
other. Otherness is not something to be transgressed; it is something
foreign or threatening for the self, but the self has to find itself by
means of the other. Without this otherness there is no dialogic construction of the self. The otherness of the other is the groundless
ground of the responsibility that the self has for the other. It is this
moral ground of subjective irreducibility of the other that is central
to an ethics of nearness. We will give two illustrations of this in
modern ethics from the work of Levinas and Bakhtin.

A central concept for Levinas is 'subjection' (Levinas, 1961). Before
I respond, I am subject to something other than myself. Responsibility
is beyond the free and not-free. I am responsible for the other before
freedom exists. Responsibility is not something that I choose or do
not choose. I find my self within dialogic intersubjectivity as a self
responsible to the other. For Levinas I come into being only as subjected to a social network of signification or substitution for-the-other
(Nealon, 1997, p. 136). We are always already in a social network,
which is for Levinas not an abstract notion but incorporated in time
and space. The authentic model for this response is the face-to-face
encounter between persons. This face-to-face encounter is, according to Levinas, asymmetrical and non-reciprocal.

> The essence of dialogue is that it demands a response—not for *what* was
> said (. . .) but in terms of the nature of the *relation* it forges. This implies
> responsibility, but not a responsibility that is contingent upon reci-
> procity or justice. Responsibility to the Other pre-exists self-consciousness;
> it bypasses rational, calculative thought. I do not grasp the Other so
> as to dominate, but I respond to the face's epiphany as if to a sum-
> mons that cannot be ignored. Levinas asserts that this unconditional
> responsibility is announced in the statement 'Here I am', which announces
> my essential 'openness' to the Other' (Gardiner, 1996, pp. 131–132).

Passivity and asymmetry characterize the response that one offers to
the other in dialogue. According to Levinas, subjectivity is being
hostage of the other. I am subject to something other than myself
before I respond. I cannot escape my responsibility for the other,
because in a face to face encounter, I am related to the other before
I can make the choice not to be related. This connection makes me
responsible for the other. I have to respond to the other.

According to Gardiner, the notion of proximity is the key to understanding the relationship between otherness and ethics. He quotes

Levinas and says that proximity 'is not a coincidence or a lost union, but signifies all the surplus or all the goodness of an original sociality' (Gardiner, 1996, p. 132). Insofar as the other and I must share proximity, my being-in-the-world cannot be a usurpation of the other's right to be. In my response to the call of the other, I divest myself of all rational calculation and must leave behind all the power that is connected with my particular social role. In the face to face encounter the naked self is revealed as the groundless ground of ethics. Proximity is not the same as homogeneity. Homogeneity is an index of domination. The other is swallowed up in a collective we. By preserving the absolute exteriority of the self-Other encounter, proximity strips the ego of its dominating characteristic. Proximity can be characterized as an 'I-Thou' collectivity, which protects difference and otherness.

Central to the Bakhtinian framework is the concept of 'answerability' (Bakhtin, 1981; 1986). The Bakhtinian self is a dialogic self, a relation. The self needs the other to know his- or herself. I-for-myself is an unconsummated fluidity. I need the outsidedness of the other in order to understand myself. There is a surplus of vision of the other towards 'I-for-myself'. I-for-myself am in a process of becoming which I cannot escape. After this moment there is always a next moment, an interpretation of this moment. I-for-myself do not have the possibility to give a final meaning of my actions or my words. I depend on the other to complete, in his or her response, the meaning of my actions or my words. The same is true for my life-story. I cannot finalize the story of my life because I cannot step outside the process of becoming. I need the other to construct the meaning of my life.

The self needs to manifest itself through his or her actions. I-for-myself am an ocean of possibilities. I could be anything and anybody, but in order to become somebody, I need to manifest myself. In my actions, I affirm my own singularity and irreplaceability within the whole of being (Bakhtin, 1993, p. 41). I am obligated to act, and by doing so manifest myself within the world. 'An answerable act or deed is precisely that act which is performed on the basis of an acknowledgement of my obligative (ought-to-be) uniqueness' (Bakhtin, 1993, p. 42). Answerability refers to the necessity for the self to manifest its uniqueness in place and time. Answerability can only be concrete and situated, never abstract. The abstract is an empty possibility.

Answerability characterizes also the dialogic relation between myself and the other. The other has also uniqueness in time and place. It is this uniqueness, which resists any attempt of the self to reduce the other to myself.

> In my emotional-volitional consciousness the other is in his *own* place, insofar as I love him as *another*, and not as myself. The other's love of me sounds emotionally in an entirely different way to me—in my own personal context—than the same love of me sounds to him, and it obligates him and me to entirely different things. Yet, there is no contradiction here, of course. A contradiction could arise for some third party, namely, for a non-incarnated, detached (non-participating) consciousness. For that consciousness, there would be self-equivalent values-in-themselves—human beings, not *I* and the *other*' (Bakhtin, 1993, p. 46).

If there would not be an other-for-me, I would not be loved. I need the other to be loved, the same as the other needs me to be loved. According to Bakhtin, 'I love another, but cannot love myself; the other loves me, but does not love himself. Each one is right in his own place, and he is right answerably, not subjectively' (Bakhtin, 1993, p 46). In the answerable response of the other-for-me I receive my right to be the person that I am in my uniqueness in time and place. Without this answer of the other, I would only be in the constant flux of becoming. The self receives its axiological weight from the other. But the same is true of the other. The other is in need of my answer to his or her being in order to receive his or her axiological weight. In my answer, I confirm his or her uniqueness in time and place. What is important is that answerability implies a dialogical relation between myself and the other. Answerability is not the same as subjectivity. If there would only be an I and an other without the relationship between them, both I and the other would be of no value. We would be lost in space and time.

To summarize, subjective irreducibility of the other for Bakhtin is based on the irreplaceability or uniqueness of the other in time and place. Within the concept of answerability, I confirm this uniqueness to the other, as the other confirms my uniqueness. I am never reducible to the other, as the other is never reducible to myself.

3. *Empirical Illustration*

We will now reflect on this process of social construction of the moral self by reviewing interview-data that we gathered in fall 1999. This conversation was a discussion between four practitioners (physical therapists) on their moral identity as health care workers. A conversation between physical therapists is well suited for an examination of a construction of moral identity related to an ethics of nearness. There is always a concrete appeal of a patient to be cured or helped by the physical therapist. The relationship between a physical therapist and a patient involves direct physical contact. This brings the problem of respect for the feelings and ideas of the patient to the fore. If the subjective irreducibility of the other plays an important role in the construction of moral identity, it must be present in a conversation between physical therapists.

The recorded conversation lasted 72 minutes. We will analyze a part of the conversation, which occurred after 54 minutes. We selected this part because it was particularly relevant for the theoretical discussion of this chapter. There are other parts of the interview in which the participants touch on the same topic. We decided to select an ongoing dialogue. We have given the practitioners fictional names. There are four men and one woman working in this practice. Fritz has worked as a physical therapist since 1981; Harry since 1986; Mary since 1992 and Martin since 1996. Mary and Martin came to the practice some 4 years ago.

We will use the methodology of the so-called 'conversation analysis' to see how moral identity is constructed in the conversation between these physical therapists.[5] We think that the conversational

---

[5] The transcription symbols used in the conversation fragments are derived from Antaki and Widdicombe (1998).

(.)	The shortest hearable pause.
(2 secs)	Examples of exactly timed pauses.
(word)	Unclear part of the tape
under	Underlining indicates emphasis.
CAPITALS	Capital letters indicate speech noticibly louder than that surrounding it.
>fast<	'Greater than' and 'less than' signs indicate that the talk they encom
<slow>	pass was produced noticeably quicker or slower than the surrounding talk.
Over[lap	Square brackets between adjacent lines of concurrent speech denote
[overlap	the start of overlapping lines.

analytic perspective and the social constructionist perspective are closely related to another.

> They 'share an emphasis on construction and variability as well as an anti-essentialist and anti-realist view of identity; that is to say, identity is not presumed to be a relatively fixed property of people or societies, nor is it assumed that identity terms are simply reflections of social and psychological reality' (see Widdicombe, 1998, p. 201).

Conversation analysis is not a fixed theoretical concept. According to Antaki and Widdicombe (1998), there are five principles favored by many scholars within the conversation analytical perspective. These principles are:

1. To have an identity as a person is to be cast within a category with associated characteristics or features. In language we arrange objects in the world into categories of things. Categories imply features, and features imply categories.

2. Categories make different sense in different places and times. A good part of the meaning of an utterance is found in the occasion of its production.

3. Only those categories that people make relevant in conversation are used for analysis.

4. One can only use a certain identity-category until and unless such an identity is visibly consequential in what happens. We should analyze identities only when they seem to have some visible effect on how the interaction pans out.

5. Conversation is made up of regular structures that are generally there and available for anyone who speaks the language. Examples of these structures are a question followed by an answer, interruption, and topic shift. People use these conversation structures in their conversational construction of identity.

(*first fragment*)

1	Harry	What is most important is that you are yourself. That you do
2		not change because of the patient. That is not successful. You,
3		(.) you have to find out for yourself and have to accept for
4		yourself that you create your own population of patients.
5	Martin	Yes, and I think [that
6	Harry	[You cannot (.) cure everybody. <soft> That
7		is utopia.
8	Mary	Yes

9	Martin	And I think that it is important that you know your own weak
10		sides. If you notice that there is no improvement. (.) Then it is
11		<end of treatment>.
12	Harry	Yes, <but that does not mean that therapy doesn't help>.
13	Martin	No, but not with you.
14	Mary	No
15	Harry	That is to say (.) I often say to people, *I think*, *I* can be of no
16		help for you any more.

The focus of this fragment is the relationship between a physical therapist and a patient. In the opening line, Harry expresses what is most important for a physical therapist, namely 'that you are yourself'. This is the kind of grammar people use when they are expressing a general rule. It is the impersonal 'you' as opposed to the personal 'I'. Harry keeps up this impersonal you, throughout the lines 1–4. By using this impersonal you, Harry is forcing his listeners to ask for themselves if this rule is also implying for them. It is something that is implied in the structure of conversation.

To be yourself is connected by Harry with the characteristic of 'not to change' (line 2). Harry restricts this 'not changing' to a particular kind of change, namely change 'because of the patient'. Harry is not saying that change as such is excluded from the idea of being your self. But he argues that changing because of a patient is 'not successful'. One is puzzled by the idea what success means here. What is a successful physical therapist? Harry argues that a successful physical therapist creates his or her own population of patients. We could infer from this that to be unsuccessful is to have all possible people as your patients [but no particular group of patients]. This selection by a successful physical therapist is something that 'you have to find out for yourself' and 'you have to accept for yourself' (lines 3–4). Selection is both a cognitive and an affective activity. By the repeated 'you ... yourself' the speaker creates a strong opposition with 'because of the patient'. The physical therapist is in control. He or she decides which patient will be helped by the physical therapist. This is not a decision that a patient should make.

Harry connects selection with curing (line 6). There is a short intervention by Martin, but apparently Harry has to add something to what he has said, because he does not let Martin say what he wants to say. Physical therapists are in the business of curing patients, but you cannot cure everybody. It is still the impersonal you, which means that according to Harry this is something that counts for every physical therapist. To cure everyone is utopia. By using the label 'utopia' Harry is stressing his case: only in 'nowhere-land' a physical therapist can cure everyone. It is a moral utopia.

(second fragment)

17	Fritz:	\<But this is something I never do\>. I think that it is something
18		for the *patient* to do. (1 sec).
19	Martin:	Yes? (.) Why?
20	Fritz:	Because, it is (.) the ability to cope for oneself is, (.) people
21		have to stand for themselves. If they think that I am not good,
22		(.) they have to say this. They have to develop the *strength*
23		that they do it *themselves* and go looking for *somebody else*.
24		If not, than you get lost in the technique. (.). And, eh (.) *that*
25		*part*, I [think
26	Harry:	[But you do have your restrictions?
27	Fritz:	Yes, but they must feel it. I say (.), I [invest
28	Harry	[They feel that the
29		complaint is still there, and (.) eh (.).
30	Fritz:	For example. (.) Or they feel things are going to slow.
31	Harry:	Yes.
32	Fritz:	I mean, if they point out something. Maybe that or that. Than
32		I will always help developing (.) in that direction to help
33		them, as one may say. They point out the road, and I want to
34		execute a part [of it.
35	Mary	[But don't you leave them longer in the medical system
36		this way.
37	Fritz:	I do *not* think so. I do *not* think so. Because *you* know (.) less
38		sure, what they want technically. Sometimes people come (.)
39		from the doctor, of whom I think: They do not want to be with
40		me. But if I (.) if I should say, you have to go to that of that,
41		than this is the same. I think (.), I think that people *themselves*
42		also (eh) (eh) have to put energy in which *road* they want the
43		*cure* to happen.

Fritz breaks the consensus that exists among the three physical therapists. The confessional grammar of Martin (lines 15–16) seems to
evoke an attestation by Fritz of his moral identity (lines 17–18). If
one person makes a confession then this opens up the way for another
person to confess his or her personal ideas. Fritz uses the structure
of conversation to make his point. He already had his words in his
mind, so he is speaking fast. His statement is in direct opposition to
the statement of Martin: the patient has to decide when a physical
therapist can be of no help.

When Fritz is pressed to give arguments for his ideas, it is clear
that he is searching for words to express him self. Fritz begins by
stating a general principle, namely the ability of patients to cope for
oneself. Implied in this principle is the strength to stand for themselves (lines 22–23). Within this conversation, this strength of the
patient stands in opposition to the strength of the professionals. It
is the patient who must say that he wants to change and go to
another physical therapist (line 23). So, change is not the issue. The
question is who decides. According to Fritz, if you do not let the
patient decide, then you get lost in the technical part of physical
therapy (line 24). Fritz is suggesting a relationship between the necessity of the patient to decide (as part of his ability to cope with his
or her situation) and not getting lost in the technical. By doing this,
he is in opposition with the reverse position: the decision by the
physical therapist is related to the getting lost in technique.

Harry is backing up this opposite position. The physical therapist
decides because of restrictions on the part of the physical therapist
(line 26). Fritz agrees with this possibility, but he uses this argument
for his own position. The restrictions of the physical therapist are
something to be experienced by the patient (line 27). Harry and
Fritz (move?) toward a process of mutual understanding about restrictions of a physical therapist. This implies that the patient feels that
the complaint is still there (Harry, line 29) or that things go to slow
(Fritz, line 30). For Fritz, the patient decides (points out the road, line
33), and the physical therapist executes a part of it. Not the reverse.

Mary questions the position of Fritz. Are you not keeping the
patients longer within the medical system? (line 35) The meaning of
this question is not clear. According to the principles of conversa-
tion-analysis, it is the reaction of the respondent who decides what
this meaning is. The answer of Fritz is that the most important thing
is that patients put energy in the road the want to be cured. Without

this energy of the patient, there is no cure, and thus the patient will stay longer in the medical system. So it is not just the fact that the patient decides, but also that this decision is an expression of the energy that the patient puts into his or her process of recovery. Fritz also returns to the idea of 'getting lost in the technique' (line 24). As a physical therapist, you are less sure what the patient wants (lines 37–38). The answer to the question of what the patient wants is not to be found within the technique of the treatment. Only the patient can answer this question.

(third fragment)
44 Martin: But at the end, it is all about the patient and not. (.)
45 Eh (.) [(syll syll).
46 Fritz   [But I keep that involvement always
47 Martin: Okay, but you are saying. I think that people themselves have to
48   come with (.) with it (.) with it has no use any longer this
49   treatment. Because they (.) finally have learned something.
50 Fritz: M m
51 Martin: But what is the goal of physical therapy.(.) Is it to learn
52   something mentally at that moment?
53 Fritz: M m
54 Martin: Or that they (.) experience improvement of their complaint.
55   (2 secs)
56 Fritz: Eh
57 Mary: But maybe, maybe both things are related?
58 Fritz: <Both things are related>. I can't see them separated. I can't see
59   them separated. And, eh, and that is why (.) they, (.) they hire me
60   as technical. That (.) that is what I give them. And if they are
61   looking for more (.)
62 Martin: (syll syll syll)
63 Fritz: Than they can try to find it somewhere else
64 Martin: So, they will say that it (.) it is sufficient at a certain moment.
66 Fritz: Yes (.) yes.
67 Harry: And even chronic people do that.

Martin formulates an opposition: is it all about the patient, and not (line 44). He cannot finish his words because Fritz confesses again his involvement with the patient (line 46). It is Fritz who derives his identity from his commitment to the patient, and the increase of the ability of the patient to cope with his or her sickness. Martin agrees with this involvement. As a health care worker it is impossible not to agree with it. Involvement is also something that is important for him. So, that is not the question?

Martin formulates two goals of physical therapy: to learn something mentally (lines 51–52), and to experience improvement of a complaint (line 54). He formulates these goals in opposition to one another. Is it either this or that? After his question is remains silent for some seconds (line 55). The reason for this silence becomes clear in line 57. Mary reformulates the idea of Martin, in the sense that she asks if both goals are not related.

Fritz agrees with this: there is no separation (line 58). Fritz is referring to himself as somebody that is hired as a technical professional. The category 'to hire' is remarkable in connection to physical therapy. One hires an electrician or a plumber but not a physical therapist. The category 'to hire' implies that the customer is in charge. This is in clear opposition with the concept of the professional who decides what needs to be done.

Martin returns again to the problem of who decides when the treatment is sufficient and can be stopped (line 64). He has identified himself as a physical therapist who wants to decide for the patient. He questions the ability of the patient to decide this. In questioning this idea, he is trying to weaken the opposite position of Fritz, who wants to keep the patient in charge of his or her own cure. According to Fritz, patients can make this decision (line 66). Harry supports him by saying that 'even chronic people do that' (line 67). For the physical therapists in this conversation this is a strong argument, because the image (prejudiced?) of chronic patients is that they prolong their treatment.

(*fourth fragment*)

68	Martin:	But why would you not say: "I think, I can be of no help for you
69		any more."
70	Fritz:	Because that doesn't work. (.) I don't know. *I* don't know.
71	Harry:	If I treat somebody, I have clear view what I want to do. I give,
72		<I, I, We do this together>, Or you do that and that. There has to
73		be a specific reaction at a certain time. If this doesn't come, (.)
74		then, then I can try another entry. But if that is not successful
75		either, (.)

76	Fritz:	M m
77	Harry:	I can no longer explain what I am doing.
78	Fritz:	I can't. I can never explain what I am doing. I, I mean, (.) it is
79		possible to work with many systems. And then you are talking
80		about a system. I work with different systems. I can take a mental
81		road, I can take a physical road. I can take still other roads. I (.) I
82		(.) I don't have any goal-directedness that this is better and this is
83		not better. <I do not know>. Because the patient feels *himself*
84		what is better. [I think.
85	Martin:	[But you.
86	Fritz:	I do not [know
87	Martin:	[But you know, you can (.). What did you (.). You just
88		said I do not know (2 sec).
89	Fritz:	I do not know what is right. I do not know what pain is?
90	Harry:	Sometimes, and that is irritating. If I think: "Oh, what a nag." He
91		is coming for attention. So I try to (.) not to concentrate on this
92		aspect of moaning, because he evidently still (.) wants something
93		from me.

This fragment starts with Martin repeating what he said before. Instead of a declaration (see lines 17–18), he now asks his opponents for counter arguments. The answer Fritz gives is that it does not work (line 70). Fritz has identified, as a working principle, that people have to invest energy in their cure. But then he adds that he does not know. He repeats this again and puts stress on the fact that '*I* do not know' (line 70). It is he, the physical therapist, who does not know.

Harry begins his reaction with the idea, that he as physical therapist has a clear view on what he wants to do (line 71). When he continues, there is a shift from the 'I' to 'we'. By doing this he is identifying himself as a physical therapist, who works together with a patient. Both the patient and the physical therapist do something. Related to this goal of the therapy, is the necessity of a reaction in a certain time (line 73). If this reaction does not come, as a physical therapist he can try another entry. There is a shift in these lines from the 'we together' back to the 'I'. If there is no reaction, he is left without an explanation of what he is doing (line 77). Whether this is positive of negative is left undecided.

For Fritz, the not knowing is fundamental. He confesses that he never can explain what he is doing (line 78). This is a puzzling remark for a physical therapist. He explains himself by saying that it is possible to do different things, which he calls systems and roads. A road is a different category than a goal. A road is a way to reach a certain destination, but it is not in itself this destination. We know from Fritz that he is only hired. His expertise is his technical knowledge of the different roads. As a professional, he knows which goal a certain road can reach. But he does not know what is better for the patient. He gives two reasons for this, both moral categories. 'I do not know what is right. I do not know what the pain is?' (line 89). Pain is used here not as a physical category, but a moral category. The patient feels what is better (lines 83–84).

In his response, Harry interprets the fact that only the patient knows what his of her pain is as 'irritating'. Apparently, as a professional he is uncomfortable with this. This is especially the case when a patient is moaning. He wants to see the patient and his or her need. It is because of this need that the patient comes to him. He wants to focus on this appeal of the patient, not his feeling of irritation. This is a different position than is expressed by him in the first lines of this conversation. There he stressed a general rule that a physical therapist should not change because of the patient (line 2). His position is actually more complex. If he can recognize the appeal for help by the patient, he will go beyond this general rule.

4. *Towards a Social Constructionist Conception of Moral Identity*

4.1 *Reflection on the Empirical Illustration*

Does the subjective irreducibility of the other play a role in the construction of moral identity of physical therapists? And if so, how does this manifest itself in the conversational construction of identity?

The discussion between the four physical therapists that we analyzed is concerned with the relationship between practitioner and patient. Physical therapists are characterized as people who cure people. But when are people cured? Who decides when a patient is cured? Can a good physical therapist cure everybody? These questions are put forward as major questions for the moral identity of physical therapists.

The analysis shows different conceptions of the moral identity of physical therapists. One position, represented by Martin, is characterized by the following categories. A good practitioner is in control of the goal of the therapy he or she is giving. He or she does not change his or her idea because of the patient. The physical therapist is in charge of the whole process. The physical therapist sets the goal of the therapy, and decides if a patient is cured. The physical therapist is the professional who knows which technical methods will be used. The physical therapist must also be the one to decide to use an alternative method if the chosen method does not yield the desired result. But a good physical therapist cannot help everybody. This does not mean that some patients cannot be cured. There is a difference between physical therapy and the physical therapist. As a physical therapist one may not be able to help a patient. This does not mean that there is no cure in physical therapy for some patients. A good physical therapist will refer a patient to another physical therapist, who could possibly be of help. This gives a good physical therapist a way out of the iron claim that chronic patients put on a physical therapist. The same process that makes the patient dependent on the therapy makes the therapist dependent on the patient. A good practitioner does not enter this circle of dependency by deciding unilaterally what happens and if something is going to happen. We could characterize this type of moral identity as a self-oriented model of moral identity.

Fritz constructs another moral identity in opposition to this moral identity of the professional. The core of this moral identity is the idea that the patient should decide what the goal of the physical therapy is. The patient should also decide if this goal has been reached. The physical therapist cannot decide this, because the patient is the one who feels the pain. The physical therapist is seen as a technician hired by the patient to help cure him of her. This technical knowledge is the professional knowledge of the physical therapist. On the basis of this knowledge, one cannot decide if a patient is cured. One can only decide on the technical quality of the physical therapy. Only the patient can answer the question of whether it has worked or not. Only the patient, therefore, can decide to seek help from another physical therapist. But as long as the patient appeals for the help of the physical therapist, the physical therapist has to stay involved to the patient. A good physical therapist cannot withdraw this involvement unilaterally. The cure of the patient is seen as physical as well as mental. If the patient is not putting energy into his or her cure, then this goal will not be reached. With the physical techniques of physical therapy, one can only reach the physical part of the patient. If he or she is not mentally investing in his of her improvement, then it is all in vein. One needs the patient to take control over his or her cure. This is important for all patients, but especially for chronic patients. A good physical therapist expects, even from these patients, that patients take control over their own process of cure. One could characterize this type of moral identity as an other-oriented model of moral identity.

As is clear from the above description, the question of the subjective irreducibility of the other plays an important role in the construction of the moral identity of Fritz. He understands his actions as physical therapist as a response to the appeal of the patients, who come to him. He cannot escape this concrete appeal of the other. It is the other who decides if and when this appeal ends. If the practitioner does not accept this, he reduces the other to himself. Now, Fritz also experiences the appeal of his patients, but he resists their claim on him in order not to become their hostage. If he accepted the subjective irreducibility of the other as moral criterion for his actions, patients would have a hold on him. Therefore he reduces the otherness of the other: he sets the goal; he decides if a person is cured; he chooses the means to reach the goal. His greatest fear concerns chronic patients: they do not know which goal to set and how to end their dependency on the physical therapy. Fritz refuses to except the other as the ultimate moral criterion because of the possibility that he would become a plaything of his patients. He wants to hold onto universal rules for everyone in the same situation. This is characteristic for what we have called a rational ethic (see section 2.1). It is important to see that both reflexivity and commitment are aspects of this ethical orientation. Fritz also expresses himself as a professional committed to his patients, but this commitment is controlled by reflection aimed at finding general prescriptions.

The moral identity of Martin and Fritz seem to stand in opposition to one another. Do they exclude each other? In the next section, we will return to this question from an ethical perspective. From a social constructionist perspective one has to be careful with this conclusion. In the conversation between Martin and Fritz, they construct their identity in opposition to each other. In a dialogue to somebody else (such as a certain patient or a friend who needs help) their respective positions would be different. Does this mean that they are not telling the truth? It depends on how the question of truth is understood. There is no such thing as a 'real self', a self outside the dialogical relation between people which could be determined objectively, as if there existed. Only within relationships can a moral identity be constructed.

In this regard, Harry takes an interesting position. The interview fragments start with an utterance from Harry 'not to change because of patients' (line 2). It is not possible to help every patient as a physical therapist. This moral rule finds its strongest protagonist in Martin. In the last interview fragment (lines 90–92) Harry talks about a reaction on a concrete patient who is moaning. He tries not to concentrate on this aspect of moaning, because he evidently wants something from him. In the first lines, Harry speaks about an impersonal 'you'. The grammar that he uses makes it clear that he is stating a general rule for everyone in every situation. In the last lines, Harry manifests himself as being sensitive to a concrete person in a situation. The grammar that he uses, is the personal 'I' (line 91: 'I try to'). The appeal of a patient on him can make him change. The moral identity of Harry seems to include both conceptions of a good physical therapist: a self-oriented and other-oriented conception.

One of the general principles in 'conversation analysis' is that the identity of people is visible in the structure of the conversation (Antaki & Widdicombe, 1998). Fritz manifests himself as an empathic listener in the conversation (see line 50; 53; 66 and 76). By humming he lets the other know that he understands what they are saying. This type of response is congruent with his moral identity. He wants to respect the otherness of the other. Martin manifests himself as somebody who puts people on the defensive. Five times, he starts his response with 'but you . . .' (lines 44; 51; 68; 85; 87). He attacks a position, which is different with the one he holds. He is not trying to understand the other, but to get approval for his own position.

4.2   *Discussion*

In section 1.2 we mentioned four points of criticism of a social constructionist account of moral identity. We will reflect shortly on these points. We will try to show that a social constructionist perspective connected with an ethics of nearness is a fruitful direction for responding to these critiques. At the same time we will point to some important questions for further research.

A first point of critique was the absence of a moral criterion. In this chapter we have focussed on the subjective irreducibility of the concrete other as moral criterion for a dialogical construction of moral identity. This criterion is relevant in situations within the health care system, a context in which there is always a face to face contact with patients. This moral criterion plays an important role in the construction of moral identity of health care workers, in this case physical therapists). We called this an other-oriented type of moral identity. Health care workers also construct an opposite moral identity, one closer to rational ethics. They look for general prescriptions that are the same for all people in the same circumstances.

According to Taels, in every ethical position reflexivity and commitment must be present. The difference between these positions is based on the question of which aspect dominates the other. There are different theoretical positions in this debate. Some scholars argue for the dominance of one type of ethics. Others think that they can be included in a procedural model without one being in a dominant position (see Ricoeur, 1992). We will not go deeper into this debate in the context of this chapter, but the question of the relationship between these different types of moral rationality is important for a social construction of identity in view of an ethics of nearness. Is a concrete ethics just one ethical position, or can it include other positions? Is there a more inclusive position than a concrete ethics?

A second point of critique was that rationality is necessary to deal with the complexity of a situation, a complexity reflected in the polyphony of voices that can be heard in a situation. Social constructionism aims at finding one's own voice. But this can lead to a simplification of the situation. In our empirical illustration, we saw that all the different voices are heard when people construct their moral identity within relationship. Finding one's own voice does not necessarily imply a simplification of the situation. This can be seen most clearly in Harry's position, whichseems to voice different ethical positions. But Fritz and Martin also manifest in their utterances different voices, although they prefer one voice before the other. The self is not a monologue of one voice but a polyphony of voices (Hermans, 1996). If this is true, than the debate is not so much

about simplification, but a debate about the conditions in which people construct their moral identity while taking account of the richness
of voices in their cultural situation. The social constructionist perspective with its focus on identity-construction within relationship is
a fruitful theoretical perspective for further research into this question.[6]

Thirdly, the narrative of caring is not rigid enough to break the
oppression, which exists, on a personal and institutional level. We
will not get into the question of whether this is an accurate assessment. However, we can see is that an ethics of nearness in its different
forms (Levinas, Bakhtin) is focussed on preserving the otherness of
the other. In our empirical illustration, we saw that Fritz, when considering the moral criterion of the subjective irreducibility of the
other, is very keen on maintaining his position of power. He is 'hired
by the patient to do a job'. In the literature, there is a growing
number of publications in which this moral criterion of subjective
irreducibility plays a central role in analyzing unjust power relations
in the field of multiculturalism, racism, and social injustice (Arnsperger,
2000; Nealon, 1996; Gardiner, 1996; Visker, 2000). This does not
mean that there are no remaining questions . One major question
regards the focus of face to face relationships in ethics. Is this a
sufficient base from which to tackle ethical problems on an institutional level? In institutions people make decisions regarding the anonymous other, such as who gets what kind of social benefit in what
kind of situation. Is the criterion of the subjective irreducibility of
the other a sufficient ethical basis for these kinds of questions?

A fourth point of critique regards the polyphony of voices of care
and the lack of a clear concept of care. In our research, we used
another ethical theory, namely an ethics of nearness. We have given
two examples of a concrete ethics, namely Levinas and Bakhtin. This
ethical background seems to be more robust compared with the concept of care. However, we are well aware of the differences between
the ethics of Levinas and Bakhtin, and these differences seem to mat-

---

[6] According to Hermans, there are two principles at work within this process of
dominance (Hermans, 1996). First, the principle of tension reduction points to a
simultaneous decrease in dominance of two opposites or contrasting meanings that
a person holds. The second principle is the idea that polar opposites are mutually
complementing. The tension between the opposites is not reduced, but rather functions as a challenge for their integration. The opposites are treated as mutually
enriching, like a countermelody in a polyphonic melody (idem, p. 22).

ter for the construction of moral identity of persons. For example, Levinas focuses on an asymmetrical relationship between self and other. A person is held hostage by the moral appeal of the other, an appeal from which he or she cannot escape. It is precisely this point where the debate starts (see the position of Martin in the above empirical illustration). Does this not end in a monologue of the other, which suppresses the self? Is it possible to change the asymmetry for a symmetry and reciprocity in a relationship without loosing the moral criterion of subjective irreducibility of the other? Does the self and not the other take reverse positions in a relationship at the same time? There are different answers to these questions within the type of concrete ethics coming from the ethics of Levinas or Bakhtin (Gardiner, 1996; Nealon, 1996).

Bibliography

Antaki, Ch. & S. Widdicombe (1998). Identity as an Achievement and as a Tool. In: Antaki, Ch. & S. Widdicombe (eds.). *Identities in Talk* (pp. 1–14). London: Sage.

Arnsperger, C. (2000). Homo Oecumenicus, Social Order, and the Ethics of Otherness. *Ethical Perspectives.*

Auer, A. (1977). Die Bedeutung des christlichen bei der Normfindung [The significance of Christian in the Discovery of Norms]. In: J. Sauer (Ed.). *Normen im Konflikt* [Norms in Conflict] (pp. 29–55). Freiburg: Herder.

Bakhtin, M. (1981). *The Dialogic Imagination. Four Essays.* Austin: Un. of Texas Press.

—— (1986). *Speech Genres and Other Late Essays.* Austin: Un. of Texas Press.

—— (1990). *Art and Answerability. Early philosophical essays.* Austin: Un. of Texas Press.

—— (1993). *Towards a Philosophy of the Act.* Austin: Un. Of Texas Press.

Blum, L. (1992). Vocation, Friendship, and Community: Limitations of the Personal-Impersonal Framework. In: Flanagan, O. & Oksenberg Rorty, A. (eds.). *Identity, Character and Morality. Essays in Moral Psychology* (pp. 173–197). Cambridge Mass.: MIT Press.

Böckle, F. (1981). Werte und Normbegründing [Values and the grounding of norms]. In: Böckle, F. (a.o.) (Eds.). *Christlicher Glaube in moderner Gesellschaft* [Christian faith in modern society] (pp. 37–89). Freiburg: Herder.

Brown, L.M., Tappan, M.B., Gilligan, C, Miller, B.A. & Argyris, D.E. (1989). Reading for Self and Moral Voice: A Method for Interpreting Narratives of Real-Life Moral Conflict and Choice. In: Packer, M.J. & Addison, R.B. (Eds.) *Entering the circle. Hermeneutic Investigation in Psychology* (pp. 141–164). New York: State University of new York Press.

Cox, L.M. & Lyddon, W.J. (1997). Constructivist Conceptions of Self: A Discussion of Emerging Identity Constructs. *Journal of Constructivist Psychology* 10, 201–219.

Day, J.M. (1991). The Moral Audience: On Narrative Mediation of Moral "Judgment" and Moral "Action". In: Tappan, M.B. & Packer, M.J. (Eds.). *Narrative and Storytelling: Implications for Understanding Moral Development* (pp. 27–42). San Francisco: Jossey-Bass.

—— (1996). Recognition and Responsivity: Unlearning the Pedagogy of Estrangement for a Catholic Moral Education. In: McLaughlin, T.H., O'Keefe, J. & O'Keeffe, B.

(Eds.). *The Contemporary Catholic School. Context, Identity and Diversity* (pp. 162–173). London: Falmer Press.

Day, J.M. & Tappan, M. (1996). The Narrative Approach to Moral Development: From Epistemic Subject to Dialogical Selves. *Human Development* 39, 67–82.

Dreyfuss, H.L. & Dreyfuss, S.E. (1990). What is morality? A phenomenological account of the development of ethical expertise. In: Ramussen, D. (Ed.). *Universalism vs Communitarianism. Contemporary Debates in Ethics* (pp. 237–264). Cambridge Mass.: MIT Press.

Gardiner, M. (1996). Alterity and Ethics: A Dialogical Perspective. *Theory, Culture and Society* 13(2), 121–143.

Gergen, K.J. & M.M. Gergen (1988). Narrative and the Self as Relationship. In: L. Berkowitz (ed.). *Advances in Experimental Social Psychology* (pp. 28–51). New York: Academic Press.

Gergen, K.J. (1991). The *Saturated Self*. New York: Basic Books.

—— (1993). Belief as relational resource. *The international journal for the psychology of religion* 3(4), 231–235.

—— (1994). The communal Creation of Meaning. In: W.F. Overton & D.S. Palermo (eds.). *The nature and Ontogenesis of Meaning* (pp. 19–39). Hillsdale N.J.: Lawrence Erlbaum.

—— (1999). *An invitation to social constructionism*. London: Sage

Gergen, K. (1998). Erzählung, moralische Identität und historisches Bewusstsein. Eine sozialkonstruktionistische Darstellung [Narrative, moral identity and historical consciousness. A social canstructionist perspective]. In: J. Straub (Ed.). *Erinnerung, Geschichte, Identität: Die psychologische Konstruktion von Zeit und Geschichte* [Memory, History, Identity: The psychological construction of time and history] (pp. 170–202). Frankfurt a.M.: Suhrkamp.

Hermans, H.J.M. (1996). Opposites in a dialogical self: Constructs as characters. *Journal of Constructivist Psychology* 9, 1–26.

Lapsley, D.K. (1996). Commentary. *Human Development* 39, 100–107.

Leeman, Y. (1996). *Interculturele communicatie in het onderwijs* [Intercultural communication in education]. Amsterdam: Het Spinhuis.

Levinas, E. (1961). Totalité et infini: essai sur l'extériorité. Den Haag: Martinus Nijhoff.

Lourenco, O. (1996). Reflections on Narrative Approaches to Moral Development. *Human Development* 39, 83–99.

Nealon, J.T. (1996). The Ethics of Dialogue: Bakhtin and Levinas. *College English* 59(2), 129–148.

Puka, B. (1996). Commentary. *Human Development* 39, 108–116.

Rest, J. & Narvaez, D. (eds.) (1994). *Moral Development in the Professions: Psychology and Applied Ethics*. Hillsdale N.J.: Lawrence Erlbaum.

Ricoeur, P. (1992). *Oneself as Another*. Chicago: Un. of Chicago Press.

Schüller, B. (1976). Types van fundering van zedelijke normen [Different types of grounding of moral norms]. *Concilium* 12(10), 61–72.

Taels, J. (1998). Ethiek van veraf en van dichtbij. Reflectie en zelfdistantie: drie modellen [Ethics of distance and of nearness. Reflection and self-distantiation: three models]. *Bijdragen. Tijdschrift voor Filosofie en Theologie* 59, 369–390.

Tappan, M.B. (1991). Narrative, Authorship, and Development of Moral Authority. In: Tappan, M.B. & Packer, M.J. (Eds.). *Narrative and Storytelling: Implications for Understanding Moral Development* (pp. 5–26). San Francisco: Jossey-Bass.

—— (1993). Relational Voices and Moral Development: Reflections on Change. In: Kahancy, P., Perry, I. & Jangelo, J. (Eds.). *Theoretical and Critical Perspectives on Teacher Change* (pp. 1–18). Norwood N.J.: Ablex.

Visker, R. (2000). Levinas, Multiculturalim, and Us. *Ethical Perspectives*

Widdicombe, S. (1998). Identity as an Analysts'and a Participants' Resource. In: Antaki, Ch. & S. Widdicombe (eds.). *Identities in Talk* (pp. 1–14). London: Sage.

PART THREE

REFLECTIONS

REFLECTING ON/WITH MY COMPANIONS

Kenneth J. Gergen

My encounter with these offerings from my theological colleagues has been one of the most gratifying experiences of my scholarly career. In many respects writing is a lonely and fearful activity. One carries into the act a community of dialogue, and one imagines a caring audience. But the actual reader is never present, and one can never be certain that he or she will not respond with indifference or disdain. Beyond the manuscript lies the void. Thus to encounter the work of eleven scholars from neighboring domains of inquiry, all of whom have devoted themselves to a serious dialogue with my writing—and the writing with allies in the constructionist dialogues— is a joyous affirmation of relationship. To be sure there are many differences and disagreements; yet in the caring way they have been offered here, they are to be cherished. But most exciting for me is the many ways in which these scholars have creatively extended the range of ideas. In their dialogue with constructionist ideas new vistas are opened—both conceptual and practical. Do we not approach the ecstasy of dialogue when our conjunction brings forth realities never imagined in isolation?

And now the conversational turn falls to me once again. I am blessed with the enormous riches represented in these chapters. Yet, the same plenitude also defies the possibility for a fully responsible reply. By virtue of publisher's requirements I am forced to be selective. In what directions shall the dance then move? I find myself drawn in three particular directions. In part these choices reflect themes centrally wound through many of the essays. However, my colleagues also stimulate and invite me to extend a range of concerns latent within my initial offering, but important to the future of constructionist and theological endeavours. First I address the problem of moral action. Many of the present papers are directly or indirectly concerned with the roots of morality and the place of religion within moral development. Many have also found constructionist ideas useful in generating accounts of morality. At the same time we are left with what appears to be a theory itself without moral investment. What are we to make, then of the moral relativism that seems inherent in constructionist theoretics? Second, and more briefly, I take up the question of *The Real*. Perhaps the most frequent criticism raised by my colleagues stems from their investment in realities that are so very obvious to them, and yet seem wholly disregarded or discredited by constructionism. There is special resistance in these chapters to what seems to be a constructionist demolition of the self. How can we productively move past these differences? Finally, and perhaps most importantly, I address the challenge of the sacred. Here we confront a major question for social construction and for many of my theological colleagues: is the realm of the sacred simply a construction, and if so, does this not lead to an ultimate delegitimation of theology and its manifestations in religious practices? I shall argue quite the contrary. In my view a sophisticated constructionism will lead to the abolition of the distinction between the sacred and the profane, and in doing so open new possibilities for the sacralization of everyday life.

Toward Morally Generative Practices

Religion and morality are often viewed as two sides of the same coin—with religion serving as a chief vehicle for generating and sustaining moral action, and the necessity for moral conduct in society serving as a major justification for religious institutions. It is within this context that theologians have long attempted to articulate moral principles or foundational rationales for ethical conduct, and religious institutions have offered codes, dictums, or commandments to guide our actions. The need for such foundations has become all the more acute in recent decades. Increasingly we find the value neutral stance of the empirico/scientific orientation—so central to cultural modernism—to be ethically infertile. In the scientific splitting of *is* from *ought* we have lost ethical compass. In any case, the outcome of almost all attempts to provide such direction have been *content-full* ethics. That is, the efforts culminate in articulated accounts of the good—honoring *this* and not *that*, favoring certain kinds of conduct while condemning others. Rendered rationale are guides to specific forms of moral being.

These concerns with ethical foundations have also played an important role in several contributions to the present volume. In his offering, for example, Mark Wallace (Chapter 2) writes in support of a

Levinasian view that establishes as a first principle, "taking responsibility for the welfare of the other." Favoring much the same idea,
Hermans and Dupont (Chapter 8) argue for the "subjective irreducibility of the other as the groundless ground" for what they propose as a "concrete ethics." James Day's analysis (Chapter 11) of
religious development is also apposite; for him a constructionist
account of development is viable replacement for traditional cognitive views of moral development. For Day, the challenge of building toward a more morally secure society is paramount. Much the
same concerns are reflected in Friedrich Schweitzer's exploration
(Chapter 5) of religious education.

At the same time, in the intellectual world more broadly there is
abiding concern with the limits of content ethics. For example, Alisdair
MacIntyre (1984) has described ethical theory as rife with conflict
among ethical incommensurables, and in a later volume labors over
the question of *Whose Justice, Whose Rationality?*. In his volume, *Ethics
After Babel*, Jeffrey Stout (1988) also struggles with the problem ethical commitment in the context of competing claims. More radically
John Caputo's *Against Ethics* (1993) proposes that ethical principles
can neither dictate nor account for the sense of obligation that binds
people together in specific circumstances. Social constructionist writings have added further dimension to such misgivings. Elsewhere I
have written, for example, about problem of deducing specific actions
from abstract principles of the good; given a set of ethics, nothing
necessarily follows in terms of action (Gergen, 1994). Indeed, many
contributions to the present volume also echo doubts in the possibility of a foundational ethic. Wallace proposes that in light of much
postmodern/constructionist thought, "theology becomes a vital undertaking" primarily when it "avoids the temptation to ground its enterprise on a philosophical foundation." Hermans and Dupont worry
that their attempt to establish a concrete ethics of nearness may be
just one more ethical standpoint among many competitors. This concern with multiple, competing standpoints also informs Schweitzer's
views on religious education. He makes excellent use of Berger's
(1979) "heretical imperative" in arguing for religious education sensitive to the "context of multicultural and multireligious society and
of the interreligious communication needed in this situation." In a
similar vein, Chris Hermans (Chapter 3) argues for a conception of
a polyphonic as opposed to an authoritative vision of God in religious communication.

With a strong impetus toward affirming a moral society, on the one hand, and rampant doubt in the possibility of univocal ethical codes on the other, how are we to proceed? How can we, in effect, have morality without moral standards? In my view constructionist thought can carry us past this impasse and into a more promising and viable space of possibility. It can enable us to press beyond commitments to singular (authoritative) ethical codes or credos, while simultaneously honoring those commitments. In particular, it can provide us with a means of addressing issues of moral traditionalism in the face of global incommensurability. Interestingly, it is precisely in what is often assailed as a "constructionist relativism" (see chapters by both Wallace and Hermans) that this potential is to be located. It is first in its lack the constructionist lack of commitment to any one content ethic, and second in its focus on the communicative process from which ethics derive, that we locate a means of orienting ourselves in a pluralist world.

To appreciate the possibilities, consider again the various ways in which constructionist accounts have been used in this volume to describe and explain moral and religious development. James Day, for example, provides an excellent account of religious development in terms of discursive construction; this account is quite congenial with Ulrike Popp-Baier's (Chapter 3) understanding of religious conversion through narration, and the importance placed by Wallace on narration and the vitality of theology. In a similar vein, Hans Schilderman (Chapter 10) provides a sensitive portrait of the way in which religious identity may be formed within an extended process of relationship. Finally, on a more communal level, Aad de Jong (Chapter 9) demonstrates how a constructionist approach can be used to understand the emergence of religious organization.

In all these cases we find an emphasis on the processes of coordination from which spring valued patterns of relationship. We must also suppose that when people wish to protect such patterns from erosion or defection, from outside interference or annihilation, they will often develop codes of conduct. Such codes are often unwritten and informally maintained—as in the case of standards for moral behavior. However, they may also be publicly articulated in systems of rules, regulations, organizational values, ethical standards, and laws—in effect, content ethics. We must realize, however, that the codes are not themselves "the good," which the participants wish to sustain, but rather, serve as security or policing measures. This is to say that content ethics are not in themselves the ethical conduct that is so important to our lives; they are but a possible means to an end that lies elsewhere. There is no principled need, then, for codes of good conduct—for "ethical principles," "value clarification," "the bill of rights," or a "code of professional ethics." Such efforts come into play primarily when there are threats to the valued order.

At this point we must inquire into the potentials and limits of such codes in sustaining the cultural forms we so deeply value. If they are optional in principle, we may be justifiably explore their shortcomings and their alternatives. I scarcely wish to propose that content ethics are inconsequential. In many cases, particularly in matters of societal laws, their existence may essential, both in sustaining tradition and in achieving desirable social change. The argument here is in no way intended to challenge the development of abstract prescriptions—particularly when these are pressed into the service of dialogue. However, we must also confront the following difficulty: Content ethics are created within social enclaves for sustaining its own ways of life. In this sense they always stand in a potentially alienated or antagonistic relationship to that which lies outside.

Exacerbating the potential for conflict is the fact that codifications of principles, ethics, or standards are not easily negotiable. They function as articulated limits—"beyond this point we do not go"— with the implicit subtext, "if you go beyond this limit and you are no longer one of us." In other terms, codifications serve as terminators of conversation. Additional words—of critique, reflexivity, doubt, or emendation—are often threatening and unwelcome. There are "principles at stake," as it is said. Such terminating tendencies are especially problematic in a world in which there are multiple and disparate enclaves of meaning making. If we look across the array of ethnicities, religions, geographical regions, sexual preference groups, professions, and specialized political communities that make up any society, we are likely to find vast differences in the sense of the ethical. To the extent that content ethics function as matters of principle, productive dialogue across the borders is curtailed. Antagonism and hostility prevail, and impulses toward suppression (or eradication) are set in motion.

In this sense, while content ethics may function to secure traditions within groups, they often lend themselves to alienation and conflict between. Or to put it another way, ethical stipulations may have a corrosive effect on the very forms of relationships out of which ethical value can take root. Commitment to content ethics may imperil the forms of coordination from which values are birthed, and unleash processes of mutual destruction—the very silencing of the ethical impulse. It is at this point that we begin to appreciate possibility of moving beyond the tradition of content ethics. Rather, our attention is directed to those processes of relationship that can provide the *ethically generative moment*. We require means of conversation—and related actions—enabling us to move more felicitously across the boundaries of colliding commitments, opening possibilities for growthful dialogue across otherwise antagonistic communities. It is here that social constructionism joins the dialogue of *process ethics*, concerned as it is with the achievement of ethics within ongoing relationships. We draw sustenance, for example, from Carol Gilligan's (1982) attempt to locate moral decision making within dialogue as opposed to abstract principles. We are challenged by Jürgen Habermas' (1979) articulation of ideal speech conditions, and its implications for settling conflicts among competing claims to the good. And we take inspiration from those attempting to locate within Martin Buber's (1947) work guidelines to ethically informed dialogue.

At the same time, process ethics are only a beginning. From a constructionist perspective much of the literature on process ethics still carries strong remnants of the foundationalism that imperils the content tradition. That is, there remains a pervasive tendency to establish ethical foundations—imperatives or first principles—for securing generative dialogue. From a constructionist standpoint there is again reason to avoid such tendencies. Foundations of practice function much like content ethics, only one step removed. They place *a priori* limits over "the good" in human relationships, and thus lead ultimately toward division and antagonism. Of course, one might argue that the present account suffers from this problem; does constructionism not invite us to place a transcendent value on forms of action that are responsible to the sustenance of relatedness itself? Or, in other terms, do we not affirm here the priority of *relational responsibility*? Perhaps, but not in a way that demands any particular form of practice. At any point a promising form of relational practice creates an antagonistic other, the invitation to re-create is reinstigated. We may view relational responsibility not as an ethical imperative, but rather, as an invitation for continuous and mutual exploration. Here indeed is a challenge for a *practical* theology.

Much may be said about the forms of practice that may contribute to the generative process of relationship. The discourses of conflict resolution, mediation, and consensus building are all rich in possibilities. Much that I have described as *transformative dialogue* (Gergen, 1999) is similarly dedicated. Whenever our actions as individuals are coordinated with the communities of which we are apart, and communities act so as to realize their interdependency with those outside, and as a community of the whole we act in ways that appreciate the environments giving us sustenance, so do we establish a space for ethical generativity. However, the search for ethically generative practices must remain forever unfinished; we must avoid concretizing the possibilities, for each solidification of practice may be the silencing of yet another tradition of relationship. It is to the human capacities for improvisation that we must look for sustenance. It is improvisation that enables new adjustments to be continuously made, and thus the possibility for a continuous prizing of our lives *together*.

Resistant Realisms and the Self

One of the most radical aspects of constructionist thought is its destablization of all truth claims and/or foundational ontologies. Rather, we are constantly entreated to explore the communal processes from which our taken for granted worlds emerge. All that seemed *natural* in our understanding we may now understand in terms of *cultural* location and function. And in doing so we thereby open new worlds of potential. By and large my interlocutors in this volume have drawn significant sustenance from this liberatory aspect of constructionist thought. They have demonstrated the culturally contingent presumptions of a bounded self (Wallace, Hermans, Schweitzer), cognitive development (Day), the psychology of religion (van der Lans), psychological conversion (Popp-Baier), and more. At the same time, I am especially pleased that most of my colleagues have looked beyond the deconstructive moment to explore the more positive potentials of constructionism. As they variously demonstrate, the same forms of argument used to destabilize the potentially stultifying voices of monologic authority can also be used to understand the positive creation of beliefs, morality, religious experience, conversion, and church organization.

Yet, I am also unsettled by a certain tendency within many of these contributions. It is a tendency that sometimes gives rise to unnecessary distances and doubts, or misleading grievances with one or another aspect of constructionist thought. It is also a tendency that can ultimately undermine the positive potentials of these offerings. And finally, it is a tendency that gives rise to one of the major issues of contention within this volume: the status of the self. The tendency may usefully be viewed as a vestigial commitment to a realist epistemology. A particular form of realism lies somewhere toward the center of modernist institutions of science, education, and governance. Put simply, it is a belief in the reality of a material world, a world that exists independently of the minds of those seeking to understand this world. Science, as an institution, is dedicated to establishing knowledge of this world, education seeks to impart such knowledge to new generations, and government decision making (within the West) is largely carried out in terms of "real world" parameters. The declaration of "the real" also establishes the grounds for what is "true." True propositions are those which accurately reflect or picture the real. Truth and reality walk hand in hand.

In an important sense the drama of constructionism derives from its contrast to the realist tradition and the allied conception of truth. For constructionists the distinction between a world "out there," and a mind "in here" is already subject to question. Scientific knowledge is not an accurate reflection of what exists, but a communal tradition of representation with deep roots in cultural suppositions, values, and institutions. This is scarcely to abandon the realist tradition, but rather, to realize that it is indeed a tradition. Such realization creates a context in which we can reflect on the implications of its practices for western culture and the world. At the same time, what for me is one of the most important elements of a constructionist orientation is often disregarded by those carrying out constructionist inquiry. It is an element also obscured in many of the preceding chapters. This is the caveat that *constructionist proposals are not themselves truth bearing* about such matters as mind/world dualism, material reality, knowledge, and the like. There is no foundation upon which constructionism rests. Rather, constructionist proposals constitute a domain of intelligibility that invites, enables, or facilitates certain forms of cultural practice. The question is not whether constructionist proposals are accurate or "true," any more or less than realist claims. Rather, from a constructionist standpoint we are moved to reflect on the value of the various forms of cultural practice invited by the way we talk—both realist and constructionist.

In my view, many of the minor vexations appearing in these chapters can be traced to the tendency of the authors to read constructionism in realist terms. That is, constructionist writings are assumed to be truth posits of the traditional realist kind. It is in this fashion that Aad de Jong (Chapter 6), for example, takes me to task for my insufficient attention to "institutional facts," such as the reality of the Catholic Church as an organization. Gerrit Immink (Chapter 4) faults me for "underestimating the role of illocutionary force." And, in an interesting variation on this form of criticism, he finds constructionism deficient because it fails to recognize metaphysical facts. He holds to the view that propositional content is noetic, which is to say "neither in the mind nor physical reality" but inhering in "ideal objects." These forms of objection are unnecessary, in a certain sense, because my view of constructionism would not reject talk about institutional facts or ideal objects. Again, the question is not whether such "facts" exist but what are the consequences of putting things in this way. Or, more broadly, we may inquire into the ramifications of realist discourse. For my own part, I fear that pronouncements of what is "real" and "true" too often function to terminate dialogue. They tend to set limits over what can be admitted into the realm of possibility; they suppress those traditions in which these realities and truths are not self evident.

I fear that this same tendency to reify constructionist theory may also serve to undermine the significance of many of the positive proposals offered by my colleagues. We have here compelling accounts of religious development (Day), the conversion process (Popp-Baier), the act of preaching (Schweitzer), religious education (Schweitzer), and the organizing process in religion (de Jong). But one must be cautious in generating such accounts, because the very form of our scholarly/scientific discourse is itself realist. Whether we subscribe to realism or not, common language use serves to declare "X is the case and not Y." If the reflexive moment is deleted from such discourse, it will enter the world in the form of a truth posit. (This has been a problem in my own writing as well, even when I have been at pains to add the necessary disclaimers). And when such proposals are cast in realist terms they become simply one further entry into the vast compendium of social science hypotheses. They place us again in the role of the expert—the monologic authority—and undermine the possibilities for genuine dialogue among traditions. It is in this same vein that many social scientists participating in the constructionist dialogues have sought means of simultaneously saying and unsaying, situating their claims within traditions or contexts, or calling attention to their own participation in the constructions. And, to reply to Jan van der Lans concerns (Chapter 9) with methodology, it is also in this context that numerous constructionist investigators are contributing to a virtual renaissance in collaborative, performative, and reflexive methodologies (cf. Denzin and Lincoln, 2000).

Vestiges of the realist commitment are especially relevant to a central issue in a number of the preceding chapters—the status of the self. By and large, my colleagues join in the constructionist critique of the traditional conception of the "self-contained individual." They add fascinating new chapters to our understanding of the ways in which self is embedded within and inseparable from relationship. At the same time, there is a strong reluctance to abandon the private, agentive, psychological self. Although Wallace's account of conscience is deeply relational, he wishes in the end to preserve room for a personal conscience that can "tear apart the fabric of one's social relations in an effort to work out the meaning and truth of one's ownmost, radically individualistic, and oftentimes antisocial sense of the good," and that can "press beyond the limited confines and orthodoxies of (one's) communal groups in order to realize new expressions of truth and goodness." Echoing Wallace's Levinasian treatment of conscience, Hermans and Dupont's concrete ethics proposes a "subjective irreducibility of the other . . ." In Day's account of successful religious development, the culmination is an individual who is competent to speak as an author. While agreeing in some degree with Day, Schweitzer does not wish to see an abandonment of cognitive development. Similarly, van der Lans wishes to retain the assumption of "human beings" as "conscious, reflective animals. " And both de Jong and Immink hold to the view that words and actions are in the former's terms, "realizations of intentions. . . . of individual people."

I can well appreciate the desires of my colleagues here to retain something of the essential self so central to the western tradition—its theologies, its dualist epistemology, and its humanism. And I deeply admire the steps taken in many of these essays to explore the socially constituted character of individual being. Their deliberations on the work of Bakhtin, Levinas, Taylor, Harre, Searle and others are welcome additions to the current dialogues. At the same time, if we foreground the self-reflexive moment in constructionist theory, we realize that we do not confront a problem here of whether and to what extent there *is* an autonomous self, a social self, or no self at all. We need not ask whether there is, in reality, individual cognition, an autonomous consciousness, the sense of irreducible otherness, or human intention. We need not be concerned that in the social/discursive accounts of self certain constructionists (myself included) are "blind" to psychological process. Rather, the significant questions concern the implications for societal life of constructing the person within these various forms of intelligibility.

Thus, I have deep respect for my colleagues' wishes to sustain various elements of the western ethnopsychology of the self. I also live within the forms of life of which these elements are an integral part. In no way do I wish to see us abandon the vocabulary of love, hope, experience, intention, and the like. And we must savor those theories—psychological and theological—that offer support for these discourses and their respective institutions. However, with this said we must also be prepared to address the limitations. There is abundant and growing concern over the extent to which the reification of the mental world lends itself to loneliness, narcissism, antagonism, and instrumentalism in society, and the ways in which the assumption of a self-directing agent impedes the development of cooperation, commitment, and community. Such issues have been addressed in many of my previous writings (cf. Gergen, 1994, 1999), and by many before me.

With this said, for me the paramount challenge is to hammer out alternative conceptions of the person that do not recapitulate the problems inherent in the traditional views of private, independent minds. As I see it, our special charge is to articulate and render intelligible a conception of persons as inherently tissued one with another. Various chapters in the present volume surely move in this direction. I tend in my own writings, however, to go somewhat beyond what many of these authors are willing to permit. I do this not because I somehow "know" about the true nature of the self, but because the further we can press into the space of a relational intelligibility, the greater the reflexive challenge to the existing traditions. And with this challenge also comes an opening to new, more communal forms of practice. Already such practices are beginning to emerge within the worlds of narrative and postmodern therapy,

community conflict reduction programs, collaborative educational practices, and appreciative inquiry in the organization. And there are signs
within the present chapters of their emergence within religious institutions. At this point I can only enjoin my colleagues to travel this path
toward relational being, not as a replacement to the subjective self,
but as an alternative discourse with potentially powerful implications
for the conjoining of people, enriching dialogue, and enhancing ethics
in the making. In what follows I shall also propose that there are
within the conception of relational being intimations of the sacred.

The Relational Real/ization of the Sacred

In his widely acclaimed volume, *The Sacred and the Profane*, Merciade
Eliade (1959) argues cogently for the significance of sacred experience in human history. For Eliade the sacralization of space is essential, for example, because "it reveals the fixed point, the central axis
for all future orientation." (p. 21) The experience of the sacred is
set against the tradition of the profane, in which all "space is homo-
geneous and neutral" (p. ??) It is simply there to be dissected by
various rational tools. This is the space that we typically identify with
the "common stock of philosophical and scientific thought" (p. 22).
We might suppose that Eliade was moved to justify the significance
of sacred experience primarily because such experience was under
siege. This was Carl Jung's (1933) view, as he wrote with passion
about the loss of the mysteries of the spirit through science. "It is
easy enough to drive the spirit out of the door," he wrote, "but
when we have done so the salt of life grows flat—it loses its savour."
(p. 142). Even more trenchantly, Morris Berman argues in *The
Reenchantment of the World* that the modernist vision of the world—
most fully represented in the scientific perspective—has robbed humanity of its major source of valuing. As Berman sees it, the scientific
perspective distances the person from nature. We observe nature as
if independent from us, and as a result, we study and use nature
for our own purposes. The result has been disastrous for the ecol-
ogy and for human relationships. Again, we are drawn to the call
of the sacred.

   In my view the domain of practical theology carries with it a tension between the traditions of the sacred and the profane. There is
within the preceding chapters a strong impetus to realize the sacred.

Such intimations of the sacred are especially apparent in the contributions of Wallace and of Hermans. For Wallace the significance
of the sacred may be carried by narratives, and for Hermans by
silence. Both Schweitzer and Immink hold fast to an ontology of the
sacred in religious and ministerial practice. At the same time, most
of the contributions to the present volume are framed in the common argot of contemporary social science: a language of the profane.
The discussions of religious development, the relational construction
of the self, the conversion process, religious organizing and the like,
would be congenial companions to dialogues within the social sciences more generally. In my view there is an important tension here:
as in the scholarly world and society more generally, the discourse
of the profane is in ascendance. As it expands to fill the domain of
intelligibility, so does the realm of the sacred recede. Sacred discourse is squeezed into "quaint" corners; its profundity is recast as
mere rhetoric—misleading, magical, an opiate. In the same vein,
those concerned with the realm of the sacred might also be resistant to social constructionist ideas. After all, constructionist texts
largely grow from secular roots, and in this respect (among others),
share much with 20th century science. And certainly one's resistance
might be reinforced by the way in which constructionist arguments
remove any fundamental warrant from ontological, logical, or moral
claims issuing from religious or theological spheres. Constructionism
casts a suspicious eye toward serious eschatology.

Yet, in my view this account is incomplete. Further probing reveals
a far more promising relationship between constructionism and "the
realm of the sacred." This is so, in part, because the constructionist dialogues restore parity between the scientific and the spiritual
worlds of understanding. The traditional binaries used to elevate science over religion—with the material over the spiritual, objectivity
over subjectivity, determinism over voluntarism—are rendered invalid.
Such distinctions create our realities rather than reflect them. Constructionism not only invites the scientific and religious traditions
to the table as equals, but simultaneously asks us to consider the
societal consequences of religious and spiritual discourses. The question here is not one of truth, for both science and religion generate
their own truths within their own spheres of practice. The primary
question is how do scientific and spiritual discourses (and practices)
function within our relationships; what are the reverberations for our
lives together—here and now and beyond? And, if we find that some

of these consequences are unfortunate, we should open new dialogues, generate new interpretations, and consider alternative practices. In this vein, one might even venture that the discourses and practices of the sacred have contributed more to cultural well-being than the practices of science. However, the ways in which this may be so—or not—should be the subject of continuing dialogue. And these dialogues should be open to a multiplicity of evaluative criteria. In this way we remain responsible to the very process of meaning making itself.

Yet, in my view the constructionist dialogues can carry us still further. The preceding chapters have demonstrated a variety of ways in which constructionism can be used to explain religion, morality, worship, and so on. As pointed out, these efforts have rendered the otherwise sacred in a profane language. Is there a way in which the opposite case can be made, in which the constructionist dialogues may contribute to the real/ization of the sacred—giving the spiritual world a palpability rivaling that of the secular? I believe there is. For me the pivotal concept in the constructionist movement is *relational process*. The significance of social construction largely derives from its replacement of the individual as the fundamental atom of cultural life with relational process. To bring this view into full intelligibility, and to secure a range of congenial practices, would transform the face of cultural life. Yet, we may ask, given its critical role in societal life, what is the nature of relational process? Here the constructionist falters. Surely, there is much that has been said about relational processes, and the vistas of future exploration are enormous. The chapters of the present volume bear important witness. However, the constructionist also understands that anything said about relationship is inevitably issuing from a particular culture, tradition, and historical era. The reflexive moment in action. Thus, we may develop compelling discourses of relationship—of negotiation, narration, rhetoric and the like—but such discourses can in no way picture, map or contain the phenomenon. In fact, to presume that relational process is "a phenomenon" is already to objectify the otherwise inarticulable, that which must inevitably remain beyond our descriptive possession.

Let me offer a provocative reconstruction: that source from which all meaning is made possible—all that we deem to exist, that we hold valuable, that we cherish, that gives our lives a sense of worth and direction—issues from a source that is unfathomable. Placed in these terms, we locate a significant space for dialogically linking the domains of the profane and the sacred: daily life is altogether an immersion in relational process, but simultaneously a process that is the unfathomable source of being. In confronting the enormity of the impenetrable source, we approach the register of the sublime—resistant to logical limning—and commanding of our awe. And it is in precisely this space of wonderment that theology and social construction begin to merge. For this sense of the sacred—as an indescribable font of existence—is itself a theme entwined with centuries of theological sensibility. The view is certainly present in the Judao-Christian tradition. "How unsearchable are his judgments and how inscrutable his ways!" we find in the book of Romans (11:33). It reemerges in the 4th century writings on negative theology, in which humans are deemed incapable of direct comprehension of the Deity. We are linked to our fellow beings by bonds of love, it was advanced, and we cannot ascertain the source of this communion through acts of reason. Much the same theme now emerges in postmodern theology (cf. Coward and Foshay, 1992). As Mark Taylor (1984) avers, "The *radical* codependence of all things negates the possibility of an absolutely primal origin from which everything descends." (p. 154). And there are important links as well to Chris Hermans' vision of "ultimate meaning" as residing "in silence as unuttered truth." Many will also find in these recognitions of the relational unfathomable, echoes of the Asian traditions of Buddhism and Taoism.

As we move into this space of understanding we are prepared as well for a transformation in our sense of relationship to a Deity. We can understand the traditional conception of God as Supreme Being—an identifiable entity possessed with power, love, anger, wisdom and other attributes garnered from our discourse on human agents—as a communal construction. As a construction, there is no absolute demand that such a view be embraced. In fact, a fundamental commitment to such a view would set the conditions for alienation and conflict. In contrast, if we are sensitized to the sacred dimension of relatedness, we can glimpse the possibility that God is not a separate Being—out there, in the heavens—but that God is immanent in a *process* from which we cannot be separated (see also Marion, 1991). We need not view God as distinct and distant from humankind, as our relationships in the here and now possess hierophanic potential—the capacity to manifest the sacred. In this sense, God is the reality "in (which) we live and move and have our being." (Acts

17:28) In our every action we possess the potential to share in this
process. Nor, must we view the relational process as limited to the
human domain. In the generation of meaning we cannot ultimately
separate that which is human from the non-human. Required for
the creation of meaning—and thus the immanence of the sacred—
is a generative relationship with all that we call natural and material. In Martin Buber's terms, "the relation with God . . . includes
and encompasses the possibility of relation with all otherness." (1958,
p. 81) Our relations with our natural environment, then, have sacred
potentials. As we extend the conversation of construction, we see
that "all otherness" becomes "one" in relational process.

The implications of this view for a *practical* theology are significant.
Rather than understanding the realm of the sacred as distinct from
daily life, we are invited to see our participation in daily life as
potentially an emanation or realization of the sacred. In particular,
when our actions contribute to the continuous generation of meaning—which is to say, to generative as opposed to destructive coordination—we are *manifesting the sacred*, we are participants in the divine.
We are contributing to those very processes from which domains of
value, morality, and theology issue forth. In this sense, living with
God is not a postponement to some future and unspecified time; in
Christian terms we need not await Christ's coming. We have the
potential to reveal Christ in every momentary action. In Taylor's
(1984) terms, "Within the unending play of the divine milieu, 'wait-
ing is the final losing game.'" (p. 155) The sacred inhabits the full
flowing of relatedness, and is thus most apparent in those actions
that rescue the flows of relationship from the inevitability of opposing cross-currents. Thus, we approach the sacred in forms of ethically generative practice, of relational responsibility, of moving from
singularity of self to co-construction and collaboration. In these terms,
we may manifest the sacred in many of the practices described by
my colleagues in the preceding chapters: in religious and moral development, preaching, church organizing, and religious education. Aad
de Jong's chapter ends with an exhortation for "practical theologians
to cultivate participatory attitudes and skills." In extending and real-
izing the call, so do we cultivate the sacred.

References

Arnett, R.C. (1986). *Communication and community*. Carbondale, IL: Southern Illinois University Press.

Berger, P.L. (1979). *The heretical imperative: Contemporary possibilities for religious affirmation*. New York: Doubleday.

Berman, M. (1981). *The reenchantment of the world*. Ithica: Cornell University Press.

Buber, M. (1947). *Between man and man*. London: Kegan Paul.

Caputo, J. (1993). *Against ethics*. Bloomington: Indiana University Press.

Coward, H. & Foshay, T. (1992) (Eds.) (1992). *Derrida and negative theology*. Albany: State University of New York Press.

Denzin, N. & Lincoln, Y. (2000). *Handbook of Qualitative Methods* (2nd ed.). Thousand Oaks, CA: Sage.

Eliade, M. (1959). *The sacred and the profane*. New York: Harcourt Brace.

Gergen, K.J. (1994). *Realities and relationships*. Cambridge: Harvard University Press.
—— (1999). *An invitation to social construction*. London: Sage.

Gilligan, C. (1982). *In a different voice*. Cambridge: Harvard University Press.

Habermas, J. (1979). *Communication and the evolution of society*. Boston: Beacon Press.

Jung, C.J. (1933). *Modern man in search of a soul*. New York: Harvest.

MacIntyre, A. (1984). *After virtue*. 2nd ed. Notre Dame, IN: University of Notre Dame Press.

Marion, J. (1991). *God without being*. Chicago: University of Chicago Press.

McNamee, S. & Gergen, K.J. (1999). *Relational responsibility, resources for sustainable dialogue*. Thousand Oaks, CA.: Sage.

Nishitani, K. (1982). *Religion and nothingness*. Berkeley: University of California Press.

Stout, J. (1988). *Ethics after Babel*. Boston: Beacon Press.

SOCIAL CONSTRUCTIONISM AND THEOLOGY: A DANCE TO BE POSTPONED?

Johannes A. van der Ven

The title of this contribution, in which I reflect on some previous articles in this volume inasmuch as they deal with the relation between social constructionism and theology, expresses a certain ambivalence. It is a response to the title of Gergen's first article in this book, "Social constructionism and theology: the dance begins".

Social constructionism makes some interesting points, especially the general insight that every kind of human activity—from perceiving, thinking and feeling to interpreting, evaluating and communicating—is socio-historically and socio-culturally determined. This also applies to activities that we tend to consider extremely individual, private and intimate such as meditation and prayer. It applies equally to those aspects of human existence that relate to the self, such as the moral and religious self, and to what—also in the moral and religious domains—constitutes the individual's personal identity. This general insight is so fundamental that it seems worth while continually to wrest it from oblivion, expose it, polish it and make it sparkle in all its self-evidence, like a crystal whose multifaceted reflection of light does not blind but attracts and fascinates us.

What we are saying is that this insight is not new and that we should be wary of thinking that it will help us to probe a brand new, hitherto unexploited goldmine. On the contrary: the debate on the relation between the individual and society is as old as systematic philosophy itself, judging by metaphysical, philosophical and social anthropological discourse; it is as old as the debate on Durkeim's *The rules of sociological method* (1908); it is as old as the tradition of symbolic interactionism established by George Herbert Mead's *Mind, self and society* (1934); and, finally, it is as old as the debate on the paradigm of the historian Maurice Halbwachs that has been raging ever since his *La mémoire collective* (1950). This is not to repudiate social constructionism, but rather to acknowledge that we are dealing with an ageless theme, an ever recurring problem or even—as I am inclined to think—an insoluble aporia. Whatever your starting point, let's say it is the individual self, sooner or later you come up against the limits imposed by the relational self, the group, the collectivity, the institution. Or, if you start with the relational self, group or community, sooner or later you come up against the limits imposed by the individual self. These historical references of mine are simply a caveat that it may be wise to incorporate the history of philosophy and the social sciences into any discussion of social constructionism in order to protect oneself against the pitfalls of facile, one-sided statements.

That brings me to the other side of my ambivalence. If proponents of social constructionism were to ask me to dance, I would for the time being decline the invitation—albeit courteously and chivalrously—and suggest to them that we first go to a dancing school together for lessons, some five of them. These are the critical comments offered below, which, as mentioned already, are directed only to those articles in the book which pertain to the dance with theology and, more particularly, to practical theology. In so doing I focus on some ontological, epistemological, ethical and theological facets; that is, after pointing out the relation between practical theology and practical philosophy. From the articles in this book it struck me, moreover, that some colleagues (at least, that is what I suspect) are inclined not just to postpone the dance but to write it off altogether, or may even have done so already. Personally I would not go that far. To me this experiment—on the fictitious dance floor—is far too appealing.

1   *Theology as a Practical Discipline*

Readers may well wonder why I should head my commentary on the articles in this volume with a title referring to an age-old problem which appears to have no bearing on social constructionism; that is to say, the problem of whether, and in what sense, theology is a speculative or a practical discipline. Let me explain its relevance right away. As we know, medieval theologians grappled with the question of whether theology should continue in the Augustinian tradition, or whether it should proceed from what was at that time a "modern", albeit axiomatic and deductive, notion of science derived from newly discovered Aristotelian philosophy. The Augustinian tradition reflected on the Bible and the biblical concept of faith with a view to human well-being, a virtuous life and surrender to God.

In that tradition Alexander of Hales and Albertus Magnus developed what came to be known as pre-Thomist theology, which thus had a practical orientation. Thomas Aquinas himself, however, assimilated major facets of Aristotelian philosophy, not only into his ethics but also into his ontology and epistemology, and the dogmatic analyses in his theology attained great speculative heights. But Aquinas would not be Aquinas if his argument on the speculative versus the practical character of theology did not display a certain balance. In the first article of the first *quaestio* of his *Summa theologia* he maintains that theology deals with God in terms of the salvation of human beings, with God from the perspective of human well-being. In the fourth article, however, he concludes that it is both a speculative and a practical science, even though its speculative character may predominate. Later Duns Scotus made an excellent case for the opposite view, holding that the *cognitio practica* in theology exceeds any speculative understanding in truth and value.

Why cite this debate here? I do so because Thomas, in the aforementioned fourth article, refers to the distinction between a speculative and a practical approach, not only in theology but also in philosophy, or between what we would now call speculative and practical disciplines. And it seems to me that this distinction is pre-eminently relevant to a discussion of the importance of social constructionism for theology, and certainly for practical theology which is the discipline practised by the contributors to this volume. This is not the place to examine the meaning of the distinction in detail. I merely mention the dichotomy that one can introduce as far back as Aristotle between speculative writings (e.g. his *Categories, Topics, Analytics, Metaphysics*) on the one hand and practical writings (e.g. his *Nicomachean Ethics, Politics, Rhetoric, Poetics*) on the other. But if it is true—and I am becoming increasingly convinced that it is—that judicious use of philosophy is indicated for the mediation between the social sciences and theology generally, and practical theology in particular, then we cannot evade the question: which philosophical disciplines does practical theology draw on for this mediation? My answer would be that for the cross-border traffic between practical theology and the social sciences—in this case social constructionism—practical philosophy at any rate is needed. This is not to exclude speculative (or systematic or fundamental) philosophy, but merely to assert that practical philosophy is prerequisite for any such interaction with practical theology.

Does this mean that I am sidestepping the critical questions in this book regarding the ontological, epistemological, fundamental ethical and theo-logical implications of social constructionism? Am I failing to deal with objections in this regard? Emphatically not. I simply prefer to deal with them primarily in terms of the categories and concepts of practical philosophy rather than those of speculative philosophy. For practical philosophy, too, has something to say—obviously in a poly-vocal rather than a univocal way—in the domains of ontology, epistemology, fundamental ethics and theology, albeit on the basis of its own material and formal object. Clearly it is extremely difficult to present this material and formal object in a nutshell, let alone in a single sentence, but for the sake of this argument I proceed on the following assumption: practical philosophy is about human action (material object) with due regard to freedom (formal object). The definition needs to be amplified, for instance as regards the relation between action and behaviour; between freedom, intentionality and causality; between consciousness and reconstruction, to mention but a few topics. The point is, however, that this definition of the material and formal objects of practical philosophy entails a number of ontological, epistemological, fundamental ethical and theo-logical aspects that are of the utmost importance for a consideration of the relevance of social constructionism to (practical) theology, as I hope to demonstrate below.

2 Ontological Aspects

There is some confusion among practical theologians about the discipline's most elementary basic concept: is it action or interaction, act or communication? The exchange with social constructionism does not improve matters, particularly since it further justifies the route followed by practical theologians since the 1960s (a route I have vigorously pursued myself in other respects): "Interaction, communication, naturally," they would respond. On this premise one could substantiate ontological statements such as "being human *consists* in interacting" or "a human being *is* a dialogical self: that is his/her very existence". But this is to ignore the fact that "act" and "action" are inherent in the concept of praxis, for which practical theology professes to provide a basis, and that "interaction" and "communication" should be approached from this perspective (and not the other way round). This insight applies even more forcefully if one brings practical philosophy into one's practical theology. Following the philosopher at the vanguard of the Enlightenment, Baruch Spinoza, Ricoeur developed a claim which, freely interpreted, states that the very essence of being human consists in acting: I act so I am, as I am, because I am and, conversely, I am so I act, while I act, because I act. Ontologically this is a more profound claim than Gergen's "communicamus ergo sum"—a proposition that is perfectly understandable in terms of his argument but which, logically and ontologically, would be more aptly expressed by "communicamus ergo sumus". After all, this implies "ergo sum". (Of course, he would then forfeit his polemical tone, which I would consider an advantage.)

What do we gain by making action rather than interaction our basic concept, as social constructionism in fact does? At least three things. Firstly, it is not only groups and collectivities that act—in a derived sense—but also, and primarily, the individual person. In this way, and at this level, one at least maintains the polarity between the individual self and the relational self without reducing it simply to interaction between individuals. Secondly, focussing on the concept "action" compels one to reflect on the significance and meaning of human intentionality and, following from that, to determine its relation to causality in human life and society. I find nothing about these two concepts and their interrelationship in the articles in this volume, whereas it strikes me as a fundamental problem in practical theology. Translated into social constructionist terms, one might put it thus: should the interaction between people be seen as reciprocal intentionality or does it also contain elements of reciprocal causal influencing? The question is obviously rhetorical, but it pinpoints the really pressing problem: how do the two relate to each other? If and inasmuch as we can speak of causal influencing, that takes us back to the study of individuals and their background variables, which is (superficially and unilaterally) challenged in some articles) but which conflicts directly with the principles of social constructionism. Let us define this knotty philosophical problem explicitly: are causality and intentionality mutually exclusive (as Gergen would have it), or can/should causality be explained in terms of causality (as Searle maintains), or (as cognition theorists insist) the other way round: can/should intentionality be explained in terms of causality? Or are they (merely?) different perspectives which may or may not be included simultaneously in a path-analytical model and, therefore, can function side by side? These are not simple questions, particularly since they touch on the issues of human freedom and autonomy. Thirdly, if one speaks of action (*actio*)—at any rate according to one age-old tradition—one is also speaking of passion (*passio*). This concept, too, does not feature in the various articles, with the exception of Schilderman's. The two terms should be viewed dialectically, for one party's action implies the other's passion; after all, the latter is subjected to the action of the former. This is a significant insight, for if one ignores the term "passion", one loses sight of the power relations and power structures which determine human life and society—not, I hasten to add, in an original but in a radical sense—under which all of us, one way or another, suffer all the time. But by the same token, if one disregards passion, one loses sight of the passions (*passiones*) which accompany actions: while acting I am subject to feelings. At the same time, if one disregards passion, one is overlooking the passions of those who tolerate, permit or accept one's actions. I am not saying that social constructionism disregards passions, but the connection with the more fundamental concept of passion is not explicit enough.

Altogether these reasons suffice to declare action a basic concept, as social constructionists in fact do, and to explain interaction and communication in terms of the concept of action, not the other way round. I not only construct but am constructed, and this happens in relations of power, right down to my feelings. And, besides intentional aspects, there are all sorts of causal aspects involved which influence both the self and the other, as well as the interaction between them.

3   *Epistemological Aspects*

In some articles I was struck by their epistemological weakness, which is one of the objections levelled at social constructionism. In particular I was struck by the area in which the epistemological discourse is conducted, namely that of fundamental or systematic philosophy rather than practical philosophy. The latter is the area into which I venture in this article, without declaring the area of fundamental or systematic philosophy irrelevant—on the contrary. To my mind practical philosophy also has something to offer when it comes to the question of whether we can know reality in terms of reference.

This question is raised specifically in the articles by Immink and De Jong, although they do so in different ways and also offer different answers, at any rate in terms of different paradigms.

The question is: can we know reality in terms of reference? This is clearly an extremely complex epistemological problem, one in which realism and nominalism grapple with each other and in whose tug of war I am caught up almost daily, in both interpersonal and intrapersonal dialogues. I am content merely to clarify some aspects of it from a practical philosophical point of view. In so doing I proceed on the assumption—which in itself, of course, requires (none too readily forthcoming) substantiation—that our knowledge is loaded with and constructed in language, and that knowledge is linguistic in character.

The first point is this. The linguistic expressions in which our knowledge is contained have—at least from a practical philosophical angle of approach—the status of speech acts. Whatever the substance of the philosophy of language and philosophical linguistics, in a practical philosophical approach the focus is on language as speech acts, which underscores yet again the basic character of the concept "act" in practical philosophy and practical theology. According to my interpretation of Searle—who is cited in several articles—he distinguishes between different aspects of speech acts: an illocutionary/perlocutionary aspect and a locutionary aspect. The illocutionary aspect relates to the speaker's intention (the speaker is intent on asserting, arguing, warning, requesting) and the speaker's aim of being understood by the listener (i.e. that the listener should understand asserting as asserting, arguing as arguing, etc). The perlocutionary aspect relates to the intended reception by the listener (asserting as convincing, arguing as persuading, warning as alarming, requesting as making the listener do something) and to the effect that the speaker wants to have on the listener (getting the listener to agree with the assertion or argument, or accept the warning or request). One could also call it the rhetorical aspect, referred to in various articles. The illocutionary and perlocutionary aspects are extensions of each other and are sometimes difficult if not impossible to tell apart. But there is a third aspect as well: the locutionary aspect. This relates to the propositional content of the illocutionary/perlocutionary speech act. If I open a meeting in my capacity as chairperson (thus performing an illocutionary act belonging to the class of declaratives) or when I express assent to affirm a promise (thus

performing an illocutionary act belonging to the class of commissives), then the propositional implication in the first case is that a
group of people are present along with me in a given space at a
given time, and in the second case that I and someone else are
together in the same place at a given moment and that the promise
refers to a book which that person is giving me on loan and which
I promise to return. Can one speak of reference in such instances?
In his article, which has a clear epistemological slant, Immink answers
the question affirmatively: naturally one can speak of reference, he
would say. I am there, there are other people, there is a book. From
a practical philosophical angle, with the accent on actions and speech
acts, I would be inclined to say that one can only speak of reference insofar as it is implicit in the illucutionary/perlocutionary structure of the speech act, not separate from it. In other words, the
locutionary aspect that relates to reference does not exist independently of, or in isolation from, the language utterance as a speech
act but is actually an aspect *of* the speech act itself. To make it quite
plain: from a practical philosophical point of view all language utterances are illocutionary/perlocutionary speech acts; there is no other
kind. We act in and through our language utterances: that is the
meaning of the terms "illocutionary" and "perlocutionary"; there are
no language utterances in which, or through which, we do not act.
The term "locutionary" indicates an aspect of these speech acts: it
does not exist independently of our linguistic actions in illocutio-
nary/perlocutionary speech acts or apart from them, but is implicit
in them. Does that mean that we cannot make any assertions about
the world around us? To be sure we can, but according to speech
act theory assertives are illocutionary/perlocutionary speech acts and
not simply speech acts, for there is no such thing. As noted already,
the illocutionary intention of the speaker's assertions consists in being
understood by the listener in terms of asserting, and the perlocutionary
effect consists in persuasively convincing and persuasively making the
listener agree. And *within* these illocutionary/perlocutionary speech
acts of assertives there is a locutionary aspect which does refer to
the extralinguistic world at issue. My response to social constructionism boils down to this: one certainly can speak of reference, but
only as an aspect of the interlocution between speaker and listener.

   This can be explicated further by looking at the nature and meaning of narratives, the second point I want to examine. This is a topic
for which social constructionists rightly have a distinct predilection,

particularly because it features prominently in human praxis. A narrative may be regarded as a complex speech act unit, along with other complex speech units such as argumentation, description, judgment and discourse. Here it should be noted that these complex speech units, however clearly they may be distinguishable from each other, can display all sorts of combinations. That is to say, narratives may contain elements of argumentation, description and/or judgment and they may also be created in and through certain forms of discourse. But the point is that narratives in themselves are not meant to refer to any extralinguistic state of affairs or seek to offer a one-to-one portrayal of that extralinguistic reality. Their primary aim is to offer a perspective for action—the basic concept!—by means of a reconstruction of past and present actions, plus events occurring beyond the volition of the person concerned, the incidental circumstances in which that person is caught up, the people influencing him or her and the broad social context in which she or he is situated. The aim is not to create knowledge for its own sake in terms of reference, but to introduce some sort of coherence in what happened recently or long ago, and to see whether chance can be turned into challenge and fate into destiny. And, as we noted in the case of simple speech acts, these narrative complex speech acts units also have locutionary aspects: there *is* a situation in which they were enacted, which is enacted in the narrative; there *are* people who have acted as they act in the narrative; there *were* opportunities that were not seized and which are left unseized in the narrative. It would be foolish to deny it; it would be equally foolish to divorce this referential content from the narrative and pretend that it exists independently.

Of course this does not mean that all narratives are "true" or "conflict-free". This is the third aspect. That is by no means the case, which becomes clear when one considers that it is not just I who tell my story but that others tell my story as well: I am narrated in my turn. It becomes even clearer when we take into account that I told my story about "the same events" differently ten years ago from the way I am telling it now (I reconstruct it differently now), that the people around me will tell my story differently ten years hence from the way they used to tell it, and that there will be diverse versions and interpretations among them. What is truth? What is narrative truth? If there were no such thing as truth, or narrative truth, then one cannot explain why people are forever struggling to find truth even when their own versions and interpretations differ from other people's. Is it a matter of power? Of whose story is the most forceful, most potent, the dominant one? It would not be the first time that stories are inspired by power, are influenced by power struggles in their evolution, are directed by a lust for power. But that cannot be the final verdict, for hermeneutic ideological criticism and the hermeneutics of suspicion, which also apply to narratives, perform their purifying task here as well. No, there must be some regulatory notion of truth that drives people to reconstruct the "real" confluence of circumstances and determine the "real" role played in it by the dramatis personae. In this process the narrator acts as some sort of judge who listens to the various attestations competing with each other in a situation of contestation and, having listened to everything, makes an evaluation and eventually arrives at a narrative verdict. This is a verdict which is always subject to appeal, for the narrative verdict is never final: it remains open, as Aristotle pointed out, even after the death of the person concerned; the web of meaning of his or her life continues to be woven after the character has died. There is no criterion of truth other than the narrative verdict which continually comes up for narrative and argumentative review when new facts come to light or when new, unsuspected contexts emerge, as social constructionism rightly points out.

4   *Ethical Aspects*

I don't know whether I am being altogether fair to social constructionism if I say that it is based on a twofold claim: firstly, that the self is a social construct, which it indisputably is provided it is not reduced to just that; and secondly, that it is itself constructed in terms of, and even by, the alterity of the other, which is likewise not disputed, again provided it is not reduced to that. In order to prevent such reduction I consider it necessary briefly to put the various "dramatis personae" in the spotlight.

First of all there is the I. This I is indeed a social construct, but it is more than just that. It would be absurd to ignore the body that the I calls "mine" and not "yours" or "hers". Of course one could object that this body, and bodiliness generally, certainly are also social constructs, but again one has to add that they are more than just social constructs. There is something like a physical substratum comprising a trunk, a head and limbs which together constitute "my" body and do so in terms of the dialectic that I both *have* and *am* my body. In philosophy the concept "body" is called a primitive concept, referring to the body as a basic particular situated within the irreducible parameters of time and space. The bodily I forms the basis of the individual—in the sense of indivisible and irreducible—person that I am, the centre of knowledge and action. Of course, the individual person that is "I" cannot be divorced from its interaction with others, but that does not mean that this I is simply a result of that interaction. Here the dialectic tension between "I" and "the other" must be kept intact.

But who or what is the other'? Here one has to differentiate, from six distinct perspectives. This is important, because a purely abstract approach to the other (especially if that other is embellished, aesthetically but not analytically enough, with such epithets as "the voice of the other", the "otherness" of the other or, even more abstractly, "alterity") makes us lose sight of the multiplicity of the other.

First, the term "the other" may represent the rest of the group to which I belong—the first person plural "we". Inasmuch as the I is a social construct, this is partly because that I belongs to a group of other I's who, for whatever reason, also have a sense of belonging and develop a sense of "us". Despite this the I remains distinct from the other I's in this group. Again it is a matter not of a reduction, but of a dialectic between "I" and "we", between "mine" and "ours". Classically, the fundamental question is what causes a group to cohere. There is no simple answer. Is it a shared belief (cultural) or is it a need to belong (social)? Or must we maintain the same tension as before, this time between the cultural and the social aspect? There could be other factors involved as well, like a contract or ruling (juridical), a goal or plan (political), or the distribution of scarce material and/or personal resources (economic). It is important not simply to dump all one's eggs in the basket of the social and/or cultural relations that the I maintains with the others in "our" group. The social construct may just as well be based on juridical, political or economic factors in the interaction between me and the rest of us, or among ourselves.

Secondly, there is the second person singular, "you", and more particularly the personal you, the intimate you, the you of the small community and close circle of friends. This you is undoubtedly the party that prompts the keenest awareness of alterity: the otherness of the other, the other who is not equivalent to, or identical with, me but, as another I, differs fundamentally from me. This aware-ness is sharpened, not so much in the group to which I belong as part of a "we", but in the intimate relationship in which I and you look each other in the eye as two absolutely unique, unrepeatable people who are contingently present to each other. It is the other's look which makes her or him a you and me an I. Is this a matter of reciprocity or mutuality? Does the one act and the other suffer, and vice versa (reciprocity), or is there a permanent equivalence of simultaneous action and suffering (mutuality)? Either way, it is social construction, but who is constructing whom?

Besides this, in this encounter with others in their otherness, the I becomes aware of its own otherness: I become aware of my own riddle, enigma, mystery. I am another to myself. Again it is a mat-ter of social construction, in this case of my own unfathomable depths, my own inhospitable abyss, but they do not belong to some-one else but to me-as-the-other. This other is intrapersonal, which ultimately refers simply to "me".

Just as the other may be regarded as representing an extension of the I in the direction of the first person plural "we", so taking it further—the you can be extended in the direction of the second person "you", plural . These others differ in their turn from the "others" considered up to now: the other that I am to myself, the others that form part of "us", and you, the intimate other. One might call this plural "you" the group to which you, not I, belong.

Finally there are two forms of what Ricoeur calls the institutional other, namely the third person singular "he" or "she" and the third person plural "they". These others have no interpersonal relation-ship with the I, they have no face, no name or surname. One could also call them the anonymous other, for they form part of the same geographical, judicial or political territory to which I belong, but without either their or my uniqueness and unrepeatability affecting it. We are all part of civil society and located cadastrally; we have the same rights and obligations; and we are all equal before the law. They, like me, are simply numbers in the institutions within that territory. Yet they, too, are other than me.

In the context of ethics it is extremely important to make sure that each of the dramatis personae in question, which we have traced back to the three agencies denoted by the personal pronouns "I/we", "you" (singular and plural) and "he/she/they", can form the basis for distinctive ethical principles, values and norms. This is important because social constructionism might tempt us to focus on the other exclusively as the interpersonal other, which, as mentioned before, refers mainly to the intimate other. This would push not only the I, but also the institutional other (the anonymous he/she/they) to the periphery or even completely outside our field of vision.

By identifying the three agencies—I/we, you (singular and plural), and he/she/they—and associating distinct ethical attitudes with each of them we avoid the risk of reducing the entire field of ethics to two principles: those of care and justice. In our brief exploration of the ethical significance of the three agencies indicated by the personal pronouns it is noteworthy that all the ethical attitudes and values mentioned below have the I as their author, their agent, and more particularly the I as the centre of ethical claims, as the seat of conscience and source of action. How could it be otherwise, however much of a social construct that I may be!

According to a long tradition dating back at least to Kant, the ethical attitudes that one should adopt to the self, the I, are those of the drive for self-preservation (as opposed to e.g. self-mutilation), self-esteem (as opposed to e.g. self-neglect) and integrity (as opposed to e.g. obsequiousness). One might say that the I that is the other to oneself—the enigmatic dimension of the I—is presented with a new task: that of self-knowledge, "know yourself". This self-knowledge is of a dialectical, vertiginous profundity: the better the I comes to know itself, the more the mystery deepens. The attitude that the I should adopt towards the other who belongs to "us" is one of friendship. The attitudes that the I should adopt towards the other as a you are those of care (as opposed to e.g. indifference) and love (as opposed to e.g. hatred). Do the friendship, care and love also apply to others who belong to the "you" (plural) category? Not necessarily, maybe not at all, even though the adage that my friends' friends are my friends as well has some validity. At all events, the rule is that the I is bound to express its respect for the other as a human being with human dignity.

Finally, what attitudes must the I adopt towards institutional or anonymous others? Here the dominant factor is a sense of justice and its expression in the moral principles of human rights. These comprise three "generations": civil, socio-economic and group rights. They include negative rights (e.g. freedom of association, i.e. the right to non-intervention by government) and positive rights (e.g. the right to food and work), as well as passive rights (e.g. receiving something from others) and active rights (e.g. to do things oneself).

My reason for mentioning the three agencies (I/we, you [singu-lar and plural], and he/she/they), as well as the concomitant ethi-cal attitudes, is that they act as a counterweight to the tendency towards ethical relativism or even ethical aestheticism which, as Hermans and Dupont points out, does lurk in social constructionism, and which could be fatal for theology if it were to be injected into the discipline along with social constructionism. Ethics has always been a discipline that is critical of the notion that cultural-historical conventions on which everyone belonging to a particular culture agrees are, for that reason, ethically acceptable and/or permissible. Even the invocation of *consensus gentium* is not an adequate argument to validate an ethical principle, any more than lack of consensus would be an adequate refutation. The consensus of the Nazi state in Germany and of the apartheid regime in South Africa illustrates the casuistry of this kind of reasoning.

5   *God Talk*

The previous articles point out that Gergen allows little scope for reflec-tion on religion in his social constructionism. In itself this is no reason for not critically assimilating his insights into theology. The question is, however, whether his theory creates adequate conditions for the God talk which he himself does not engage in nor needs to engage in, but which is a crucial part of theology. I shall deal with three points that struck me while reading the various articles in this book.

The first point has to do with the reference theme which I have already touched on in the section on epistemology but which resur-faces cogently in the present context of God talk. The question is this: do religious statements refer to an extra linguistic reality which is God, or does social constructionism dismiss this question as irre-levant and absurd because referential truth is declared nonexistent? From the epistemological point of view that I sought to clarify in terms of a practical philosophical approach, my answer would be as follows. Religious statements should be seen as religious speech acts or religious performances, which display illocutionary/perlocutionary attributes and which, like all speech acts (according to Searle), can be classified into five categories: assertives, directives, commissives, expressives and declaratives. Thus we confess that God exists (assertive), we ask him to bless us or challenge him, as Job did (directive), we promise that we will be faithful to his word (commissive), we express our gratitude to him or our sorrow at his absence (expressive), and, lastly, we declare that this word is the word of God, or that this bread and this wine are the body and blood of his son (declarative). Now *within* these illocutionary/perlocutionary speech acts, we have said, there is a locutionary aspect with a propositional load. This propositional load does not exist independently of the speech act but is embedded and implicit in it. In other words, our religious speech acts most definitely *contain* a reference to God but it does not lie outside them. Hence we know God only insofar as we confess him (assertive); we know him only insofar as we ask him to bless us (directive); we know him only insofar as we promise to remain faithful to him (commissive); we known him only insofar as we express our gratitude or sorrow to him (expressive); we know him only insofar as we declare this word to be his word (declarative). After all, how could we know God except in the relationship that we establish, maintain and develop with him through our speech acts? How could we possibly know God outside this relationship? How can I know my lover outside my relationship with him or her?

This does not detract from the fundamental social constructionist tenet that we can apply to this problem, namely that the religious self-definition contained in these religious utterances, like the religious identity to which they give rise, is a product of social construction. In my religious speech acts I address God or put myself in his presence *because* I learned to do so in my early religious socialisation, *because* there are people around me who engage in a similar kind of talk and thus provide social plausibility for my utterances, and *because* my interaction with them and our environing culture puts me in a state of constant development and change. All this is true, but the polyphonous reality of religious speech cannot be reduced to this alone, and *one* aspect of that reality is the reference to the extralinguistic reality which is God, to whom I am actually addressing myself *in* my religious performances.

Yet this still leaves us with a host of problems. One of them is the distinction between reference and representation, in the sense that the latter concept adds a certain modulation to the first one. Put differently, reference is not unmediated but representative reference. What does that mean? Generally speaking, representation means that the actual object being represented is not present. That

is why it is being represented: it is not there itself, it is absent. At
the same time it *is* represented, implying that it is present at least
in the representation, *in the mode* of representation. In other words,
the object being represented is both absent and present. This does
not only apply to religious language. It applies to language generally, whether about the past or the present, as the following examples illustrate. The stories we dig up from memory do not call the
actual characters and events that they narrate into our field of vision;
the are and remain absent, yet at the same time they are portrayed.
The same applies to the history we write: the past is and remains
in the pluperfect tense, yet historiography does open it up for us
and gives us access to it. The writings of social scientists, too, can
be described in terms of representation: they do not bring the contemporary social world that they refer to into our range of vision,
yet they do give us a picture of it. By analogy this dialectic of
absence/presence that applies to all our representative knowledge—
and there is no other kind—can be applied to speech acts in the
religious domain. As mentioned already, in its propositional orientation the locutionary aspect embedded in illocutionary/perlocutio-
nary speech employs images which partly indicates the absence of
God (otherwise we would not need images), and partly represent
God as present *within* the images. God is both absent and present.
Probably the loveliest image to convey God's simultaneous absence
and presence is the silence of God, the silent God cited by Hermans.
But this, too, is an image—an image in its turn complemented by
other images, because God cannot be captured by just one image
but requires a whole polyphony of images, through which, as Ricoeur
points out, he coordinates his constant withdrawal from the images.
Be that as it may, the reference to God is representative, not direct.
True, the images themselves are products of social interaction and
cultural construction, as social constructionism avers; but this does
not detract from the fundamental fact of a dialectic between absence
and presence, and hence from representative reference.

Finally, is God himself a social construction? Actually, in view of
what we have said above, this is a silly, nonsensical question. If—I
repeat, *if*—social constructionists were to reply, "Yes, just that and
nothing besides", then I shall for now refuse the invitation to join
the dance; I would even refuse an invitation to a dance deferred to
a later occasion. But I don't think the social constructionists' answer
is that silly. Of course the images that religious people employ in

their religious speech acts, and even the form and content of the speech acts themselves, are social constructions. But after all we have said, that still leaves the door open, even though—I hasten to concede—for some theologians it can never be left open enough. And of course the locutionary, propositional aspect of these religious speech acts referring to God in the mode of representative reference is a social construction. But that still does not make God himself a social construction. If I take the question of whether God is a social construction independently of, and separately from, the illocutionary/perlocutionary religious speech acts I perform, then I am bound to say that outside these religious speech acts I can neither affirm nor deny God's existence. As one who performs these speech acts myself, I deny and must deny that God is only a social construction; but beyond these religious speech acts I leave the question open.

AUTHOR REFERENCE

James M. Day is Professor in the Department of Psychology and Educational Sciences at the Université catholique de Louvain, Louvain-la-Neuve, Belgium, Adjunct Professor in the Center for Social Science and Policy Studies and the Department of Communication at the University of New Hampshire, Durham, and Associate of the Taos Institute, Taos, New Mexico. He holds degrees from Oberlin College (A.B.), Harvard University (ED.M), and the University of Pennsylvania (PH.D.) has completed additional study at Columbia and Yale, and has been a visiting scholar at Cambridge, Princeton, and Union Theological Seminary, New York. He is co-founder of the European Inter-University Research Network in Psychology of Religion, supported in part by the SOCRATES Programme of the European Union. Professor Day is co-editor and co-author of four books including most recently 'Human Development Across the Life Span: Educational and Psychological Applications (2001)', of numerous chapters published in scholarly books, and articles in peer-reviewed journals, including 'Human Development', 'American Psychologist', 'The International Journal for the Psychology of Religion', and 'The Journal of Counseling and Development'.

Joost Dupont (1959) studied philosophy at the University of Nijmegen. He is now working on a thesis about 'the collective identity of a Catholic school' at the University of Nijmegen. In 2001 he published a study about professional ethics of healthcare workers (physiotherapists and nurses).

Kenneth J. Gergen is the Mustin Professor of Psychology at Swarthmore College, and the Director of the Taos Institute, a non-profit organization working at the intersection of social constructionist theory and societal change practices. He is the author of numerous books and articles, including 'The Saturated Self' (1991), 'Toward Transformation in Social Knowledge' (1982, 1994), 'Realities and Relationships' (1996), and 'An Invitation to Social Construction' (1999). Gergen holds honorary doctorates from Tilburg University, and the Saybrook Institute, and is an Honorary Professor at the University of Buenos Aires.

Gerrit Immink holds the chair of Practical Theology at Utrecht University (The Netherlands) since 1993. He wrote his Ph.D. in Philosophy of Religion on Divine Simplicity (Kampen 1987). From 1979–1987 he was a pastor in the Dutch Reformed Church and from 1987–1993 he was a rector of the Theological Seminary of this church. He is now working on a theory of Practical Theology and his main interests are homiletics and liturgy.

Aad de Jong is from the Netherlands. He is presently an Associate Professor of Practical Theology at the Catholic University of Nijmegen in the Netherlands. He holds a Ph.D. (practical theology) from this university. He had previously taught in the University for Theology and Pastoral Work (UTP) in Heerlen in the Netherlands. Dr. de Jong is visiting professor for practical theology at the Duta Wacana University in Yogyakarta in Indonesia. He is a member of the AAR (American Association of Religion) and one of the founding members of ISERT (the International Society for Empirical Research in Theology). He has been the coordinator of the curriculum reform of Religious Studies at the University of Nijmegen. He presently coordinates the research program 'Religious Education of Adults and Pluralism' and teaches on several practical theological subjects. He has written several books and articles about religious education, the history and fundamentals of practical theology and interreligious dialogue. His main publication is 'Weerklank van Job' [The Echo of Job] (1990) about the problem of religious language in teaching the bible. Now he is preparing a monography about interreligious dialogue from a practical theological point of view.

Chris A.M. Hermans is professor of identity of Catholic schools and religious education at the Catholic University of Nijmegen. Since 2001, he is also scientific director of the Institute of Catholic Education at the same university. He is the author of several books, such als 'Morele vorming' [Moral education] (1986), 'Wie werdet Ihr die Gleichnisse verstehen?' [How to Understand Parables] (1990), 'Vorming in perspectief' [Education in perspective] (1993) and 'Participerend leren' [Participatory learning] (2001). He is executive editor of the International Journal of Education and Religion (Brill).

Jan M. van der Lans (1933) is emeritus professor in Psychology of Religion in the Faculty of Social Sciences of the Catholic University of Nijmegen (Netherlands). After his PhD thesis on Meditation and Religious Experience (1978), the three main topics of his empirical research were affiliation of young adults to new religious movements, literal vs metaphorical interpretation of religious language, and acculturation and religion among second generation muslim migrants.

Ulrike Popp-Baier is Associate Professor of Psychology at the University of Amsterdam in The Netherlands and "Privatdozentin" in psychology at the University of Erlangen-Nürnberg in Germany. Publications include 'Das Heilige im Profanen. Religiöse Orientierungen im Alltag' (1998) and (ed.) 'Religiöses Wissen und alltägliches Handeln— Assimilationen, Transformationen, Paradoxien' (1999). Current research interests are cultural psychology, psychology of religion, theoretical psychology, qualitative methods in the social sciences.

Hans Schilderman (1959) studied theology at the University of Nijmegen, and was researcher both at the Faculty of Philosophy and at the Faculty of Theology in Nijmegen. He was subsequently appointed University Teacher at the Theological Faculty of Tilburg, with a teaching assignment in practical theology, empirical methodology and pastoral care and counselling. His PhD thesis 'Pastorale professionalisering' (1998) studies pastoral ministery on the basis of an empirical theological survey among Dutch Catholic pastors. At this moment he is associate professor in pastoral theology, research coordinater in empirical theology, and Director of Research at the Faculty of Theology, University of Nijmegen.

Friedrich Schweitzer, Dr.rer.soc.theol.habil. was professor of practical theology and religious education in Mainz from 1992 until 1995. Since 1995 to the present he has worked at the Evangelical-theological Faculty in Tuebingen (Germany). He is the author of 'Identitaet und Erziehung' [Identity and education] (1985); 'Lebensgeschichte und Religion' [Life-history and religion] (1987); 'Die Religion des Kindes' [The religion of children] (1992); 'Die Suche nach eigenem Glauben' [The search for own belief] (1996) and 'Das Recht des Kindes auf Religion' [The right of children to religion] (2000).

Johannes A. van der Ven, Ph.D. in Theology (1973), is professor of Practical and Empirical Theology at the university of Nijmegen and extraordinary professor at the university of South Africa, Pretoria.

He has written numerous books, including 'Practical Theology: An Empirical approach' (1993), 'Ecclesiology in context' (1996), 'Formation of the Moral Self' (1998), 'Education for Reflective Ministry' (1998) and 'God reinvented?' (1998). He holds a honorary doctorate from the University of Lund (Sweden) and at this moment he is dean of the Faculty of Theology at the University of Nijmegen.

Mark I. Wallace is Chair and Associate Professor in the Department of Religion at Swarthmore College. He is the author of *Fragments of the Spirit: Nature, Violence, and the Renewal of Creation* (1996) and *The Second Naïveté: Barth, Ricoeur, and the New Yale Theology* (1990), editor of *Paul Ricoeur's Figuring the Sacred: Religion, Narrative, and Imagination* (1995), and co-editor of *Curing Violence: Essays on René Girard* (1994). He is a member of the Constructive Theology Workgroup and active in the environmental justice movement in the Philadelphia area.

SUBJECT INDEX

NAMES INDEX

Allport, G., 27
Alma, H.A., xvii, xxiii
Alston, W.P., 154, 156, 169
Ambert, A.-M., xvii, xxiii
Anderson, H., 80, 86, 231, 235
Antaki, Ch., 12, 20, 256, 270, 271
Aristotle, 50, 94, 300
Arnold, F.X., 189, 209
Arnsperger, C., 268, 270
Aquinas, Th., 94, 110
Auer, A., 242, 270
Austin, 155, 192

Bakhtin, M., xx, xxii, 80–82, 86, 114,
    120, 124–127, 129, 130, 132–140,
    142, 144, 192, 206, 251, 253, 254,
    269, 270
Barker, E., 47, 59
Barth, K., 162
Bartkowsky, B., 31
Barton, J., 160, 169
Bartow, C.L., 163, 169
Bauman, Z., 248
Beck, U., 172, 183
Beckford, J.A., 48, 59
Bellah, R.N., 214, 235
Benhabib, S., 175, 183
Berger, P.L., xii, xiii, xvii, xxiii, 5, 20,
    36, 37, 171, 182, 183, 275, 289
Berman, M., 284, 289
Berry, P., 11, 20
Billig, M., 24
Bilu, Y., 30, 37
Blum, L., 245, 246, 270
Böckle, F., 242, 244, 270
Boeve, L., 140, 144
Bolton, B., 27, 38
Bonhoeffer, D., 109, 110
Bricmont, J., 42, 61
Bromley, D., 30, 37
Brown, L., 70, 86, 87
Browning, D., viii, ix, xxiii
Bruner, J., 25, 37
Brunner, E., 148
Buber, M., 173, 183, 278, 288, 289
Butler, J., 43, 59, 99
Buttrick, D., 162, 169

Campbell, C.L., 164, 169
Capps, D., 214, 235
Caputo, J., 143, 144, 275, 289
Carnap, R., 156
Carse, J., 16, 20
Chatelion Counet, P., 114, 117, 140,
    143, 144
Chisholm, R., 156, 169
Clebsch, W.A., 229, 230, 235
Coates, R., 129,130, 132–134, 137,
    144
Conway, F., 46, 60
Coward, H., 289, 291
Craddock, F.B., 160, 169
Cronin, W., 99
Csordas, Th.J., 55, 60
Czarniawska-Jeorges, B., 17, 21

Dana, R.H., 27, 38
Dawson, L.L., 47, 60
Day, J.M., 29, 30, 37, 60, 64–72, 76,
    78, 81, 82, 86, 87, 239, 242, 249,
    270, 275, 276, 279, 281, 282
Denzin, N., 13, 21, 284, 291
Derrida, J., 96, 110, 143
Descartes, R., 103, 105, 119
Dewey, J., 231
Desimpelaere, P., 71, 87
Di Loreto, O., 68, 87
Dobbelaere, K., 113, 121, 144
Dostoljevsky, F.M., 131, 134
Dreyfuss, H.L., 270
Dreyfuss, S.E., 270
Duijker, H.C.J., 37
Dumont, V., 70, 87
Dupont, J.A.P., 277, 282, 304
Duns Scotus, 132, 293
Durkheim, E., 291

Edwards, D., 12, 21
Eliade, M., 284, 289
Engemann, W., 169
Epston, D., 17, 21
Erickson, E., 65

Fenn, R.K., 214, 235
Firet, J., 189